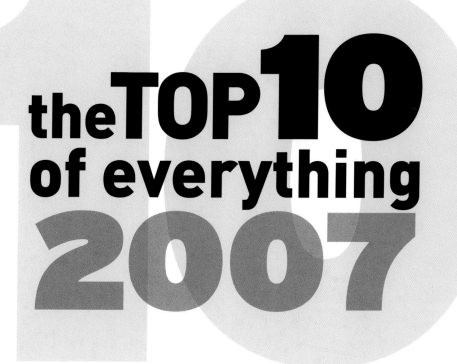

the TOP 10 of everything 2007

the TOP10
of everything
2007

Russell Ash

hamlyn

Contents

Produced for Hamlyn by
Palazzo Editions Ltd
15 Gay Street, Bath BA1 2PH

Publishing director: Colin Webb
Art director: Bernard Higton
Project editor: Sonya Newland
Editor: Marion Dent
Picture researcher: David Penrose
Indexer: Michael Dent

First published in Great Britain in 2006 by
Hamlyn, a division of Octopus Publishing
Group Ltd
2–4 Heron Quays, London E14 4JP

Copyright © Octopus Publishing Group Ltd
2006
Copyright text © Russell Ash 2006

Distributed in the United States
and Canada by
Sterling Publishing Co., Inc.
387 Park Avenue South, New York,
NY 10016-8810

ISBN-13: 978-0-600-61557-6
ISBN-10: 0-600-61557-X

A CIP catalogue record for this book is
available from the British Library

Printed and bound in China

10 9 8 7 6 5 4 3 2 1

Introduction

Coming of Age

Like my elder son, *The Top 10 of Everything* has reached its age of majority, having been published annually for 18 years. To those of you who have loyally bought it every year, I would like to extend my thanks. You now have nearly 5,000 pages of Top 10 lists and have filled 20 inches (50 cm) of shelving.

Top 10 – the Ground Rules

The Top 10 of Everything is a book of definitive, quantifiable Top 10 lists. It is not a book of "bests," except those that are measurably bestsellers, while "worsts" such as disasters are similarly ranked by cost or the number of victims. All the lists are all-time and global unless a year or territory are stated. Film lists are based on cumulative global earnings, irrespective of production or marketing budgets, and inflation – that eternal bugbear of those who compile such lists – is not taken into account. Figures for country and city populations are based on the latest available census, with estimates for increases where officially available, while in most instances "countries" should be taken as meaning "countries, colonies, and dependent territories." The only detours from strict Top 10-ism are found in occasional "asides." Amazing Fact features on everything from giant squids to extraordinary names, the most-married man to the first airmail letter.

Why Lists?

We are constantly assailed with lists. Newspapers and TV programs present rankings based on market research and polls, lists of the best places to live, the greatest films, the bestselling books, the worst crime rates, and so on. Ranked lists have become a journalistic shorthand overview of what might otherwise be a daunting mass of facts and figures. *The Top 10 of Everything* provides a unique collection of lists in a diverse array of categories.

The Rate of Change

In my work in compiling *The Top 10 of Everything*, I am constantly aware of just how much the world is changing and how the rate and scale of change seem inexorably to accelerate. For example, not many more than 40 films have ever earned over $\$^1/_2$ billion worldwide, but 25 of them have done so since 2000. In 2006 a single photograph was sold at auction for $2.9 million and the world's largest passenger ship, *Freedom of the Seas*, was launched. It was predicted that the US population will top 300 million as this book is published and that 2007 will mark the year in which the balance of the world's population tips from predominantly rural to a majority of urban dwellers.

Caught in the Web

In 2006 world Internet usage topped 1 billion and, for the first time, music tracks reached No.1 in the chart based solely on downloads, rather than physical record sales. As is often stated, the Internet is both a blessing and a curse. Information that was previously unavailable or not released until often years later, now becomes accessible almost instantaneously, so, for example, my film database which was once updated as and when figures were released can now be updated almost daily – and because it can be, I do.

Source Material

My sources encompass international organizations, commercial companies and research bodies, specialized publications, and, especially, a network of individuals around the world who have shared their knowledge of everything from snakes and skyscrapers to ships and skateboarding. As ever, I gladly acknowledge their invaluable contribution (see page 255 for a full list of credits), as well as the many people who have been involved with the book at all stages of its development.

Want to be in the Book?

★ Become an actor and get nominated for at least six Oscars (you will be in two lists if you win one before your 21st birthday).

★ Make at least 20 films, such as the James Bond series, that earn over $3.7 billion worldwide.

★ Be worth more than $18 billion, or earn over $7 million a year after your death.

★ Drive a car at over 763 mph (1,228 km/h).

★ Become a monarch and rule for over 59 years, or serve as a president for over 22 years.

★ Record a single that sells at least 8 million copies, or if you are a female singer, have over 12 Top 10 hits.

★ Win more than 8 Olympic medals if you are a woman or 11 if you are a man, or run 100 m in under 9.86 seconds.

★ Score over 14 goals in soccer World Cup matches. This will probably also guarantee you a transfer fee of $60 million-plus, and a place in yet another Top 10 list.

Contact Me

Your comments, corrections, and suggestions for new lists are always welcome. Please contact me via the publishers or visit my website:

http://www.top10ofeverything.com

Russell Ash

THE UNIVERSE &
THE EARTH

1

Space Bodies

top10 LARGEST BODIES IN THE SOLAR SYSTEM

BODY	MAXIMUM DIAMETER MILES	KM	SIZE COMPARED WITH EARTH
1 Sun	865,036	1,392,140	109.136
2 Jupiter	88,846	142,984	11.209
3 Saturn	74,898	120,536	9.449
4 Uranus	31,763	51,118	4.007
5 Neptune	30,775	49,528	3.883
6 Earth	7,926	12,756	1.000
7 Venus	7,521	12,104	0.949
8 Mars	4,228	6,805	0.533
9 Ganymede	3,270	5,262	0.413
10 Titan	3,200	5,150	0.404

Along with Mercury, with a diameter of 3,032 miles (4,879 km), most of the planets are visible with the naked eye. The exceptions are Uranus and Neptune and, outside the Top 10, Pluto. Its diameter is approximately 1,485 miles (2,390 km), but its status as a planet is argued. A newly discovered body known as 2003 UB313 is larger, at some 1,678 miles (2,700 km), and is described by some astronomers as the "10th planet."

top10 STARS NEAREST TO THE EARTH

STAR*	LIGHT YEARS	DISTANCE MILES (MILLIONS)	KM (MILLIONS)
1 Proxima Centauri	4.22	24,792,500	39,923,310
2 Alpha Centauri	4.39	25,791,250	41,531,595
3 Barnard's Star	5.94	34,897,500	56,195,370
4 Wolf 359	7.78	45,707,500	73,602,690
5 Lalande 21185	8.31	48,821,250	78,616,755
6 Sirius	8.60	50,525,000	81,360,300
7 Luyten 726-8	8.72	51,230,000	82,495,560
8 Ross 154	9.69	56,928,750	91,672,245
9 Ross 248	10.32	60,630,000	97,632,360
10 Epsilon Eridani	10.49	61,628,750	99,240,645

* Excluding the Sun

Source: Peter Bond, Royal Astronomical Society

A spaceship traveling at 25,000 mph (40,237 km/h) – faster than any human has yet reached in space – would take over 113,200 years to reach the Earth's closest star, Proxima Centauri. Even stars within the Milky Way are as much as 2,500 light years from us, while our own galaxy may span 100,000 light years end to end, with the Sun some 25,000 to 30,000 light years from its center.

top10 LONGEST YEARS IN THE SOLAR SYSTEM

BODY*	LENGTH OF YEAR# YEARS	DAYS
1 Pluto	247	256
2 Neptune	164	298
3 Uranus	84	4
4 Saturn	29	168
5 Jupiter	11	314
6 Mars		687
7 Earth		365
8 Venus		225
9 Mercury		88
10 Sun		0

* Excludes satellites
\# Period of orbit round the Sun, in Earth years/days

⊕ *Ceres launches series*
The first and largest asteroid was discovered by Italian astronomer Giuseppe Piazzi and called Ceres after the patron goddess of Sicily, the location of Palermo Observatory. The element cerium, identified in Sweden two years later, was named after it.

top10 LARGEST ASTEROIDS

NAME	NO.	DISCOVERED	MAXIMUM DIAMETER* MILES	KM
1 Ceres	1	Jan 1, 1801	584	940
2 Vesta	4	Mar 29, 1807	357	576
3 Pallas	2	Mar 28, 1802	334	538
4 Hygeia	10	Apr 12, 1849	267	430
5 Interamnia	704	Oct 2, 1910	210	338
6 Davida	511	May 30, 1903	201	324
7 Cybele	65	Mar 8, 1861	191	308
8 Europa	52	Feb 4, 1858	181	292
9 Sylvia	87	May 16, 1866	175	282
10 Patienta	451	Dec 4, 1899	173	280

* Most asteroids are irregular in shape

Asteroids, sometimes known as "minor planets," are fragments of rock orbiting between Mars and Jupiter. Up to November 16, 2005, some 305,624 had been found: 120,437 with orbits calculated and assigned numbers and 12,712 named. Each of the four Beatles has an asteroid named after him, as do Walt Disney, Frank Zappa, James Bond, and the Monty Python team members.

top10 LARGEST PLANETARY **MOONS**

MOON	PLANET	MILES	KM
		DIAMETER	

1 **Ganymede** Jupiter 3,269.9 5,262.4
Discovered by Galileo on January 11, 1610, Ganymede – one of Jupiter's 63 known satellites and the largest moon in the Solar System – is thought to have a surface of ice about 60 miles (97 km) thick.

2 **Titan** Saturn 3,200.1 5,150.0
Titan is the largest of Saturn's 49 moons and is larger than two of the planets in the Solar System, Mercury and Pluto. We have no idea what its surface looks like, because it has a dense atmosphere containing nitrogen, ethane, and other gases, which shroud its surface – not unlike that of the Earth four billion years ago.

3 **Callisto** Jupiter 2,995.4 4,820.6
Possessing a similar composition to Ganymede, Callisto is heavily pitted with craters, perhaps more so than any other body in the Solar System.

4 **Io** Jupiter 2,263.4 3,642.6
Most of what we know about Io was reported back by the 1979 *Voyager 1* probe, which revealed a crust of solid sulfur with massive volcanic eruptions in progress, hurling sulfurous material 186 miles (300 km) into space.

5 **Moon** Earth 2,160.0 3,476.2
Our own satellite is a quarter of the size of the Earth, the fifth largest in the Solar System, and, to date, the only one to have been explored by Man.

6 **Europa** Jupiter 1,939.7 3,121.6
Although Europa's ice-covered surface is apparently smooth and crater-free, it is covered with mysterious black lines, with some of them 40 miles (64 km) wide and resembling canals.

7 **Triton** Neptune 1,681.9 2,706.8
Discovered on October 10, 1846 by British brewer and amateur astronomer William Lassell, 17 days after German astronomer Johann Galle had discovered Neptune itself, Triton is the only known satellite in the Solar System that revolves around its planet in the opposite direction to the planet's rotation.

8 **Titania** Uranus 980.4 1,577.8
The largest of Uranus's 27 moons, Titania was discovered by William Herschel (who had discovered the planet six years earlier) in 1787 and has a snowball-like surface of ice.

9 **Rhea** Saturn 947.6 1,528.0
Saturn's second-largest moon was discovered in 1672. *Voyager 1*, which flew past Rhea in November 1980, confirmed that its icy surface is pitted with craters, one of them 140 miles (225 km) in diameter.

10 **Oberon** Uranus 946.2 1,522.8
Oberon was discovered by Herschel and given the name of the fairy king husband of Queen Titania, both characters in Shakespeare's *A Midsummer Night's Dream*.

⬆ *Mighty moons*
Our own Moon (shown immediately above) is smaller than the other natural satellites Ganymede, Callisto, and Io (top to bottom), as well as Saturn's Titan, whose appearance is shrouded by a dense layer of gases.

Star Gazing

⬆ **Roving reporter**
NASA's Mars Exploration Rovers are the latest planetary probes.

➡ **Moon Ranger**
Ranger 7 was one of several successful US lunar launches.

top10 FIRST **PLANETARY PROBES**

PROBE / COUNTRY*	PLANET	ARRIVAL#
1 Venera 4	Venus	Oct 18, 1967
2 Venera 5	Venus	May 16, 1969
3 Venera 6	Venus	May 17, 1969
4 Venera 7	Venus	Dec 15, 1970
5 Mariner 9, USA	Mars	Nov 13, 1971
6 Mars 2	Mars	Nov 27, 1971
7 Mars 3	Mars	Dec 2, 1971
8 Venera 8	Venus	Jul 22, 1972
9 Venera 9	Venus	Oct 22, 1975
10 Venera 10	Venus	Oct 25, 1975

* USSR, unless otherwise stated
\# Successfully entered orbit or landed

This list excludes "fly-bys" – probes that passed by but did not land on the surface of another planet. The USA's *Pioneer 10*, for example, launched on March 2, 1972, flew past Jupiter on December 3, 1973, but did not land. *Venera 4* was the first unmanned probe to land on a planet, and *Venera 9* the first to transmit pictures from a planet's surface. *Mariner 9* was the first to orbit another planet and transmit photographs.

top10 FIRST UNMANNED **MOON LANDINGS**

NAME	COUNTRY	DATE (LAUNCH/IMPACT)
1 Luna 2	USSR	Sep 12/13, 1959
2 Ranger 4	USA	Apr 23/26, 1962
3 Ranger 6	USA	Jan 30/Feb 2, 1964
4 Ranger 7	USA	Jul 28/31, 1964
5 Ranger 8	USA	Feb 17/20, 1965
6 Ranger 9	USA	Mar 21/24, 1965
7 Luna 5	USSR	May 9/12, 1965
8 Luna 7	USSR	Oct 4/8, 1965
9 Luna 8	USSR	Dec 3/7, 1965
10 Luna 9	USSR	Jan 31/Feb 3, 1966

The first nine on this list were the first successful Moon landings – but all impacted at speed and were destroyed. *Luna 9* was the first to make a soft landing and transmit photographic images back to Earth. Among subsequent US landings were seven *Surveyors* (1966–68) and five *Lunar Orbiters* (1966–67). Before crashing onto the Moon, the 838-lb (380-kg) *Orbiters* relayed detailed photographic images of the surface, mapping suitable sites for the manned *Apollo* landings that followed.

the 10 FIRST PLANETARY MOONS TO BE DISCOVERED

	MOON	PLANET	DISCOVERER	YEAR
1	Moon	Earth	—	Ancient
2	=Io	Jupiter	Galileo Galilei, Italy	1610
	=Europa	Jupiter	Galileo Galilei	1610
	=Ganymede	Jupiter	Galileo Galilei	1610
	=Callisto	Jupiter	Galileo Galilei	1610
6	Titan	Saturn	Christian Huygens, Netherlands	1655
7	Iapetus	Saturn	Giovanni Cassini, Italy/France	1671
8	Rhea	Saturn	Giovanni Cassini	1672
9	=Tethys	Saturn	Giovanni Cassini	1684
	=Dione	Saturn	Giovanni Cassini	1684

While the Earth's Moon has been observed since ancient times, it was not until the development of the telescope that Galileo was able to discover (on January 7, 1610) the first moons of another planet. These, which are Jupiter's four largest, were named by German astronomer Simon Marius and are known as the Galileans.

🌑 *Mirror image*
Comprising 91 hexagonal mirrors, the internationally funded SALT (South African Large Telescope) is so powerful that it is capable of detecting light from distant stars a billion times fainter than the human eye can see.

the 10 FIRST ASTEROIDS TO BE DISCOVERED

ASTEROID / DISCOVERER / COUNTRY — DISCOVERED

1 Ceres — Jan 1, 1801
Giuseppe Piazzi, Italy

2 Pallas — Mar 28, 1802
Heinrich Olbers, Germany

3 Juno — Sep 1, 1804
Karl Ludwig Harding, Germany

4 Vesta — Mar 29, 1807
Heinrich Olbers, Germany

5 Astraea — Dec 8, 1845
Karl Ludwig Hencke, Germany

6 Hebe — Jul 1, 1847
Karl Ludwig Hencke, Germany

7 Iris — Aug 13, 1847
John Russell Hind, UK

8 Flora — Oct 18, 1847
John Russell Hind, UK

9 Metis — Apr 25, 1848
Andrew Graham, UK

10 Hygeia — Apr 12, 1849
Annibale de Gasparis, Italy

top 10 LARGEST REFLECTING TELESCOPES

	TELESCOPE NAME (YEAR BUILT)	LOCATION	APERTURE FT	APERTURE M
1	Southern African Large Telescope (2005)	Sutherland, South Africa	36.1	11.0
2	Gran Telescopio Canarias (2005)	La Palma, Canary Islands, Spain	34.1	10.4
3	=Keck I Telescope* (1993)	Mauna Kea, Hawaii	32.2	9.8
	=Keck II Telescope* (1996)	Mauna Kea, Hawaii	32.2	9.8
5	Hobby-Eberly Telescope (1997)	Mt. Fowlkes, Texas	30.2	9.2
6	Large Binocular Telescope* (2004)	Mt. Graham, Arizona	27.6	8.4
7	Subaru Telescope (1999)	Mauna Kea, Hawaii	27.2	8.3
8	=Antu Telescope# (1998)	Cerro Paranal, Chile	26.9	8.2
	=Kueyen Telescope# (1999)	Cerro Paranal, Chile	26.9	8.2
	=Melipal Telescope# (2000)	Cerro Paranal, Chile	26.9	8.2
	=Yepun Telescope# (2001)	Cerro Paranal, Chile	26.9	8.2

* Twin
# Combine to form VLT (Very Large Telescope)

Based on a c.1670 design by Sir Isaac Newton, reflecting telescopes are optical telescopes with mirrors, offering greater power and accuracy than the lenses of refractors. Recent technology has enabled progressive increases in the size of the world's research reflectors.

Space Explorers

top10 LONGEST **SPACE SHUTTLE** FLIGHTS*

	FLIGHT	DATES	DAYS	DURATION HRS	MINS	SECS
1	STS-80 Columbia	Nov 19–Dec 7, 1996	17	8	53	18
2	STS-78 Columbia	Jun 20–Jul 7, 1996	16	21	48	30
3	STS-67 Endeavour	Mar 2–18, 1995	16	15	9	46
4	STS-107 Columbia#	Jan 16–Feb 1, 2003	15	22	20	32
5	STS-73 Columbia	Oct 20–Nov 5, 1995	15	21	53	16
6	STS-90 Columbia	Apr 17–May 3, 1998	15	21	15	58
7	STS-75 Columbia	22 Feb–9 Mar 1996	15	17	41	25
8	STS-94 Columbia	Jul 1–17, 1997	15	16	46	1
9	STS-87 Atlantis	Sep 25–Oct 6, 1997	15	16	35	1
10	STS-65 Columbia	Jul 8–23, 1994	14	17	55	0

* To Jan 1, 2006
# Destroyed on reentry

● *Monkey around*
Named for USAF's School of Aviation Medicine, Miss Sam orbited in a Mercury capsule.

top10 FIRST **ANIMALS** IN SPACE

	NAME / ANIMAL / STATUS	COUNTRY	DATE
1	Laika (name used by Western press: actually the name of the breed to which the dog named Kudryavka, a female Samoyed husky, belonged). *Died in space*	USSR	November 3, 1957
2 =	Laska and Benjy (mice) *Reentered Earth's atmosphere, but not recovered*	USA	December 13, 1958
4 =	Able and Baker (female rhesus monkey/female squirrel monkey). *Successfully returned to Earth*	USA	May 28, 1959
6 =	Otvazhnaya (female Samoyed husky) and an unnamed rabbit. *Recovered*	USSR	July 2, 1959
8	Sam (male rhesus monkey). *Recovered*	USA	December 4, 1959
9	Miss Sam (female rhesus monkey). *Recovered*	USA	January 21, 1960
10 =	Belka and Strelka (female Samoyed huskies), plus 40 mice, and two rats. *First to orbit and return safely*	USSR	August 19, 1960

top10 COUNTRIES WITH THE **MOST SPACEFLIGHT** EXPERIENCE

	COUNTRY	ASTRONAUTS	TOTAL DURATION OF MISSIONS* DAYS	HRS	MINS	SECS
1	USSR/Russia	97	16,858	17	8	24
2	USA	275	9,380	10	4	48
3	France	9	384	23	38	0
4	Kazakhstan	2	349	14	59	3
5	Germany	10	309	17	8	56
6	Canada	8	122	13	30	58
7	Japan	5	88	6	0	40
8	Italy	4	76	6	34	9
9	Switzerland	1	42	12	5	32
10	South Africa	1	24	22	28	22

* To Oct 24, 2004 landing of Soyuz TMA-4

The long-duration stays of its cosmonauts on board the *Mir* Space Station have given the USSR (now Russia) its lead. The USA has had many more astronauts in space, but its missions were shorter.

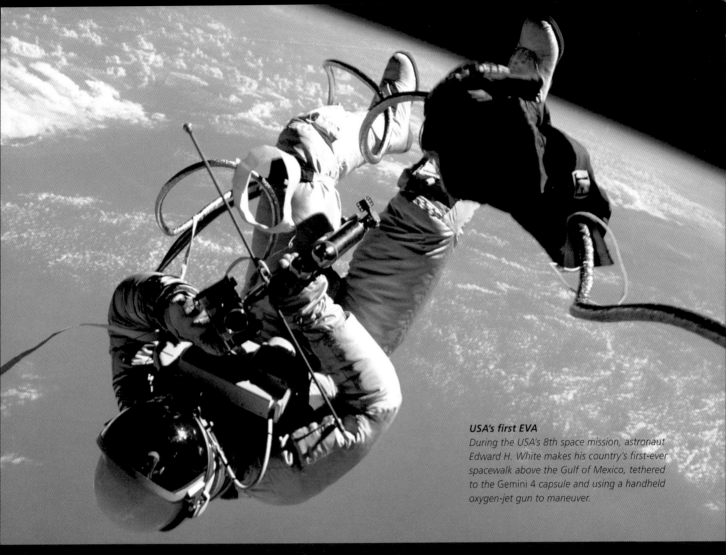

USA's first EVA
During the USA's 8th space mission, astronaut Edward H. White makes his country's first-ever spacewalk above the Gulf of Mexico, tethered to the Gemini 4 capsule and using a handheld oxygen-jet gun to maneuver.

top10 FIRST **SPACEWALKERS**

	ASTRONAUT*	SPACECRAFT	EVA# HR:MIN	EVA DATE
1	Alexei A. Leonov	Voskhod 2	0.23	Mar 18, 1965
2	Edward H. White	Gemini 4	0:36	Jun 3, 1965
3	Eugene A. Cernan	Gemini 9	2:07	Jun 3, 1966
4	Michael Collins	Gemini 10	0:50	Jul 19, 1966
5	Richard F. Gordon	Gemini 11	0:33	Sep 13, 1966
6	Edwin E. ("Buzz") Aldrin	Gemini 12	2:29	Nov 12, 1966
7	= Alexei S. Yeliseyev	Soyuz 5	0:37	Jan 16, 1969
	= Yevgeny V. Khrunov	Soyuz 5	0:37	Jan 16, 1969
9	= Russell L. Schweickart	Apollo 9	0:46	Mar 6, 1969
	= David R. Scott	Apollo 9	0:46	Mar 6, 1969

* Excluding repeat spacewalks on same mission
\# Extra Vehicular Activity

Leonov's first-ever spacewalk almost ended in disaster when his spacesuit "ballooned," and he was unable to return through the airlock into the *Voskhod 2* capsule until he reduced the pressure in his suit to a dangerously low level. Edward H. White, the first American to walk in space, was killed in the *Apollo* spacecraft fire of January 27, 1967.

top10 MOST EXPERIENCED **SPACEWOMEN**

	SPACEWOMAN*	MISSIONS	TOTAL DURATION OF MISSIONS# DAYS	HOURS	MINS
1	Shannon W. Lucid	5	223	2	50
2	Susan J. Helms	5	210	23	6
3	Peggy A. Whitson	1	184	22	15
4	Yelena V. Kondakova, USSR	2	178	10	41
5	Tamara E. Jernigan	5	63	1	24
6	Marsha S. Ivins	5	55	21	48
7	Bonnie J. Dunbar	5	50	8	24
8	Janice E. Voss	5	49	3	49
9	Nancy J. Currie	4	41	15	32
10	Ellen L. Ochoa	4	40	19	37

* All USA, except Kondakova (USSR)
\# To Jan 1, 2006

In 1996, Shannon Lucid became both America's most experienced astronaut and the world's most experienced female astronaut, through a combination of Shuttle missions and a 75-million-mile (121-million-km), 188-day stay on the Russian *Mir* Space Station – itself a record duration for a single mission by a US astronaut.

Seas & Lakes

top10 DEEPEST DEEP-SEA TRENCHES

	TRENCH*	DEEPEST POINT FT	M
10	Yap	27,973	8,527
9	Puerto Rico	28,229	8,605

Each of the eight deepest ocean trenches would be deep enough to submerge Mount Everest, which is 29,035 ft (8,850 m) above sea level.

8	Izu	31,805	9,695
7	Kuril	31,985	9,750
6	New Britain	32,609	9,940
5	Bonin	32,786	9,994
4	Kermadec#	32,960	10,047
3	Philippine	34,436	10,497
2	Tonga#	35,430	10,800
1	Marianas	35,797	10,911

* With the exception of the Puerto Rico (Atlantic), all the trenches are in the Pacific
\# Some authorities consider these parts of the same feature

top10 DEEPEST OCEANS AND SEAS

SEA / OCEAN	AVERAGE DEPTH FT	M
1 Pacific Ocean	12,925	3,939
2 Indian Ocean	12,598	3,840
3 Atlantic Ocean	11,730	3,575
4 Caribbean Sea, Atlantic Ocean	8,448	2,575
5 Sea of Japan, Pacific Ocean	5,468	1,666
6 Gulf of Mexico, Atlantic Ocean	5,297	1,614
7 Mediterranean Sea, Atlantic Ocean	4,926	1,501
8 Bering Sea, Pacific Ocean	4,893	1,491
9 South China Sea, Pacific Ocean	4,802	1,463
10 Black Sea, Atlantic Ocean	3,906	1,190

top10 LARGEST OCEANS AND SEAS

SEA / OCEAN	APPROXIMATE AREA* SQ MILES	SQ KM
1 Pacific Ocean	64,186,600	166,242,500
2 Atlantic Ocean	33,420,160	86,557,800
3 Indian Ocean	28,350,640	73,427,800
4 Arctic Ocean	5,105,740	13,223,800
5 South China Sea	1,148,499	2,974,600
6 Caribbean Sea	971,400	2,515,900
7 Mediterranean Sea	969,120	2,510,000
8 Bering Sea	873,020	2,261,100
9 Sea of Okhotsk	589,800	1,527,570
10 Gulf of Mexico	582,100	1,507,600

* Excluding tributary seas

AMAZING FACT

The World's Deepest Dive

Only two people have ever descended to the deepest point in the world's oceans – the Challenger Deep in the Marianas Trench in the Pacific. On January 23, 1960 the 58-ft-long (17.7-m) bathyscaphe *Trieste* took Jacques Piccard (Swiss – the son of its designer Auguste Piccard) and Donald Walsh (American) to the seabed, a depth of almost 7 miles (10 km), or 29 times the height of the Empire State Building, where the pressure is 16,883 lb/sq in (11,869,924 kg/sq m). The descent stage lasted 4 hours 48 minutes and the ascent 3 hours 17 minutes.

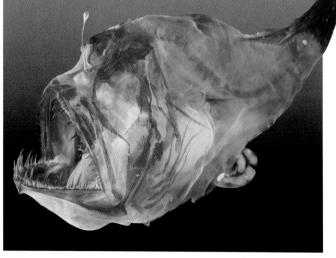

⬆ Denizen of the deep
Anglerfish (Melanocetus johnsoni) *use bioluminescence to lure prey.*

top10 SHALLOWEST OCEANS AND SEAS

SEA* / OCEAN	AVERAGE DEPTH FT	M
1 Yellow Sea, Pacific Ocean	121	36.8
2 Baltic Sea, Atlantic Ocean	180	54.8
3 Hudson Bay, Atlantic Ocean	305	92.9
4 North Sea, Atlantic Ocean	308	93.8
5 Persian Gulf, Indian Ocean	328	99.9
6 East China Sea, Indian Ocean	620	188.9
7 Red Sea, Indian Ocean	1,764	537.6
8 Gulf of California, Pacific Ocean	2,375	723.9
9 Sea of Okhotsk, Pacific Ocean	3,192	972.9
10 Arctic Ocean	3,407	1,038.4

* Excludes landlocked seas

The Yellow Sea, or Huang Hai, an arm of the Pacific Ocean, north of the China Sea between China and Korea, is so-called for the color of mineral deposits from the rivers that discharge into it. With a maximum depth of 500 ft (152 m), ice fields form during the winter and shifting sandbanks make it treacherous to shipping. It has been predicted that environmental changes in the next few millennia will result in its total disappearance.

top10 LARGEST LAKES

LAKE / LOCATION	APPROX. AREA SQ MILES	SQ KM
1 Caspian Sea, Azerbaijan/Iran/Kazakhstan/Russia/Turkmenistan	143,000	371,000
2 Michigan/Huron*, Canada/USA	45,342	117,436
3 Superior, Canada/USA	31,700	82,103
4 Victoria, Kenya/Tanzania/Uganda	26,828	69,485
5 Tanganyika, Burundi/Tanzania/Dem. Rep. of Congo/Zambia	12,700	32,893
6 Baikal, Russia	12,162	31,500
7 Great Bear, Canada	12,096	31,328
8 Malawi (Nyasa), Tanzania/Malawi/Mozambique	11,150	28,880
9 Great Slave, Canada	11,030	28,568
10 Lake Erie, Canada/USA	9,910	25,667

* Now considered two lobes of the same lake

Lake Michigan/Huron is the world's largest freshwater lake. As recently as 1960, the Aral Sea (Kazakhstan/Uzbekistan), which has an area (including several lake islands) of some 26,371 sq miles (68,300 sq km) was the fourth largest lake in the world, but as a result of the diverting of rivers for irrigation, it has dropped to 6,625 sq miles (17,158 sq km) and thus fallen out of the Top 10.

⊕ *Scratching the surface*
An ice-hockey game on Siberia's frozen Baikal, the world's deepest lake.

top10 DEEPEST LAKES

	LAKE / LOCATION	GREATEST DEPTH FT	M
10	Hornindals Norway	1,686	514
9	Toba Sumatra, Indonesia	1,736	529
8	Crater Oregon, USA	1,932	589
7	Matana Sulawesi, Indonesia	1,936	590
6	Great Slave Canada	2,015	614
5	Issyk-kul Kyrgyzstan	2,191	668
4	Malawi Malawi/Mozambique/Tanzania	2,316	706
3	Caspian Sea Azerbaijan/Iran/Kazakhstan/Russia/Turkmenistan	3,363	1,025
2	Tanganyika Burundi/Tanzania/Dem. Rep. of Congo/Zambia	4,825	1,471
1	Baikal Russia	5,712	1,741

Rivers & Waterfalls

top10 **LONGEST** RIVERS

RIVER / LOCATION	APPROXIMATE LENGTH MILES	KM
1 Nile, Burundi/Dem. Rep. of Congo/ Egypt/Eritrea/Ethiopia/Kenya/ Rwanda/Sudan/Tanzania/Uganda	4,160	6,695
2 Amazon, Peru/Brazil	4,007	6,448
3 Yangtze (Chang Jiang), China	3,964	6,378
4 Huang He (Yellow), China	3,395	5,464
5 Amur, China/Russia	2,744	4,415
6 Lena, Russia	2,734	4,400
7 Congo, Angola/Dem. Rep. of Congo	2,718	4,373
8 Irtysh, China/Kazkhakstan/Mongolia/Russia	2,640	4,248
9 Mackenzie, Canada	2,635	4,241
10 Mekong, Tibet/China/Myanmar/Laos/ Thailand/Cambodia/Vietnam	2,600	4,183

⊙ *Egyptian enigma*
Its precise length the subject of debate among geographers, the River Nile flows through Egypt and nine other countries.

The source of the Nile was discovered in 1858 when British explorer John Hanning Speke reached Lake Victoria Nyanza, in what is now Burundi. The river is today generally accepted to be the world's longest, with an overall length of 4,160 miles (6,695 km). It was not until almost 100 years later, in 1953, that the source of the Amazon was identified as a stream called Huarco flowing from the Misuie glacier in the Peruvian Andes mountains. After following a series of feeders, it joins the Amazon's main tributary at Ucayali, Peru, giving a total length of 4,007 miles (6,448 km). By following the Amazon from its source and up the Rio Pará, it is possible to sail for some 4,195 miles (6,750 km), which is a greater distance than the length of the Nile, but because experts do not regard this entire route as part of the Amazon basin, the Nile is still considered the world's longest river.

top10 **LONGEST** RIVERS IN THE US

RIVER	LENGTH MILES	KM
1 Missouri-Red Rock	2,540	4,088
2 Mississippi	2,348	3,779
3 Missouri	2,315	3,726
4 Yukon	1,979	3,185
5 Rio Grande	1,760	2,832
6 Arkansas	1,459	2,348
7 Colorado	1,450	2,334
8 Ohio-Allegheny	1,306	2,102
9 Red	1,290	2,076
10 Columbia	1,243	2,000

top10 **WIDEST** WATERFALLS

WATERFALL / RIVER / COUNTRY	WIDTH FT	M
1 Chutes de Khône, Mekong River, Laos	35,376	10,783
2 Salto Pará, Rio Caura, Venezuela	18,400	5,608
3 = Salto del Guaíra, Rio Paraná, Brazil	15,840	4,828
= Chutes de Livingstone, Congo River, Congo	15,840	4,828
5 Celilo Falls, Columbia River, USA	10,560	3,219
6 Kongou Falls, Ivindo River, Gabon	10,500	3,200
7 Salto de Iguaçu, Rio Iguaçu, Argentina/Brazil	8,858	2,700
8 = Saltos dos Patos e Maribondo, Rio Grande, Brazil	6,600	2,012
= Salto do Urubupungá, Rio Paraná, Brazil	6,600	2,012
10 Victoria Falls, Zambezi River, Zimbabwe/Zambia	5,700	1,737

top10 **HIGHEST** WATERFALLS

WATERFALL RIVER / LOCATION	TOTAL DROP	
	FT	M
1 Angel Carrao, Venezuela	3,212*	979
2 Tugela Tugela, South Africa	2,800	850
3 Utigård Jostedal Glacier, Nesdale, Norway	2,625	800
4 Mongefossen Monge, Mongebekk, Norway	2,540	774
5 Mutarazi Mutarazi River, Zimbabwe	2,499	762
6 Yosemite Yosemite Creek, California	2,425	739
7 Østre Mardøla Foss Mardals, Eikisdal, Norway	2,152	656
8 Tyssestrengane Tysso, Hardanger, Norway	2,120	646
9 Cuquenán Arabopo, Venezuela	2,000	610
10 Sutherland Arthur, South Island, New Zealand	1,904	580

* Longest single drop 2,648 ft (807 m)

Although earlier explorers may have seen it, American adventurer James Crawford Angel (1899–1956) first sighted the Angel Falls, Venezuela, from the air on November 16, 1933, noting in his logbook, "I found myself a waterfall." When Angel's report was investigated, the falls on the River Churún were confirmed as the world's highest and named Salto Angel (Angel Falls) in his honor.

top10 **HIGHEST** WATERFALLS IN THE US

WATERFALL / RIVER / STATE	HIGHEST DROP	
	FT	M
1 Ribbon (Yosemite), Ribbon Creek, California	1,612	491
2 Upper Yosemite, Yosemite Creek, California	1,430	436
3 Widow's Tears, Meadow Brook, California	1,170	357
4 Middle Cascade, Yosemite Creek, California	909	277
5 Fairy, Stevens Creek, Washington	700	213
6 Feather, Fall River, California	640	195
7 Bridalveil, Bridalveil Creek, California	620	189
8 Nevada, Merced, California	594	181
9 Multnomah, Multnomah Creek, Oregon	542	165
10 Sentinel, Sentinel Creek, California	500	152

◄ *Angel Falls*
These dramatic falls are over 10 times the height of the Statue of Liberty.

The Lie of the Land

top10 DEEPEST CAVES

The world's deepest cave is a comparatively recent discovery: in January 2001 a team of Ukrainian cave explorers in the Arabikskaja system in the western Caucasus mountains of the Georgian Republic found a branch of the Voronja, or "Crow's Cave," and established that its depth of 5,610 ft (1,710 m) far exceeded anything previously known. Progressively deeper penetrations have taken its extent to more than seven times the height of the Eiffel Tower.

	CAVE SYSTEM / LOCATION	DEPTH FT	M
10	Sistema Huautla, Mexico	4,839	1,475
9	Sistema Cheve (Cuicateco), Mexico	4,869	1,484
8	Shakta Vjacheslav Pantjukhina, Georgia	4,948	1,508
7	Cehi 2, Slovenia	5,033	1,533
6	Sarma, Georgia	5,062	1,543
5	Torca del Cerro del Cuevon/ Torca de las Saxifragas, Spain	5,213	1,589
4	Réseau Jean Bernard, France	5,256	1,602
3	Gouffre Mirolda, France	5,335	1,626
2	Lamprechtsofen Vogelschacht Weg Schacht, Austria	5,354	1,632
1	Krubera (Voronja), Georgia	7,021	2,140

top10 LARGEST METEORITE CRATERS

	CRATER / LOCATION	DIAMETER MILES	KM
1	Vredefort, South Africa	186	300
2	Sudbury, Ontario, Canada	155	250
3	Chicxulub, Yucatán, Mexico	107	170
4	= Manicougan, Quebec, Canada	62	100
	= Popigai, Russia	62	100
6	= Acraman, Australia	56	90
	= Chesapeake Bay, Virginia	56	90
8	Puchezh-Katunki, Russia	50	80
9	Morokweng, South Africa	43	70
10	Kara, Russia	40	65

Source: Earth Impact Database, Planetary and Space Science Centre, University of New Brunswick

Unlike on the Solar System's other planets and moons, many astroblemes (collision sites) on Earth have been weathered over time and obscured, and debate continues as to whether certain crater-like structures are of meteoric origin or the remnants of long-extinct volcanoes. The Vredefort Ring, once thought to be meteoric, was declared in 1963 to be volcanic, but has since been claimed as a definite meteor crater, as are all the giant meteorite craters in the Top 10, as listed by the International Union of Geological Sciences Commission on Comparative Planetology.

top10 LARGEST ISLANDS

	ISLAND / LOCATION	AREA* SQ MILES	SQ KM
1	Greenland (Kalaatdlit Nunaat), North Atlantic	840,004	2,175,600
2	New Guinea, Southwest Pacific	303,381	785,753
3	Borneo, West midPacific	288,869	748,168
4	Madagascar, Indian Ocean	226,917	587,713
5	Baffin Island, North Atlantic	194,574	503,944
6	Sumatra, Northeast Indian Ocean	171,068	443,065
7	Great Britain, off coast of Northwest Europe	88,787	229,957
8	Honshu, Sea of Japan	87,805	227,413
9	Victoria Island, Arctic Ocean	83,897	217,292
10	Ellesmere Island, Arctic Ocean	75,767	196,236

* Mainlands, including areas of inland water, but excluding offshore islands

Australia is regarded as a continental land mass, rather than an island; otherwise it would rank first, at 2,941,517 sq miles (7,618,493 sq km), or 35 times the size of Great Britain.

top10 HIGHEST **MOUNTAINS**

MOUNTAIN / LOCATION	FIRST ASCENT	TEAM NATIONALITY	HEIGHT* FT	HEIGHT* M
1 Everest, Nepal/China	May 29, 1953	British/New Zealand	29,035	8,850
2 K2 (Chogori), Pakistan/China	July 31, 1954	Italian	28,238	8,607
3 Kangchenjunga, Nepal/India	May 25, 1955	British	28,208	8,598
4 Lhotse, Nepal/China	May 18, 1956	Swiss	27,923	8,511
5 Makalu I, Nepal/China	May 15, 1955	French	27,824	8,481
6 Lhotse Shar II, Nepal/China	May 12, 1970	Austrian	27,504	8,383
7 Dhaulagiri I, Nepal	May 13, 1960	Swiss/Austrian	26,810	8,172
8 Manaslu I (Kutang I), Nepal	May 9, 1956	Japanese	26,760	8,156
9 Cho Oyu, Nepal	Oct 19, 1954	Austrian	26,750	8,153
10 Nanga Parbat (Diamir), Kashmir	July 3, 1953	German/Austrian	26,660	8,126

* Height of principal peak; lower peaks of the same mountain are excluded

When the results of the 19th-century Great Trigonometrical Survey of India were studied, it was first realized that Everest was Earth's tallest mountain. Its height originally was computed as 29,002 ft (8,840 m), adjusted in 1955 to 29,029 ft (8,848 m) and in 1993 to 29,028 ft (8,848 m). In 1999 an analysis of data beamed from sensors on Everest's summit to GPS (Global Positioning System) satellites established a new height of 29,035 ft (8,850 m), which is now accepted as the current "official" figure.

top10 LARGEST **DESERTS**

DESERT / LOCATION	APPROX. AREA SQ MILES	APPROX. AREA SQ KM
1 Sahara, Northern Africa	3,500,000	9,100,000
2 Australian, Australia*	1,300,000	3,400,000
3 Arabian Peninsula, Southwest Asia#	1,000,000	2,600,000
4 Turkestan, Central Asia†	750,000	1,900,000
5 = Gobi, Central Asia	500,000	1,300,000
= North American Desert, USA/Mexico☆	500,000	1,300,000
7 Patagonia, Southern Argentina	260,000	670,000
8 Thar, Northwest India/Pakistan	230,000	600,000
9 Kalahari, Southwestern Africa	220,000	570,000
10 Takla Makan, Northwestern China	185,000	480,000

* Includes Gibson, Great Sandy, Great Victoria, and Simpson
# Includes an-Nafud and Rub al-Khali
† Includes Kara-Kum and Kyzylkum
☆ Includes Great Basin, Mojave, Sonorah, and Chihuahuan

top10 COUNTRIES WITH THE **LOWEST ELEVATIONS**

COUNTRY*	HIGHEST POINT	ELEVATION FT	ELEVATION M
1 Maldives	Unnamed on Wilingili Island in the Addu Atoll	7.8	2.4
2 Tuvalu	Unnamed	16.4	5
3 Marshall Islands	Unnamed on Likiep	32.8	10
4 The Gambia	Unnamed	173.9	53
5 Nauru	Unnamed on plateau rim	200.1	61
6 The Bahamas	Mount Alvernia on Cat Island	206.7	63
7 Vatican City	Unnamed	246.1	75
8 Kiribati	Unnamed on Banaba	265.7	81
9 Qatar	Qurayn Abu al Bawl	337.9	103
10 Singapore	Bukit Timah	544.6	166

* Excludes overseas possessions, territories, and dependencies

Source: CIA, "The World Factbook 2005"

Weather

top10 COLDEST PLACES IN THE US

CITY / STATE	MEAN ELEVATION FT/M	TEMPERATURE °F	°C
1 Mt. Washington, New Hampshire	6,266/1,910	27.2	-2.7
2 International Falls, Minnesota	1,184/361	37.4	3.0
3 Marquette, Michigan	1,415/431	38.7	3.7
4 Duluth, Minnesota	1,426/435	39.1	3.9
5 Caribou, Maine	623/190	39.2	4.0
6 Sault St. Marie, Michigan	715/218	40.1	4.5
7 Grand Forks, North Dakota	843/257	40.3	4.6
8 Alamosa, Colorado	7,539/2,298	40.8	4.9
9 Williston, North Dakota	1,982/604	40.9	4.9
10 Fargo, North Dakota	899/274	41.5	5.3

Source: National Climatic Data Center

These chilly temperatures are 30-year averages for the period 1971–2000 and for the contiguous states (excluding Hawaii and Alaska).

top10 LOWEST TEMPERATURES RECORDED IN THE US

STATE* / YEAR	AVERAGE TEMPERATURE* °F	°C
1 Alaska, 1971	-80	-62.2
2 Montana, 1954	-70	-56.7
3 Utah, 1985	-69	-56.1
4 Wyoming, 1933	-66	-54.4
5 Colorado, 1985	-61	-51.7
6 = Idaho, 1943	-60	-51.1
= North Dakota, 1936	-60	-51.1
= Minnesota, 1996	-60	-51.1
9 South Dakota 1936	-58	-50.0
10 Wisconsin, 1996	-55	-48.3

* Extreme low for each state

Source: National Climatic Data Center

top10 WETTEST PLACES IN THE US

CITY / STATE
MEAN ANNUAL PRECIPITATION (INCHES / MM)

5 Annette, Alaska 100.83 / 2,561

7 Valdez, Alaska 67.41 / 1,712

9 Mobile, Alabama 66.29 / 1,683

2 Hilo, Hawaii 126.27 / 3,207

4 Quillayute, Washington 101.72 / 2,583

6 Kodiak, Alaska 75.35 / 1,913

3 Mt. Washington, New Hampshire 101.91 / 2,588

8 Astoria, Oregon 67.13 / 1,705

10 Pensacola, Florida 64.28 / 1,632

1 Yakutat, Alaska 160.38 / 4,073

Source: National Climatic Data Center

the 10 DRIEST PLACES IN THE US

CITY / STATE	MEAN ANNUAL PRECIPITATION*	
	INCHES	MM
1 Yuma, Arizona	3.01	76
2 Barrow, Alaska	4.16	105
3 Las Vegas, Nevada	4.49	114
4 Bishop, California	5.02	127
5 Bakersfield, California	6.49	164
6 Alamosa, Colorado	7.25	184
7 Reno, Nevada	7.48	189
8 Winslow, Arizona	8.03	203
9 Yakima, Washington	8.26	209
10 Phoenix, Arizona	8.29	210

* Based on 30-year averages for the period 1971–2000

Source: National Climatic Data Center

top 10 HOTTEST PLACES IN THE US*

 1 78.1 / 25.6
Key West, Florida

 2 77.5 / 25.3
Honolulu, Hawaii

 3 76.7 / 24.8
Miami, Florida

 4 75.8 / 24.3
Kahului, Hawaii

 5 75.7 / 24.2
Lihue, Hawaii

 6 75.3 / 24.0
= West Palm Beach, Florida
= Yuma, Arizona

 8 74.9 / 23.8
Fort Myers, Florida

 9 73.9 / 23.3
Hilo, Hawaii

 10 73.3 / 23.0
Brownsville, Texas

* Based on mean temperatures for the period 1971–2000; first temperature is Fahrenheit, second Celsius

Source: National Climatic Data Center

top 10 SUNNIEST PLACES IN THE US

CITY / STATE	SUNSHINE AVERAGE AS PERCENTAGE OF POSSIBLE %
1 Yuma, Arizona	90
2 = Las Vegas, Nevada	85
= Phoenix, Arizona	85
= Tucson, Arizon	85
5 El Paso, Texas	84
6 = Fresno, California	79
= Reno, Nevada	79
8 = Flagstaff, Arizona	78
= Sacramento, California	78
10 = Albuquerque, New Mexico	76
= Key West, Florida	76
= Pueblo, Colorado	76

The maximum percentage of sunshine is 100, so Yuma has cloud cover for just 10 percent of the year.

Natural Disasters

The eruption of Tambora on the island of Sumbawa killed about 10,000 islanders immediately, with a further 82,000 dying subsequently (38,000 on Sumbawa, 44,000 on neighboring Lombok) from disease and famine resulting from crops being destroyed.

the 10 WORST EARTHQUAKES

1 Near East/Mediterranean
May 20, 1202, 1,100,000

2 Shenshi, China
Feb 2, 1556, 820,000

3 Calcutta, India
Oct 11, 1737, 300,000

4 Antioch, Syria
May 20, 526, 250,000

5 Tangshan, China
Jul 28, 1976, 242,419

6 Nan Shan, China
May 22, 1927, 200,000

7 Yeddo, Japan
Dec 30, 1703, 190,000

8 Kansu, China
Dec 16, 1920, 180,000

9 Messina, Italy
Dec 28, 1908, 160,000

10 Tokyo/Yokohama, Japan
Sept 1, 1923, 142,807

There are some discrepancies between the "official" death tolls in many of the world's worst earthquakes. For example, 750,000 is sometimes quoted for the Tangshan earthquake of 1976, and totals of 58,000– 250,000 are given for the quake that devastated Messina in 1908.

the 10 WORST TSUNAMIS

1 Southeast Asia,
Dec 26, 2004, 287,534

2 Krakatoa, Sumatra/Java*,
Aug 27, 1883, 36,380

3 Sanriku, Japan,
Jun 15, 1896, 28,000

4 Agadir, Morocco#,
Feb 29, 1960, 12,000

5 Lisbon, Portugal,
Nov 1, 1755, 10,000

6 Papua New Guinea,
Jul 18, 1998, 8,000

7 Chile/Pacific islands/Japan,
May 22, 1960, 5,700

8 Philippines,
Aug 17, 1976, 5,000

9 Hyuga to Izu, Japan,
Oct 28, 1707, 4,900

10 Sanriku, Japan,
Mar 3, 1933, 3,000

Often mistakenly called tidal waves, tsunamis (from the Japanese *tsu*, port, and *nami*, wave) are powerful waves caused by undersea disturbances, such as earthquakes or volcanic eruptions, often resulting in massive devastation of low-lying coastal settlements.

* Combined effect of volcanic eruption and tsunamis
\# Combined effect of earthquake and tsunamis

the 10 WORST HURRICANES, TYPHOONS AND CYCLONES

1 East Pakistan (Bangladesh)
Nov 13, 1970, 500,000–1,000,000

2 Bengal, India
Oct 7, 1737, >300,000

3 Haiphong, Vietnam
Oct 8, 1881, 300,000

4 Bengal, India
Oct 31, 1876, 200,000

5 Bangladesh
Apr 29, 1991, 138,000

6 Bombay, India
June 6, 1882, >100,000

7 Southern Japan
Aug 23, 1281, 68,000

8 Northeast China
Aug 2–3, 1922, 60,000

9 Calcutta, India
Oct 5, 1864, 50,000–70,000

10 Bengal, India
Oct 15–16, 1942, 40,000

The cyclone of 1970 hit the Bay of Bengal with winds of over 120 mph (190 km/h). Loss of life was worst in the Bhola region, so it is often known as the Bhola cyclone. The cyclone that struck India in 1737 churned the sea into a 40-ft (12-m) storm surge, flooding land and destroying ships.

LIFE ON EARTH

2

Dinosaurs

top10 DINOSAUR **DISCOVERERS**

	DISCOVERER / COUNTRY	PERIOD	DINOSAURS NAMED*
1	Friedrich von Huene (Germany)	1902–61	46
2	Othniel Charles Marsh (USA)	1870–94	39
3	Dong Zhiming (China)	1973–2003	35
4	= Edward Drinker Cope (USA)	1866–92	30
	= Harry Govier Seeley (UK)	1869–98	30
6	José Fernando Bonaparte (Argentina)	1969–2000	28
7	Richard Owen (UK)	1841–84	23
8	= Barnum Brown (USA)	1873–1963	17
	= Henry Fairfield Osborn (USA)	1902–24	17
	= Yang Zhong-Jian ("C.C. Young") (China)	1937–82	17

* Including joint namings

top10 **LONGEST** DINOSAURS EVER DISCOVERED

This Top 10 is based on the most reliable recent evidence of dinosaur lengths and indicates the probable ranges. As more information is assembled, these are undergoing constant revision. To compare the sizes of these dinosaurs with living animals, note that the largest recorded crocodile measured 20 ft 4 in (6.2 m) and the largest elephant 35 ft (10.7 m) from trunk to tail and weighed about 12 tonnes.

NAME
ESTIMATED WEIGHT (TONNES) / LENGTH (FT/M)

1 Argentinosaurus huinculensis
80–100 / 115–148/ 35–45
An Argentinian farmer discovered a 6-ft (1.8-m) bone in 1988. It was found to be the shinbone of a previously unknown dinosaur, which was given the name *Argentinosaurus*.

↻ *African elephants at approximately same scale.*

2 Seismosaurus
50–80 / 108/33
A skeleton of this colossal planteater was excavated in 1985 near Albuquerque, New Mexico, by US paleontologist David Gillette and given a name that means "earth-shaking lizard."

3 Paralititan stromeri
70 / 82–98/25–30
Remains discovered in 2001 in the Sahara Desert in Egypt suggest that it was a giant plant-eater. Its name means "Stromer's tidal giant," and commemorates the site's discoverer, Bavarian geologist Ernst Stromer von Reichenbach.

4 Sauroposeidon
50–60 / 98/30
From vertebrae discovered in 1994, it has been estimated that this creature was probably the tallest ever to walk on Earth, able to extend its neck to 60 ft (18 m). Its name means "Earthquake lizard-god."

5 Supersaurus vivianae
50 / 79–98/24–30
The remains of *Supersaurus* were found in Colorado in 1972. Some scientists have suggested a length of up to 138 ft (42 m) and a weight of perhaps 75–100 tonnes.

Gentle giants
Two Brachiosaurus *graze on tree tops. Although of fearsome size, they were docile vegetarians.*

the 10 FIRST DINOSAURS TO BE NAMED

	NAME	MEANING	NAMED BY	YEAR
1	Megalosaurus	Great lizard	William Buckland	1824
2	Iguanodon	Iguana tooth	Gideon Mantell	1825
3	Hylaeosaurus	Woodland lizard	Gideon Mantell	1833
4	Macrodontophion	Large tooth snake	A. Zborzewski	1834
5	Palaeosaurus	Ancient lizard	Henry Riley and Samuel Stutchbury	1836
6	Thecodontosaurus	Socket-toothed lizard	Henry Riley and Samuel Stutchbury	1836
7	Plateosaurus	Flat lizard	Hermann von Meyer	1837
8	Poekilopleuron	Varying side	Jacques Armand Eudes-Deslongchamps	1838
9	= Cetiosaurus	Whale lizard	Richard Owen	1841
	Cladeiodon	Branch tooth	Richard Owen	1841

The 10 first dinosaurs were all identified and named within a quarter of a century – although subsequent research has since cast doubt on the authenticity of certain specimens. The name *Megalosaurus*, the first to be given to a dinosaur, was proposed by William Buckland (1784–1856), an English geologist, in an article published in 1824 in the *Transactions of the Geological Society of London*. Then the *Iguanodon* was identified by Gideon Algernon Mantell (1790–1852) in 1825. A doctor in his home town of Lewes in Sussex, he devoted much of his life to the study of geology. Mantell (or, according to some authorities, his wife Mary) found the first *Iguanodon* teeth in 1822 in a pile of stones being used for road repairs. After much detailed study, he concluded that they resembled an enormous version of the teeth of the Central American iguana lizard, and hence he suggested the name *Iguanodon*.

top 10 SMALLEST DINOSAURS

	DINOSAUR	MAX. SIZE IN	CM
1	Micropachycephalosaurus	20	50
2	= Saltopus	23	60
	= Yandangornis	23	60
4	Microraptor	30	77
5	= Lesothosaurus	35	90
	= Nanosaurus	35	90
7	= Bambiraptor	36	91
	= Sinosauropteryx	36	91
9	Wannanosaurus	39	99
10	Procompsognathus	47	120

AMAZING FACT

The Name of the Beasts

A number of dinosaurs had been named before the word "dinosaur" itself was invented. "Dinosauria," or "terrible lizards," was proposed in April 1842 by British anatomist Richard Owen (1804–92) in a report for the British Association for the Advancement of Science.

6 Andesaurus delgadoi
12.5 / 59–98/18–30
Found in Argentina and named in 1991 by Calvo and José Bonaparte, its vertebrae alone measure 2 ft (0.6 m).

7 Giraffatitan brancai
Uncertain / 82–98/ 25–30
This lightly built but long dinosaur was found in Tanzania and named by Gregory S. Paul in 1988.

8 Diplodocus
10–18 / 89/27
As it was long and thin, *Diplodocus* was a relative lightweight in the dinosaur world. It was also probably one of the most stupid dinosaurs, having the smallest brain in relation to its body size.

9 Barosaurus
40 / 66–89/20–27
Barosaurus (meaning "heavy lizard," so named by Othniel C. Marsh in 1890) has been found in both North America and Africa, thus proving the existence of a land link in Jurassic times (205–140 million years ago).

10 Brachiosaurus
30–80 / 85/26
Its name (given by US paleontologist Elmer S. Riggs in 1903) means "arm lizard." A mounted skeleton of the dinosaur in the Humboldt Museum, Berlin, is the largest in the world.

Nature's Heavyweights

top10 **HEAVIEST** BIRDS

BIRD* / SCIENTIFIC NAME	HEIGHT INCHES	CM	WEIGHT LB	KG
1 Ostrich (male) (*Struthio camelus*)	100.4	255	343	156.0
2 Northern cassowary (*Casuarius unappendiculatus*)	59.1	150	127	58.0
3 Emu (female) (*Dromaius novaehollandiae*)	61.0	155	121	55.0
4 Emperor penguin (female) (*Aptenodytes forsteri*)	45.3	115	101	46.0
5 Greater rhea (*Rhea americana*)	55.1	140	55	25.0
6 Mute swan# (*Cygnus olor*)	93.7	238	49	22.5
7 Kori bustard# (*Ardeotis kori*)	106.3	270	41	19.0
8 = Andean condor# (*Vultur gryphus*)	126.0	320	33	15.0
= Great white pelican# (*Pelecanus onocrotalus*)	141.7	360	33	15.0
10 European black vulture# (Old World) (*Aegypius monachus*)	116.1	295	27	12.5

* By species
# Flighted; all others are flightless

Source: Chris Mead

top10 LAND ANIMALS WITH THE **BIGGEST BRAINS**

ANIMAL SPECIES	AVERAGE BRAIN WEIGHT LB	OZ	GM
1 Elephants (genus *Elephantidae*)	13	4	6,000
2 Adult human (*Homo sapiens*)	3	0	1,350
3 Camels (*Camelus* species)	1	11	762
4 Giraffe (*Giraffa camelopardalis*)	1	8	680
5 Hippopotamus (*Hippopotamus amphibius*)	1	4	582
6 Horses (*Equus* species)	1	3	532
7 Gorilla (*Gorilla gorilla gorilla*)	1	1	500
8 Polar bear (*Ursus maritimus*)	1	1	498
9 Cows (*Bos* species)	0	15	445
10 Chimpanzee (*Pan troglodytes*)	0	15	420

The sperm whale has the heaviest brain of all animals, weighing in at a massive 17 lb 3 oz (7.8 kg).

top10 **HEAVIEST** TERRESTRIAL MAMMALS

MAMMAL* / SCIENTIFIC NAME
LENGTH FT/M / WEIGHT LB/KG

African elephant
(*Loxodonta africana*)
24.6 / 7.5   16,534 / 7,500

Hippopotamus
(*Hippopotamus amphibius*)
16.4 / 5.0   9,920 / 4,500

White rhinoceros
(*Ceratotherium simum*)
13.7 / 4.2   7,937 / 3,600

Giraffe
(*Giraffa camelopardalis*)
15.4 / 4.7   4,255 / 1,930

American buffalo
(*Bison bison*)
11.4 / 3.5   2,205 / 1,000

Moose (*Alces alces*)
10.1 / 3.1   1,820 / 825

Brown (grizzly) bear
(*Ursus arctos*)
9.8 / 3.0   1,720 / 780

Arabian camel (dromedary)
(*Camelus dromedarius*)
11.3 / 3.45   1,521 / 690

Siberian tiger
(*Panthera tigris altaica*)
10.8 / 3.3   793 / 360

Gorilla
(*Gorilla gorilla gorilla*)
6.5 / 2.0   606 / 275

* Heaviest species per genus

The list excludes domesticated cattle and horses, focusing on the heavyweight champions within distinctive large mammal groups or megafauna. Chief among them, the elephant, is 357,000 times as heavy as the smallest mammal, the pygmy shrew.

top10 LARGEST SPECIES OF **FRESHWATER FISH** CAUGHT

SPECIES	ANGLER / LOCATION / DATE	LB	OZ	KG	GM
			WEIGHT		
1 Mekong giant catfish (*Pangasianodon gigas*)	Team of five anglers, Mekong River, Thailand, May 1, 2005	646	0	293	0
2 White sturgeon (*Acipenser transmontanus*)	Joey Pallotta III, Benicia, California, Jul 9, 1983	468	0	212	28
3 Alligator gar (*Atractosteus spatula*)	Bill Valverde, Rio Grande, Texas, Dec 2, 1951	279	0	126	55
4 Nile perch (*Lates niloticus*)	William Toth, Lake Nasser, Egypt, Dec 20, 2000	230	0	104	32
5 Beluga sturgeon (*Huso huso*)	Ms Merete Lehne, Guryev, Kazakhstan, May 3, 1993	224	13	102	0
6 Flathead catfish (*Pylodictis olivaris*)	Ken Paulie, Withlacoochee River, Florida, May 14, 1998	123	9	55	79
7 Blue catfish (*Ictalurus furcatus*)	William P. McKinley, Wheeler Reservoir, Tennessee, Jul 5, 1996	111	0	50	35
8 Redtailed catfish (*Phractocephalus hemioliopteru*)	Gilberto Fernandes, Amazon River, Brazil, Jul 16, 1988	97	7	44	20
9 Chinook salmon (*Oncorhynchus tshawytscha*)	Les Anderson, Kenai River, Alaska, May 17, 1985	97	4	44	11
10 Giant tigerfish (*Hydrocynus goliath*)	Raymond Houtmans, Zaïre River, Kinshasa, Zaïre, Jul 9, 1988	97	0	44	0

Source: International Game Fish Association, "World Record Game Fishes, 2005"

top10 CARNIVORES WITH THE **HEAVIEST NEWBORN**

MAMMAL / SCIENTIFIC NAME	LB	OZ	GM
		BIRTH WEIGHT	
1 African lion (*Panthera leo*)	3	10	1,650
2 Spotted hyena (*Crocuta crocuta*)	3	5	1,500
3 Tiger (*Panthera tigris*)	2	11	1,255
4 Brown (grizzly) bear (*Ursus arctos*)	2	3	1,000
5 Jaguar (*Panthera onca*)	1	13	816
6 Polar bear (*Ursus maritimus*)	1	7	641
7 Leopard (*Panthera pardus*)	1	3	549
8 Snow leopard (*Panthera uncia*)	1	0	442
9 Grey wolf (*Canis lupus*)	0	15	425
10 Mountain lion (*Puma concolor*)	0	14	400

The ratio in size between a tiny, newborn kangaroo (under 1 inch/2.5 cm long) and an adult is the greatest of all mammals.

➔ Big babies
While carnivores produce relatively large offspring, tiger cubs are only 40 percent of the weight of a newborn human.

Great Lengths

top10 **LARGEST** BUTTERFLIES AND MOTHS

	BUTTERFLY / MOTH (SCIENTIFIC NAME)	APPROX. WINGSPAN INCHES	MM
● **1**	Atlas moth (*Attacus atlas*)	11.8	300
● **2**	Owlet moth (*Thysania agrippina*)*	11.4	290
○ **3**	Queen Alexandra's birdwing (*Ornithoptera alexandrae*)	11.0	280
● **4**	Chickweed geometer (*Haematopis grataria*)	10.2	260
○ **5**	African giant swallowtail (*Papilio antimachus*)	9.1	230
○ **6**	=Goliath birdwing (*Ornithoptera goliath*)	8.3	210
●	=Hercules emperor moth (*Coscinocera hercules*)	8.3	210
○ **8**	=Buru opalescent birdwing (*Troides prattorum*)	7.9	200
○	=Birdwing (*Trogonoptera trojana*)	7.9	200
○	=Birdwing (*Troides hypolitus*)	7.9	200

* Exceptional specimen measured at 12.2 in (308 mm)

○ Butterfly   ● Moth

top10 MAMMALS WITH THE **LONGEST GESTATION** PERIODS

	MAMMAL	AVERAGE GESTATION (DAYS)
1	African elephant (*Loxodonta africana*)	660
2	Asiatic elephant (*Elephas maximus*)	600
3	Baird's beaked whale (*Berardius bairdii*)	520
4	White rhinoceros (*Ceratotherium simum*)	490
5	Walrus (*Odobenus rosmarus*)	480
6	Giraffe (*Giraffa camelopardalis*)	460
7	Tapir (*Tapirus*)	400
8	Arabian camel (dromedary) (*Camelus dromedarius*)	390
9	Fin whale (*Balaenoptera physalus*)	370
10	Llama (*Lama glama*)	360

The 480-day gestation of the walrus includes a delay of up to five months while the fertilized embryo is held as a blastocyst (a sphere of cells), but it is not implanted until later in the wall of the uterus. This option enables offspring to be produced at a more favorable time of the year. Other mammals capable of this "delayed implantation" trick include the roe deer and the badger.

top10 BIRDS WITH THE **LARGEST WINGSPANS**

	BIRD*	MAXIMUM WINGSPAN INCHES	CM
1	Great white pelican (*Pelecanus onocrotalus*)	141	360
2	Wandering albatross# (*Diomedea exulans*)	138	351
3	Andean condor (*Vultur gryphus*)	126	320
4	Himalayan griffon (vulture) (*Gyps himalayensis*)	122	310
5	Black vulture (Old World) (*Coragyps atratus*)	116	295
6	Marabou stork (*Leptoptilos crumeniferus*)	113	287
7	Lammergeier (*Gypaetus barbatus*)	111	282
8	Sarus crane (*Grus antigone*)	110	280
9	Kori bustard (*Ardeotis kori*)	106	270
10	Steller's sea eagle (*Haliaeetus pelagicus*)	104	265

* By species
 # Royal albatross, a close relative, is the same size

Source: Chris Mead

The measurements are, as far as can be ascertained, for wingtip to wingtip of live birds measured in a natural position. Much bigger wingspans have been claimed for many species, but dead specimens may be stretched by 15 to 20 percent.

top10 LONGEST **LAND ANIMALS**

	ANIMAL*	MAXIMUM LENGTH FT	M
1	Reticulated (royal) python (*Python regius*)	35	10.7
2	Tapeworm (*Cestoda* class)	33	10.0
3	African elephant (*Loxodonta africana*)	24	7.3
4	Estuarine crocodile (*Crocodylus porosus*)	19	5.9
5	Giraffe (*Giraffa camelopardalis*)	19	5.8
6	White rhinoceros (*Ceratotherium simum*)	14	4.2
7	Hippopotamus (*Hippopotamus amphibius*)	13	4.0
8	American bison (*Bison bison*)	13	3.9
9	Arabian camel (dromedary) (*Camelus dromedarius*)	12	3.5
10	Siberian tiger (*Panthera tigris altaica*)	11	3.3

* Longest representative of each species

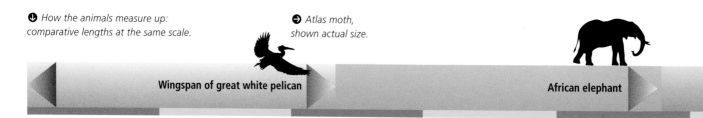

⊙ *How the animals measure up: comparative lengths at the same scale.*

➲ *Atlas moth, shown actual size.*

Wingspan of great white pelican

African elephant

top10 LONGEST **SNAKES**

SNAKE / SCIENTIFIC NAME / MAXIMUM LENGTH FT/M

Although the South American anaconda is sometimes claimed to be the longest snake, this has never been authenticated: reports of monsters up to 120 ft (36.5 m) have been published, but without material evidence. Former US President and hunting enthusiast Theodore Roosevelt once offered $5,000 to anyone who could produce the skin or vertebra of an anaconda of over 30 ft (9 m), but the prize was never won.

1 Reticulated (royal) python (*Python regius*) 35 / 10.7 **2** Anaconda (*Eunectes murinus*) 28 / 8.5

3 Indian python (*Python molurus molurus*) 25 / 7.6 **4** Diamond python (*Morelia spilota spilota*) 21 / 6.4

5 King cobra (*Opiophagus hannah*) 19 / 5.8 **6** Boa constrictor (*Boa constrictor*) 16 / 4.9

7 Bushmaster (*Lachesis muta*) 12 / 3.7 **8** Giant brown snake (*Oxyuranus scutellatus*) 11 / 3.4

9 Diamondback rattlesnake (*Crotalus atrox*) 9 / 2.7 **10** Indigo or gopher snake (*Drymarchon corais*) 8 / 2.4

top10 LONGEST **MOLLUSKS***

MOLLUSK / SCIENTIFIC NAME	CLASS	LENGTH INCHES	MM
1 Giant squid (*Architeuthis* species)	Cephalopod	660#	16,764
2 Giant clam (*Tridacna gigas*)	Marine bivalve	51	1,300
3 Australian trumpet (*Syrinx aruanus*)	Marine snail	30	770
4 Sea slug (*Hexabranchus sanguineus*)	Sea slug	20	520
5 Heteropod (*Carinaria cristata*)	Heteropod	19	500
6 Steller's Coat of Mail shell (*Cryptochiton stelleri*)	Chiton	18	470
7 Freshwater mussel (*Cristaria plicata*)	Freshwater bivalve	11	300
8 Giant African snail (*Achatina achatina*)	Land snail	7	200
9 Tusk shell (*Dentalium vernedi*)	Scaphopod	5	138
10 Apple snail (*Pila werneri*)	Freshwater snail	4	125

* Largest species within each class # Estimated; actual length unknown

AMAZING FACT

Monster of the Deep

Although the giant squid heads the list of longest mollusks, the Norwegian legend of the monstrous kraken and tales told by sailors in Jules Verne's *Twenty Thousand Leagues Under the Sea* have given rise to the myth of creatures of vast size capable of dragging ships to the bottom. However, even the graphically named "colossal squid" seldom exceeds 46 ft (14 m), and such stories should be taken with a pinch of sea salt.

Reticulated python

At the same scale, the blue whale is twice this length

Giant squid

Animal Speed

top10 FASTEST **BIRDS**

Recent research reveals that, contrary to popular belief, swifts are not fast fliers, but efficient with long, thin, glider-like wings and low wing-loading. Fast fliers generally have a combination of high wing-loading and fast wing beats.

 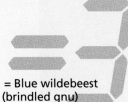

Common eider
(*Somateria mollissima*)
47 / 76

Bewick's swan
(*Cygnus columbianus*)
44 / 72

= Barnacle goose
(*Branta leucopsis*)
42 / 68

= Common crane
(*Grus grus*)
42 / 68

top10 FASTEST **MAMMALS***

The cheetah can deliver its astonishing maximum speed over only relatively short distances. For comparison, the human male 100-m record (Asafa Powell, Jamaica, 2005) stands at 9.77 seconds, equivalent to a speed of 23 mph (37 km/h).

Cheetah
(*Acinonyx jubatus*)
71 / 114

Pronghorn antelope
(*Antilocapra americana*)
57 / 95

= Blue wildebeest (brindled gnu)
(*Connochaetes taurinus*)
50 / 80

= Lion
(*Panthera leo*)
50 / 80

top10 FASTEST **FISH**

Flying fish are excluded: they have a top speed in the water of only 23 mph (37 km/h), but airborne they can reach 35 mph (56 km/h). Many sharks qualify for this list, but only two (the blue and the tiger) are given here to prevent the list becoming overly shark-infested.

Sailfish
(*Istiophorus platypterus*)
69 / 112

Striped marlin
(*Tetrapturus audax*)
50 / 80

Wahoo
(peto, jack mackerel)
(*Acanthocybium solandri*) 48 / 77

Southern bluefin tuna
(*Thunnus maccoyii*)
47 / 76

top10 SLOWEST **MAMMALS**

MAMMAL / SCIENTIFIC NAME*	AVERAGE SPEED MPH	KM/H
1 Three-toed sloth (*Bradypus variegatus*)	0.06–0.19	0.1–0.3
2 Short-tailed (giant mole) shrew (*Blarina brevicauda*)	1.4	2.2
3 = Pine vole (*Pitymis pinetorum*)	2.6	4.2
= Red-backed vole (*Clethrionomys gapperi*)	2.6	4.2
5 Opossum (genus *Didelphis*)	2.7	4.4
6 Deer mouse (genus *Peromyscus*)	2.8	4.5
7 Woodland jumping mouse (*Napaeozapus insignis*)	3.3	5.3
8 Meadow jumping mouse (*Zapus hudsonius*)	3.4	5.5
9 Meadow mouse or meadow vole (*Microtus pennsylvanicus*)	4.1	6.6
10 White-footed mouse (*Peromyscus leucopus*)	4.2	6.8

* Of those species for which data available

top10 HIBERNATING MAMMALS WITH THE **SLOWEST HEARTBEATS***

SPECIES	HEARTBEATS PER MINUTE NONHIBERNATING	HIBERNATING
1 Franklin's ground squirrel (*Spermophilus franklinii*)	n/a	2–4
2 Olympic marmot (*Marmota olympus*)	130–140	4
3 Syrian (golden) hamster (*Mesocricetus auratus*)	500–600	6
4 American black bear# (*Ursus americanus*)	40–50	8
5 Hedgehog (*Erinaceus europaeus*)	190	20
6 Garden dormouse (*Eliomys quercinus*)	n/a	25
7 Eastern pigmy possum (dormouse possum, possum mouse) (*Cercartetus nanus*)	300–650	28–80
8 Birch mouse (*Sicista betulina*)	550–600	30
9 Big brown bat (*Eptesicus fuscus*)	450	34
10 Edible dormouse (*Glis glis*)	450	35

* Of those species for which data are available; one species per genus listed
# Not considered true hibernators by some experts — the heartbeat drops, although body temperature is not significantly lowered

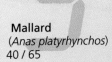 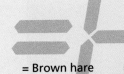 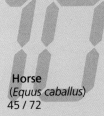

Mallard
(*Anas platyrhynchos*)
40 / 65

= Red-throated diver
(*Gavia stellata*)
38 / 61

= Wood pigeon
(*Columba palumbus*)
38 / 61

Oystercatcher
(*Haematopus ostralegus*)
36 / 58

= Ring-necked pheasant
(*Phasianus colchichus*)
33 / 54

= White-fronted goose
(*Anser albifrons*)
33 / 54

Source: Chris Mead

  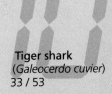

= Springbok
(*Antidorcas marsupialis*)
50 / 80

= Brown hare
(*Lepus capensis*)
48 / 77

= Red fox
(*Vulpes vulpes*)
48 / 77

= Grant's gazelle
(*Gazella granti*)
47 / 76

= Thomson's gazelle
(*Gazella thomsonii*)
47 / 76

Horse
(*Equus caballus*)
45 / 72

* Of those species for which data available

Yellowfin tuna
(*Thunnus albacares*)
46 / 74

Blue shark
(*Prionace glauca*)
43 / 69

= Bonefish
(*Albula vulpes*)
40 / 64

= Swordfish
(*Xiphias gladius*)
40 / 64

Tarpon (ox-eye herring)
(*Megalops cyprinoides*)
35 / 56

Tiger shark
(*Galeocerdo cuvier*)
33 / 53

Source: Lucy T. Verma

⊃ Flying fins
As many anglers have discovered to their cost, the marlin is one of the fastest and most powerful of all fish.

Nature by the Numbers

⊙ A pot of gold
Although its average litter size is about nine, extreme instances of golden hamsters producing as many as 26 have been recorded. In theory, a single pair could produce up to 100,000 descendants in a single year.

top10 MOST EXPENSIVE THREATENED AND ENDANGERED **MAMMAL PROGRAMS** IN THE US

MAMMAL / SCIENTIFIC NAME	EXPENDITURE, 2004 ($)
1 Steller's sea-lion (*Eumetopias jubatus*)	42,557,321
2 Right whale (*Balaena glacialis* and *australis*)	12,369,623
3 West Indian manatee (*Trichechus manatus*)	9,861,677
4 Grizzly bear (*Ursus arctos*)	7,743,129
5 Gray wolf (*Canis lupus*)	6,665,669
6 Indiana bat (*Myotis sodalis*)	4,920,682
7 Louisiana black bear (*Ursus americanus luteolus*)	3,811,626
8 Black-footed ferret (*Mustela nigripes*)	3,081,889
9 Canas lynx (*Lynx canadensis*)	3,012,982
10 San Joaquin kit fox (*Vulpes macrotis mutica*)	2,641,027
Mammals total	122,205,860

Source: US Fish & Wildlife Service

top10 WILD MAMMALS WITH THE **LARGEST LITTERS**

MAMMAL / SCIENTIFIC NAME	AVERAGE LITTER
1 Common tenrec (*Tenrec ecaudatus*)	25
2 Virginia (common) opossum (*Didelphis virginiana*)	21
3 Southern (black-eared) opossum (*Didelphis marsupialis*)	10
4 = Ermine (*Mustela erminea*)	9
= Prairie vole (*Microtus ochrogaster*)	9
= Syrian (golden) hamster (*Mesocricetus auratus*)	9
7 African hunting dog (*Lycaon pictus*)	8.8
8 = Dhole (Indian wild dog) (*Cuon alpinus*)	8
= Pygmy opossum (*Marmosa robinsoni*)	8
= South American mouse opossum (*Gracilinanus agilis*)	8

The prairie vole probably holds the world record for most offspring produced in a season. It has up to 17 litters in rapid succession, bringing up to 150 young into the world. Rabbits, despite their reputation as fast breeders, fail to make the list with an average litter size of six. All the numbers in the list are averages: the tiny tenrec can produce as many as 31 in a single litter, and instances of domestic pigs producing 30 or more piglets at one go are not uncommon. Despite these prodigious reproductive peaks, mammalian litter sizes appear minute when compared with those of other animal groups. Many fish, for instance, can lay over 10,000 eggs at a time and many amphibians over 1,000.

top10 MOST EXPENSIVE, THREATENED AND ENDANGERED **BIRD PROGRAMS** IN THE US

BIRD / SCIENTIFIC NAME	EXPENDITURE, 2004 ($)
1 Red-cockaded woodpecker (*Picoides borealis*)	14,125,085
2 Southwestern willow flycatcher (*Empidonax traillii extimus*)	11,911,824
3 Bald eagle (*Haliaeetus leucocephalus*)	9,837,240
4 Northern spotted owl (*Strix occidentalis caurina*)	6,980,570
5 Marbled murrelet (*Brachyramphus marmoratus marmoratus*)	5,646,695
6 Mexican spotted owl (*Strix occidentalis lucida*)	5,276,995
7 Black-capped vireo (*Vireo atricapilla*)	4,606,463
8 Western snowy plover (*Charadrius alexandrinus nivosus*)	4,530,614
9 Golden-cheeked warbler (*Dendroica chrysoparia*)	4,452,326
10 Piping plover (*Charadrius melodus*)	3,913,981
Birds total	103,170,863

Source: US Fish & Wildlife Service

the 10 FIRST LAND **MAMMALS** DECLARED ENDANGERED IN THE US

MAMMAL / SCIENTIFIC NAME

1 Black-footed ferret *(Mustela nigripes)*

2 Delmarva Peninsula fox squirrel *(Sciurus niger cinereus)*

3 Florida panther *(Felis concolor coryi)*

4 Grizzly bear *(Ursus arctos)*

5 Indiana bat *(Myotis sodalis)*

6 Key deer *(Odocoileus virginianus clavium)*

7 Red wolf *(Canis niger)*

8 San Joaquin kit fox *(Vulpes macrotis mutica)*

9 Sonoran pronghorn *(Antilocapra americana sonoriensis)*

10 Timber wolf *(Canis lupus lycaon)*

Arranged alphabetically, these were the first 10 US land animals to be identified as threatened with extinction under the Endangered Species Preservation Act of October 15, 1966.

❯ A plague of locusts
Individual swarms containing an estimated 12.5 trillion locusts provide a pointer to the sheer numbers of insect species.

top 10 LARGEST **ENTOMOLOGICAL COLLECTIONS**

COLLECTION* / COUNTRY	APPROX. NO. OF SPECIMENS
1 = Muséum d'Histoire Naturelle Paris, France	30,000,000
= Smithsonian Institution Washington, DC	30,000,000
3 Natural History Museum London, UK	28,000,000
4 Zoologische Staatssammlung Munich, Germany	16,566,000
5 American Museum of Natural History New York, NY	16,204,000
6 Canadian National Collection Ottawa, Canada	15,000,000
7 Zoologisches Forschungsinstitut & Museum Alexander König, Bonn, Germany	14,000,000
8 Bernice P. Bishop Museum Honolulu, Hawaii	13,250,000
9 Musée Royal de l'Afrique Centrale Tervuren, Belgium	10,510,000
10 = Australian National Insect Collection Canberra, Australia	10,000,000
= Museum für Naturkunde der Humboldt-Universität Berlin, Germany	10,000,000

* Excluding Russian collections, for which data not available at time of collection

top 10 MOST COMMON **INSECTS***

ORDER / SCIENTIFIC NAME	APPROXIMATE NO. OF KNOWN SPECIES
1 Beetles *(Coleoptera)*	400,000
2 Butterflies and moths *(Lepidoptera)*	165,000
3 Ants, bees and wasps *(Hymenoptera)*	140,000
4 True flies *(Diptera)*	120,000
5 Bugs *(Hemiptera)*	90,000
6 Crickets, grasshoppers and locusts *(Orthoptera)*	20,000
7 Caddisflies *(Trichoptera)*	10,000
8 Lice *(Phthiraptera/Psocoptera)*	7,000
9 Dragonflies and damselflies *(Odonata)*	5,500
10 Lacewings *(Neuroptera)*	4,700

* By number of known species

This list includes only species that have been discovered and named: it is surmised that many thousands of species still await discovery. It takes no account of the absolute numbers of each species, which are truly colossal, if speculative – one authority suggests that there are 5,000,000,000,000,000 (5,000 trillion) individuals, or 770,000 for every one of the Earth's 6.5 billion humans, which together would weigh at least 12 times as much as the human race and at least three times more than the combined weight of all other living animals.

Deadly Creatures

top10 **DEADLIEST** SPIDERS

SPIDER / SCIENTIFIC NAME	RANGE
1 Banana spider (*Phoneutria fera*)	Central and South America
2 Sydney funnel web (*Atrax robustus*)	Australia
3 Wolf spider (*Lycosa raptorial erythrognatha*)	Central and South America
4 Black widow (*Latrodectus* species)	Widespread
5 Violin spider/Recluse spider (*Loxesceles reclusa*)	Widespread
6 Sac spider (*Cheiracanthium punctorium*)	Central Europe
7 Tarantula (*Eurypelma rubropilosum*)	Neotropics
8 Tarantula (*Acanthoscurria atrox*)	Neotropics
9 Tarantula (*Lasiodora klugi*)	Neotropics
10 Tarantula (*Pamphobetus* sp.)	Neotropics

This list ranks spiders according to their "lethal potential" – their venom yield divided by their venom potency. The banana spider, for example, yields 6 mg of venom, with 1 mg being the estimated lethal dose for humans. However, the venom yield of most is low compared with that of the most dangerous snakes: the tarantula, for example, produces 1.5 mg of venom, but its lethal dose for an adult human is 12 mg.

top10 SNAKES WITH THE **DEADLIEST BITES**

SNAKE / LATIN NAME	EST. LETHAL DOSE FOR HUMANS (MG)	AVE. VENOM PER BITE (MG)	POTENTIAL HUMANS KILLED PER BITE
1 Coastal taipan (*Oxyuranus scutellatus*)	1	120	120
2 Common krait (*Bungarus caeruleus*)	0.5	42	84
3 Philippine cobra (*Naja naja philippinensis*)	2	120	60
4 = King cobra (*Ophiophagus hannah*)	20	1,000	50
= Russell's viper (*Daboia russelli*)	3	150	50
6 Black mamba (*Dendroaspis polyepis*)	3	135	45
7 Yellow-jawed tommygoff (*Bothrops asper*)	25	1,000	40
8 = Multibanded krait (*Bungarus multicinctus*)	0.8	28	35
= Tiger snake (*Notechis scutatus*)	1	35	35
10 Jararacussu (*Bothrops jararacussu*)	25	800	32

Source: Russell E. Gough

In comparing the danger posed by poisonous snakes, this takes account of such factors as venom strength – hence its lethality – and the amount injected per bite (most snakes inject about 15 percent of their venom per bite).

the10 TYPES OF SHARK THAT HAVE **KILLED THE MOST** HUMANS

SHARK SPECIES	UNPROVOKED ATTACKS* (TOTAL)	(FATALITIES#)
1 Great white (*Carcharodon carcharias*)	212	61
2 Tiger (*Galeocerdo cuvieri*)	83	28
3 Bull (*Carcharhinus leucas*)	68	21
4 Requiem (family *Carcharhinidae*)	33	7
5 Blue (*Prionace glauca*)	12	4
6 = Sand tiger (*Carcharias taurus*)	31	2
= Shortfin mako (*Isurus* species)	8	2
8 = Dusky (*Carcharhinus obscurus*)	3	1
= Galápagos (*Carcharhinus galapagensis*)	1	1
= Ganges (*Glyphis gangeticus*)	1	1
= Oceanic whitetip (*Carcharhinus longimanus*)	5	1

* 1580–2004
# Where fatalities are equal, entries are ranked by total attacks

Source: International Shark Attack File, Florida Museum of Natural History

These are the only species of shark that are on record for having actually killed humans, although there have been a total of 32 species involved in attacks that have not proved fatal.

top10 COUNTRIES REGISTERING THE **MOST NEW PLANT** VARIETIES

COUNTRY / VARIETIES REGISTERED*

* As recorded by World Intellectual Property Organization, 2002

1 USA 1,510	2 Japan 1,321
3 Russia 479	4 Australia 286
5 Poland 264	6 Germany 254
7 France 246	8 Canada 228
9 South Africa 196	10 Israel 124

the10 OLDEST **BOTANIC GARDENS** IN NORTH AMERICA

GARDEN	FOUNDED
1 Pierce's Park*, Kennett Square, Pennsylvania	1800
2 United States Botanic Garden, Washington, D.C.	1820
3 Painter's Arboretum#, Media, Pennsylvania	1830
4 Missouri Botanical Garden, St. Louis, Missouri	1859
5 Arnold Arboretum, Jamaica Plain, Massachusetts	1872
6 W.J. Beal Botanical Garden, East Lansing, Michigan	1873
7 Dominion Arboretum & Botanic Garden, Ottawa, Ontario, Canada	1886
8 University of California – Berkeley Botanic Garden, Berkeley, California	1890
9 New York Botanical Garden, Bronx, New York	1891
10 Botanic Garden of Smith College, Northampton, Massachusetts	1893

* Now Longwood Gardens

Now Tyler Arboretum

Source: American Association of Botanical Gardens and Arboreta

The first botanic gardens for the study of plants date from the medieval era. Plants were then widely used in the preparation of remedies, so gardens were often attached to medical schools, such as that at the first European medical school at Salerno, Italy, dating from 1309; it became the model for gardens set up in Venice, Pisa, and Padua. Other European universities, such as Leiden, Leipzig, and Heidelberg, followed suit, with the University of Oxford creating the first in the British Isles in 1621. In the 18th century botanic gardens were set up in various parts of the world, including Pamplemousses, Mauritius (1735); Sibpur, India (1787); and the Dublin National Botanic Gardens, Glasnevin (1795). Several further botanic gardens in the US are no longer extant, among them Elgin Botanic Gardens, New York (founded in 1801); the Botanic Garden of Harvard, Massachusetts (1807); and Lindsey Botanic Garden, Georgia (1810).

the10 COUNTRIES WITH THE **MOST THREATENED** PLANT SPECIES

COUNTRY / TOTAL NO. OF THREATENED PLANTS

1	Ecuador	1,815
2	Malaysia	683
3	China	443
4	Indonesia	383
5	Brazil	381
6	Cameroon	334
7	Sri Lanka	280
8	Madagascar	276
9	Peru	274
10	Mexico	261

USA 240
Canada 1

Source: 2004 IUCN Red List of Threatened Species

Of 11,824 species of plants evaluated by the IUCN in 2004 (out of a total 287,655 known), some 8,321, or 70 percent of the total, were considered threatened. Of these, the most threatened are flowering plants belonging to the class *Magnoliopsida*, of which 7,025 were so-categorized.

Trees & Forests

top10 LARGEST **NATIONAL FORESTS** IN THE US

FOREST / LOCATION	AREA SQ MILES	AREA SQ KM
1 Tongass National Forest, Sitka, Alaska	25,913	67,114
2 Chugach National Forest, Anchorage, Alaska	8,433	21,841
3 Toiyabe National Forest, Sparks, Nevada	5,051	13,082
4 Tonto National Forest, Phoenix, Arizona	4,489	11,626
5 Gila National Forest, Silver City, New Mexico	4,232	10,961
6 Boise National Forest, Boise, Idaho	4,145	10,736
7 Humboldt National Forest, Elko, Nevada	3,878	10,044
8 Challis National Forest, Challis, Idaho	3,851	9,974
9 Shoshone National Forest, Cody, Wyoming	3,808	9,863
10 Flathead National Forest, Kalispell, Montana	3,682	9,536

Source: Land Areas of the National Forest System

Established in 1907 by President Roosevelt, the Tongass National Forest is larger than all 10 of the smallest states and the Dictrict of Columbia. Even the much smaller No.2 is larger than Connecticut.

top10 COUNTRIES WITH THE LARGEST AREAS OF **TROPICAL FOREST**

COUNTRY	AREA SQ MILES	AREA SQ KM
1 Brazil	1,163,222	3,012,730
2 Dem. Rep. of Congo	521,512	1,350,710
3 Indonesia	343,029	887,440
4 Peru	292,032	756,360
5 Bolivia	265,012	686,380
6 Venezuela	214,730	556,150
7 Columbia	205,352	531,860
8 Mexico	176,700	457,650
9 India	171,622	444,500
10 Angola	145,035	375,640

Source: Food and Agriculture Organization of the United Nations, "State of the World's Forests, 2005"

top10 **MOST COMMON** TREES IN THE US

TREE / SCIENTIFIC NAME

1 **Silver maple** (*Acer saccharinum*)
2 **Black cherry** (*Prunus serotina*)
3 **Box elder** (*Acer negundo*)
4 **Eastern cottonwood** (*Populus deltoides*)
5 **Black willow** (*Salix nigra*)
6 **Northern red oak** (*Quercus rubra*)
7 **Flowering dogwood** (*Cornus florida*)
8 **Black oak** (*Quercus velutina*)
9 **Ponderosa pine** (*Pinus ponderosa*)
10 **Coast Douglas fir** (*Pseudotsuga meniesii*)

Source: American Forests

Hardwood trees native to the eastern and southern states prevail in this list, while the Ponderosa pine and Douglas fir are softwoods most typical of the northwest coast forests.

top10 **COUNTRIES** WITH THE LARGEST AREAS OF FOREST

COUNTRY / AREA SQ MILES / SQ KM

The world's forests occupy 29.6 percent of the total land area of the planet. Just under half of Russia is forested, a total area that is almost the size of the whole of Brazil.

1 Russia 3,287,243 / 8,513,920

2 Brazil 2,100,359 / 5,439,905

3 Canada 944,294 / 2,445,710

4 USA 872,564 / 2,259,930

5 China 631,200 / 1,634,800

6 Australia 596,678 / 1,545,390

7 Dem. Rep. of Congo 522,037 / 1,352,070

8 Indonesia 405,353 / 1,049,860

9 Angola 269,329 / 697,560

10 Peru 251,796 / 652,150

Source: Food and Agriculture Organization of the United Nations, "State of the World's Forests, 2005"

⊕ Clinging on
Even the extensive forest cover of Surinam is dwindling, threatening the natural habitats of creatures such as the red-bellied tree frog.

top10 **MOST FORESTED** COUNTRIES

COUNTRY	PERCENTAGE FOREST COVER
1 Surinam	90.5
2 Solomon Islands	88.8
3 Gabon	84.7
4 Brunei	83.9
5 Guyana	78.5
6 Palau	76.1
7 Finland	72.0
8 North Korea	68.2
9 Papua New Guinea	67.6
10 Seychelles	66.7
USA	*24.7*
Canada	*26.5*

Source: Food and Agriculture Organization of the United Nations, "State of the World's Forests, 2005"

These are the 10 countries with the greatest area of forest and woodland as a percentage of their total land area. With increasing deforestation, the world average has fallen from about 32 percent in 1972 to its present 29.6 percent. The least forested large countries in the world are the desert lands of the Middle East and North Africa, such as Oman, which has none, and Egypt and Qatar, each with just 0.1 percent.

top10 **DEFORESTING** COUNTRIES

COUNTRY	ANNUAL FOREST COVER LOSS, 1990–2000 SQ MILES	SQ KM
1 Brazil	8,915	23,090
2 Indonesia	5,065	13,120
3 Sudan	3,702	9,590
4 Zambia	3,286	8,510
5 Mexico	2,436	6,310
6 Dem. Rep. of Congo	2,054	5,320
7 Myanmar	1,996	5,170
8 Nigeria	1,537	3,980
9 Zimbabwe	1,235	3,200
10 Argentina	1,100	2,850

Source: Food and Agriculture Organization of the United Nations, "State of the World's Forests, 2005"

THE HUMAN WORLD

Healthcare

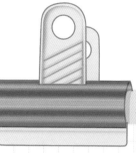

the 10 LEAST HEALTHY COUNTRIES

	COUNTRY	HEALTHY LIFE EXPECTANCY AT BIRTH*
1	Sierra Leone	28.6
2	Lesotho	31.4
3	Angola	33.4
4	Zimbabwe	33.6
5	Swaziland	34.2
6 =	Malawi	34.9
=	Zambia	34.9
8	Burundi	35.1
9	Liberia	35.3
10 =	Afghanistan	35.5
=	Niger	35.5

* Average number of years expected to be spent in good health

Source: World Health Organization

top 10 HEALTHIEST COUNTRIES

	COUNTRY	HEALTHY LIFE EXPECTANCY AT BIRTH*
1	Japan	75.0
2	San Marino	73.4
3	Sweden	73.3
4	Switzerland	73.2
5	Monaco	72.9
6	Iceland	72.8
7	Italy	72.7
8 =	Australia	72.6
=	Spain	72.6
10 =	Canada	72.0
=	France	72.0
=	Norway	72.0
	USA	69.3

* Average number of years expected to be spent in good health

Source: World Health Organization

HALE (Health Adjusted Life Expectancy) differs from life expectancy in that an adjustment is made for years spent in ill health as a result of poor diet, disease, lack of healthcare, and other factors. It is the method used by the World Health Organization to compare the state of health of nations and graphically illustrates the contrast between the HALEs of Western countries – over double those of developing countries, especially sub-Saharan Africa.

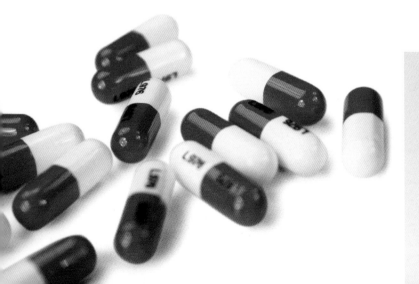

AMAZING FACT

Life Expectancy

Average life expectancy at birth in prehistoric times was about 20 years. During the Greek and Roman era it increased to 28 and in the Medieval period to 33. By the end of the 19th century it was 37, steadily rising during the 20th century to the present-day figure of about 65 years, and predicted to reach 75 by 2050. Today, the greatest disparity is between the 80 years of many developed countries to under 50 in others.

the10 COUNTRIES SPENDING THE LEAST ON HEALTHCARE

	COUNTRY	HEALTH SPENDING PER CAPITA IN 2002 ($)
1	North Korea	0.3
2	Burundi	3
3	= Dem. Rep. of Congo	4
	= Liberia	4
5	= Ethiopia	5
	= Madagascar	5
7	= Sierra Leone	6
	= Somalia [2001]	6
	= Tajikistan	6
10	Niger	7

Source: World Health Organization

top10 COUNTRIES THAT SPEND THE MOST ON HEALTHCARE

	COUNTRY	HEALTH SPENDING PER CAPITA IN 2002 ($)
1	USA	5,274
2	Switzerland	4,219
3	Norway	4,033
4	Monaco	3,656
5	Luxembourg	2,951
6	Iceland	2,916
7	Denmark	2,835
8	Germany	2,631
9	Sweden	2,489
10	Japan	2,476

Source: World Health Organization

top10 COUNTRIES WITH THE FEWEST PATIENTS PER DOCTOR

	COUNTRY	PATIENTS PER DOCTOR
1	Italy	162
2	Cuba	165
3	Georgia	206
4	Greece	220
5	Belgium	223
6	Russia	235
7	Lithuania	252
8	Uruguay	256
9	Israel	272
10	Kazakhstan	273
	USA	*358*

Source: World Health Organization

top10 MOST COMMON REASONS FOR VISITS TO A PHYSICIAN IN THE US

	REASON FOR VISIT*	VISITS, 2003
1	General medical examination	59,938,000
2	Cough	28,759,000
3	Routine prenatal examination	24,457,000
4	Postoperative visit	24,202,000
5	Throat symptoms	23,314,000
6	Gynecological examination	15,553,000
7	Knee symptoms	15,501,000
8	Back symptoms	15,023,000
9	Vision dysfunctions	13,568,000
10	Stomach pains, cramps, and spasms	13,429,000

* Excluding nonspecific and progress visits

Source: National Center for Health Statistics

top10 OVER-THE-COUNTER* HEALTHCARE PRODUCTS IN THE US

	PRODUCT	ANNUAL SALES, 2004 ($)
1	Cough, cold, and related products	3,406,000,000
2	Internal analgesics (painkillers)	2,364,000,000
3	Oral-care products (toothpaste, etc.)	1,259,000,000
4	Heartburn remedies	1,169,000,000
5	Laxatives	708,000,000
6	Oral antiseptics (throat sprays, etc.)	666,000,000
7	First aid	615,000,000
8	Antismoking products	514,000,000
9	Eye care	422,000,000
10	Foot-care products	353,000,000
	Total (including products not in Top 10)	*15,100,000,000*

* Nonprescription, excluding vitamin, mineral, and dietary supplements

Source: AC Nielsen/Consumer Healthcare Products Association

Healthy Living

top10 **FAT** CONSUMERS

COUNTRY	AVERAGE DAILY FAT CONSUMPTION PER CAPITA, 2002 OZ	GMS
1 France	6.02	170.8
2 Belgium	5.62	159.6
3 Austria	5.58	158.2
4 Italy	5.57	158.1
5 USA	5.52	156.5
6 Switzerland	5.51	156.2
7 Greece	5.38	152.7
8 Spain	5.32	150.9
9 Hungary	5.19	147.2
10 Germany	5.16	146.4
World average	*2.73*	*77.5*

Source: Food and Agricultural Organization of the United Nations

top10 **CALORIE** CONSUMERS

COUNTRY	AVERAGE DAILY CALORIE CONSUMPTION PER CAPITA, 2002
1 USA	3,774.1
2 Portugal	3,740.9
3 Greece	3,721.1
4 Austria	3,673.3
5 Italy	3,670.6
6 Israel	3,666.1
7 Ireland	3,656.4
8 France	3,653.9
9 Canada	3,589.3
10 Malta	3,586.9
World average	*2,804.4*

Source: Food and Agriculture Organization of the United Nations

The Calorie requirement of the average man is 2,700 and of a woman 2,500. Inactive people need less, while those engaged in heavy labor require more. The countries in the Top 10, as well as many others, are consuming over 30 percent more than they need – hence the rise of obesity and related medical problems. However, the Calorie consumption of over 10 of the poorest African nations falls below 2,000, with Eritrea's average of 1,512.8 standing at just 40 percent of the figure for the USA.

top10 **PROTEIN** CONSUMERS

COUNTRY	AVERAGE DAILY PROTEIN CONSUMPTION PER CAPITA, 2002 OZ	GMS
1 Israel	4.53	128.6
2 Iceland	4.38	124.4
3 France	4.20	119.2
4 Malta	4.19	118.9
5 Portugal	4.17	118.4
6 Greece	4.08	115.7
7 Ireland	4.03	114.2
8 USA	4.02	114.0
9 Italy	3.98	113.1
10 Spain	3.94	111.7
World average	*2.65*	*75.3*

the10 MOST **OBESE** COUNTRIES

COUNTRY	PERCENTAGE OF OBESE ADULTS* MEN	WOMEN	COUNTRY	PERCENTAGE OF OBESE ADULTS* MEN	WOMEN
1 Nauru	80.2	78.6	**6** Qatar	34.6	45.3
2 Tonga	46.6	70.3	**7** French Polynesia	36.3	44.3
3 Samoa	32.9	63.0	**8** Saudi Arabia	26.4	44.0
4 Jordan#	32.7	59.8	**9** Palestine	23.9	42.5
5 Nieue	15.0	46.0	**10** United Arab Emirates	25.9	39.9
			USA	*27.7*	*34.0*

* Ranked by percentage of obese women (those with a BMI greater than 30) in those countries and latest year for which data available
\# Urban population only

Source: International Obesity Task Force (IOTF)

top10 COUNTRIES WITH THE HEAVIEST SMOKERS

	COUNTRY	AVERAGE ANNUAL CIGARETTE CONSUMPTION PER ADULT, 1992–2000*
1	Greece	3,230
2	Bulgaria	3,222
3	Japan	2,950
4	Switzerland	2,880
5	Spain	2,826
6	Netherlands	2,775
7	Slovenia	2,742
8	Hungary	2,697
9	Russia	2,691
10	South Korea	2,686
	USA	2,092

* Smokers aged over 15, in those countries for which data available

Source: World Health Organization

top10 VITAMIN AND DIETARY SUPPLEMENT CONSUMERS

	COUNTRY	$ PER CAPITA PER ANNUM, 2004
1	Japan	89.93
2	USA	51.34
3	Norway	49.84
4	Taiwan	41.17
5	South Korea	30.53
6	Australia	29.76
7	Singapore	25.64
8	Belgium	24.79
9	Sweden	23.74
10	Italy	22.50

Source: Euromonitor

the10 MOST EFFECTIVE KEEP-FIT ACTIVITIES

1 Swimming
2 Cycling
3 Rowing
4 Gymnastics
5 Judo
6 Dancing
7 Football
8 Jogging
9 Walking (briskly!)
10 Squash

Source: Sports Council (now Sport England)

These are the sports and activities recommended by keep-fit experts as the best means of acquiring all-round fitness, building stamina and strength, and increasing suppleness.

Disease & Illness

the10 WORST

	DISEASE, ETC	% OF DALYS*
1	HIV/AIDS	7.4
2	Coronary heart disease	6.8
3	Stroke	5.0
4	Depression	4.8
5	Road traffic injuries	4.3
6	Tuberculosis	4.2
7	Alcohol abuse	3.4
8	Violence	3.3
9	Obstructive pulmonary disease	3.1
10	Hearing loss	2.7

* Percentage of people's healthy lifespans that are lost
as a result of these diseases, among men aged over 15

Source: World Health Organization

DALYs – Disability-adjusted Life Years – are potential healthy years of life that are lost as a result of contracting diseases or as a result of an injury or other disability. This is used as a measure of the "burden of disease" that affects not only the individual sufferer but also has an affect on the cost of the provision of health services and consequent loss to a country's economy. These are world averages, but there are variations from country to country, with 10 percent of DALYs lost as a result of cardiovascular disease in low- and middle-income countries, but as much as 18 percent in high-income countries.

the10 MOST **COMMON CAUSES** OF ILLNESS

	CAUSE	NEW CASES ANNUALLY
1	Diarrhoea (including dysentery)	4,002,000,000
2	Malaria	up to 500,000,000
3	Acute lower respiratory infections	395,000,000
4	Occupational injuries	350,000,000
5	Occupational diseases	217,000,000
6	Trichomoniasis	170,000,000
7	Mood (affective) disorders	122,865,000
8	Chlamydial infections	89,000,000
9	Alcohol-dependence syndrome	75,000,000
10	Gonococcal (bacterial) infections	62,000,000

Source: World Health Organization

AMAZING FACT

History's Worst Disease

Malaria has killed more people than any other disease. Its cause – a mosquito-borne parasite – was unknown until discovered by Charles Laveran (1845–1922), for which he received the 1907 Nobel Prize. Malaria remains a major killer and in 2005 the Bill & Melinda Gates Foundation pledged $258.3 million to fund research in combating it through prevention, drugs, and a vaccine.

the10 COUNTRIES WITH THE MOST CASES OF MALARIA

	COUNTRY	MALARIA CASES PER 100,000 PEOPLE*, 2000
1	Guinea	75,386
2	Botswana	48,704
3	Burundi	48,098
4	Zambia	34,204
5	Malawi	25,948
6	Mozambique	18,115
7	Gambia	17,340
8	Ghana	15,344
9	Solomon Islands	15,172
10	Yemen	15,160

* Data refer to malaria cases reported to the World Health Organization (WHO) and may represent only a fraction of the true number in a country

Source: United Nations, "Human Development Report 2005"

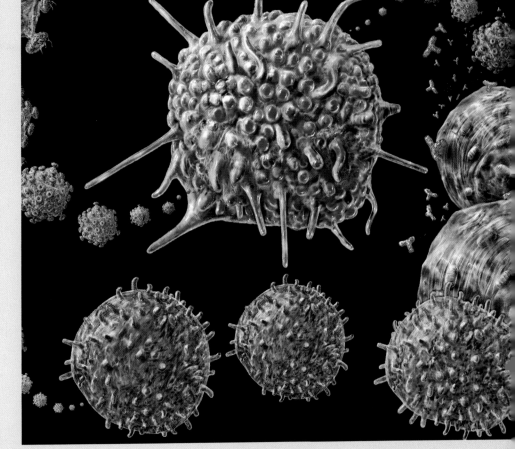

the10 COUNTRIES WITH THE MOST CASES OF TUBERCULOSIS

	COUNTRY	TUBERCULOSIS CASES PER 100,000 PEOPLE*, 2000
1	Djibouti	1,161
2	Swaziland	769
3	Cambodia	734
4	Mali	695
5	Togo	688
6	Ivory Coast	634
7	Sierra Leone	628
8	Indonesia	609
9	Rwanda	598
10	Dem Rep of Congo	594
	World average	*257*
	USA	*4*

* Data refer to the prevalence of all forms of tuberculosis

Source: United Nations, "Human Development Report 2004"

the10 COUNTRIES WITH THE MOST CASES OF AIDS

	COUNTRY	DEATHS, 2003	EST. NO. OF CASES
1	South Africa	370,000	5,300,000
2	India	N/A	5,100,000
3	Nigeria	310,000	3,600,000
4	Zimbabwe	170,000	1,800,000
5	Ethiopia	120,000	1,500,000
6	Tanzania	160,000	1,400,000
7	Mozambique	110,000	1,300,000
8	= Kenya	150,000	1,200,000
	= Zambia	170,000	1,200,000
10	Dem. Rep. of Congo	100,000	950,000
	World	*3,000,000*	*37,800,000*
	USA	*15,000*	*950,000*

Source: UNAIDS, "2004 Report on the Global AIDS Epidemic"

First identified in 1981, AIDS has killed over 25 million and affected the social and economic fabric of many African countries by orphaning children, decimating labor forces, and stretching medical resources to their limit.

🡱 *Deadly virus*
The HIV (Human Immunodeficiency Virus) that causes AIDs (Acquired Immunodeficiency Syndrome) attacks healthy cells. Worldwide, some five million people become infected with AIDS every year.

Birth to Death

the10 COUNTRIES WITH THE MOST BIRTHS

COUNTRY	EST. BIRTHS, 2007
1 India	24,073,392
2 China	17,778,908
3 Nigeria	5,428,253
4 Indonesia	4,960,256
5 Pakistan	4,919,004
6 Bangladesh	4,417,163
7 USA	4,264,142
8 Brazil	3,097,174
9 Ethiopia	2,860,779
10 Dem. Rep. of Congo	2,798,765
World	131,698,130

Source: US Census Bureau, International Data Base

As India's birth rate is maintained and China's is subject to curbs, the population of India is set to overtake that of China by 2030.

the10 COUNTRIES WITH THE HIGHEST BIRTH RATE

COUNTRY	ESTIMATED BIRTH RATE (LIVE BIRTHS PER 1,000, 2007)
1 Niger	50.16
2 Mali	49.57
3 Uganda	47.32
4 Afghanistan	46.61
5 Sierra Leone	45.51
6 Chad	45.30
7 Burkina Faso	45.28
8 Angola	44.61
9 Somalia	44.60
10 Liberia	43.73
World	20.00
USA	14.16

Source: US Census Bureau, International Data Base

The countries with the highest birth rates are among the poorest countries in the world. In these countries, people often deliberately have large families, so that the children can help earn income for the family when they are older. The 10 countries with the highest birth rate therefore corresponds very closely with the list of countries with the highest fertility rate – the average number of children born to each woman in the country.

the10 COUNTRIES WITH THE LOWEST BIRTH RATE

COUNTRY	ESTIMATED BIRTH RATE (LIVE BIRTHS PER 1,000, 2007)
1 Hong Kong	7.34
2 Andorra	8.45
3 Italy	8.54
4 Germany	8.65
5 Austria	8.69
6 Bosnia and Herzegovina	8.80
7 Lithuania	8.87
8 Czech Republic	8.96
9 Slovenia	9.00
10 Monaco	9.12

Source: US Census Bureau, International Data Base

top10 YEARS WITH MOST BIRTHS IN THE US

YEAR	BIRTHS
1 1957	4,308,000
2 1961	4,268,000
3 1960	4,258,000
4 1958	4,255,000
5 1959	4,245,000
6 1956	4,218,000
7 1962	4,167,000
8 1990	4,158,000
9 2004	4,116,000
10 1991	4,111,000

The total number of births in the US first exceeded 3 million in 1921, but then remained below this figure throughout the 1920s and 1930s, and until 1943 when it hit a new peak of 3,104,000. The first year in which it topped 4 million was 1954, with 1957 remaining the all-time peak; a postwar low of 3,137,000 was experienced in 1973, but by 2000 the figure once again exceeded the 4-million mark.

the10 COUNTRIES WITH THE HIGHEST DEATH RATE

COUNTRY	ESTIMATED DEATH RATE (DEATHS PER 1,000, 2007)
1 Swaziland	30.35
2 Botswana	29.43
3 Lesotho	28.57
4 Angola	23.90
5 Sierra Leone	22.64
6 South Africa	22.45
7 Liberia	22.26
8 Zimbabwe	21.76
9 Mozambique	21.68
10 Niger	20.59
World average	*8.60*
USA	*8.26*

Source: US Census Bureau, International Data Base

All 10 of the countries with the highest death rates are in sub-Saharan Africa. A decade ago, South Africa had a rate of 10.7, but the AIDS toll has changed its demographic profile as a high proportion of young people have fallen victim.

the10 COUNTRIES WITH THE LOWEST DEATH RATE

COUNTRY	ESTIMATED DEATH RATE (DEATHS PER 1,000, 2007)
1 Kuwait	2.39
2 Saudi Arabia	2.55
3 Jordan	2.68
4 Libya	3.47
5 Brunei	3.49
6 Oman	3.78
7 Solomon Islands	3.87
8 = Bahrain	4.21
= Ecuador	4.21
10 Costa Rica	4.39

Source: US Census Bureau, International Data Base

The crude death rate is derived by dividing the total number of deaths in a given year by the total population and multiplying by 1,000. Because countries with young populations appear to have low death rates and older populations high rates, statisticians also use age-standardized death rates, which factor in the age structure for a more accurate assessment.

the10 COUNTRIES WITH THE MOST CREMATIONS

COUNTRY	PERCENTAGE OF DEATHS	CREMATIONS*
1 China	52.70	4,349,000
2 Japan	99.61	1,072,977
3 USA	28.63	693,742
4 UK	70.83	424,956
5 Germany	40.10	338,469
6 France	21.80	120,037
7 Canada	47.30	107,673
8 Czech Republic	76.54	85,180
9 Netherlands	50.90	71,815
10 Sweden	72.12	67,040

* In latest year for which data available

Source: The Cremation Society of Great Britain

Cremation is least practiced in traditionally Roman Catholic countries, such as Italy (7.49 percent), and the Republic of Ireland (6.78 percent), whereas land shortages for burial and cultural factors have led to cremation being the dominant means of disposal of the dead in Japan.

the10 MOST COMMON CAUSES OF DEATH IN THE US

CAUSE	TOTAL, 2002
1 Diseases of the heart	696,947
2 Cancer	557,271
3 Cerebrovascular diseases	162,672
4 Chronic lower respiratory diseases	124,816
5 Accidents	106,742
6 Diabetes	73,249
7 Pneumonia and influenza	65,681
8 Alzheimer's disease	58,866
9 Nephritis, nephrotic syndrome, and nephrosis	40,974
10 Septicemia	33,865
Total deaths from all causes (including some that do not appear in the Top 10)	*2,443,387*

Source: National Center for Health Statistics

Accidents include 44,065 deaths resulting from motor vehicle accidents. The category "Homicide and legal intervention" (which includes murders, executions, and deaths resulting from actions by members of the police force), formerly at No.10, has fallen to 13th place with 17,638 deaths, while the number of deaths from diabetes has shown a notable increase. Those from each of the major causes varies considerably according to age and sex – accidents, for example, are the No.1 cause of death for people aged from 1 to 24, cancer in the age group 45 to 64, and heart disease for persons aged over 65.

Names

top10 MALE FIRST NAMES PER MILLION IN THE US

	NAME	PER MILLION
1	Robert	18,164
2	James	15,920
3	John	15,862
4	Michael	15,131
5	David	14,186
6	William	12,107
7	Richard	11,122
8	Donald	7,442
9	Thomas	7,131
10	Charles	6,657

Unlike the baby names of a particular year, those appearing in the names per million lists are based on a sample of some 1.85 million US citizens of all ages, hence limiting the effect of naming fashions. Robert was the No.1 US name from 1924 to 1938, overtaking John, No.1 from 1880 to 1923, thus ensuring their prominence in the long-term name stock, whereas Jacob has been No.1 only since 1999, rising from a low of 369th place in 1966.

top10 FEMALE FIRST NAMES PER MILLION IN THE US

	NAME	PER MILLION
1	Mary	11,024
2	Patricia	7,125
3	Linda	6,651
4	Barbara	6,148
5	Susan	5,710
6	Jennifer	4,834
7	Karan	4,404
8	Nancy	4,291
9	Margaret	4,121
10	Carol	4,096

Although Mary's rank in 2004 was 63rd, it was consistently No.1 from 1880 to 1961, which accounts for its place at the head of this list. Although currently US No.1, Emily did not even enter the Top 100 until 1974, and so does not appear prominently among names overall.

top10 SURNAMES IN THE US

	SURNAME	% OF ALL NAMES
1	Smith	1.006
2	Johnson	0.810
3	Williams	0.699
4 =	Brown	0.621
=	Jones	0.621
6	Davis	0.480
7	Miller	0.424
8	Wilson	0.339
9	Moore	0.312
10 =	Anderson	0.311
=	Taylor	0.311
=	Thomas	0.311

The Top 10 (or, in view of those in equal 10th place, 12) surnames together make up over six percent of the US population. Extending the list, some 28 different names comprise 10 percent of the population, and 115 names 20 percent.

top10 NAMES OF TWINS BORN IN THE US IN 2004

	NAMES	NUMBER
1	Jacob/Joshua	103
2	Taylor/Tyler	75
3	Matthew/Michael	74
4	Daniel/David	63
5	Faith/Hope	60
6	Madison/Morgan	41
7 =	Ethan/Evan	37
=	Mackenzie/Madison	37
9 =	Alexander/Andrew	34
=	Nathan/Nicholas	34

top10 **BABIES' NAMES** IN THE US, 2004

GIRLS		BOYS
Emily	1	Jacob
Emma	2	Michael
Madison	3	Joshua
Olivia	4	Matthew
Hannah	5	Ethan
Abigail	6	Andrew
Isabella	7	Daniel
Ashley	8	William
Samantha	9	Joseph
Elizabeth	10	Christopher

top10 **FIRST NAMES** IN THE US 100 YEARS AGO

GIRLS		BOYS
Mary	1	John
Helen	2	William
Margaret	3	James
Ruth	4	Joseph
Anna	5	George
Elizabeth	6	Charles
Dorothy	7	Robert
Marie	8	Frank
Alice	9	Henry
Florence	10	Edward

AMAZING FACT

Names to Conjure With

In his book *The American Language* (1937), the American journalist H.L. Mencken listed a number of bizarre but genuine personal names. Taken from sources such as insurance companies' policies, they included names like Oscar R. Apathy, Barnum B. Bobo, Emil E. Buttermilk, Christian Girl, George Goatleg, Memory B. Orange, Chintz Royalty, Ansen B. Outhouse, Dagmar Sewer, G.H. Upthegrove, and Mary Lou Wham.

Marriage & Divorce

	COUNTRY	MARRIAGES PER ANNUM*
1	USA	2,254,000
2	Bangladesh	1,181,000
3	Russia	1,001,589
4	Vietnam	964,701
5	Japan	757,331
6	Brazil	710,120
7	Iran	650,960
8	Ethiopia	630,290
9	Mexico	570,060
10	Egypt	525,412

* In those countries/latest year for which data available

Source: United Nations

◉ *Chinese wedding belle*
Exotic costumes are typical of weddings in China, the country that has the world's highest marriage rate.

top10 COUNTRIES WITH THE **HIGHEST** MARRIAGE RATE

	COUNTRY	MARRIAGES PER 1,000 PER ANNUM*
1	China	35.9
2	Cook Islands	32.8
3	Barbados	13.1
4	Cyprus	12.9
5	Vietnam	12.1
6	Seychelles	10.7
7	Jamaica	10.4
8	Ethiopia	10.2
9	Fiji	10.1
10	Iran	9.9
	USA	*7.8*

* In those countries/latest year for which data available

Source: United Nations

the10 COUNTRIES WITH THE **LOWEST MARRIAGE** RATE

	COUNTRY	MARRIAGES PER 1,000 PER ANNUM*
1	Peru	2.4
2	United Arab Emirates	2.5
3	Georgia	2.7
4	Andorra	2.8
5	Dominican Republic	2.9
6	French Guiana	3.0
7	= Argentina	3.2
	= Armenia	3.2
	= Saudi Arabia	3.2
10	Venezuela	3.3

* In those countries/latest year for which data available

Source: United Nations

AMAZING FACT

Till Death Us Do Part

On June 20, 1996 America's most married man, Baptist minister Glynn "Scotty" Wolfe (b.1908) of Blythe, California, married America's most married woman, Linda Essex of Anderson, Indiana. It was the Rev. Wolfe's 29th marriage since 1927 and Ms Essex's 23rd. Rumored to be a publicity stunt, their wedding was filmed for a TV program, but the couple separated shortly afterwards. Sadly, Glynn Wolfe died a year later – unmarried.

top10 **MONTHS** FOR MARRIAGES IN THE US

MONTH / MARRIAGES, 2004

JULY 246,000 — **1**

JUNE 243,000 — **2**

AUGUST 226,000 — **3**

MAY 224,000 — **4**

SEPTEMBER 214,000 — **5**

OCTOBER 212,000 — **6**

APRIL 174,000 — **7**

MARCH 159,000 — **8**

DECEMBER 154,000 — **9**

NOVEMBER 153,000 — **10**

Source: National Center for Health Statistics

Figures are estimates for 2004 from a US total of some 2,279,000 weddings, an decrease of 33,000 compared with the previous year. February was at No.11 with 151,000, and January the least popular month with 123,000 marriages.

top10 COUNTRIES WITH THE **LOWEST DIVORCE** RATES

COUNTRY / DIVORCE RATE PER 1,000*

1 Guatemala 0.12
2 Belize 0.17
3 Mongolia 0.28
4 Libya 0.32
5 Georgia 0.40
6 Chile 0.42
7 St. Vincent and the Grenadines 0.43
8 Jamaica 0.44
9 Armenia 0.47
10 Turkey 0.49

* In those countries/latest year for which data available

Source: United Nations

The countries that figure among those with the lowest rates represent a range of cultures and religions, which either condone or condemn divorce to varying extents, thus affecting its prevalence or otherwise. In some countries, legal and other obstacles make divorce difficult or costly, while in certain societies, such as Jamaica, where the marriage rate is also low, partners often separate without the formality of divorce.

the10 COUNTRIES WITH THE **HIGHEST DIVORCE** RATES

COUNTRY / DIVORCE RATE PER 1,000*

1 Russia 5.30
2 Aruba 5.27
3 USA 4.19
4 Ukraine 3.79
5 Belarus 3.77
6 Moldova 3.50
7 Cuba 3.16
8 Czech Republic 3.11
9 =Lithuania 3.05
   =South Korea 3.05

* In those countries/latest year for which data available

Source: United Nations

Religion

top10 RELIGIOUS BELIEFS

	RELIGION	FOLLOWERS
1	Christianity	2,135,784,198
2	Islam	1,313,983,654
3	Hinduism	870,047,346
4	Chinese folk-religions	404,922,244
5	Buddhism	378,809,103
6	Ethnic religions	256,340,652
7	New religions	108,131,713
8	Sikhism	25,373,879
9	Judaism	15,145,702
10	Spiritists	13,030,538

Source: World Christian Database

While some mainstream religious groups have experienced a decline in formal attendance, certain fringe religions have grown. Today, about one-third of the world's population are nominally, if not practicing, Christians, and one-fifth are followers of Islam. At least 15 percent of the world's population profess no religious beliefs of any kind.

top10 LARGEST CHRISTIAN POPULATIONS

	COUNTRY	CHRISTIANS
1	USA	252,394,312
2	Brazil	166,847,207
3	China	110,956,366
4	Mexico	102,011,835
5	Russia	84,494,596
6	Philippines	73,987,348
7	India	68,189,739
8	Germany	61,833,042
9	Nigeria	61,437,608
10	Dem. Rep. of Congo	53,370,662
	World total	*2,135,784,198*

Source: World Christian Database

Christian populations of these countries comprise almost half the world total. Christians exist in almost every country. Precise estimates of nominal membership (declared religious persuasion), rather than active participation (regular attendance at a place of worship), are inevitably vague.

top10 LARGEST JEWISH POPULATIONS

	COUNTRY	JEWS
1	USA	5,764,208
2	Israel	4,772,138
3	France	607,111
4	Argentina	520,130
5	Palestine	451,001
5	Canada	414,452
7	Brazil	383,837
8	UK	312,173
9	Russia	244,719
10	Germany	222,689
	World	*15,145,702*

Source: World Christian Database

The Diaspora (scattering of the Jewish people) has established Jewish communities in almost every country in the world. In 1939 the estimated total Jewish population was 17 million, but six million fell victim to Nazi persecution, reducing the figure to about 11 million.

top10 LARGEST MUSLIM POPULATIONS

	COUNTRY	MUSLIMS
1	Pakistan	154,563,023
2	India	134,149,817
3	Bangladesh	132,868,312
4	Indonesia	121,606,358*
5	Turkey	71,322,513
6	Iran	67,724,004
7	Egypt	63,503,397
8	Nigeria	54,665,801
9	Algeria	31,858,555
10	Morocco	31,000,895
	World	*1,313,983,654*
	USA	*4,657,005*

* An additional 46 million people are considered Muslims by the Indonesian government but are more properly categorized as New Religionists (Islamicized syncretistic religions)

Source: World Christian Database

top10 LARGEST HINDU POPULATIONS

	COUNTRY	HINDUS
1	India	810,387,411
2	Nepal	19,020,312
3	Bangladesh	17,029,336
4	Indonesia	7,632,941
5	Sri Lanka	2,173,114
6	Pakistan	2,100,342
7	Malaysia	1,855,194
8	USA	1,143,864
9	South Africa	1,078,667
10	Myanmar	1,006,804
	World	*870,047,346*

Source: World Christian Database

top10 LARGEST BUDDHIST POPULATIONS

	COUNTRY	BUDDHISTS
1	China	111,358,666
2	Japan	70,722,505
3	Thailand	53,294,170
4	Vietnam	40,780,825
5	Myanmar	37,151,956
6	Sri Lanka	13,234,600
7	Cambodia	12,697,958
8	India	7,596,701
9	South Korea	7,281,110
10	Taiwan	4,823,361
	World	*378,809,103*
	USA	*2,721,335*

Source: World Christian Database

top10 LONGEST-SERVING POPES

	POPE	PERIOD IN OFFICE	DURATION YRS	MTHS	DAYS
1	Pius IX	Jun 16, 1846–Feb 7, 1878	31	7	22
2	John Paul II	Oct 16, 1978–Apr 2, 2005	26	5	17
3	Leo XIII	Feb 20, 1878–Jul 20, 1903	25	5	0
4	Pius VI	Feb 15, 1775–Aug 29, 1799	24	6	14
5	Adrian I	Feb 1, 772–Dec 25, 795	23	10	24
6	Pius VII	Mar 14, 1800–Aug 20, 1823	23	5	6
7	Alexander III	Sep 7, 1159–Aug 30, 1181	21	11	23
8	Sylvester I	Jan 31, 314–Dec 31, 335	21	11	0
9	Leo I	Sep 29, 440–Nov 10, 461	21	1	12
10	Urban VIII	Aug 6, 1623–Jul 29, 1644	20	11	23

↑ John Paul II
Among the 265 Popes, John Paul II's 26-year pontificate places him second among the longest-serving, with twice the 13-year average of incumbents of the office since 1700.

Popes are usually chosen from the ranks of cardinals, who are customarily men of mature years (Pope Benedict IX, elected in 1033, was said by some to have been as young as 12, but in all probability was in his twenties). As a result, it is unusual for a pope to remain in office for over 20 years. Although St. Peter is regarded as the first pope, the historical accuracy of his reign and its dates are questionable. Pius IX, the longest-serving pope, was 85 years old at the time of his death. The longest-lived in the Top 10 was Leo XIII at 93. Although he served for less than two years, it is said, but with little evidence, that Pope Agatho was at least 100 when he was elected and died in 681 at the age of 106.

top10 RELIGIONS 100 YEARS AGO

	RELIGION*	FOLLOWERS, 1900
1	Christians	558,130,722
2	Chinese universists#	380,006,038
3	Hindus	203,003,440
4	Muslims	199,913,833
5	Buddhists	127,076,771
6	Jews	12,292,210
7	Shintoists	6,720,000
8	Sikhs	2,962,300
9	Jains	1,323,280
10	Confucianists	640,050

* Excluding folk religions and miscellaneous groups
# Followers of traditional Chinese religion

Source: World Christian Database

top10 COUNTRIES WITH MOST ATHEISTS

	COUNTRY	ATHEISTS
1	China	104,076,894
2	Russia	7,107,848
3	Vietnam	5,777,868
4	Japan	3,672,367
5	North Korea	3,564,162
6	France	2,411,946
7	Italy	2,069,806
8	Ukraine	1,993,168
9	India	1,816,622
10	Germany	1,689,417
	World total	*768,598,424*
	USA	*1,423,787*

top10 RELIGIOUS BELIEFS IN THE US

	RELIGION	FOLLOWERS
1	Christianity	252,394,312
2	Agnosticism	27,794,387
3	Judaism	5,764,208
4	Islam	4,657,005
5	Buddhism	2,721,335
6	New religions	1,508,925
7	Atheism	1,423,787
8	Ethnic religions	1,157,804
9	Hinduism	1,143,864
10	Baha'ism	829,260

Source: World Christian Database

Kings & Queens

top10 LARGEST MONARCHIES*

COUNTRY	POPULATION
1 Japan	127,654,000
2 Britain#	124,522,000
3 Thailand	62,833,000
4 Spain	41,060,000
5 Morocco	30,566,000
6 Nepal	25,164,000
7 Malaysia	24,425,000
8 Saudi Arabia	24,217,000
9 Netherlands	16,149,000
10 Cambodia	14,144,000

* By population
# Commonwealth

The world's 29 monarchies rule over more than 540 million subjects, almost nine percent of the population of the planet, with Monaco (pop. 32,000) the smallest.

top10 LONGEST-REIGNING LIVING MONARCHS*

	MONARCH	COUNTRY	DATE OF BIRTH	ACCESSION
1	Bhumibol Adulyadej	Thailand	Dec 5, 1927	Jun 9, 1946
2	Elizabeth II	UK	Apr 21, 1926	Feb 6, 1952
3	Malietoa Tanumafili II	Samoa	Jan 4, 1913	Jan 1, 1962#
4	Taufa'ahau Tupou IV	Tonga	Jul 4, 1918	Dec 16, 1965†
5	Haji Hassanal Bolkiah	Brunei	Jul 15, 1946	Oct 5, 1967
6	Sayyid Qaboos ibn Said al-Said	Oman	Nov 18, 1942	Jul 23, 1970
7	Margrethe II	Denmark	Apr 16, 1940	Jan 14, 1972
8	Jigme Singye Wangchuk	Bhutan	Nov 11, 1955	Jul 24, 1972
9	Carl XVI Gustaf	Sweden	Apr 30, 1946	Sep 15, 1973
10	Juan Carlos	Spain	Jan 5, 1938	Nov 22, 1975

* Including hereditary rulers of principalities, dukedoms, etc.
# Sole ruler since Apr 15, 1963
† Full sovereignty from Jun 5, 1970 when British protectorate ended

the10 LATEST COUNTRIES TO ABOLISH MONARCHIES

	COUNTRY	MONARCHY ABOLISHED
1	Iran	1979
2	Laos	1975
3	Ethiopia*	1974
4	= Afghanistan	1973
	= Greece#	1973
6	Cambodia†	1970
7	Libya	1969
8	Maldives	1968
9	Burundi	1966
10	Zanzibar☆	1964

* Emperor deposed 1974
# King exiled 1967
† Restored 1993
☆ Joined with Tanganyika to form Tanzania

the10 SHORTEST-REIGNING BRITISH MONARCHS

	MONARCH	REIGN	DURATION
1	Jane	1553	9 days
2	Edward V	1483	75 days
3	Edward VIII	1936	325 days
4	Richard III	1483–85	2 years
5	James II	1685–88	3 years
6	= Mary I	1553–58	5 years
	= Mary II	1689–94	5 years
8	Edward VI	1547–53	6 years
9	William IV	1830–37	7 years
10	Edward VII	1901–10	9 years

AMAZING FACT

The Kingdom of Hawaii

Hawaii is the only part of the USA that was once an independent monarchy. It ended when, within two years, its last king, Kalākaua, died in 1891 and was succeeded by his sister Queen Lili'uokalani. With the support of various businesses protecting sugar and other interests in the country, she was deposed in 1893 and the Republic of Hawaii declared, with the country becoming a US territory and, in 1959, the 50th state of the USA.

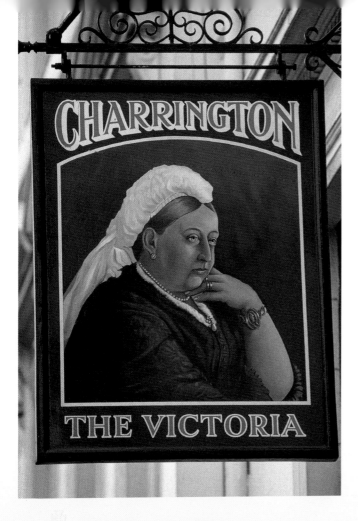

Victoria and Albert
Queen Victoria, the longest-reigning queen, on an inn sign; Prince Albert II of Monaco, one of the most recent incumbents among the world's 29 monarchies, is Queen Victoria's 8th cousin five times removed.

top10 LONGEST-REIGNING MONARCHS

	MONARCH / COUNTRY	REIGN	AGE AT ACCESSION	REIGN YEARS
1	King Louis XIV, France	May 1643–Sep 1715	5	72
2	King John II, Liechtenstein	Nov 1858–Feb 1929	18	71
3	Emperor Franz-Josef Austria-Hungary	Dec 1848–Nov 1916	18	67
4	Queen Victoria, UK	Jun 1837–Jan 1901	18	63
5	Emperor Hirohito, Japan	Dec 1926–Jan 1989	25	62
6	Emperor K'ang Hsi, China	Feb 1661–Dec 1722	7	61
7	= King Sobhuza II*, Swaziland	Dec 1921–Aug 1982	22	60
	= Emperor Ch'ien Lung, China	Oct 1735–Feb 1796	25	60
9	= King Christian IV, Denmark	Apr 1588–Feb 1648	11	59
	= King George III, UK	Oct 1760–Jan 1820	22	59

* Paramount chief until 1967, when Great Britain recognized him as king with the granting of internal self-government

Although historically unsubstantiated, King Harald I of Norway is said to have ruled for 70 years from 870–940, while reigns of 95 years and 94 years, respectively, are claimed for King Mihti of Arakan (Myanmar), c.1279–1374, and Pharaoh Phiops (Pepi) II of Egypt (Neferkare), c.2269–2175 BC.

the10 LATEST MONARCHS TO ASCEND THE THRONE

	TITLE/NAME	COUNTRY	ACCESSION
1	Emir Sabah al-Ahmad al-Saba	Kuwait	Jan 29, 2006
2	Prince Abdullah	Saudi Arabia	Aug 1, 2005
3	Prince Albert II	Monaco	Apr 6, 2005
4	King Norodom Sihamoni	Cambodia	Oct 14, 2004
5	Prince Alois	Liechtenstein	Aug 25, 2004
6	Supreme Head of State Saiyid Sirajuddin ibni al-Marhum Saiyid Putra Jamalullail*	Malaysia	Dec 13, 2001
7	King Gyanendra Bir Bikram Shah Deva	Nepal	Jun 4, 2001
8	Grand Duke Henri	Luxembourg	Oct 7, 2000
9	King Sayyidi Muhammad (VI) ibn al-Hasan	Morocco	Jul 23, 1999
10	King (formerly Emir) Hamad ibn 'Isa al-Khalifah	Bahrain	Mar 6, 1999

* Elected king

Malaysia has a unique system of "revolving monarchy," which was established following Malaysia's independence from Britain in 1957. Each of the nine state sultans takes a five-year turn as king.

Politics

the10 FIRST FEMALE PRIME MINISTERS AND PRESIDENTS

	PRIME MINISTER / PRESIDENT	COUNTRY	FIRST PERIOD IN OFFICE
1	Sirimavo Bandaranaike (PM)	Sri Lanka	Jul 21, 1960–Mar 27, 1965
2	Indira Gandhi (PM)	India	Jan 19, 1966–Mar 24, 1977
3	Golda Meir (PM)	Israel	Mar 17, 1969–Jun 3, 1974
4	Maria Estela Perón (President)	Argentina	Jul 1, 1974–Mar 24, 1976
5	Elisabeth Domitien (PM)	Central African Republic	Jan 3, 1975–Apr 7, 1976
6	Margaret Thatcher (PM)	UK	May 4, 1979–Nov 28, 1990
7	Dr Maria Lurdes Pintasilgo (PM)	Portugal	Aug 1, 1979–Jan 3, 1980
8	Mary Eugenia Charles (PM)	Dominica	Jul 21, 1980–Jun 14, 1995
9	Vigdís Finnbogadóttir (President)	Iceland	Aug 1, 1980–Aug 1, 1996
10	Gro Harlem Brundtland (PM)	Norway	Feb 4–Oct 14, 1981

Following the assassination of her husband Solomon West Ridgeway Dias Bandaranaike, Sirimavo Ratwatte Dias Bandaranaike (1916–2000) took over as leader of the Ceylon (later Sri Lanka) Freedom Party, won the election, and became the world's first female prime minister. She served in this office three times (1960–65, 1970–77, and 1994–2000), while her daughter Chandrika Kumaratunga became the country's first female president in 1994.

First lady
Margaret Thatcher became Britain and Europe's first female prime minister in 1979.

top10 PARLIAMENTS WITH THE HIGHEST PERCENTAGE OF WOMEN MEMBERS*

	PARLIAMENT (LATEST ELECTION)	WOMEN MEMBERS	TOTAL MEMBERS	PERCENTAGE WOMEN
1	Rwanda (2003)	39	80	48.8
2	Sweden (2002)	158	349	45.3
3	Norway (2005)	64	169	37.9
4	Finland (2003)	75	200	37.5
5	Denmark (2005)	66	179	36.9
6	Netherlands (2003)	55	150	36.7
7 =	Cuba (2003)	219	609	36.0
=	Spain (2004)	126	350	36.0
9	Costa Rica (2006)	20	57	35.1
10	Argentina (2005)	90	257	35.0

* As at Feb 27, 2006

Source: Inter-Parliamentary Union

This list is based on the most recent general election results for all democratic countries, and based on the lower chamber where the parliament comprises two chambers. A total of 99 countries have at least 10 percent female members of parliament, 40 countries over 20 percent, and 19 countries over 30 percent.

AMAZING FACT

Votes for Women!

Women's suffrage – the right to vote in national elections – was extremely slow to be adopted. A few territories granted a limited form – only unmarried women and widows who owned property could vote in New Jersey in 1776, but this right was rescinded in 1807. New Zealand was first to grant this universal, unqualified right to women on September 19, 1893 – but they could not stand for election. The following year, in South Australia all women could vote and stand for parliament. It took until 1918 in Great Britain and Ireland (for women over 30), and 1920 in the USA, before women could vote.

top10 LONGEST-SERVING PRESIDENTS TODAY

	PRESIDENT	COUNTRY	TOOK OFFICE
1	El Hadj Omar Bongo	Gabon	Dec 2, 1967
2	Colonel Mu'ammar Gadhafi	Libya	*Sep 1, 1969
3	Fidel Castro	Cuba	Nov 2, 1976
4	Ali Abdullah Saleh	Yemen	Jul 17, 1978
5	Maumoon Abdul Gayoom	Maldives	Nov 11, 1978
6	Teodoro Obiang Nguema Mbasogo	Equatorial Guinea	Aug 3, 1979
7	José Eduardo Dos Santos	Angola	Sep 21, 1979
8	Hosni Mubarak	Egypt	Oct 6, 1981
9	Paul Biya	Cameroon	Nov 7, 1982
10	Lansana Conté	Guinea	Apr 3, 1984

* Since a reorganization in 1979, Colonel Gadhafi has held no formal position, but continues to rule under the ceremonial title of "Leader of the Revolution"

All the presidents in this list have been in power for over 20, some for almost 40 years. Fidel Castro became prime minister of Cuba as long ago as February 1959. As he was also chief of the army and there was no opposition party, he effectively ruled as dictator from then, but he was not technically president until the Cuban constitution was revised in 1976. Similarly, Robert Mugabe has ruled Zimbabwe since April 18, 1980, but only became president in 1987 (prior to this he held the title of prime minister).

Vice-President Theodore Roosevelt assumed the office of President following the assassination of William McKinley. John F. Kennedy was the youngest President to be elected. The US Constitution insists that a President must be at least 35 years old on taking office. George W. Bush was aged 54 years 6 months 14 days when he took office in 2001. Despite his appearance in this youthful group, Polk holds the record for the shortest lifespan after leaving office: he ended his four-year term on March 3, 1849, and died 103 days later at the age of 53 years 6 months 17 days.

top10 OLDEST US PRESIDENTS

	PRESIDENT	LEFT OFFICE	AGE ON TAKING OFFICE		
			YEARS	MONTHS	DAYS
1	Ronald W. Reagan	Jan 20, 1989	77	11	14
2	Dwight D. Eisenhower	Jan 20, 1961	70	3	6
3	Andrew Jackson	Mar 3, 1837	69	11	16
4	James Buchanan	Mar 3, 1841	69	10	8
5	Harry S. Truman	Jan 20, 1953	68	8	10
6	George H. W. Bush	Jan 20, 1993	68	7	8
7	William H. Harrison	Apr 4, 1841*	68	1	26
8	Zachary Taylor	Jul 9, 1850*	65	7	15
9	John Adams	Mar 3, 1801	65	4	3
10	Gerald R. Ford	Jan 20, 1977	63	6	6

* Died in office

top10 YOUNGEST US PRESIDENTS

	PRESIDENT	TOOK OFFICE	AGE ON TAKING OFFICE		
			YEARS	MONTHS	DAYS
1	Theodore Roosevelt	Sep 14, 1901	42	10	18
2	John F. Kennedy	Jan 20, 1961	43	7	22
3	Bill Clinton	Jan 20, 1993	46	5	1
4	Ulysses S. Grant	Mar 4, 1869	46	10	5
5	Grover Cleveland	Mar 4, 1893	47	11	14
6	Franklin Pierce	Mar 4, 1804	48	3	9
7	James A. Garfield	Mar 4, 1881	49	3	13
8	James K. Polk	Mar 4, 1845	49	4	2
9	Millard Fillmore	Jul 10, 1850	50	6	3
10	John Tyler	Apr 6, 1841	51	0	8

Crime & Punishment

top10 MOST **COMMON MURDER WEAPONS** AND METHODS IN THE US

WEAPON / METHOD	VICTIMS, 2004
1 Firearms	9,326
2 Knives or cutting instruments	1,866
3 "Personal weapons" (hands, feet, fists, etc.)	933
4 Blunt objects (hammers, clubs, etc)	663
5 Strangulation	155
6 Fire	114
7 Asphyxiation	105
8 Narcotics	76
9 Drowning	15
10 Poison	11
Other weapons not stated	*856*
Total	*14,121*

Source: FBI Uniform Crime Reports

the10 COUNTRIES WITH THE **HIGHEST MURDER RATES**

COUNTRY / MURDERS PER 100,000 POP.

1 Colombia 61.8	**6** Mexico 13.0
2 South Africa 49.6	**7** Estonia 10.7
3 Jamaica 32.4	**8** Latvia 10.4
4 Venezuela 31.6	**9** Lithuania 10.3
5 Russia 20.2	**10** Belarus 9.8

Source: United Nations

the10 **WORST YEARS** FOR MURDER IN THE US

	YEAR	MURDER RATE PER 100,000 POP.	TOTAL*
1	1991	9.8	24,703
2	1993	9.5	24,526
3	1992	9.3	23,760
4	1990	9.4	23,438
5	1994	9.0	23,326
6	1980	10.2	23,040
7	1981	9.8	22,520
8	1989	8.7	21,500
9	1979	9.7	21,460
10	1982	9.1	21,010

* Includes nonnegligent manslaughter victims; victims of September 11, 2001, terrorist attacks are excluded

Source: Bureau of Justice Statistics

Murders in the US first exceeded 2,000 in 1910 and increased rapidly as a result of gang warfare during the Prohibition era, topping 10,000 in 1930. The total rose to over 20,000 for the first time in 1974.

the10 COUNTRIES WITH THE HIGHEST PRISON POPULATIONS

	COUNTRY	PRISONERS PER 100,000 OF POP.	TOTAL PRISONERS*
1	USA	724	2,135,901
2	China	118	1,548,498
3	Russia	581	828,900
4	Brazil	183	336,358
5	India	31	322,357
6	Mexico	191	201,931
7	Ukraine	364	170,057
8	Thailand	264	168,264
9	South Africa	344	156,175
10	Iran	191	135,132

* As at date of most recent data

Source: International Centre for Prison Studies,'"World Prison Population List" (6th edition, 2005)

the10 US STATES WITH THE MOST PRISONERS ON DEATH ROW

	STATE	PRISONERS UNDER DEATH SENTENCE*
1	California	649
2	Texas	409
3	Florida	338
4	Pennsylvania	231
5	Ohio	196
6	= Alabama	190
	= North Carolina	190
8	Arizona	125
9	Georgia	109
10	Tennessee	108
	Total	3,380

* As at Jan 1, 2006

the10 STATES WITH THE MOST EXECUTIONS*

	STATE	1608–1976	EXECUTIONS SINCE 1976
1	Texas	755	362
2	Virginia	1,277	95
3	Oklahoma	132	80
4	Missouri	285	66
5	Florida	314	60
6	North Carolina	784	42
7	Georgia	950	39
8	South Carolina	641	35
9	Alabama	708	34
10	= Arkansas	478	27
	= Louisiana	632	27

* To May 1, 2006

Source: Death Penalty Information Center

the10 WORST STATES FOR MURDER IN THE US

	STATE	FIREARMS USED	TOTAL MURDERS, 2004
1	California	1,724	2,391
2	Texas	882	1,362
3	New York	500	864
4	Michigan	456	638
5	Pennsylvania	449	632
6	Louisiana	442	557
7	Georgia	342	528
8	Maryland	386	520
9	North Carolina	282	477
10	Ohio	245	464
	Total	9,326	14,121

Source: FBI Uniform Crime Reports

the10 FIRST COUNTRIES TO ABOLISH CAPITAL PUNISHMENT

	COUNTRY	ABOLISHED
1	Russia	1826
2	Venezuela	1863
3	San Marino	1865
4	Portugal	1867
5	Costa Rica	1877
6	Brazil	1889
7	Panama	1903
8	Norway	1905
9	Ecuador	1906
10	Uruguay	1907

the10 COUNTRIES WITH THE MOST EXECUTIONS

	COUNTRY	EXECUTIONS PER 100 MILLION POP.	EXECUTIONS, 2004
1	China	260	3,400
2	Iran	230	159
3	Vietnam	77	64
4	USA	20	59
5	Saudi Arabia	130	33
6	Pakistan	9	15
7	Kuwait	400	9
8	Bangladesh	5	7
9	= Egypt	8	6
	= Singapore	140	6
	= Yemen	30	6

Source: Amnesty International/Death Penalty Information Center

World World I

the 10 LARGEST ARMED FORCES OF WORLD WAR I

	COUNTRY	PERSONNEL*
1	Russia	12,000,000
2	Germany	11,000,000
3	British Empire	8,904,467
4	France	8,410,000
5	Austria-Hungary	7,800,000
6	Italy	5,615,000
7	USA	4,355,000
8	Turkey	2,850,000
9	Bulgaria	1,200,000
10	Japan	800,000

* Total at peak strength

Among the total of over 65 million combatants, Russia's forces were relatively small in relation to the country's population at some six percent, compared with 17 percent in Germany. Several small European nations had large forces in relation to their populations, Serbia's representing 14 percent of its population.

the 10 SMALLEST ARMED FORCES OF WORLD WAR I

	COUNTRY	PERSONNEL*
1	Montenegro	50,000
2	Portugal	100,000
3	Greece	230,000
4	Belgium	267,000
5	Serbia	707,343
6	Romania	750,000
7	Japan	800,000
8	Bulgaria	1,200,000
9	Turkey	2,850,000
10	USA	4,355,000

* Total at peak strength

the 10 COUNTRIES WITH THE MOST PRISONERS OF WAR, 1914–18

	COUNTRY	CAPTURED*
1	Russia	2,500,000
2	Austria-Hungary	2,200,000
3	Germany	1,152,800
4	Italy	600,000
5	France	537,000
6	Turkey	250,000
7	British Empire	191,652
8	Serbia	152,958
9	Romania	80,000
10	Belgium	34,659
	Total of all nations	*7,750,919*
	USA	*3,937*

* Nationals of each country held prisoner

the 10 COUNTRIES SUFFERING THE GREATEST MILITARY LOSSES IN WORLD WAR I

1 CROSS = 100,000 KILLED / COUNTRY / KILLED

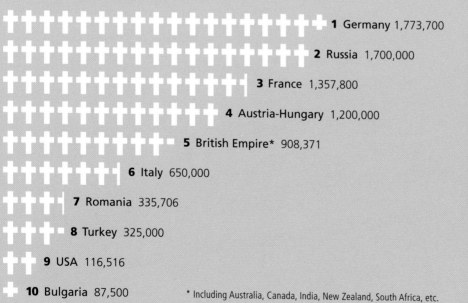

1 Germany 1,773,700
2 Russia 1,700,000
3 France 1,357,800
4 Austria-Hungary 1,200,000
5 British Empire* 908,371
6 Italy 650,000
7 Romania 335,706
8 Turkey 325,000
9 USA 116,516
10 Bulgaria 87,500

* Including Australia, Canada, India, New Zealand, South Africa, etc.

the 10 COUNTRIES WITH THE GREATEST MERCHANT SHIPPING LOSSES IN WORLD WAR I

	COUNTRY	VESSELS SUNK NUMBER	TONNAGE
1	UK	2,038	6,797,802
2	Italy	228	720,064
3	France	213	651,583
4	USA	93	372,892
5	Germany	188	319,552
6	Greece	115	304,992
7	Denmark	126	205,002
8	Netherlands	74	194,483
9	Sweden	124	192,807
10	Spain	70	160,383

⊘ The Red Baron
Seen here wearing his Pour le Mérite, *or "Blue Max," medal (Germany's highest military award) and his Iron Cross, Manfred Albrecht Freiherr (Baron) von Richthofen (1892–1918) was the leading fighter pilot of World War I. With fellow fliers, including Nazi leader Herman Goering, he formed the Jasta 11 (11th Chasing Squadron), nicknamed the "Flying Circus," with their aircraft (including "Red Baron" Richthofen's Fokker triplane) flamboyantly painted crimson. Germany's foremost pilot was shot down on April 21, 1918, aged just 25.*

top10 **AIR ACES** OF WORLD WAR I

	PILOT	NATIONALITY	KILLS CLAIMED*
1	Rittmeister Manfred Albrecht Freiherr von Richthofen#	German	80
2	Capitaine René Paul Fonck	French	75
3	Maj William Avery Bishop	Canadian	72
4	Maj Edward Corringham "Mick" Mannock#	British	68
5	= Maj Raymond Collishaw	Canadian	62†
	= Oberleutnant Ernst Udet	German	62
7	Maj James Thomas Byford McCudden#	British	57
8	= Capt Anthony Wetherby Beauchamp-Proctor	South African	54
	= Capt Donald Roderick MacLaren	Canadian	54
	= Capitaine George Marie Ludovic Jules Guynemer#	French	54

* Approximate – some kills disputed
# Killed in action
† Including two in Russian Civil War, 1919

The term "ace" – or, more precisely, "fighter ace" – was first used during World War I to describe a pilot who had brought down at least five enemy aircraft. The first-ever reference in print to an air "ace" appeared in an article in *The Times* of September 14, 1917, which described Raoul Lufbery as "the 'ace' of the American Lafayette Flying Squadron." The German equivalent was *Oberkanone*, which means "top gun." Although the definition varied from country to country and was never officially approved, it was used during both World Wars, with aces universally hailed as heroes.

World War II

the 10 LARGEST ARMED FORCES OF WORLD WAR II

1 SOLDIER=1,000,000 PERSONNEL / COUNTRY / PERSONNEL*

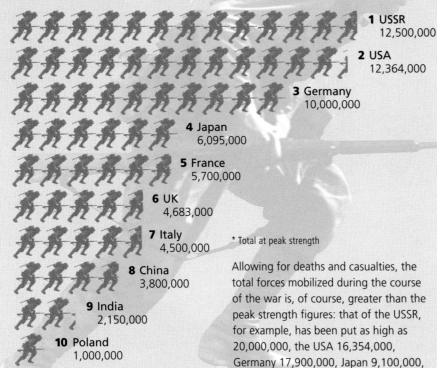

1 USSR 12,500,000

2 USA 12,364,000

3 Germany 10,000,000

4 Japan 6,095,000

5 France 5,700,000

6 UK 4,683,000

7 Italy 4,500,000

8 China 3,800,000

9 India 2,150,000

10 Poland 1,000,000

* Total at peak strength

Allowing for deaths and casualties, the total forces mobilized during the course of the war is, of course, greater than the peak strength figures: that of the USSR, for example, has been put as high as 20,000,000, the USA 16,354,000, Germany 17,900,000, Japan 9,100,000, and the UK 5,896,000.

the 10 SMALLEST ARMED FORCES OF WORLD WAR II

	COUNTRY	PERSONNEL*
1	Costa Rica	400
2	Liberia	1,000
3 =	El Salvador	3,000
=	Honduras	3,000
=	Nicaragua	3,000
6	Haiti	3,500
7	Dominican Republic	4,000
8	Guatemala	5,000
9 =	Bolivia	8,000
=	Paraguay	8,000
=	Uruguay	8,000

* Total at peak strength

The smallest European armed force was that of Denmark, with a maximum strength of 15,000, just 13 of whom were killed during the one-day German invasion of April 9, 1940. Several South American countries did not declare war until the closing stages, in order to become eligible to join the fledgling United Nations.

the 10 COUNTRIES SUFFERING THE GREATEST MILITARY LOSSES IN WORLD WAR II

	COUNTRY	KILLED
1	USSR	13,600,000*
2	Germany	3,300,000
3	China	1,324,516
4	Japan	1,140,429
5	British Empire# (UK 264,000)	357,116
6	Romania	350,000
7	Poland	320,000
8	Yugoslavia	305,000
9	USA	292,131
10	Italy	279,800

* Total, of which 7.8 million battlefield deaths
# Including Australia, Canada, New Zealand, India, etc.

The actual numbers killed in World War II have been the subject of intense argument for 60 years. The immense level of the military casualty rate of the USSR, in particular, is hard to comprehend. Most authorities now reckon that of the 30 million Soviets who bore arms, there were 13.6 million military deaths. This includes a battlefield deaths total of approximately 7.8 million, plus up to 2.5 million who died later of wounds received in battle and disease and, of the 5.8 million who were taken prisoner, as many as 3.3 million who died in captivity. It should also be borne in mind that these were military losses: to these should be added many untold millions of civilian war deaths, while recent estimates have suggested an additional figure of up to 25 million civilian deaths as a result of Stalinist purges, which began just before the outbreak of war.

the 10 COUNTRIES SUFFERING THE GREATEST CIVILIAN LOSSES IN WORLD WAR II

	COUNTRY	APPROX. NO. KILLED
1	China	8,000,000
2	USSR	6,500,000
3	Poland	5,300,000
4	Germany	2,350,000
5	Yugoslavia	1,500,000
6	France	470,000
7	Greece	415,000
8	Japan	393,400
9	Romania	340,000
10	Hungary	300,000

During World War II, many deaths among civilians, especially in China and the USSR, resulted from famine and internal purges.

the 10 WORST MILITARY SHIP LOSSES OF WORLD WAR II

SHIP*	COUNTRY	DATE	APPROX. NO. KILLED
1 Wilhelm Gustloff	Germany	Jan 30, 1945	7,800
2 Goya	Germany	Apr 16, 1945	6,202
3 Cap Arcona	Germany	Apr 26, 1945	6,000
4 Junyo Maru	Japan	Sep 18, 1944	5,620
5 Toyama Maru	Japan	Jun 29, 1944	5,400
6 Arcona	Germany	May 3, 1945	5,000
7 Lancastria	Great Britain	Jun 17, 1940	3,050
8 Steuben	Germany	Feb 9, 1945	3,000
9 Thielbeck	Germany	May 3, 1945	2,750
10 Yamato	Japan	Apr 7, 1945	2,498

* Includes warships and passenger vessels used for troop and refugee transport

The German liner *Wilhelm Gustloff*, laden with civilian refugees and wounded German soldiers and sailors, was torpedoed off the coast of Poland by a Soviet submarine, S-13. Although imprecise, some sources even suggest a figure as high as 9,400, the probable death toll being some five times as great as that of the *Titanic*.

top 10 BRITISH AND COMMONWEALTH AIR ACES OF WORLD WAR II

PILOT	NATIONALITY	KILLS CLAIMED
1 Sqd Ldr Marmaduke Thomas St John Pattle	South African	40+
2 Gp Capt James Edgar "Johnny" Johnson	British	33.91
3 Wng Cdr Brendan "Paddy" Finucane	Irish	32
4 Flt Lt George Frederick Beurling	Canadian	31.33
5 Wng Cdr John Randall Daniel Braham	British	29
6 Gp Capt Adolf Gysbert "Sailor" Malan	South African	28.66
7 Wng Cdr Clive Robert Caldwell	Australian	28.5
8 Sqd Ldr James Harry "Ginger" Lacey	British	28
9 Sqd Ldr Neville Frederick Duke	British	27.83
10 Wng Cdr Colin F. Gray	New Zealander	27.7

Uniquely to Western air forces in World War II, kills that are expressed as fractions refer to those that were shared with others, the number of fighters involved and the extent of each pilot's participation determining the proportion allocated to him.

← **War at sea**
While many ship losses resulted from sea battles, some of the highest death tolls were caused by the bombing and torpedoing of vessels carrying refugees and other civilians.

Modern Conflict

top10 LARGEST ARMED FORCES

COUNTRY	ARMY	ESTIMATED ACTIVE FORCES NAVY	AIR	TOTAL
1 China	1,600,000	255,000	400,000	2,255,000
2 USA	502,000	376,750	379,500	1,473,960*
3 India	1,100,000	55,000	170,000	1,325,000
4 North Korea	1,106,000	46,000	110,000	1,262,000
5 Russia	395,000	142,000	170,000	1,037,000#
6 South Korea	560,000	63,000	64,700	687,700
7 Pakistan	550,000	24,000	45,000	619,000
8 Turkey	402,000	52,750	60,100	514,850
9 Vietnam	412,000	42,000	30,000	484,000
10 Egypt	340,000	18,500	30,000	468,500†

* Includes 175,350 Marine Corps, 40,360 Coast Guard
# Includes 80,000 Strategic Deterrent Forces, 250,000 Command and Support
† Includes 80,000 Air Defense Command

Source: The International Institute for Strategic Studies, "The Military Balance 2005–2006"

Several countries also have substantial reserves on standby: South Korea's has been estimated at some 4.5 million plus 3.5 million Paramilitary, Vietnam's at 3 to 4 million, and China's 800,000.

⬆ **High rank**
Indian troops in Kashmir celebrate Republic Day, January 26. India's highly trained military forces are entirely voluntary, and rank third in the world in total size and ninth in defense budget. India is nuclear-capable and has a substantial armory of conventional weapons.

the10 SMALLEST ARMED FORCES*

COUNTRY	ESTIMATED TOTAL ACTIVE FORCES
1 Antigua and Barbuda	170
2 Seychelles	450
3 Barbados	610
4 Gambia	800
5 Bahamas	860
6 Luxembourg	900
7 Belize	1,050
8 Guyana	1,100
9 Cape Verde	1,200
10 East Timor	1,250

* Includes only those countries that declare a defence budget

Source: The International Institute for Strategic Studies, "The Military Balance 2005–2006"

A number of small countries maintain military forces for ceremonial purposes, national prestige, or reasons other than national defense and would clearly be inadequate to resist an invasion by their much larger neighbors.

top10 COUNTRIES WITH THE LARGEST DEFENSE BUDGETS

	COUNTRY	BUDGET ($)*
1	USA	465,000,000,000
2	China	62,500,000,000
3	Russia	61,900,000,000
4	France	51,600,000,000
5	UK	51,100,000,000
6	Japan	44,700,000,000
7	Italy	30,500,000,000
8	Germany	30,200,000,000
9	India	22,000,000,000
10	Saudi Arabia	21,300,000,000

* Estimated 2004 expenditure or 2005 budget

Source: The International Institute for Strategic Studies, "The Military Balance 2005–2006"

the10 COUNTRIES WITH THE SMALLEST DEFENSE BUDGETS

	COUNTRY*	BUDGET ($)#
1	Gambia	2,300,000
2	Antigua and Barbuda	4,810,000
3	Guyana	5,920,000
4	Cape Verde	6,800,000
5	Equatorial Guinea	7,300,000
6	Suriname	7,700,000
7	Guinea-Bissau	8,600,000
8	Moldova	9,200,000
9	Seychelles	12,600,000
10	Malawi	12,800,000

* Includes only those countries that declare defense budgets
# Estimated 2004 expenditure or 2005 budget

Source: The International Institute for Strategic Studies, "The Military Balance 2005–2006"

top10 NOBEL PEACE PRIZE-WINNING COUNTRIES

	COUNTRY	PEACE PRIZES
1	= International institutions	19
	= USA	19
3	UK	10
4	France	9
5	= Germany	5
	= Sweden	5
7	= Belgium	3
	= Israel	3
	= South Africa	3
	= Switzerland	3

Since 1901 it has been awarded for "...the most or best work for fraternity between the nations, for the abolition or reduction of standing armies, and for the holding and promotion of peace congresses."

top10 ARMS EXPORTERS

	COUNTRY	EXPORTS, 2004 ($)
1	Russia	26,925,000,000
2	USA	25,930,000,000
3	France	6,358,000,000
4	Germany	4,878,000,000
5	UK	4,450,000,000
6	Ukraine	2,118,000,000
7	Canada	1,692,000,000
8	China	1,436,000,000
9	Sweden	1,290,000,000
10	Israel	1,258,000,000

Source: Stockholm International Peace Research Institute

top10 ARMS IMPORTERS

	COUNTRY	IMPORTS, 2004 ($)
1	China	11,677,000,000
2	India	8,526,000,000
3	Greece	5,263,000,000
4	UK	3,395,000,000
5	Turkey	3,298,000,000
6	Egypt	3,103,000,000
7	South Korea	2,755,000,000
8	United Arab Emirates	2,581,000,000
9	Australia	2,177,000,000
10	Pakistan	2,018,000,000
	USA	1,760,000,000

Source: Stockholm International Peace Research Institute

top10 COUNTRIES WITH THE HIGHEST MILITARY/CIVILIAN RATIO

	COUNTRY	RATIO*, 2004
1	North Korea	558
2	Israel	251
3	Qatar	199
4	Jordan	189
5	Syria	171
6	Oman	160
7	Bahrain	157
8	South Korea	144
9	Taiwan	128
10	United Arab Emirates	125
	USA	50

* Military personnel per 10,000 population

TOWN & COUNTRY

4

Countries of the World

COUNTRY	SQ MILES	AREA SQ KM	% OF WORLD TOTAL
1 Russia	6,592,772	17,075,200	11.5
2 Canada	3,855,103	9,984,670	6.7
3 China	3,719,731	9,634,057	6.5
4 USA	3,718,712	9,631,418	6.5
5 Brazil	3,286,488	8,511,965	5.7
6 Australia	2,967,910	7,686,850	5.2
7 India	1,269,346	3,287,590	2.2
8 Argentina	1,068,302	2,766,890	2.1
9 Kazakhstan	1,049,156	2,717,300	1.9
10 Sudan	967,499	2,505,810	1.7
World total	57,506,062	148,940,000	100.0

Source: Central Intelligence Agency, "The World Factbook 2005"

This list is based on the total area of a country within its borders, including offshore islands, inland water such as lakes, rivers, and reservoirs. It may thus differ from versions in which these are excluded. Antarctica has an approximate area of 5,096,549 sq miles (13,200,000 sq km) but is discounted, as it is not considered a country. The countries in the Top 10 collectively comprise 50 percent of the total Earth's surface.

top10 LARGEST DIVIDED ISLANDS

ISLAND	DIVIDED BETWEEN	AREA SQ MILES	SQ KM
1 New Guinea	Indonesia/ Papua New Guinea	303,380	785,753
2 Borneo	Indonesia/Malaysia/ Brunei	288,869	748,168
3 Cuba	Cuba/USA (Guantánamo Bay)	42,803	110,861
4 Ireland	Ireland/United Kingdom	31,520	81,638
5 Hispaniola	Dominican Republic/ Haiti	28,544	73,929
6 Tierra del Fuego	Chile/Argentina	18,301	47,401
7 Timor	Indonesia/East Timor	10,972	28,418
8 Cyprus	Greece/Turkey	3,565	9,234
9 Sebatik Island	Indonesia/Malaysia	174	452
10 Usedom (Uznan)	Germany/Poland	172	445

Most islands are either countries or parts of larger (often, although not always, adjacent) countries, but some are divided between two or more countries. This may result from or remain the cause of political disputes, as with Ireland and Cyprus. Outside the Top 10, the island of St. Martin is divided between Guadeloupe (a French overseas territory) and the Netherlands Antilles, while tiny Märket is split between Finnish-administered Åland and Sweden.

top10 SMALLEST COUNTRIES

COUNTRY	AREA SQ MILES	SQ KM
1 Vatican City	0.17	0.44
2 Monaco	0.75	1.95
3 Nauru	8.18	21.20
4 Tuvalu	9.89	25.63
5 San Marino	23.63	61.20
6 Liechtenstein	61.77	160.00
7 Marshall Islands	70.05	181.43
8 St Kitts and Nevis	104.01	269.40
9 Maldives	115.05	298.00
10 Malta	121.66	315.10

Although recognized as an independent state by a treaty of February 1929, the Vatican's "country" status is questionable, since its government and other functions are intricately linked with those of Italy.

top10 COUNTRIES WITH THE LONGEST COASTLINES

COUNTRY	TOTAL COASTLINE LENGTH MILES	KM
1 Canada	125,566	202,080
2 Indonesia	33,999	54,716
3 Russia	23,396	37,653
4 Philippines	22,559	36,289
5 Japan	18,486	29,751
6 Australia	16,007	25,760
7 Norway	15,626	25,148
8 USA	12,380	19,924
9 New Zealand	9,404	15,134
10 China	9,010	14,500

Including its islands, the coastline of Canada is over six times as long as the distance round the Equator (24,9012 miles/40,076 km). Greece and the UK fall just outside the Top 10.

the10 MOST RECENT INDEPENDENT COUNTRIES

COUNTRY	INDEPENDENCE
1 East Timor	May 20, 2002
2 Palau	Oct 1, 1994
3 Eritrea	May 24, 1993
4 = Czech Republic	Jan 1, 1993
= Slovakia	Jan 1, 1993
6 Serbia and Montenegro	Apr 27, 1992
7 Bosnia-Herzegovina	Mar 1, 1992
8 Kazakhstan	Dec 16, 1991
9 Turkmenistan	Oct 27, 1991
10 Armenia	Sep 21, 1991

Source: Central Intelligence Agency, "The World Factbook 2005"

The breakup of the former Soviet Union was the main factor in the creation of some 28 new nation states since 1990.

⬆ **Remote region** *Landlocked Kazakhstan is some 800 miles (1,300 km) from the nearest seaport.*

top10 **LARGEST LANDLOCKED** COUNTRIES

COUNTRY / NEIGHBORS	AREA SQ MILES	SQ KM
1 Kazakhstan China, Kyrgyzstan, Russia, Turkmenistan, Uzbekistan	1,049,156	2,717,300
2 Mongolia China, Russia	603,908	1,564,116
3 Niger Algeria, Benin, Burkina Faso, Chad, Libya, Mali, Nigeria	489,075	1,266,699
4 Chad Cameroon, Central African Republic, Libya, Niger, Nigeria, Sudan	486,180	1,259,201
5 Mali Algeria, Burkina Faso, Côte d'Ivoire, Guinea, Mauritania, Niger, Senegal	471,044	1,219,999
6 Ethiopia Djibouti, Eritrea, Kenya, Somalia, Sudan	435,186	1,127,127
7 Bolivia Argentina, Brazil, Chile, Paraguay, Peru	424,164	1,098,580
8 Zambia Angola, Dem. Rep. of Congo, Malawi, Mozambique, Namibia, Tanzania, Zimbabwe	290,585	752,614
9 Afghanistan China, Iran, Pakistan, Tajikistan, Turkmenistan, Uzbekistan	250,001	647,500
10 Central African Republic Cameroon, Chad, Congo, Dem. Rep. of Congo, Sudan	240,535	622,984

There are 42 landlocked countries in the world. Both Turkmenistan and Kazakhstan have coasts on the Caspian Sea (also landlocked).

top10 **SMALLEST LANDLOCKED** COUNTRIES

COUNTRY / NEIGHBORS	AREA SQ MILES	SQ KM
1 Vatican City Italy	0.17	0.44
2 San Marino Italy	23.63	61.20
3 Liechtenstein Austria, Switzerland	61.77	160.00
4 Andorra France, Spain	180.70	468.00
5 Luxembourg Belgium, France, Germany	998	2,586
6 Swaziland Mozambique, South Africa	6,704	17,363
7 Macedonia Albania, Bulgaria, Greece, Yugoslavia	9,781	25,333
8 Rwanda Burundi, Dem. Rep. of Congo, Tanzania, Uganda	10,169	26,338
9 Burundi Dem. Rep.of Congo, Rwanda, Tanzania	10,745	27,830
10 Armenia Azerbaijan, Georgia, Iran, Turkey	11,506	29,800

Lacking direct access to the sea, landlocked countries rely on their neighbors for trade routes. At times of political conflict their geography may make them vulnerable to blockades.

Country Populations

⬆ **Rush hour, Bangladesh-style** *A quarter of the country's densely packed population lives in the cities.*

top10 **MOST DENSELY POPULATED** COUNTRIES

	COUNTRY	AREA (SQ KM)	POPULATION (2007 EST.)	POPULATION PER SQ KM
1	Macau	25	456,989	18,279.6
2	Monaco	1.95	32,671	16,754.4
3	Singapore	693	4,553,009	6,570.0
4	Hong Kong	1,092	6,980,412	6,392.3
5	Vatican City	0.44	921	2,093.2
6	Malta	315.10	401,880	1,275.4
7	Maldives	298.00	369,031	1,238.4
9	Bangladesh	133,911	150,448,339	1,123.5
8	Bahrain	665	708,573	1,065.5
10	Taiwan	35,980	23,174,294	644.1
	World	*148,940,000*	*6,600,115,810*	*44.3*
	USA	*9,631,418*	*301,139,947*	*31.3*

Source: US Census Bureau, International Data Base

Macau and Hong Kong are special Administrative Regions within China, but for the purposes of statistical comparison many agencies still consider them as countries.

top10 **LEAST DENSELY POPULATED** COUNTRIES

	COUNTRY	AREA (SQ KM)	POPULATION (2007 EST.)	POPULATION PER SQ KM
1	Mongolia	1,564,116	2,874,127	1.84
2	Namibia	825,418	2,055,080	2.49
3	Australia	7,686,850	20,434,176	2.66
4	Suriname	163,270	439,894	2.69
5	Botswana	600,370	1,639,131	2.73
6	Iceland	103,000	301,931	2.93
7	Mauritania	1,030,700	3,270,065	3.17
8	Canada	9,984,670	33,390,141	3.34
9	Libya	1,759,540	6,036,914	3.43
10	Guyana	214,970	769,095	3.58

Source: US Census Bureau, International Data Base

In marked contrast to the many countries that have population densities in the hundreds (and, in a few instances, thousands) per square kilometre, these sparsely populated countries of the world generally present environmental disadvantages that make human habitation challenging: some contain large tracts of mountain, desert, or dense forest, or have extreme climates.

top10 COUNTRIES WITH **LARGEST POPULATIONS**

COUNTRY	POPULATION (2007 EST.)
1 China	1,321,851,888
2 India	1,110,396,331
3 USA	301,139,947
4 Indonesia	248,883,917
5 Brazil	190,010,647
6 Pakistan	169,270,617
7 Bangladesh	150,448,339
8 Russia	142,369,485
9 Nigeria	135,031,164
10 Japan	127,467,972
World	*6,600,115,810*

Source: US Census Bureau, International Data Base

top10 COUNTRIES WITH **SMALLEST POPULATIONS**

COUNTRY	POPULATION (2007 EST.)
1 Vatican City	921
2 Tuvalu	11,992
3 Nauru	13,528
4 Palau	20,842
5 San Marino	28,615
6 Monaco	32,671
7 Liechtenstein	34,247
8 St. Kitts and Nevis	39,349
9 Marshall Islands	61,782
10 Dominica	68,925

Source: US Census Bureau, International Data Base

⬆ *City and country*
Vatican City's power and world status contrast with its position as the world's smallest and least populated country.

The US Census Bureau projects that by 2034 India's population will reach 1,464,048,216, overtaking China's then 1,461,598,160 – and the USA's will be 375,273,474 – but the populations of many small countries, such as San Marino and Monaco, will barely alter.

top10 COUNTRIES WITH THE **YOUNGEST** POPULATIONS

COUNTRY	PERCENTAGE UNDER 15 (2007 EST.)
1 Uganda	49.8
2 Mali	48.2
3 Chad	47.8
4 = Dem. Rep. of Congo	47.3
= São Tomé and Príncipe	47.3
6 Niger	46.9
7 Burkina Faso	46.7
8 Malawi	46.5
9 = Burundi	46.3
= Congo	46.3
= Yemen	46.3
World average	*27.2*
USA	*20.2*

Source: US Census Bureau, International Data Base

Countries with high proportions of their population under the age of 15 are usually characterized by high birth rates and high death rates. Although not a country, in the Gaza strip almost one in two people (47.6 percent) are aged under 15.

top10 COUNTRIES WITH THE **OLDEST** POPULATIONS

COUNTRY	PERCENTAGE OVER 65 (2007 EST.)
1 Monaco	22.7
2 Japan	20.6
3 Italy	19.9
4 Germany	19.8
5 Greece	19.0
6 Sweden	17.9
7 Spain	17.8
8 = Belgium	17.4
= Bulgaria	17.4
10 Portugal	17.3
World	*7.5*
USA	*12.6*

Source: US Census Bureau, International Data Base

With lower death rates and a higher life expectancy than the rest of the world, nine of the 10 countries with the oldest populations are in Europe. On average, in Western Europe, 16.3 percent of people are over 65, 4.8 percent over 80 – Africa's average is only 3.3 percent for over 65s.

top10 COUNTRIES THAT WILL **DOUBLE THEIR POPULATIONS** SOONEST

COUNTRY	POPULATION DOUBLING TIME (YEARS)
1 Niger	20
2 = Mali	21
= Uganda	21
= Yemen	21
5 = Congo	22
= Malawi	22
7 = Comoros	23
= Dem. Rep. of Congo	23
= Guinea-Bissau	23
= Marshall Islands	23
= Mayotte	23

Source: Population Reference Bureau, "2005 World Population Data Sheet"

People on the Move

top10 COUNTRIES WITH THE **MOST REFUGEES**

	COUNTRY	RATIO OF REFUGEE POP. TO TOTAL POP.	REFUGEE TOTAL
1	West Bank and Gaza	1:2	1,635,000
2	Iran	1:64	1,046,100
3	Pakistan	1:164	968,800
4	Syria	1:26	701,700
5	Tanzania	1:60	602,300
6	Thailand	1:38	460,000
7	China	1:3,257	401,500
8	India	1:2,763	393,300
9	Kenya	1:120	269,300
10	Lebanon	1:18	265,800
	USA	*1:1,261*	*232,000*

Source: US Committee for Refugees and Immigrants

top10 COUNTRIES OF ORIGIN OF **REFUGEES TO THE US**, 2004

	COUNTRY OF ORIGIN	REFUGEES, 2004*
1	Somalia	13,331
2	Liberia	7,140
3	Laos	6,005
4	Sudan	3,500
5	Ukraine	3,482
6	Cuba	2,959
7	Ethiopia	2,710
8	Iran	1,747
9	Moldova	1,711
10	Russia	1,446
	Total all countries	*52,835*

* Financial year

Source: Office of Immigration Statistics, "Yearbook of Immigration Statistics: 2004"

In 2004, over 55 percent of all refugee arrivals to the US were from Africa (a total of 29,129), 10,896 from Asia, and 9,254 from Europe – compared with 1995 total of 98,520 (32,244 from Vietnam).

top10 COUNTRIES OF ORIGIN FOR **REFUGEES AND ASYLUM SEEKERS***

	COUNTRY	REFUGEES
1	Former Palestine	2,985,500
2	Afghanistan	2,088,200
3	Sudan	703,500
4	Myanmar	691,800
5	Burundi	482,200
6	Dem. Rep. of Congo	469,100
7	Iraq	366,100
8	Liberia	328,300
9	Somalia	324,900
10	Vietnam	310,300

* As of January 1, 2005

Source: US Committee for Refugees and Immigrants

top10 **FOREIGN BIRTHPLACES** OF THE US POPULATION*

	BIRTHPLACE	POPULATION
1	Mexico	9,177,487
2	China	1,518,652
3	Philippines	1,369,070
4	India	1,022,552
5	Vietnam	988,174
6	Cuba	872,716
7	Korea (North and South)	864,125
8	Canada	820,711
9	El Salvador	817,336
10	Germany	706,704

* US Bureau of the Census 2000 figures

At the time of the 2000 US Census, 31,107,889 people were foreign-born, with the Top 10 comprising 18,157,587, or 58.4 percent of the total. The most notable change since the previous (1990) Census is the prominence of persons born in China and India, neither of which previously featured in the Top 10.

top10 COUNTRIES RECEIVING THE **MOST INCOME** FROM MIGRANTS*

	COUNTRY	RECEIPTS, 2004 ($)
1	India	21,700,000,000
2	China	21,300,000,000
3	Mexico	18,100,000,000
4	France	12,700,000,000
5	Philippines	11,600,000,000
6	Spain	6,900,000,000
7	Belgium	6,800,000,000
8	Germany	6,500,000,000
9	UK	6,400,000,000
10	Morocco	4,200,000,000
	USA	*3,000,000,000*

* Nationals working overseas

Source: International Monetary Fund/World Bank

AMAZING FACT

US Immigration

Emma Lazarus's poem, *The New Colossus*, inscribed on the Statue of Liberty, contains the lines, "Give me your tired, your poor, Your huddled masses yearning to breathe free," and for many years the USA was the magnet that attracted vast numbers of immigrants. The first great immigration decade was 1901–10, when a total of 8,795,386 arrivals were recorded. The first year in which it topped a million was 1905, with 1,026,499, and a peak of 1,285,349 in 1907. This figure was not exceeded until 1990, when 1,536,483 were received, with 1991 the record year at 1,827,167, and a total of 9,095,417 for the decade 1990–2000. From 1820, when detailed records were first kept, until 2004, the total number of immigrants to the USA was 69,869,450.

⊙ *Fleeing to safety*
Refugees displaced within their own countries or fleeing to neighboring territories have become an all-too familiar feature of the world's recent conflict zones.

Urban World

top10 LARGEST CAPITAL CITIES

CITY / COUNTRY	EST. POPULATION, 2006
1 Tokyo (including Yokohama and Kawasaki), Japan	34,200,000
2 Mexico City (including Nezahualcóyotl, Ecatepec and Naucalpan), Mexico	22,800,000
3 Seoul (including Bucheon, Goyang, Incheon, Seongnam and Suweon), South Korea	22,300,000
4 Delhi (including Faridabad and Ghaziabad), India	19,700,000
5 Jakarta (including Bekasi, Bogor, Depok and Tangerang), Indonesia	16,550,000
6 Cairo (including Al-Jizah and Shubra al-Khaymah), Egypt	15,600,000
7 Manila (including Kalookan and Quezon City), Philippines	14,950,000
8 Moscow, Russia	13,750,000
9 Buenos Aires (including San Justo and La Plata), Argentina	13,450,000
10 Dhaka, Bangladesh	13,250,000

Source: Th. Brinkhoff: The Principal Agglomerations of the World, http://www.citypopulation.de, 2006-01-28

top10 LARGEST CITIES IN THE US

CITY / STATE	POPULATION, 2006*
1 New York (including Newark and Paterson), New York	21,900,000
2 Los Angeles (including Riverside and Anaheim), California	18,000,000
3 Chicago, Illinois	9,750,000
4 Washington (including Baltimore), DC	8,150,000
5 San Francisco (including Oakland and San Jose), California	7,250,000
6 =Dallas (including Fort Worth), Texas	6,000,000
=Philadelphia, Pennsylvania	6,000,000
8 Detroit (including Windsor, Canada), Michigan	5,800,000
9 Boston, Massachusetts	5,700,000
10 Miami (including Fort Lauderdale), Florida	5,550,000

* Of urban agglomeration

Source: Th. Brinkhoff: The Principal Agglomerations of the World, http://www.citypopulation.de , 2006-01-28

top10 COUNTRIES WITH THE LARGEST URBAN POPULATIONS

COUNTRY	EST. TOTAL URBAN POPULATION, 2005*
1 China	535,958,000
2 India	312,887,000
3 USA	232,080,000
4 Brazil	151,925,000
5 Indonesia	104,048,000
6 Russia	102,731,000
7 Japan	101,831,000
8 Mexico	80,073,000
9 Germany	72,405,000
10 Nigeria	62,623,000
World	*3,176,892,000*

* In those countries for which data available

Source: United Nations Population Division, "World Urbanization Prospects: The 2003 Revision"

top10 CITIES WITH THE HIGHEST PROPORTION OF A COUNTRY'S POPULATION

CITY / COUNTRY	% OF TOTAL COUNTRY POPULATION
1 Singapore	100.0
2 San Juan, Puerto Rico	60.1
3 Beirut, Lebanon	49.1
4 Kuwait City, Kuwait	48.5
5 Tel Aviv, Israel	45.3
6 Montevideo, Uruguay	39.3
7 Tripoli, Libya	36.1
8 Yerevan, Armenia	35.3
9 Santiago, Chile	34.7
10 Buenos Aires, Argentina	34.0
New York, USA	*6.2*

Source: United Nations Population Division, "Urban Agglomerations 2003"

These are all capital cities (the United Nations and international law regard Tel Aviv as Israel's capital). If Puerto Rico were excluded as a dependency of the USA, Athens, Greece, with 29.3 percent of the country's population, would enter the list.

top10 HIGHEST CITIES

CITY / COUNTRY	HEIGHT FT	HEIGHT M
1 Wenchuan, China	16,730	5,099
2 Potosí, Bolivia	13,045	3,976
3 Oruro, Bolivia	12,146	3,702
4 Lhasa, Tibet	12,087	3,684
5 La Paz, Bolivia	11,916	3,632
6 Cuzco, Peru	11,152	3,399
7 Huancayo, Peru	10,660	3,249
8 Sucre, Bolivia	9,301	2,835
9 Tunja, Colombia	9,252	2,820
10 Quito, Ecuador	9,249	2,819

Lhasa was formerly the highest capital city in the world, a role now occupied by La Paz, the capital of Bolivia. Wenchuan is situated at over half the elevation of Everest, and even the towns and cities at the bottom of this list are more than one-third as high.

top10 **LARGEST** CITIES

CITY / COUNTRY	EST. POPULATION, 2006
1 Tokyo, Japan	34,200,000
2 Mexico City, Mexico	22,800,000
3 Seoul, South Korea	22,300,000
4 New York, USA	21,900,000
5 São Paulo, Brazil	20,200,000
6 Mumbai (Bombay), India	19,850,000
6 Delhi, India	19,700,000
8 Shanghai, China	18,150,000
9 Los Angeles, USA	18,000,000
10 Osaka, Japan	16,800,000

Source: Th. Brinkhoff: The Principal Agglomerations of the World, http://www.citypopulation.de, 2006-01-28

top10 LARGEST CITIES **100 YEARS AGO**

CITY / COUNTRY	POPULATION, 1907
1 London, UK	4,758,218
2 New York, USA	4,285,435
3 Paris, France	2,735,165
4 Tokyo, Japan	2,433,000
5 Chicago, USA	2,107,620
6 Berlin, Germany	2,096,318
7 Vienna, Austria	1,979,003
8 Osaka, Japan	1,765,000
9 St. Petersburg, Russia	1,505,200
10 Philadelphia, USA	1,500,595

Censuses and population estimates conducted in or around 1907 indicated that these cities, plus a handful of others including Beijing (then spelled Peking), China; Buenos Aires, Argentina; Constantinople, Turkey; and Moscow, Russia, were the only ones with populations in excess of one million. Today, there are almost 440 world cities with million-plus populations.

⬆ *Population center*
Tokyo replaced New York as the world's most populous city in 1965, a position it has maintained ever since.

⬇ *New York, New York*
Photographed in 1907 as the skyscraper age began, New York's population was then in second place after London's. Less than 20 years later, New York had overtaken it.

Place Names

Krung Thep Mahanakhon Amon Rattanakosin Mahir
Burirom Udomratchaniwet Mahasathan Amon Piman

top10 LONGEST PLACE NAMES*

NAME	LETTERS

1 Krung Thep Mahanakhon Amon Rattanakosin Mahinthara Ayuthaya Mahadilok Phop Noppharat Ratchathani Burirom Udomratchaniwet Mahasathan Amon Piman Awatan Sathit Sakkathattiya Witsanukam Prasit **168**

It means "The city of angels, the great city, the eternal jewel city, the impregnable city of God Indra, the grand capital of the world endowed with nine precious gems, the happy city, abounding in an enormous Royal Palace that resembles the heavenly abode where reigns the reincarnated god, a city given by Indra, and built by Vishnukarn." When the poetic name of Bangkok, capital of Thailand, is used, it is usually abbreviated to "Krung Thep" (city of angels).

2 Taumatawhakatangihangakoauauotamateaturipukakapiki-maungahoronukupokaiwhenuakitanatahu **85**

This is the longer version (the other has a mere 83 letters) of the Maori name of a hill in New Zealand. It translates as "The place where Tamatea, the man with the big knees, who slid, climbed, and swallowed mountains, known as land-eater, played on the flute to his loved one."

3 Gorsafawddachaidraigddanheddogleddollônpenrhynareur-draethceredigion **67**

A name contrived by the Fairbourne Steam Railway, Gwynedd, North Wales, for publicity purposes and in order to outdo its rival, No.4. It means "The Mawddach station and its dragon teeth at the Northern Penrhyn Road on the golden beach of Cardigan Bay."

4 Llanfairpwllgwyngyllgogerychwyrndrobwllllantysiliogo-gogoch **58**

This is the place in Gwynedd famed especially for the length of its railway tickets. It means "St. Mary's Church in the hollow of the white hazel near to the rapid whirlpool of the church of St. Tysilo near the Red Cave." Questions have been raised about its authenticity, since its official name comprises only the first 20 letters, and the full name appears to have been invented as a hoax in the 19th century by a local tailor.

5 El Pueblo de Nuestra Señora la Reina de los Ángeles de la Porciúncula **57**

The site of a Franciscan mission and the full Spanish name of Los Angeles; it means "The town of Our Lady the Queen of the Angels of the Little Portion." Nowadays it is customarily known by its initial letters, "LA," making it also one of the shortest-named cities in the world.

6 Chargoggagoggmanchaugagoggchaubunagungamaug **43**

America's longest place name, a lake near Webster, Massachusetts. Its Indian name, loosely translated, is claimed to mean "You fish on your side, I'll fish on mine, and no one fishes in the middle." It is said to be pronounced "Char-gogg-a-gogg (pause) man-chaugg-a-gog (pause) chau-bun-a-gung-a-maug." It is, however, an invented extension of its real name (Chabunagungamaug, or "boundary fishing place"), devised in the 1920s by Larry Daly, the editor of the *Webster Times*.

7 = Lower North Branch Little Southwest Miramichi **40**

Canada's longest place name – a short river in New Brunswick.

= Villa Real de la Santa Fé de San Francisco de Asis **40**

The full Spanish name of Santa Fe, New Mexico, translates as, "Royal city of the holy faith of St. Francis of Assisi."

9 Te Whakatakanga-o-te-ngarehu-o-te-ahi-a-Tamatea **38**

The Maori name of Hammer Springs, New Zealand; like the second name in this list, it refers to a legend of Tamatea, explaining how the springs were warmed by "the falling of the cinders of the fire of Tamatea." Its name is variously written either hyphenated or as a single word.

10 Meallan Liath Coire Mhic Dhubhghaill **32**

The longest multiple name in Scotland, a place near Aultanrynie, Highland, alternatively spelled Meallan Liath Coire Mhic Dhughaill (30 letters).

* Including single-word, hyphenated, and multiple names

ra Ayuthaya Mahadilok Phop Noppharat Ratchathani tan Sathit Sakkathattiya Witsanukam Prasit (Bangkok)

top10 MOST COMMON STREET NAMES IN THE US

1 Second Street
2 Third Street
3 First Street
4 Fourth Street
5 Park Street
6 Fifth Street
7 Main Street
8 Sixth Street
9 Oak Street
10 Seventh Street

Source: US Bureau of the Census

top10 LONGEST PLACE NAMES IN THE US*

NAME / STATE / (LETTERS)

1 Chargoggagoggmanchauggagoggchaubunagungamaugg, Massachusetts (45)
2 Nunathloogagamiutbingoi Dunes, Alaska (23)
3 =Kleinfeltersville, Pennsylvania (17)
   =Mooselookmeguntic, Maine 17)
5 =Chancellorsville, Virginia (16)
   =Chickasawhatchee, Georgia (16)
   =Eichelbergertown, Pennsylvania (16)
   =Nollidewabticook, Maine (16)
9 Pongowayhaymock, Maine (15)
10 Anasagunticook, Maine (14)

* Nonhyphenated

Source: US Geological Survey Geographical Names Information System (GNIS)

top10 MOST COMMON PLACE NAMES IN THE US

	NAME	STATES* / PLACES
1	Midway	39 / 211
2	Fairview	40 / 202
3	Oak Grove	31 / 160
4	Five Points	28 / 147
5	=Pleasant Hill	29 / 119
	=Riverside	46 / 119
7	Mount Pleasant	32 / 115
8	Bethel	34 / 110
9	Centerville	43 / 108
10	New Hope	25 / 105

* No. of states with at least one example

Source: US Geological Survey Geographical Names Information System (GNIS)

Fairview figures prominently in certain states – there are 27 in Tennessee alone. It is also one of the most common cemetery names in the USA, with no fewer than 59 examples; there are also 81 cemeteries called Riverside and 43 called Oak Grove.

top10 LARGEST COUNTRIES THAT CHANGED THEIR NAMES IN THE PAST 100 YEARS

	FORMER NAME	CURRENT NAME	YEAR CHANGED	AREA SQ MILES	AREA SQ KM
1	Zaïre	Dem. Rep. of Congo	1997	905,567	2,345,409
2	Persia	Iran	1935	630,577	1,633,188
3	Tanganyika/Zanzibar	Tanzania	1964	364,900	945,087
4	South West Africa	Namibia	1990	318,261	824,292
5	Northern Rhodesia	Zambia	1964	290,586	752,614
6	Burma	Myanmar	1989	261,218	676,552
7	Ubanghi Shari	Central African Republic	1960	240,535	622,984
8	Bechuanaland	Botswana	1966	224,607	581,730
9	Siam	Thailand	1939	198,115	513,115
10	Mesopotamia	Iraq	1921	169,235	438,317

Although not a country, Greenland (840,004 sq miles/2,175,600 sq km) has been officially known as Kalaallit Nunaat since 1979.

Skyscrapers

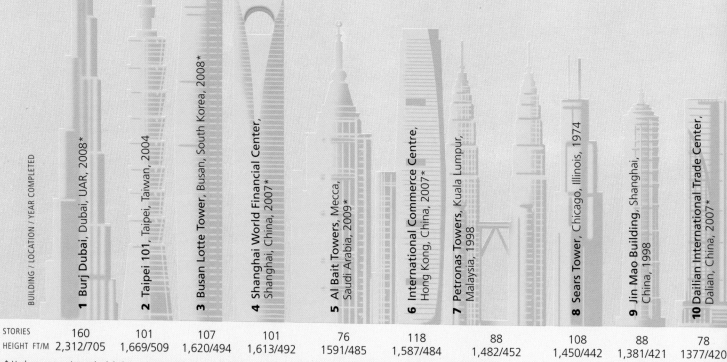

top10 **TALLEST** HABITABLE BUILDINGS

Although much debated by skyscraper experts, according to rules established by the Chicago-based Council on Tall Buildings and Urban Habitat, a building's height is measured from street level to its structural top. This includes spires, but not subterranean floors or nonstructural additions, such as masts, antennae, or flagpoles. The CTBUH separately identifies such categories as highest occupied floor, top of roof, and top of pinnacle or antenna.

BUILDING / LOCATION / YEAR COMPLETED

1 Burj Dubai, Dubai, UAR, 2008*
2 Taipei 101, Taipei, Taiwan, 2004
3 Busan Lotte Tower, Busan, South Korea, 2008*
4 Shanghai World Financial Center, Shanghai, China, 2007*
5 Al Bait Towers, Mecca, Saudi Arabia, 2009*
6 International Commerce Centre, Hong Kong, China, 2007*
7 Petronas Towers, Kuala Lumpur, Malaysia, 1998
8 Sears Tower, Chicago, Illinois, 1974
9 Jin Mao Building, Shanghai, China, 1998
10 Dailian International Trade Center, Dalian, China, 2007*

	1	2	3	4	5	6	7	8	9	10
STORIES	160	101	107	101	76	118	88	108	88	78
HEIGHT FT/M	2,312/705	1,669/509	1,620/494	1,613/492	1591/485	1,587/484	1,482/452	1,450/442	1,381/421	1377/420

* Under construction, scheduled completion date

top10 TALLEST HABITABLE BUILDINGS **DESTROYED**

BUILDING / LOCATION (ALL USA) / YEAR COMPLETED	YEAR DESTROYED	STORIES	HEIGHT FT	M
1 1 World Trade Center, New York, 1972	2001	110	1,368	417.0
2 2 World Trade Center, New York, 1973	2001	110	1,363	415.4
3 Singer Building, New York, 1908	1968	47	612	186.5
4 7 World Trade Center, New York, 1987	2001	47	570	173.7
5 Morrison Hotel, Chicago, 1926	1965	45	526	160.3
6 One Meridian Plaza, Philadelphia, 1972	1999	38	492	150.0
7 City Investing Building, New York, 1908	1968	33	486	148.1
8 Hudson's Department Store, Detroit, 1924	1998	26	439	133.8
9 National Bank Building, New York, 1928	1975	32	433	132.0
10 Savoy-Plaza Hotel, New York, 1930	1964	33	420	128.0

➔ Broken record-holder
New York's Singer Building, the world's tallest from 1908, was demolished in 1968 and replaced by the 743-ft (225-m) One Liberty Plaza in 1973.

Height of luxury
Modeled on the sail of an Arab dhow, the Burj al-Arab Hotel took the record as the world's tallest dedicated hotel structure.

top10 TALLEST HOTELS

	HOTEL* / LOCATION / YEAR	STORIES	HEIGHT# FT	M
1	Jin Mao Tower, Shanghai, China, 1998 Grand Hyatt Hotel occupies floors 53 to 87	88	1,214	370
2	Trump International Hotel & Tower Chicago, USA, 2008†	92	1,171	357
3	Shimao International Plaza, Shanghai, China, 2005 48 floors of hotel occupancy	60	1,093	333
4	Abbco Rotana Hotel, Dubai, UAR, 2006†	72	1,033	315
5	Baiyoke Tower 2, Bangkok, Thailand, 1997 Baiyoke Sky Hotel occupies floors 22 to 74	89	1,013	309
6	Burj Dubai Lake Hotel, Dubai, UAR, 2007†	63	984	300
7	Burj al-Arab, Dubai, UAR, 1999	60	885	270
8	Emirates Hotel Tower, Dubai, UAR, 2000	54	856	261
9	Thai Wah Tower II, Bangkok, Thailand, 1996 Westin Banyan Tree Hotel occupies floors 33–60	60	853	260
10	Mercure Grand Hotel Tower, Dubai, UAR, 2008†	62	820	250

* Including mixed occupancy (hotel + residential/office) buildings
# Excluding spire
† Under construction; scheduled completion date

top10 TALLEST CYLINDRICAL BUILDINGS

	BUILDING / LOCATION	YEAR COMPLETED	STORIES	HEIGHT FT / M	
1	Treasury Building, Singapore	1986	52	770	235
2	Tun Abdul Prazak Building, Penang, Malaysia	1985	61	760	232
3	Westin Peachtree Plaza, Atlanta, Georgia	1973	71	721	220
4	Renaissance Center, Detroit, Michigan	1977	73	718	219
5	Hopewell Centre (Hong Kong, China)	1980	64	705	215
6	Marina City Apartments (twin towers), Chicago, Illinois	1969	61	588	179
7	Australia Square Tower, Sydney, Australia	1968	46	560	170
8	Amartapura Condominium 1, Tangerang, Indonesia	1996	54	535	163
9	Shenzen City Plaza, Shenzen, China	1996	37	490	150
10	Amartapura Condominium 2, Tangerang, Indonesia	1997	36	445	136

top10 CITIES WITH MOST SKYSCRAPERS*

	CITY / LOCATION	SKYSCRAPERS
1	Hong Kong, China	188
2	New York City, New York	183
3	Chicago, Illinois	87
4	Shanghai, China	68
5	Tokyo, Japan	61
6	Singapore City, Singapore	34
7	Houston, Texas	29
8	Seoul, South Korea	26
9	=Sydney, Australia	24
10	=Kuala Lumpur, Malaysia	23

* Habitable buildings of over 500 ft (152 m)

Super Structures

top10 TALLEST **PYRAMIDS**

PYRAMID	BUILT	HEIGHT FT	HEIGHT M
1 Transamerica pyramid, San Francisco, California	1972	853	260
2 Great Pyramid, Giza, Egypt	2530 BC	483	147
3 Chefren pyramid, Giza, Egypt	2500 BC	449	137
4 Luxor Hotel and Casino, Las Vegas, Nevada	1993	351	107
5 Red Pyramid of Sneferu, Dahsûr, Egypt	2600 BC	341	104
6 Bent pyramid, Dahsûr, Egypt	2605 BC	332	101
7 Great American Pyramid, Memphis, Tennessee	1991	322	98
8 Meidum Pyramid, Meidum, Egypt	2610 BC	308	94
9 Pyramid of Mykerinos, Giza, Egypt	2480 BC	216	66
10 Pyramid of the Sun, Teotihuacán, Mexico	225	209	64

Some authorities have claimed that the so-called Great White Pyramid, Xian, China, is up to 984 ft (300 m) high. However, this manmade earth mound may measure no more than 150 ft (45 m).

top10 TALLEST **CHIMNEYS**

CHIMNEY / LOCATION	HEIGHT FT	HEIGHT M
1 Ekibastuz power station, Kazakhstan	1,377	420
2 International Nickel Company, Copper Hill, Sudbury, Ontario, Canada	1,250	381
3 Homer City Generating Station Unit 3, Minersville, Pennsylvania	1,216	371
4 Kennecott Copper Corporation, Magna, Utah	1,215	370
5 Mitchel Power Plant, Moundsville, West Virginia	1,206	368
6 Zasavje power station, Trbovlje, Slovenia	1,181	360
7 Endesa Termic, La Coruña, Spain	1,169	356
8 Syrdarya Power Plant Units 5–10, Syrdarya, Uzbekistan	1,148	350
9 Teruel Power Plant, Teruel, Spain	1,125	343
10 Plomin Power Plant, Plomin, Croatia	1,115	340

The chimney at the Ekibastuz power station, the world's largest coal-fired plant which was completed in 1991, tapers from 144 ft (44 m) at the base to 47 ft (14 m) at the top.

top10 **TALLEST** STRUCTURES ERECTED OVER **100 YEARS AGO**

STRUCTURE / LOCATION	YEAR COMPLETED	HEIGHT FT	HEIGHT M
1 Eiffel Tower, Paris, France	1889	984	300
2 Washington Memorial, Washington, DC	1885	555	169
3 Mole Antonelliana, Turin, Italy	1889	551	168
4 Philadelphia City Hall, Philadelphia, Pennsylvania	1901	548	167
5 Ulm Cathedral, Ulm, Germany	1890	528	161
6 Lincoln Cathedral, Lincoln, England (destroyed 1548)	c.1307	525	160
7 Blackpool Tower, Blackpool, England	1894	518	158
8 Cologne Cathedral, Cologne, Germany	1880	513	156.4
9 Rouen Cathedral I, Rouen, France (destroyed 1822)	1530	512	156
10 St Pierre Church, Beauvais, France (collapsed 1573)	1568	502	153

top10 TALLEST **LIGHTHOUSES** IN THE US

LIGHTHOUSE / STATE	HEIGHT* FT	HEIGHT* M
1 Cape Hatteras, North Carolina	196	59.7
2 Cape Charles, Virginia	191	58.2
3 Pensacola, Florida	171	52.1
4 = Absecon, New Jersey	170	51.8
= Cape May, New Jersey	170	51.8
6 Lookout, North Carolina	169	51.5
7 Ponce de Leon Inlet, Florida	168	51.2
8 Fire Island, New York	167	50.9
9 "New" Cape Henry, North Carolina	165	50.3
10 = Bodie Island, North Carolina	163	49.7
= Currituck, North Carolina	163	49.7

* Measurement taken from ground level to the top of the lantern

Source: US Lighthouse Society

Built in 1870, Cape Hatteras lighthouse, North Carolina, is the tallest in the USA at 196 ft (59.7 m). To save it from erosion by the sea, between 1999 and 2000 the entire 2,800-tonne lighthouse was moved 2,900 ft (884 m) inland, very slowly, on tracks.

↑ *Superstructures compared: The Great Pyramid, Giza; The Eiffel Tower, Paris; Ekibastuz power station chimney, Kazakhstan; CN Tower, Toronto, Canada.*

top10 TALLEST **TELECOMMUNICATIONS TOWERS**

TOWER / LOCATION	YEAR COMPLETED	HEIGHT FT	M
1 Guangzhou TV & Sightseeing Tower, Guangzhou, China	2007*	2,001	610
2 CN Tower, Toronto, Canada	1975	1,821	555
3 Ostankino Tower#, Moscow, Russia	1967	1,762	537
4 Oriental Pearl Broadcasting Tower, Shanghai, China	1995	1,535	468
5 Borj-e Milad Telecommunications Tower, Tehran, Iran	2003	1,426	435
6 Menara Telecom Tower, Kuala Lumpur, Malaysia	1996	1,381	421
7 Tianjin TV and Radio Tower, Tianjin, China	1991	1,362	415
8 Central Radio and TV Tower, Beijing, China	1994	1,328	405
9 Kiev TV Tower, Kiev, Ukraine	1973	1,263	385
10 TV Tower, Tashkent, Uzbekistan	1983	1,230	375

* Under construction; scheduled completion
# Severely damaged by fire, Aug 27, 2000; restored and reopened 2004

All the towers listed are self-supporting, rather than masts braced with guy wires. The completion of the Menara Telecom Tower meant that for the first time in 107 years the Eiffel Tower – which once headed the list – dropped out of the Top 10.

⬆ *Towering achievement*
Higher than the Eiffel Tower, Millau Viaduct, the world's tallest road bridge, has seven towers ranging in height from 574 ft (175 m) to 1,125 ft (343 m).

top10 TALLEST **BRIDGE TOWERS**

BRIDGE / LOCATION	YEAR COMPLETED	HEIGHT FY	M
1 Millau Viaduct, Millau, France	2004	1,125	343
2 Akashi-Kaikyo, Akashi, Japan	1998	978	298
3 East Bridge, Great Belt Fixed Link, Sprogø, Denmark	1997	833	254
4 Golden Gate, San Francisco, California	1937	745	227
5 Tatara, Onomichi, Japan	1999	741	226
6 Jambatan Pulau Pinang, Penang, Malaysia	1985	739	225
7 Le Ponte de Normandie, Le Havre, France	1994	705	215
8 Verrazano Narrows, New York City, New York	1964	692	211
9 Tsing Ma, Hong Kong, China	1997	675	206
10 Mezcala-Solidaridad, Cuilapan, Mexico	1993	673	205

Scheduled for completion in 2012, the Strait of Messina Bridge between Sicily and mainland Italy will have two towers 1,256 ft (383 m) high.

CULTURE

5

World Languages

top10 LANGUAGES MOST SPOKEN IN THE US

	LANGUAGE	SPEAKERS
1	English	215,423,557
2	Spanish	28,101,052
3	Chinese	2,022,143
4	French	1,643,838
5	German	1,382,613
6	Tagalog	1,224,241
7	Vietnamese	1,009,627
8	Italian	1,008,370
9	Korean	894,063
10	Russian	706,242

Source: US Census Bureau, Census 2000

top10 MOST SPOKEN LANGUAGES*

	LANGUAGE	SPEAKERS
1	Chinese (Mandarin)	873,014,298
2	Spanish	322,299,171
3	English	309,352,280
4	Hindi	180,764,791
5	Portuguese	177,457,180
6	Bengali	171,070,202
7	Russian	145,031,551
8	Japanese	122,433,899
9	German	95,392,978
10	Chinese (Wu)	77,175,000

* Primary speakers only

Source: Raymond G. Gordon, Jr. (ed.), "Ethnologue: Languages of the World," 15th edition, 2005, Dallas, Texas: SIL International. Online version: http://www.ethnologue.com/

top10 COUNTRIES WITH THE MOST ENGLISH LANGUAGE SPEAKERS

	COUNTRY	APPROX. NO. OF SPEAKERS*
1	USA	215,423,557
2	UK	58,190,000
3	Canada	20,000,000
4	Australia	14,987,000
5	Ireland	3,750,000
6	= New Zealand	3,700,000
	= South Africa	3,700,000
8	Jamaica#	2,600,000
9	Trinidad and Tobago#	1,145,000
10	Guyana#	650,000

* People for whom English is their mother tongue
# Includes English Creole

The Top 10 represents the countries with the greatest numbers of inhabitants who speak English as their mother tongue. After the 10th entry, the figures dive to around or under 260,000 in the case of the Bahamas, Barbados, and Zimbabwe. In addition to these and others that make up a world total that is probably in excess of 500,000,000, there are perhaps as many as 1,000,000,000 who speak English as a second language: a large proportion of the population of the Philippines, for example, speaks English, and there are many countries, such as India, Nigeria, and other former British colonies in Africa, where English is either an official language or is widely understood and used in conducting legal affairs, business, and government.

hello how

hallo, wie ge

es Ihnen

ciao come siete?

top10 MOST COMMON WORDS IN ENGLISH

WRITTEN		SPOKEN
the	**1**	be
of	**2**	the
and	**3**	I
a	**4**	you
in	**5**	and
to	**6**	it
is	**7**	have
was	**8**	a
it	**9**	not
for	**10**	do

A survey of a wide range of texts containing a total of almost 90 million words indicated that, in written English, one word in every 16 is "the."

top10 LANGUAGES INTO WHICH MOST BOOKS ARE TRANSLATED

	LANGUAGE	TRANSLATIONS 1979–2002
1	German	247,631
2	Spanish	192,365
3	French	164,448
4	English	103,293
5	Japanese	90,803
6	Dutch	88,362
7	Portuguese	66,062
8	Russian	61,333
9	Polish	50,678
10	Danish	50,370

Source: UNESCO, "Index Translationum (1979–2002)"

top10 LANGUAGES FROM WHICH MOST BOOKS ARE TRANSLATED

	LANGUAGE	TRANSLATIONS 1979–2002
1	English	860,139
2	French	161,826
3	German	146,176
4	Russian	89,860
5	Italian	48,240
6	Spanish	37,380
7	Swedish	27,089
8	Latin	14,797
9	Danish	13,916
10	Ancient Greek	12,993

Source: UNESCO, "Index Translationum (1979–2002)"

top10 ONLINE LANGUAGES

	LANGUAGE	% OF ALL INTERNET USERS	INTERNET USERS*
1	English	30.6	311,241,881
2	Chinese	13.0	132,301,513
3	Japanese	8.5	86,300,000
4	Spanish	6.3	63,971,898
5	German	5.6	56,853,162
6	French	4.0	40,974,005
7	Korean	3.3	33,900,000
8	Portuguese	3.2	32,372,000
9	Italian	2.8	28,870,000
10	Russian	2.3	23,700,000
	Top 10 languages	*79.6*	*810,484,459*
	Rest of world languages	*20.4*	*207,572,930*
	World total	*100.0*	*1,018,057,389*

* As at Dec 31, 2005

Source: Internet World Stats http://www.internetworldstats.com/

Education

top10 **OLDEST** UNIVERSITIES*

	UNIVERSITY	COUNTRY	FOUNDED
1	Parma	Italy	1064
2	Bologna	Italy	1088
3	Paris	France	1150
4	Oxford	England	1167
5	Modena	Italy	1175
6	Cambridge	England	1209
7	Salamanca	Spain	1218
8	Padua	Italy	1222
9	Naples	Italy	1224
10	Toulouse	France	1229

* Only those in continuous operation since founding

⊙ *Dreaming spires*
All Souls College, Oxford, was founded over 300 years into the university's 840-year history. Teaching began as early as 1096, but the university dates its origin to a decree by Henry II forbidding English students from attending the University of Paris. All Souls' Gothic spires were designed by Nicholas Hawksmoor in the early 18th century.

top10 **LARGEST** UNIVERSITIES **IN THE US**

	UNIVERSITY / LOCATION	ENROLLMENT, 2005
1	Arizona State University, Tempe, Arizona	51,712
2	University of Minnesota Twin Cities, Minneapolis, Minnesota	51,175
3	Ohio State University, Columbus, Ohio	50,504
4	University of Florida, Gainesville, Florida	49,650
5	University of Texas at Austin, Austin, Texas	49,333
6	Michigan State University, East Lansing, Michigan	45,166
7	Texas A&M University-College Station, College Station, Texas	44,647
8	University of South Florida, Tampa, Florida	43,021
9	University of Central Florida, Orlando, Florida	42,550
10	University of Wisconsin-Madison, Madison, Wisconsin	41,480

top10 OLDEST
UNIVERSITIES AND COLLEGES
IN THE US

	UNIVERSITY / LOCATION	YEAR CHARTERED
1	Harvard University, Massachusetts	1636
2	College of William and Mary, Virginia	1692
3	Yale University, Connecticut	1701
4	University of Pennsylvania, Pennsylvania	1740
5	Moravian College, Pennsylvania	1742
6	Princeton University, New Jersey	1746
7	Washington and Lee University, Virginia	1749
8	Columbia University, New York	1754
9	Brown University, Rhode Island	1764
10	Rutgers, the State University of New Jersey	1766

the10 OLDEST
SECONDARY SCHOOLS
IN THE US

	SCHOOL / LOCATION	FOUNDED
1	Roxbury Latin School, West Roxbury, Massachusetts	1645
2	Hopkins School, New Haven, Connecticut	1660
3	= Friends Select School, Philadelphia, Pennsylvania	1689
	= William Penn Charter School, Philadelphia, Pennsylvania	1689
5	Abington Friends School, Jenkintown, Pennsylvania	1697
6	Trinity School, New York, New York,	1709
7	Moravian Academy, Bethlehem, Pennsylvania	1742
8	Linden Hall School for Girls, Lititz, Pennsylvania	1746
9	Governor Dummer Academy, Byfield, Massachusetts	1763
10	Columbia Grammar and Preparatory School, New York, New York	1764

top10 LARGEST
UNIVERSITIES

	UNIVERSITY / COUNTRY	STUDENTS
1	Kameshwara Singh Darbhanga Sanskrit, India	515,000
2	Calicut, India	300,000
3	Paris, France	279,978
4	Mexico City, Mexico	269,000
5	Mumbai, India	262,350
6	Chhatrapati Shahuji Maharaj University, India	220,000
7	Utkal, India	200,000
8	Rome, Italy	189,000
9	Buenos Aires, Argentina	183,397
10	Guadalajara, Mexico	180,776

With 594,227 students, the Indira Gandhi National Open University, India, is the world's largest distance-learning establishment, while currently some 180,000 students are enrolled with the Open University in the UK.

top10 COUNTRIES WITH
MOST FOREIGN
STUDENTS*

	COUNTRY	FOREIGN STUDENTS
1	USA	582,996
2	Germany	240,619
3	UK	227,273
4	France	221,567
5	Australia	179,619
6	Japan	74,892
7	Russia	68,602
8	Spain	53,639
9	Belgium	41,856
10	Canada	40,033

* In tertiary education

Source: UNESCO, "Global Education Digest 2005"

Books

top10 NONFICTION BOOKS IN THE US, 2005

	AUTHOR / TITLE	SALES IN 2005
1	James Frey, A Million Little Pieces	1,768,565
2	David McCullough, 1776	1,234,071
3	Thomas L. Friedman, The World is Flat	1,066,154
4	Rick Warren, The Purpose-Driven Life	983,245
5	Mehmet Oz, You: The Owner's Manual	918,239
6	Joel Osteen, Your Best Life Now	831,370
7	Malcolm Gladwell, Blink	820,087
8	Kevin Trudeau, Natural Cures "They" Don't Want You to Know About	775,682
9	Steven D. Levitt, Freakonomics	755,846
10	Greg Behrendt and Liz Tuccillo, He's Just Not That into You: The No-excuses Truth to Understanding Guys	470,135

the10 LATEST WINNERS OF THE PULITZER PRIZE FOR FICTION

YEAR	AUTHOR / TITLE
2006	Geraldine Brooks, March
2005	Marilynne Robinson, Gilead
2004	Edward P. Jones, The Known World
2003	Jeffrey Eugenides, Middlesex
2002	Richard Russo, Empire Falls
2001	Michael Chabon, The Amazing Adventures of Kavalier & Clay
2000	Jhumpa Lhiri, Interpreter of Maladies
1999	Michael Cunningham, The Hours
1998	Philip Roth, American Pastoral
1997	Steven Millhauser, Martin Dressler: The Tale of an American Dreamer

top10 BESTSELLING BOOKS

AUTHOR/BOOK / YEAR OF PUBLICATION / MINIMUM ESTIMATED SALES*

1
The Bible (c. 1451–55–)
6,000,000,000

2
Quotations from the Works of Mao Tse-tung (1966)
900,000,000

3 =
J.R.R. Tolkien, The Lord of the Rings trilogy (1954–55) 100,000,000

3 =
Noah Webster, American Spelling Book (1783) 100,000,000

5
William Holmes McGuffey, The McGuffey Readers (1836)
60,000,000

6
Benjamin Spock, The Common Sense Book of Baby and Child Care (1946)
50,000,000

7
Betty Crocker's Cookbook (1950)
45,000,000

8
Elbert Hubbard, A Message to Garcia (1899)
40,000,000

9 =
Rev. Charles Monroe Sheldon, In His Steps: "What Would Jesus Do?" (1896)
30,000,000

9 =
Jacqueline Susann, Valley of the Dolls (1966)
30,000,000

* Including translations; excluding annual publications and series

top10 COUNTRIES FOR **BOOK SALES**

COUNTRY	FICTION	FORECAST BOOK SALES, 2007 NONFICTION	TOTAL
1 China	628,838,000	7,856,761,000	8,485,599,000
2 USA	971,127,000	1,718,030,000	2,689,157,000
3 Japan	702,001,000	630,069,000	1,332,070,000
4 Russia	172,800,000	392,000,000	564,800,000
5 France	222,157,000	238,750,000	460,907,000
6 Germany	178,603,000	268,669,000	447,272,000
7 UK	150,098,000	223,768,000	373,866,000
8 Brazil	46,908,000	322,066,000	368,974,000
9 Spain	107,893,000	167,312,000	275,205,000
10 Italy	111,236,000	157,006,000	268,242,000

Source: Euromonitor

top10 **FICTION BOOKS** IN THE US, 2005

AUTHOR / TITLE	SALES IN 2005
1 J.K. Rowling, Harry Potter and the Half-Blood Prince	7,024,151
2 Khaled Hosseini, The Kite Runner	1,571,431
3 Dan Brown, The Da Vinci Code	1,087,085
4 Dan Brown, Angels & Demons	923,950
5 Christopher Paolini, Eldest	882,028
6 Sue Monk Kidd, The Secret Life of Bees	655,774
7 Mark Haddon, The Curious Incident of the Dog in the Night-Time	640,061
8 Ann Brashares, Sisterhood of the Traveling Pants	639,096
9 John Grisham, The Broker	621,310
10 Gregory Maguire, Wicked	602,583

top10 COUNTRIES FOR **ELECTRONIC BOOKS**

COUNTRY	FORECAST ELECTRONIC BOOK SALES, 2007
1 USA	129,908,000
2 China	126,682,000
3 Italy	39,976,000
4 France	27,965,000
5 UK	15,019,000
6 Canada	7,904,000
7 Brazil	5,653,000
8 Belgium	3,932,000
9 Japan	3,368,000
10 Spain	3,347,000

Source: Euromonitor

Downloads of eBooks are predicted to increase dramatically as electronic readers and titles become widely available.

The Press

top10 NEWSPAPER-READING COUNTRIES

	COUNTRY	DAILY COPIES PER 1,000 PEOPLE, 2004
1	Iceland	705.9
2	Norway	684.0
3	Japan	646.9
4	Sweden	590.0
5	Finland	524.2
6	Bulgaria	472.7
7	Macau	448.9
8	Denmark	436.6
9	Switzerland	419.6
10	UK	393.4
	USA	*263.2*

Source: World Association of Newspapers, "World Press Trends 2004," www.wan-press.org

top10 SUNDAY NEWSPAPERS IN THE US

	NEWSPAPER	AVERAGE SUNDAY CIRCULATION*
1	The New York Times	1,682,644
2	Los Angeles Times	1,247,588
3	Washington Post	965,919
4	Chicago Tribune	950,582
5	New York News	781,375
6	The Denver Post/Rocky Mountain News	725,178
7	Philadelphia Inquirer	714,609
8	Houston Chronicle	708,312
9	Detroit News & Free Press	679,484
10	The Boston Globe	652,146

* Average for six months to Sep 30, 2005

Source: Audit Bureau of Circulations/Newspaper Association of America

top10 DAILY NEWSPAPERS IN THE US

	NEWSPAPER	AVERAGE US CIRCULATION*
1	USA Today	2,222,745
2	The Wall Street Journal	2,083,660
3	The New York Times	1,126,190
4	Los Angeles Times	843,432
5	Daily News (New York)	688,584
6	Washington Post	678,779
7	New York Post	662,681
8	Chicago Tribune	586,122
9	Houston Chronicle	521,419
10	San Francisco Chronicle	419,358

* Average for six months to Sep 30, 2005

Source: Audit Bureau of Circulations/Newspaper Association of America

top10 MAGAZINES IN THE US

	MAGAZINE	AVERAGE CIRCULATION, 2005
1	AARP The Magazine	22,675,655
2	AARP Bulletin	22,075,011
3	Reader's Digest	10,111,773
4	TV Guide	8,211,581
5	Better Homes and Gardens	7,620,932
6	National Geographic	5,403,934
7	Good Housekeeping	4,634,763
8	Family Circle	4,296,370
9	Ladies' Home Journal	4,122,460
10	Woman's Day	4,048,799

Source: Audit Bureau of Circulations/Magazine Publishers of America

AMAZING FACT

Heavyweight Press

The heaviest newspaper ever published was the Sunday edition of the *New York Times* of September 14, 1987. It contained 1,612 pages and tipped the scales at over 12 lb (5.4 kg), the total edition weighing over 6,000 tonnes. At this time, it was calculated that the newspaper consumed the equivalent of a forest of 75,000 trees every Sunday, but the progressive increase in the use of recycled paper, the planting of sustainable forest, and the reduction in the page size have reduced this figure.

top10 OLDEST NEWSPAPERS IN THE US

	NEWSPAPER / CITY / STATE	YEAR ESTABLISHED
1	The Hartford Courant, Hartford, CT	1764
2 =	The Augusta Chronicle, Augusta, GA	1785
=	Poughkeepsie Journal, Poughkeepsie, NY	1785
=	The Register Star, Hudson, NY	1785
5 =	Daily Hampshire Gazette, Northampton, MA	1786
=	Pittsburgh Post-Gazette, Pittsburgh, PA	1786
7	The Berkshire Eagle, Pittsfield, MA	1789
8	Norwich Bulletin, Norwich, CT	1791
9	The Recorder, Greenfield, MA	1792
10	Intelligencer Journal, Lancaster, PA	1794

Source: "Editor and Publisher Year Book"

Among even older newspapers that are no longer extant is the *Boston News-Letter*, first published in 1704 by New England postmaster John Campbell. It measured just 7.5 x 12 inches and had a circulation of 300 copies.

top10 DAILY NEWSPAPERS

	NEWSPAPER	COUNTRY	AVERAGE DAILY CIRCULATION, 2005
1	Yomiuri Shimbun	Japan	14,532,694
2	Asahi Shimbun	Japan	12,601,375
3	Sichuan Ribao	China	8,000,000
4	Mainichi Shimbun	Japan	5,845,857
5	Bild-Zeitung	Germany	5,674,400
6	Chunichi Shimbun	Japan	4,323,144
7	The Sun	UK	3,718,354
8	Renmin Ribao	China	3,000,000
9	Sankei Shimbun	Japan	2,890,835
10	Nihon Keizai Shimbun	Japan	2,705,877

Source: World Association of Newspapers

In 2005 *Yomiuri Shimbun*, Japan's and the world's bestselling daily newspaper, achieved a record sales average of 14,532,694 copies a day. Founded in 1874, the name *Yomiuri*, "selling by reading," refers to the Japanese practice of vendors reading aloud from newssheets in the era before moveable type.

top10 MAGAZINE GENRES IN THE US

	GENRE	NO. OF PUBLICATIONS, 2005
1	College and alumni	971
2	Medicine	965
3	Religion and theological	724
4	Travel	626
5	Regional interest	596
6	Business and industry	540
7	Ethnic	534
8	Computers and automation	485
9	Automotive	426
10	Music and music trades	364
	Total (including those not in Top 10)	22,054

Source: "National Directory of Magazines, 2006"

IThe number of college and alumni magazines has more than doubled since 1999, when there were just 450 titles. During the same period, most other genres have declined, reducing the overall total by almost 30 percent from 31,076. Magazines devoted to sports and sporting goods have fallen out of the Top 10 by plummeting from 863 to 359.

🕐 *Chinese whispers*
The importance of the press in China is exemplified by the presence of two Chinese dailies among the world's Top 10.

Art on Show

top10 BEST-ATTENDED ART EXHIBITIONS IN THE US, 2005

	EXHIBITION	VENUE / CITY / DATES	ATTENDANCE* DAILY	TOTAL
1	Tutankhamun and the Pharaohs	Los Angeles County Museum of Art, Jun 16 – Nov 20	5,934	937,613
2	Chanel	Metropolitan Museum of Art, New York, May 5 – Aug 7	5,519	463,603
3	Vincent van Gogh: The Drawings	Metropolitan Museum of Art, New York, Oct 18 – Dec 31	6,571	459,972
4	Cézanne and Pissarro 1865–85	Museum of Modern Art, New York, Jun 26 – Sep 12	6,387	433,397
5	Friedlander	Museum of Modern Art, New York, Jun 5 – Aug 29	5,238	386,841
6	Salvador Dalí	Philadelphia Museum, Feb 16 – May 30	4,144	370,011
7	Matisse: His Art and his Textiles	Metropolitan Museum of Art, New York, Jun 23 – Sep 25	4,311	362,152
8	Works from the UBS Art Collection	Museum of Modern Art, New York, Feb 4 – Apr 25	4,985	346,847
9	Sol LeWitt on the Roof	Metropolitan Museum of Art, New York, Apr 26 – Oct 30	1,980	319,406
10	The Aztec Empire	Guggenheim Museum, New York, Oct 15, 2004 – Feb 13, 2005	3,040	315,294

* Approximate totals provided by museums

Source: "The Art Newspaper"

top10 BEST-ATTENDED ART EXHIBITIONS, 2005

	EXHIBITION	VENUE / CITY / COUNTRY / DATES	ATTENDANCE* DAILY	TOTAL
1	Tutankhamun and the Pharaohs	Los Angeles County Museum of Art, California, Jun 16–Nov 20	5,934	937,613
2	Tutankhamun, the Golden Beyond	Kunst der Bundesrepublik, Bonn, Germany, Nov 4, 2004–May 1, 2005	5,644	866,812
3	Art Informel and Abstract Expressionism	Guggenheim Museum, Bilbao, Spain, Mar 8–Nov 6	3,278	721,074
4	Pharaoh	Institut du Monde Arabe, Paris, France, Oct 15, 2004–Jun 12, 2005	3,396	699,483
5	19th-century Masterpieces from the Louvre	Yokohama Museum of Art, Japan, Feb 23–May 22	7,066	621,814
6	Van Gogh in Context	National Museum of Modern Art, Tokyo, Japan, Feb 23–May 22	5,890	518,307
7	Turner Whistler Monet	Grand Palais, Paris, France, Oct 13, 2004–Jan 17, 2005	6,043	501,601
8	Chanel	Metropolitan Museum of Art, New York, May 5–Aug 7	5,519	463,603
9	Vincent Van Gogh: The Drawings	Metropolitan Museum of Art, New York, Oct 18–Dec 31	6,571	459,972
10	Monet, the Seine and Water Lilies	Museum di Santa Giulia, Brescia, Italy, Oct 23, 2004–Apr 3, 2005	3,150	440,564

* Approximate totals provided by museums

Source: "The Art Newspaper"

⊙ **Head of his people**
Sioux warrior Crazy Horse (c.1837–77) is commemorated by this massive work in progress, carved out of a mountain in South Dakota and begun almost 60 years ago. The face alone took from 1987 to 1998 and stands 87.5 ft (28.7 m) high.

top10 **TALLEST FREE-STANDING** STATUES

STATUE / LOCATION	HEIGHT FT	M
1 Crazy Horse Memorial, Thunderhead Mountain, South Dakota	563	172

Started in 1948 by Polish-American sculptor Korczak Ziolkowski and continued after his death in 1982 by his widow and eight of his children, this gigantic equestrian statue, even longer than it is high (641 ft/195 m), is not expected to be completed for several years.

2 Ushiku Amida Buddha, Joodo Teien Garden, Japan	394	120

This Japan-Taiwanese project, unveiled in 1993, took seven years to complete and weighs 1,000 tonnes.

3 The Indian Rope Trick, Riddersberg Säteri, Jönköping, Sweden	337	103

Sculptor Calle Örnemark's 144-tonne wooden sculpture stands in an open-air museum and depicts a long strand of "rope" held by a fakir, while another figure ascends.

4 Peter the Great, Moscow, Russia	315	96

Georgian sculptor Zurab Tsereteli's statue of the Russian ruler on a galleon was moved from St. Petersburg in 1997.

5 Motherland, Volgograd, Russia	270	82

This 1967 concrete statue of a woman with a raised sword, designed by Yevgeniy Vuchetich, commemorates the Soviet victory at the Battle of Stalingrad (1942–43).

6 Kannon, Sanukimachi, Tokyo Bay, Japan	184	56

The immense statue of the goddess of mercy was unveiled in 1961 in honor of the dead of World War II.

7 Statue of Liberty, New York, New York	151	46

Designed by Auguste Bartholdi and presented to the USA by the people of France, the statue was shipped in sections to Liberty (formerly Bedloes) Island where it was assembled, before being unveiled on October 28, 1886.

8 Christ the Redeemer, Rio de Janeiro, Brazil	125	38

The work of sculptor Paul Landowski and engineer Heitor da Silva Costa, the figure of Christ was unveiled in 1931.

9 Tian Tan (Temple of Heaven) Buddha, Po Lin Monastery, Lantau Island, Hong Kong, China	112	34

This was completed after 20 years' work and unveiled on December 29, 1993.

10 Quantum Cloud, Greenwich, London, UK	95	29

A gigantic steel human figure surrounded by a matrix of steel struts, it was created in 1999 by Antony Gormley, the sculptor of the similarly gigantic 66-ft (20-m) Angel of the North, Gateshead, UK.

the10 MOST VISITED **ART GALLERIES** AND **MUSEUMS** IN THE US

	MUSEUM / GALLERY / LOCATION	VISITORS
1	The Smithsonian Institution*	20,100,000
2	United States Capitol Historical Society*	8,000,000
3	National Museum of American History*	5,900,000
4	National Museum of Natural History*	5,542,000
5	Metropolitan Museum of Art#	5,400,000
6	=National Gallery of Art*	4,000,000
	=American Museum of Natural History#	4,000,000
8	Statue of Liberty National Monument and Ellis Island Immigration Museum#	3,408,560
9	Museum of Modern Art#	1,585,000
10	Museum of Science¹	1,429,685

* Washington, DC   # New York, NY   ¹ Boston, MA

Source: "The Official Museum Directory"

Paintings at Auction

top 10 MOST EXPENSIVE PAINTINGS

PAINTING / ARTIST	SALE	PRICE* ($)
1 Garçon à la Pipe, Pablo Picasso (Spanish; 1881–1973)	Sotheby's, New York, May 5, 2004	93,000,000
2 Portrait du Dr. Gachet, Vincent van Gogh (Dutch; 1853–90)	Christie's, New York, May 15, 1990	75,000,000
3 Bal au Moulin de la Galette, Montmartre, Pierre-Auguste Renoir (French; 1841–1919)	Sotheby's, New York, May 17, 1990	71,000,000
4 Massacre of the Innocents, Sir Peter Paul Rubens (Flemish; 1577–1640)	Sotheby's, London, Jul 10, 2002	69,714,000 (£45,000,000)
5 Portrait de l'Artiste Sans Barbe, Vincent van Gogh	Christie's, New York, Nov 19, 1998	65,000,000
6 Rideau, Cruchon et Compôtier, Paul Cézanne (French; 1839–1906)	Sotheby's, New York, May 10, 1999	55,000,000
7 Les Noces de Pierrette, Pablo Picasso	Binoche et Godeau, Paris, Nov 30, 1989	51,796,432 (F.Fr315,000,000)
8 Femme aux Bras Croises, Pablo Picasso	Christie's Rockefeller, New York, Nov 8, 2000	50,000,000
9 Irises, Vincent van Gogh	Sotheby's, New York, Nov 11, 1987	49,000,000
10 Femme Assise Dans un Jardin, Pablo Picasso	Sotheby's, New York, Nov 10, 1999	45,000,000

* Excluding buyer's premium; converted at rate prevailing at time of sale

top 10 MOST EXPENSIVE **OLD MASTER PAINTINGS**

PAINTING / ARTIST	SALE	PRICE ($)
1 Massacre of the Innocents, Sir Peter Paul Rubens	Sotheby's, London Jul 10, 2002	69,714,000 (£45,000,000)
2 Giudecca, La Donna della Salute and San Giorgio, J.M.W. Turner	Christie's, New York, Apr 6, 2006	35,856,000
3 Portrait of Duke Cosimo I de Medici, Jacopo da Carucci (Pontormo)	Christie's, New York, May 31, 1989	32,000,000
4 Portrait of Lady aged 62, Rembrandt	Christie's, London, Dec 13, 2000	26,082,720 (£18,000,000)
5 Descent into Limbo, Andrea Mantegna	Sotheby's, New York, Jan 23, 2003	25,500,000
6 The Old Horse Guards, London, from St. James's Park, Canaletto	Christie's, London, Apr 15, 1992	16,213,160 (£9,200,000)
7 Vue de la Giudecca et du Zattere, à Venice, Francesco Guardi	Sotheby's, Monaco, Dec 1, 1989	14,015,995 (F.Fr85,000,000)
8 Portrait of Omai, Standing in a Landscape, wearing Robes and a Head-dress, Sir Joshua Reynolds	Sotheby's, London, Nov 29, 2001	13,410,040 (£9,400,000)
9 Tieleman Roosterman in Black Doublet, White Ruff, Frans Hals (elder)	Christie's, London, Jul 8, 1999	11,684,250 (£7,500,000)
10 Portrait of a Bearded Man in a Red Doublet, Rembrandt	Christie's Rockefeller, New York, Jan 26, 2001	11,500,000

↑ Portrait du Dr. Gachet
Van Gogh painted two versions of this portrait of the doctor who cared for him in 1890, in the last months of his life. One hangs in the Musée d'Orsay, Paris, while this took the then record as the world's most expensive painting in 1990 when it was sold to a Japanese businessman.

top10 MOST EXPENSIVE PAINTINGS **BY WOMEN ARTISTS**

PAINTING / ARTIST	SALE	PRICE ($)
1 Calla Lilies with Red Anemone, Georgia O'Keeffe (American; 1887–1986)	Christie's Rockefeller, New York, May 23, 2001	5,600,000
2 The Conversation, Mary Cassatt (American; 1844–1926)	Christie's, New York, May 11, 1988	4,100,000
3 Cache-cache, Berthe Morisot (French; 1841–1895)	Sotheby's, New York, Nov 9, 2000	4,000,000
4 Marche au Minho, Sonia Delaunay (French/Russian, 1885–1979)	Laurence Calmels, Paris, Jun 14, 2002	3,871,507 (€4,100,000)
5 =Black Cross with Stars and Blue, Georgia O'Keeffe	Christie's Rockefeller, New York, May 23, 2001	3,700,000
=In the Box, Mary Cassatt	Christie's, New York, May 23, 1996	3,700,000
7 =Cache-cache, Berthe Morisot	Sotheby's, New York, May 10, 1999	3,500,000
=Mother, Sara, and the Baby, Mary Cassatt	Christie's, New York, May 10, 1989	3,500,000
9 From the Plains, Georgia O'Keeffe	Sotheby's, New York, Dec 3, 1997	3,300,000
10 Après le Déjeuner, Berthe Morisot	Christie's New York, May 14, 1997	3,250,000

top10 ARTISTS WITH MOST WORKS **SOLD FOR OVER $1 MILLION**

ARTIST	TOTAL VALUE OF WORKS SOLD ($)	NO. OF WORKS SOLD FOR OVER $1 MILLION
1 Pablo Picasso (Spanish; 1881–1973)	1,399,203,108	298
2 Claude Monet (French; 1888–1926)	1,016,435,017	229
3 Pierre Auguste Renoir (French; 1841–1919)	664,578,714	206
4 Edgar Degas (French; 1834–1917)	354,635,303	108
5 Henri Matisse (French; 1869–1954)	350,639,390	91
6 Paul Cézanne (French; 1839–1906)	486,000,573	85
7 Camille Pissarro (French; 1830–1903)	152,898,994	81
8 Marc Chagall (Russian; 1887–1985)	168,593,200	76
9 Amedeo Modigliani (Italian; 1884–1920)	289,213,301	65
10 Vincent van Gogh (Dutch; 1853–90)	551,850,639	60

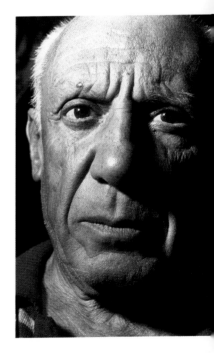

① Pablo Picasso
The works of Spanish artist Picasso (1881–1973) are among the most expensive ever sold, with more $1-million paintings than any artist at auction.

Objets d'Art

top10 MOST EXPENSIVE **WATERCOLORS**

WATERCOLOR / ARTIST / SALE	PRICE ($)
1 La Moisson en Provence, Vincent van Gogh (Dutch;1853–90), Sotheby's, London, Jun 24, 1997	13,352,000 (£8,000,000)
2 Les Toits – 1882, Vincent van Gogh, Ader Picard & Tajan, Paris, Mar 20, 1990	4,732,691 (F.Fr 27,000,000)
3 Red Canoe, Winslow Homer (American; 1836–1910), Sotheby's, New York, Dec 1, 1999	4,400,000
4 Nature Morte au Melon Vert, Paul Cézanne (French;1839–1906), Sotheby's, London, Apr 4, 1989	3,877,800 (£2,300,000)
5 Die Sangerin L. Ais Fiordiligi, Paul Klee (Swiss; 1879–1940), Sotheby's, London, Nov 28, 1989	3,744,000
6 = John Biglin in Single Scull, Thomas Eakins (American; 1844–1916), Christie's, New York, May 23, 1990	3,200,000
= The Stony Beach, Maurice Prendergast (American; 1859–1916), Christie's Rockefeller, New York, May 23, 2001	3,200,000
8 Au Moulin Rouge, La Fille du Roi d'Egypte, Pablo Picasso (Spanish; 1881–1973), Sotheby's, London, Nov 29, 1994	2,585,055 (£1,650,000)
9 Heidelberg with a Rainbow, Joseph Mallord William Turner (British; 1775–1851), Sotheby's, London, Jun 14, 2001	2,573,887 (£1,850,000)
10 Coral Divers, Winslow Homer (American; 1836–1910), Christie's, New York, Dec 2, 1998	2,400,000

top10 MOST EXPENSIVE **MINIATURES**

MINIATURE / ARTIST / SALE	PRICE ($)
1 Portrait of George Washington, John Ramage (Irish; c.1748–1802), Christie's, New York, Jan 19, 2001	1,216,000
2 Two Orientals, Francisco José de Goya y Lucientes (Spanish; 1746–1828), Christie's, London, Dec 3, 1997	580,000
3 Maja and Celestina, Francisco José de Goya y Lucientes, Sotheby's, New York, May 30, 1991	500,000
4 Portrait of George Villiers, Duke of Buckingham, Jean Petitot (French; 1607–91), Christie's, London, Apr 30, 1996	377,050 (£250,000)
5 Man Clasping Hand from Cloud, possibly Lord Thomas Howard, Nicholas Hilliard (British; 1547–1619), Christie's, London, Mar 3, 1993	232,800 (£160,000)
6 Self-portrait, Frida Kahlo (Mexican; 1907–1954), Sotheby's, New York, Nov 20, 2000	200,000
7 A Gentleman aged 52, Nicholas Hilliard, Christie's, London, May 2003	196,376 (£122,8500
8 Portrait of Henry Stuart, Earl of Ross and 1st Duke of Albany, attributed to Lievine Teerling-Bening (Flemish; 16th century) Bonhams, London, Nov 20, 1997	188,582 (£110,000)
9 King George III when Prince of Wales Wearing Order of Garter, Jean-Etienne Liotard (Swiss; 1702–89), Christie's, London, Oct 21, 1997	188,163 (£115,000)
10 Bacchic Scenes, Jean Jacques de Gault (French; c.1738–1812), Sotheby's, Geneva, Nov 13, 1995	141,069 (S.Fr.160,000)

top10 MOST EXPENSIVE **SCULPTURES**

SCULPTURE / ARTIST / SALE	PRICE ($)
1 Danaïde, Constantin Brancusi (Romanian; 1876–1956), Christie's Rockefeller, New York, May 7, 2002	16,500,000
2 Grande Femme Debout I, Alberto Giacometti (Swiss; 1901–66), Christie's Rockefeller, New York, Nov 8, 2000	13,000,000
3 La Serpentine Femme à la Stele – l'Araignée, Henri Matisse (French; 1869–1954), Sotheby's, New York, May 10, 2000	12,750,000
4 Grande Tête de Diego, Alberto Giacometti, Sotheby's, New York, May 8, 2002	12,500,000
5 La Forêt, Alberto Giacometti, Christie's Rockefeller, New York, May 7, 2002	12,000,000
6 Figure Decorative, Henri Matisse, Sotheby's, New York, May 10, 2001	11,500,000
7 Petite Danseuse de Quatorze Ans, Edgar Degas (French; 1834–1917), Sotheby's, New York, Nov 11, 1999	11,250,000
8 Petite Danseuse de Quatorze Ans, Edgar Degas, Sotheby's, New York, Nov 12, 1996	10,800,000
9 Petite Danseuse de Quatorze Ans, Edgar Degas, Sotheby's, London, Jun 27, 2000	10,484,390 (£7,000,000)
10 Nu Couche I, Aurore, Henri Matisse, Phillips, New York, May 7, 2001	9,500,000

❶ Million-dollar President
George Washington sat for this miniature on October 3, 1789 as a gift for his wife. It became the first ever to be sold for over $1 million.

◉ **Water level**
Maurice Prendergast's The Stony Beach *(1897) set a new record as the most expensive watercolor to be sold in the 21st century.*

top10 MOST EXPENSIVE **PHOTOGRAPHS**

	PHOTOGRAPH* / PHOTOGRAPHER / SALE	PRICE ($)
1	The Pond – Moonlight (1904), Edward Steichen (American; 1879–1973), Sotheby's, New York, Feb 14, 2006	2,928,000
2	Georgia O'Keeffe (Hands) (1919), Alfred Stieglitz (American; 1864–1946), Sotheby's, New York, Feb 14, 2006	1,472,000
3	Georgia O'Keeffe (Nude) (1919), Alfred Stieglitz, Sotheby's, New York, Feb 14, 2006	1,360,000
4	Untitled (Cowboy) (1989), Richard Prince (American, b.1949), Christie's, New York, Nov 8, 2005	1,320,000
5	Grande vague – sète (c.1857), Gustave le Gray (French; 1820–82), Sotheby's, London, Oct 27, 1999	838,644 (£507,500)
6	= The Breast (1921), Edward Weston (American; 1886–1958), Sotheby's, New York, Oct 10, 2005	822,400
	= White Angel Breadline (1933), Dorothea Lange (American; 1895–1965), Sotheby's, New York, Oct 11, 2005	$822,400
8	Athènes, Temple de Jupiter Olympien (1842), Joseph Philibert Girault de Prangey (French; 1804–92), Christie's, London, May 20, 2003	816,750 (£500,000)
9	Hetre, Fontainebleau (1885), Gustave le Gray, Sotheby's, London, Oct 27, 1999	693,224 (£419,500)
10	Untitled (Oriental Glasses) (1982), Richard Prince, Christie's, New York, May 12, 2005	660,000

* Single prints only

top10 PRICES FOR **FILM POSTERS** AT AUCTION

	POSTER* / AUCTION	PRICE ($)
1	The Mummy (1932) Sotheby's, New York, Mar 1, 1997	453,500
2	Metropolis (1927) Sotheby's, New York, Oct 28, 2000	357,750
3	King Kong (1933) Sotheby's, New York, Apr 16, 1999	244,500
4	Frankenstein (1931) Odyssey Auctions, Los Angeles, Oct 11, 1993	198,000
5	Babe Comes Home (1927) Heritage online auction, Nov 20, 2003	138,000
6	Men in Black (1934) Sotheby's, New York, Apr 4, 1998	109,750
7	= Play Ball with Babe Ruth (1929) Sotheby's, New York, Apr 16, 1999	96,000
	= Three Little Pigskins (1934) Sotheby's, New York, Apr 16, 1999	96,000
9	Wings (1927) Heritage online auction, Nov 12, 2005	86,250
10	Casablanca (1942) Christie's, London, Mar 27, 2000	86,130 (£54,000)

* Highest priced example of each – other versions of some have also achieved high prices

In November 2005, the Reel Poster Gallery, London, sold a 1927 *Metropolis* poster privately (not at auction, and hence not included in this Top 10) for $690,000 (£397,762), a record for any poster.

Treasured Possessions

top10 MOST EXPENSIVE **BOOKS AND MANUSCRIPTS**

BOOK / MANUSCRIPT / SALE*	PRICE ($)#
1 The Codex Hammer (formerly Codex Leicester) (1506–10), Christie's, New York, Nov 11, 1994	30,802,500

This is one of Leonardo da Vinci's notebooks, which includes many scientific drawings and diagrams. It was purchased by Bill Gates, the billionaire founder of Microsoft.

2 The Rothschild Prayerbook (c.1503) Christie's, London, Jul 8, 1999	13,369,118 (£8,581,500)

This holds the world-record price for an illuminated manuscript.

3 The Gospels of Henry the Lion (c.1173–75) Sotheby's, London, Dec 6, 1983	10,696,700 (£7,400,000)

At the time of its sale, it became the most expensive book, manuscript, or work of art other than a painting ever sold.

4 John James Audubon's The Birds of America (1827–38), Christie's, New York, Mar 10, 2000	8,802,500

The record for any printed book. A facsimile reprint of Audubon's *The Birds of America* published in 1985 by Abbeville Press, New York, was once listed at $30,000, making it the most expensive book ever published.

5 The Canterbury Tales, Geoffrey Chaucer (c.1476–77), Christie's, London, Jul 8, 1998	7,570,941 (£4,621,500)

Printed by William Caxton, and purchased by Sir Paul Getty. The record for a work of English literature. In 1776, the same volume had changed hands for just £6.

6 Comedies, Histories, and Tragedies, The First Folio of William Shakespeare (1623) Christie's, New York, Oct 8, 2001	6,166,000

This sale marks the world auction record for a 17th-century book.

7 The Gutenberg Bible (1455) Christie's, New York, Oct 22, 1987	5,390,000

One of the first books ever printed, by Johann Gutenberg and Johann Fust.

8 The Northumberland Bestiary (c.1250–60) Sotheby's, London, Nov 29, 1990	5,329,800 (£2,700,000)

9 The Burdett Psalter and Hours (c.1282–86) Sotheby's, London, Jun 23, 1998	4,175,250 (£2,500,000)

10 The Cornaro Missal (c.1503) Christie's, London, Jul 8, 1999	4,050,540 (£2,600,000)

This manuscript, formerly owned by the Barons Nathaniel and Albert Von Rothschild, achieved a world-record price for an Italian manuscript.

* Excludes collections
# Includes buyer's premium

top10 MOST EXPENSIVE **TOYS EVER SOLD** AT AUCTION

TOY / SALE	PRICE ($)
1 Kämmer and Reinhardt doll, Sotheby's, London, Feb 8, 1994	277,981 (£188,500)
2 Titania's Palace, Christie's, London, Jan 10, 1978 A doll's house with 2,000 items of furniture.	258,728 (£135,000)
3 The Charles, Christie's, New York, Dec 14, 1991 A fire hose-reel made by American manufacturer George Brown & Co (c.1875).	231,000
4 Louis Vuitton Steiff teddy bear (2000), Christie's, Monaco, Oct 14, 2000	182,550 (Euros213,720)
5 Kämmer and Reinhardt bisque character doll, German (c.1909), Sotheby's, London, Oct 17, 1996 Previously sold at Sotheby's, London, Feb 16, 1989, for £90,200 (see No.7 entry below).	171,713 (£108,200)
6 "Teddy Girl," a 1904 Steiff teddy bear, Christie's, London, Dec 5, 1994	171,600 (£110,000)
7 Kämmer and Reinhardt bisque character doll, German (c.1909), Sotheby's, London, Feb 16, 1989	159,952 (£90,200)
6 Black mohair Steiff teddy bear (c.1912), Christie's, London, Dec 4, 2000 One of a number of black Steiff bears brought out in the UK after the sinking of the *Titanic* that have since become known as "Mourning" teddies.	132,157 (£91,750)
9 Hornby 00-gauge train set, Christies, London, Nov 27, 1992 The largest train set ever sold at auction.	121,069 (£80,178)
10 Marklin train station, Noel Barrett, Carversville, Pennsylvania, May 28, 2005	110,000

● Bear market
This rare Steiff teddy bear's high price results from its association with the Titanic, the 1912 sinking of which it commemorates.

⬆ A price above rubies
The iconic ruby slippers worn by Judy Garland in The Wizard of Oz – *one of seven pairs – made a record price at auction.*

top10 ITEMS OF **FILM MEMORABILIA** SOLD AT AUCTION*

	ITEM / SALE	PRICE ($)
1	David O. Selznick's Oscar for "Gone with the Wind" (**1939**), Sotheby's, New York, Jun 12, 1999 Bought by Michael Jackson.	1,542,500
2	Marilyn Monroe's "Happy Birthday Mr. President" dress (**1962**), Christie's, New York, Oct 27, 1999	1,267,000
3	Judy Garland's ruby slippers from "The Wizard of Oz" (**1939**), Christie's, New York, May 26, 2000	666,000
4	Clark Gable's Oscar for "It Happened One Night" (**1934**), Christie's, Los Angeles, Dec 15, 1996	607,500
5	Bette Davis's Oscar for "Jezebel" (**1938**), Christie's, New York, Jul 19, 2001 Bought by Steven Spielberg.	578,000
6	Vivien Leigh's Oscar for "Gone with the Wind," Sotheby's, New York, Dec 15, 1993	562,500
7	Statue of the falcon from "The Maltese Falcon" (**1941**), Christie's, New York, Dec 6, 1994	398,500
8	Judy Garland's blue-and-white gingham dress from "The Wizard of Oz," Christie's, London, Dec 9, 1999	333,185 (£199,500)
9	Marlon Brando's script for "The Godfather" (**1972**), Christie's, New York, Jun 30, 2005	312,800
10	James Bond's Aston Martin DB5 from "Goldfinger" (**1964**), Sotheby's, New York, Jun 28, 1986	275,000

* Excluding posters and animation cels

top10 MOST EXPENSIVE **MUSICAL INSTRUMENTS**

	INSTRUMENT* / DETAILS / SALE	PRICE ($)
1	John Lennon's Steinway Model Z upright piano, Fleetwood-Owen online auction, London and New York, Hard Rock Café, Oct 17, 2000	2,100,310 (£1,450,000)
2	"Kreutzer" violin by Antonio Stradivari (1727) Christie's, London, Apr 1, 1998	1,585,452 £947,500)
3	"Cholmondeley" violincello by Antonio Stradivari Sotheby's, London, Jun 22, 1998	1,136,962 (£682,000)
4	Jerry Garcia's 'Tiger' guitar Guernsey's at Studio 54, New York, May 9, 2002	957,500
5	Eric Clapton's 1964 Gibson acoustic ES-335 Christie's, New York, Jun 25, 2004	847,500
6	Steinway grand piano, decorated by Lawrence Alma-Tadema and Edward Poynter for Henry Marquand (1884–87) Sotheby Parke Bernet, New York, Mar 26, 1980	390,000
7	Single-manual harpsichord by Joseph Joannes Couchet, Antwerp (1679), Sotheby's, London, Nov 21, 2001	379,877 (£267,500)
8	Double bass by Domenico Montagnana Sotheby's, London, Mar 16, 1999	252,423 (£155,500)
9	Verne Powell's platinum flute Christie's, New York, Oct 18, 1986	187,000
10	Viola by Giovanni Paolo Maggini Christie's, London, Nov 20, 1984	161,082 (£129,000)

* Most expensive example only for each type of instrument

AMAZING FACT

One-Dollar Oscars

It is noticeable that no post1950 Oscars figure among the Top 10 items of film memorabilia sold at auction. That is because, since 1950, the Academy of Motion Picture Arts and Sciences has compelled Oscar-winners to sign an agreement that neither they, nor their heirs, will ever dispose of their Oscars without first offering to sell them back to the Academy for one dollar. The sale of producer Mike Todd's Best Picture Oscar for *Around the World in 80 Days* (1956) was blocked, while Bette Davis's Oscar for *Jezebel* was donated back to the Academy by its purchaser, Oscar-winner Steven Spielberg.

MUSIC

Singles

TITLE / ARTIST/GROUP

1 **We Belong Together**, Mariah Carey
2 **Hollaback Girl**, Gwen Stefani
3 **Let Me Love You**, Mario
4 **Since U Been Gone**, Kelly Clarkson
5 **1, 2 Step**, Ciara featuring Missy Elliott
6 **Gold Digger**, Kanye West featuring Jamie Foxx
7 **Boulevard of Broken Dreams**, Green Day
8 **Candy Shop**, 50 Cent featuring Olivia
9 **Don't Cha**, The Pussycat Dolls featuring Busta Rhymes
10 **Behind These Hazel Eyes**, Kelly Clarkson

⊕ **All-time hit** *Elton John's tribute to Princess Diana is the bestselling single ever.*

top10 SINGLES OF **ALL TIME**

TITLE / ARTIST/GROUP	YEAR	SALES EXCEED
1 Candle in the Wind (1997)/Something about the Way You Look Tonight, Elton John	1997	37,000,000
2 White Christmas, Bing Crosby	1942	30,000,000
3 Rock Around the Clock, Bill Haley & His Comets	1954	17,000,000
4 I Want to Hold Your Hand, The Beatles	1963	12,000,000
5 = It's Now or Never, Elvis Presley	1960	10,000,000
= Hey Jude, The Beatles	1968	10,000,000
= I Will Always Love You, Whitney Houston	1992	10,000,000
8 = Diana, Paul Anka	1957	9,000,000
= Hound Dog/Don't Be Cruel, Elvis Presley	1956	9,000,000
10 = (Everything I Do) I Do it for You, Bryan Adams	1991	8,000,000
= I'm a Believer, The Monkees	1966	8,000,000

Global sales are notoriously difficult to calculate, since for many decades, little statistical research on record sales was done in a large part of the world. "Worldwide" is thus usually taken to mean the known minimum "western world" sales. It took 55 years for a record to overtake Bing Crosby's 1942 *White Christmas*, although the song, as also recorded by others and sold as sheet music, has achieved such enormous total sales that it would still appear in first position in any list of bestselling songs.

top10 **DOWNLOADS** IN THE US, 2005

TITLE / ARTIST/GROUP

1 **Beverly Hills**, Weezer
2 **Hollaback Girl**, Gwen Stefani
3 **My Humps**, Black Eyed Peas
4 **Since U Been Gone**, Kelly Clarkson
5 **Mr. Brightside**, Killers
6 **Sugar, We're Goin' Down,** Fall Out Boy
7 **Don't Phunk With My Heart**, Black Eyed Peas
8 **Gold Digger (explicit version)**, Kanye West
9 **Boulevard of Broken Dreams**, Green Day
10 **Photograph**, Nickelback

Source: Nielsen SoundScan

In 2003, annual sales of digital tracks totaled 19,200,000. Such was the growth of legal downloads and the widespread adoption of Apple iPods that, in 2004, that figure rose to 139,400,000 singles and 45,500,000 albums. In 2005, the figures were 366,900,000 and 135,700,000, respectively, valued at $503,600,00.

top10 SINGLES OF **ALL TIME** IN THE US

	TITLE / ARTIST/GROUP	EST. US SALES
1	Candle in the Wind (1997)/Something about the Way You Look Tonight, Elton John	11,000,000
2	White Christmas, Bing Crosby	8,000,000
3 =	Hey Jude, The Beatles	4,000,000
=	Hound Dog/Don't Be Cruel, Elvis Presley	4,000,000
=	I Will Always Love You, Whitney Houston	4,000,000
=	Macarena (Bayside Boys Mix), Los Del Rio	4,000,000
=	We Are the World, USA for Africa	4,000,000
=	Whoomp! (There it Is), Tag Team	4,000,000
9 =	(Everything I Do) I Do it for You, Bryan Adams	3,000,000
=	Gangsta's Paradise, Coolio	3,000,000
=	How Do I Live, LeAnnRimes	3,000,000
=	I'll Be Missing You, Puff Daddy and Faith Evans (featuring 112)	3,000,000
=	Love Me Tender/Any Way You Want Me, Elvis Presley	3,000,000

Taken from the film *Holiday Inn* (1942), Bing Crosby's *White Christmas* sold over 30 million copies worldwide, making it the bestselling single ever. In the US, it took 55 years and the death of Princess Diana to generate sales capable of overtaking it, as Elton John's specially penned tribute did, and by a considerable margin. Resting comfortably below these two megasellers is a group certified by the RIAA in the elite four-million league.

top10 SINGLES THAT STAYED **LONGEST ON THE US SINGLES CHART**

	TITLE / ARTIST/GROUP	YEAR	WEEKS
1	How Do I Live, LeAnn Rimes	1997	69
2	Foolish Games/You Were Meant For Me, Jewel	1996	65
3	Macarena (Bayside Boys Mix), Los Del Rio	1996	60
4	Smooth, Santana featuring Rob Thomas	1999	58
5	Higher, Creed	1999	57
6 =	I Don't Want to Wait, Paula Cole	1997	56
=	The Way You Love Me, Faith Hill	2000	56
8 =	Amazed, Lonestar	1999	55
=	Barely Breathing, Duncan Sheik	1996	55
=	Missing, Everything But The Girl	1996	55

Source: Music Information Database

➲ The King still rules
Fifty years after his first UK chart entry and 30 years since his death, Elvis Presley maintains his commanding lead with most weeks at No.1.

top10 ARTISTS WITH THE **MOST WEEKS AT NO. 1** IN THE US

	ARTIST/GROUP / WEEKS AT NO. 1
1	Elvis Presley 79
3	Mariah Carey* 75
2	The Beatles 59
4	Boyz II Men* 50
5	Usher# 40
6	Michael Jackson 37
7	Elton John† 34
8	Madonna 32
9	Whitney Houston 31
10	Paul McCartney/Wings 30

* Mariah Carey and Boyz II Men share a 16-week run with a duet; Carey has also had No.1s with Jay-Z and Joe & 98 Degrees
# Includes six weeks with Alicia Keys and 12 weeks with Ludacris and Lil Jon
† Includes four weeks with Kiki Dee

Source: Music Information Database

top10 ARTISTS WITH THE MOST US **NO. 1 SINGLES**

	ARTIST/GROUP / NO. 1 SINGLES
1	The Beatles 20
2	Elvis Presley 18
3	Mariah Carey 16*
4	Michael Jackson 13
5 =	Madonna 12
=	The Supremes 12
7	Whitney Houston 11
8 =	Janet Jackson 10
=	Stevie Wonder 10
10 =	The Bee Gees 9
=	Elton John 9
=	Paul McCartney/Wings 9

* Including duets with Boyz II Men, Joe & 98 Degrees, and Jay-Z

Source: Music Information Database

Albums

top10 ALBUMS WITH THE SLOWEST RISE TO NO.1

	ARTIST/GROUP / TITLE	WEEKS
1	Roberta Flack, First Take	118
2	Jim Croce, You Don't Mess Around With Jim	81
3	Paula Abdul, Forever Your Girl	64
4	Various Artists, O Brother, Where Art Thou?	63
5	Mantovani & His Orchestra, Film Encores	59
6	Fleetwood Mac, Fleetwood Mac	58
7	New Kids On The Block, Hangin' Tough	55
8 =	Bonnie Raitt, Nick of Time	52
=	Live, Throwing Copper	52
10 =	Guns 'N Roses, Appetite for Destruction	50
=	Whitney Houston, Whitney Houston	50

Source: Music Information Database

Roberta Flack's first album release, *First Take*, contained the track *The First Time Ever I Saw Your Face*, which was also released as a single. After being included in the soundtrack of the Clint Eastwood movie *Play Misty For Me*, released at the end of 1971, it went to US No.1 for six weeks and sold two million copies, projecting the *First Take* into the same position in the album chart, where it remained for five weeks.

top10 ALBUMS OF ALL TIME IN THE US

	TITLE /ARTIST/GROUP / YEAR OF ENTRY	EST. SALES
1	Their Greatest Hits, 1971–1975, The Eagles, 1976	28,000,000
2	Thriller, Michael Jackson, 1982	27,000,000
3	Led Zeppelin IV, Led Zeppelin, 1971	22,000,000
4	Back In Black, AC/DC, 1980	21,000,000
5	Come On Over, Shania Twain, 1997	20,000,000
6	Rumours, Fleetwood Mac, 1977	19,000,000
7 =	Boston, Boston, 1976	17,000,000
=	The Bodyguard, Soundtrack, 1992	17,000,000
9 =	Greatest Hits, Elton John, 1974	16,000,000
=	Hotel California, The Eagles, 1976	16,000,000
=	No Fences, Garth Brooks, 1990	16,000,000
=	Cracked Rear View, Hootie & the Blowfish, 1994	16,000,000
=	Jagged Little Pill, Alanis Morissette, 1995	16,000,000

Source: RIAA

The Eagles' *Their Greatest Hits, 1971–1975* was the first album ever to be certified platinum (for sales of over one million copies) and long vied with Jackson's *Thriller* as the US's all-time No.1.

top10 ALBUMS THAT STAYED LONGEST AT NO.1 IN THE US CHARTS

	TITLE / ARTIST/GROUP / YEAR	WEEKS AT NO.1
1	Thriller, Michael Jackson, 1982	37
2 =	Calypso, Harry Belafonte, 1956	31
=	Rumours, Fleetwood Mac, 1977	31
4 =	Saturday Night Fever, Soundtrack, 1978	24*
=	Purple Rain (Soundtrack), Prince, 1984	24*
6	Please Hammer Don't Hurt 'Em, MC Hammer, 1990	21
7 =	Blue Hawaii (Soundtrack), Elvis Presley, 1962	20*
=	The Bodyguard (Soundtrack), Whitney Houston, 1992	20
9 =	More of the Monkees, The Monkees, 1967	18*
=	Dirty Dancing, Soundtrack, 1988	18
=	Ropin' The Wind, Garth Brooks, 1991	18

* Continuous runs

Source: Music Information Database

Some sources identify the soundtrack album of *West Side Story* (1962) as the longest No.1 resident of the *Billboard* chart, but its 57-week stay was in a chart exclusively for stereo albums – then a relatively new phenomenon; the *South Pacific* soundtrack album (1958) similarly enjoyed 31 weeks in this specialist chart.

top10 ALBUMS THAT STAYED THE LONGEST ON THE US ALBUMS CHART

	TITLE	ARTIST	WEEKS
1	The Dark Side of The Moon	Pink Floyd	741
2	Johnny's Greatest Hits	Johnny Mathis	490
3	My Fair Lady	Original Cast	480
4	Highlights from The Phantom of the Opera	Original Cast	331
5	Oklahoma!	Soundtrack	305
6	Tapestry	Carole King	302
7	Heavenly	Johnny Mathis	295
8	MCMXC AD	Enigma	282
9	Metallica	Metallica	281
10 =	The King and I	Soundtrack	277
=	Hymns	Tennessee Ernie Ford	277

Source: Music Information Database

⬆ *Twain makes her mark*
Canadian singer Shania Twain's Come On Over *album has sold over 39 million copies worldwide,*
making it the bestselling of all time by a solo female artist.

top10 ALBUMS WITH MOST **CONSECUTIVE** WEEKS AT NO.1 IN THE US CHARTS

	ALBUM / ARTIST/GROUP / YEAR OF ENTRY	WEEKS AT NO.1
1	Love Me or Leave Me (Soundtrack), Doris Day, 1955	25
2	=Calypso, Harry Belafonte, 1957	24
	=Saturday Night Fever, Soundtrack, 1978	24
	=Purple Rain (Soundtrack), Prince, 1984	24
5	Blue Hawaii (Soundtrack), Elvis Presley, 1961	20
6	Rumours, Fleetwood Mac, 1977	19
7	=More of the Monkees, The Monkees, 1967	18
	=Please Hammer Don't Hurt 'Em, MC Hammer, 1990	18
9	=Thriller, Michael Jackson, 1983	17
	=Some Gave All, Billy Ray Cyrus, 1992	17

Source: Music Information Database

top10 ARTISTS WITH THE MOST **CONSECUTIVE US TOP 10 ALBUMS**

	ARTIST/GROUP	PERIOD	ALBUMS
1	The Rolling Stones	Nov 1964–Jul 1980	26
2	Johnny Mathis	Sep 1957–Dec 1960	14
3	=Frank Sinatra	Feb 1958–Mar 1962	12
	=Madonna	Apr 22, 1989–Dec 3, 2005	12
	=Garth Brooks	Mar 1991–Dec 1999	12
6	=The Beatles	June 1965–Mar 1970	11
	=Elton John	Nov 1971–Nov 1976	11
	=Van Halen	Apr 1979–Nov 1996	11
9	=Led Zeppelin	Feb 1969–Dec 1982	10
	=Chicago	Feb 1970–Oct 1977	10
	=Bruce Springsteen	Sep 1975–Mar 1995	10

Source: Music Information Database

Male Solo Artists

top10 MALE SOLO ALBUMS IN THE US, 2005

	TITLE	ARTIST/GROUP
1	The Massacre	50 Cent
2	Late Registration	Kanye West
3	The Road and The Radio	Kenny Chesney
4	In Between Dreams	Jack Johnson
5	Be Here	Keith Urban
6	Honkytonk University	Toby Keith
7	Encore	Eminem
8	Curtain Call – The Hits	Eminem
9	Get Lifted	John Legend
10	Let's Get It: Thug Motivation 101	Young Jeezy

Source: Nielsen Soundscan

➡ Curtain call?
Eminem's "greatest hits" compilation album Curtain Call *was his fourth consecutive US No.1. Its title prompted speculation that it may be his last.*

top10 MALE SOLO SINGERS WITH THE **MOST US NO.1 SINGLES**

	ARTIST	NO.1 SINGLES
1	Elvis Presley	20
2	Michael Jackson*	13
3	= George Michael#	8
	= Stevie Wonder†	8
5	= Elton John☆	7
	= Usher♦	7
7	Phil Collins◇	6
8	= Prince	5
	= Lionel Richie❋	5
10	Bobby Vinton	4

* Including two No.1s with Paul McCartney and Siedah Garrett
\# Including No.1s with Aretha Franklin, Elton John, and Wham! Featuring George Michael
† Including one No.1 with Paul McCartney
☆ Including one No. 1 with Kiki Dee and one with George Michael
♦ Including No.1s with Alicia Keys and Ludacris & Lil Jon
◇ Including one No.1 with Marilyn Martin
❋ Including one No.1 with Diana Ross

Source: Music Information Database

top10 **YOUNGEST MALE SOLO SINGERS** TO HAVE A NO. 1 SINGLE IN THE US

	ARTIST / TITLE	YEAR	YRS	AGE* MTHS	DAYS
1	Stevie Wonder, Fingertips	1963	13	2	28
2	Donny Osmond, Go Away Little Girl	1971	13	9	2
3	Michael Jackson, Ben	1972	14	1	15
4	Laurie London, He's Got the Whole World in His Hands	1958	14	3	0
5	Chris Brown, Run It!	2005	15	6	21
6	Paul Anka, Diana	1957	16	1	16
7	Brian Hyland, Itsy Bitsy Teenie Weenie Yellow Polkadot Bikini	1960	16	9	1
8	Mario, Let Me Love You	2005	17	4	7
9	Shaun Cassidy, Da Doo Ron Ron	1977	17	9	19
10	Paul Anka, Lonely Boy	1959	17	11	18

• During first week of debut No.1 US single

Source: Music Information Database

top10 ALBUMS BY MALE SOLO SINGERS IN THE US

	TITLE / ARTIST / YEAR	SALES
1	Thriller, Michael Jackson, 1982	26,000,000
2 =	Greatest Hits, Elton John, 1974	16,000,000
=	No Fences, Garth Brooks, 1990	16,000,000
4	Born in the USA, Bruce Springsteen, 1984	15,000,000
5 =	Bat Out of Hell, Meat Loaf, 1977	14,000,000
=	Ropin' the Wind, Garth Brooks, 1991	14,000,000
7 =	Greatest Hits, Kenny Rogers, 1980	12,000,000
=	No Jacket Required, Phil Collins, 1985	12,000,000
=	Breathless, Kenny G, 1992	12,000,000
10 =	Devil Without a Cause, Kid Rock, 1999	11,000,000
=	James Taylor's Greatest Hits, James Taylor, 1976	11,000,000

Source: RIAA

Within two years of its release, Michael Jackson's *Thriller* album had sold a record total of 20 million copies, but it continued to sell into its second and third decades, being certified for record sales of 26 million copies in 2000. To these US sales must be added those in other countries, bringing the world total to over 50 million.

top10 SINGLES BY MALE SOLO SINGERS IN THE US

TITLE / ARTIST(S) / YEAR

1 Candle in the Wind (1997)/Something About the Way You Look Tonight, Elton John, 1997
2 White Christmas, Bing Crosby, 1942
3 Hound Dog/Don't Be Cruel, Elvis Presley, 1956
4 Gangsta's Paradise, Coolio featuring L.V., 1995
5 (Everything I Do) I Do It For You, Bryan Adams, 1991
6 Love Me Tender/Any Way You Want Me, Elvis Presley, 1956
7 All Shook Up, Elvis Presley, 1957
8 Jailhouse Rock, Elvis Presley, 1957
9 Heartbreak Hotel/I Was the One, Elvis Presley, 1956
10 Baby Got Back, Sir Mix-A-Lot, 1992

Source: Music Information Database

As this list contains singles released before official sales figures were published, it includes those certified as having sold over two million, ranked by factoring in chart positions and longevity.

top10 TOURS IN THE US BY MALE SOLO ARTISTS, 2005*

ARTIST / TOTAL ($)

Neil Diamond
$71,339,710

Kenny Chesney
$63,029,422

Paul McCartney
$59,684,076

Rod Stewart
$48,943,773

Elton John
$45,524,280

Jimmy Buffett
$40,956,723

Toby Keith
$32,434,946

Bruce Springsteen
$31,752,514

Sting
$23,832,116

Eminem/50 Cent
$21,248,713

* November 17, 2004 to November 15, 2005

Source: "Billboard" magazine

Female Solo Artists

top10 YOUNGEST FEMALE SOLO SINGERS TO HAVE A NO. 1 SINGLE IN THE US

	SINGER / TITLE	YEAR	YRS	AGE MTHS	DAYS
1	Little Peggy March, I Will Follow Him	1963	15	1	20
2	Brenda Lee, I'm Sorry	1960	15	7	7
3	Brenda Lee, I Want to Be Wanted	1960	15	11	22
4	Tiffany, I Think We're Alone	1987	16	1	5
5	Tiffany, Could've Been	1988	16	4	4
6	Lesley Gore, It's My Party	1963	17	0	30
7	Little Eva, The Loco-Motion	1962	17	1	27
8	Britney Spears, ...Baby One More Time	1999	17	1	29
9	Monica, The First Night	1998	17	11	9
10	Shelley Fabares, Johnny Angel	1962	18	2	19

Source: Music Information Database

The ages shown are those of each artist on the publication date of the chart in which she achieved her first No.1 single. While Britney Spears and other teen singers have a place in this list, it is notable that over half the girls in the Top 10 scored their No.1 hits in the 1960s: Little Peggy March's *I Will Follow Him* was a translation of a French hit song, *Chariot*. March's real name was Margaret Annemarie Battivio, her stage name deriving from her diminutive height (4 ft 10 in) and birth month.

top10 OLDEST FEMALE SOLO SINGERS TO HAVE A NO. 1 SINGLE IN THE US

	SINGER / TITLE	YEAR	YRS	AGE MTHS	DAYS
1	Cher, Believe	1999	52	9	15
2	Tina Turner, What's Love Got to Do With It	1984	45	9	5
3	Aretha Franklin, I Knew You Were Waiting (For Me)	1987	45	0	24
4	Bette Midler, The Wind Beneath My Wings	1989	44	8	24
5	Madonna, Music	2000	42	1	0
6	Kim Carnes, Bette Davis Eyes	1981	35	9	26
7	Mariah Carey, Don't Forget About Us	2005	35	9	4
8	Gwen Stefani, Hollaback Girl	2005	35	7	4
9	Dolly Parton, 9 to 5	1981	35	1	2
10	Janet Jackson, All For You	2001	34	10	28

Source: Music Information Database

The ages shown are those of each artist on the publication date of the chart in which her last No.1 topped the Hot 100. In contrast with the male counterpart to this list, whose entries are 46 or older, it is telling that "old" here refers to veterans aged over 33.

top10 SINGLES BY FEMALE SOLO SINGERS IN THE US

	TITLE / SINGER	YEAR
1	I Will Always Love You, Whitney Houston	1992
2	How Do I Live, LeAnn Rimes	1997
3	Fantasy, Mariah Carey	1995
4	Vogue, Madonna	1990
5	Mr. Big Stuff, Jean Knight	1971
6	You were Meant for Me/ Foolish Games, Jewel	1996
7	You Light Up My Life, Debby Boone	1977
8	The Power of Love, Celine Dion	1993
9	Believe, Cher	1999
10	Physical, Olivia Newton-John	1981

Source: Music Information Database

Among these blockbusters, all of them platinum sellers, it is fitting that Whitney Houston's multiplatinum success from *The Bodyguard (Original Soundtrack)* was also written by a woman – Dolly Parton – whose original version of *I Will Always Love You* peaked in 1982 at a lowly No.53. Jean Knight's *Mr. Big Stuff*, an R&B No.1, took 25 years to reach certified sales of two million copies.

top10 ALBUMS BY FEMALE SOLO SINGERS IN THE US

	TITLE / SINGER	YEAR
1	Come On Over, Shania Twain	1997
2	The Bodyguard (Original Soundtrack), Whitney Houston	1992
3	Jagged Little Pill, Alanis Morissette	1995
4	...Baby One More Time, Britney Spears	1999
5	Whitney Houston, Whitney Houston	1985
6	The Woman in Me, Shania Twain	1995
7	Pieces of You, Jewel	1997
8	Falling Into You, Celine Dion	1996
9	Up!, Shania Twain	2003
10	Tapestry, Carole King	1971

Source: Music Information Database

top10 **FEMALE SINGERS** WITH THE MOST TOP 10 HITS IN THE US

	SINGER	TOP 10 HITS
1	Madonna	37
2	Janet Jackson (including one duet with Michael Jackson and one with Busta Rhymes)	28
3	Mariah Carey (including one duet with Boyz II Men, one with Luther Vandross, and one with Jay-Z)	25
4	Whitney Houston (including one duet with CeCe Winans and one with Faith Evans)	23
5	Aretha Franklin (including one duet with George Michael)	18
6	Connie Francis	15
7	= Olivia Newton-John (including two duets with John Travolta and one with Electric Light Orchestra)	14
	= Donna Summer	14
9	Diana Ross (including one duet with Marvin Gaye and one with Lionel Richie)	13
10	= Brenda Lee	12
	= Dionne Warwick (including one duet with the Detroit Spinners and one with "Friends" Stevie Wonder, Gladys Knight, and Elton John)	12

Source: Music Information Database

↑ Red hot
Mariah Carey's 14th album The Emancipation of Mimi *debuted at US No.1, was certified six times platinum, and won the Grammy award for "Best Contemporary R&B Album."*

top10 **FEMALE SOLO ALBUMS** IN THE US, 2005

	TITLE / ARTIST	TOTAL
1	The Emancipation Of Mimi, Mariah Carey	4,969,000
2	Breakaway, Kelly Clarkson	3,496,000
3	Love. Angel. Music. Baby., Gwen Stefani	2,505,000
4	Some Hearts, Carrie Underwood	1,637,000
5	Fireflies, Faith Hill	1,532,000
6	Goodies, Ciara	1,530,000
7	Here For The Party, Gretchen Wilson	1,215,000
8	Most Wanted, Hilary Duff	1,125,000
9	Confessions On A Dance Floor, Madonna	1,103,000
10	Greatest Hits, Shania Twain	1,019,000

Source: Nielsen Soundscan

Groups & Duos

top10 ALBUMS BY DUOS OR GROUPS IN THE US, 2005

	TITLE	ARTIST/GROUP
1	American Idiot	Green Day
2	Monkey Business	Black Eyed Peas
3	X&Y	Coldplay
4	Feels Like Today	Rascal Flatts
5	The Documentary	The Game
6	Hot Fuss	Killers
7	All The Right Reasons	Nickelback
8	From Under The Cork Tree	Fall Out Boy
9	Mesmerize	System of a Down
10	Demon Days	Gorillaz

Source: Nielsen Soundscan

Green Day's seventh studio album *American Idiot* was their first to have both US and UK No.1s. It went on to win the "Best Rock Album" Grammy. By 2006, it has sold over five million units in the US.

top10 DUOS IN THE US

	DUO	TOTAL CHART HITS
1	The Everly Brothers	38
2	Daryl Hall & John Oates	34
3	Carpenters	28
4	Jan & Dean	24
5	Righteous Brothers	23
6	Ike & Tina Turner	20
7	Sonny & Cher	18
8	Simon & Garfunkel	17
9	Peaches & Herb	16
10	Eurythmics*	15

* Including one with Aretha Franklin

Source: Music Information Database

The Everly Brothers – Don (b.1937) and Phil (b.1939) – had their first US chart hit *Bye Bye Love* in 1957, when it reached No.2, and their first No.1 the same year with *Wake Up Little Susie*.

top10 GROUPS AND DUOS WITH THE MOST US NO. 1 SINGLES

	GROUP/DUO	NO.1 SINGLES
1	The Beatles	20
2	The Supremes	12
3	The Bee Gees	9
4	The Rolling Stones	8
5	Daryl Hall & John Oates	6
6	= Boyz II Men*	5
	= The Eagles	5
	= The Four Seasons	5
	= KC & the Sunshine Band	5
10	= The Beach Boys	4
	= Blondie	4
	= Bon Jovi	4
	= Destiny's Child	4
	= The Everly Brothers	4
	= Roxette	4
	= The Temptations	4
	= TLC	4

* Including one with Mariah Carey

Source: Music Information Database

top10 SINGLES BY GROUPS IN THE US

	TITLE / GROUP	YEAR
1	Hey Jude, The Beatles	1968
2	Eye of the Tiger, Survivor	1982
3	I Wanna Sex You Up, Color Me Badd	1991
4	O.P.P., Naughty By Nature	1991
6	Let It Be, The Beatles	1970
7	Get Back, The Beatles with Billy Preston	1969
8	Come Together/Something, The Beatles	1969
9	Too Close, Next	1999
10	Wannabe, The Spice Girls	1997

Source: Music Information Database

The appearance of *Hey Jude* at the head of this list is perhaps surprising. An unusually long track (7 mins 12 secs) that disqualified it from airplay on some radio stations, it does not even figure among the Top 100 of all time in The Beatles' home country (although it did reach No.1 in both the UK and US). It nonetheless sold over 4 million copies in the US.

top10 SINGLES BY DUOS IN THE US

	TITLE / DUO	YEAR
1	Whoomp! (There It Is), Tag Team	1993
2	Macarena, Los Del Rio	1996
3	Jump, Kris Kross	1992
4	Unchained Melody, Righteous Brothers	1965/1990
5	Dazzey Duks, Duice	1993
6	Rump Shaker, Wreckx-N-Effect	1992
7	Déjà Vu (Uptown Baby), Lord Tariq & Peter Gunz	1997
8	Wake Me Up Before You Go Go, Wham!	1984
9	Reunited, Peaches & Herb	1979
10	Hey Ya!, Outkast	2003

Source: Music Information Database

Less than a year after its release, Tag Team's *Whoomp! (There It Is)* was certified with sales of 4 million copies. *Unchained Melody* by the Righteous Brothers (Bill Medley and Bobby Hatfield) made a surprise return to the charts after featuring in the soundtrack of the 1990 film *Ghost*, providing it with the Platinum status that did not even exist when it was first released.

top10 ALBUMS BY GROUPS IN THE US

TITLE / GROUP	YEAR
1 Their Greatest Hits, 1971–1975, The Eagles	1976
2 Led Zeppelin IV (untitled), Led Zeppelin	1971
3 Back in Black, AC/DC	1980
4 Rumours, Fleetwood Mac	1977
5 Boston, Boston	1976
6 Hotel California, The Eagles	1977
7 Cracked Rear View, Hootie and the Blowfish	1995
8 Dark Side of the Moon, Pink Floyd	1973
9 Appetite For Destruction, Guns 'N Roses	1987
10 Supernatural, Santana	1999

Source: Music Information Database

This list has changed considerably in recent times, with official sales figures being updated in the US on several perennially big-selling albums – most notably those by the recently resurrected Eagles, whose *Greatest Hits* and *Hotel California* albums are now certified as having sold in excess of 28 million and 16 million copies, respectively.

↑ Tour de force
Bono of U2, whose Vertigo tour topped $260 million in 2005.

top10 TOURS IN THE US, 2005*

ARTIST/GROUP	TOTAL ($)
1 U2	260,119,588
2 The Rolling Stones	140,845,375
3 The Eagles	116,907,647
4 Dave Matthews Band	45,015,384
5 Green Day	36,537,583
6 Motley Crue	33,785,715
7 Rascal Flatts	26,349,676
8 Coldplay	23,573,443
9 Trans-Siberian Orchestra	22,559,636
10 Tom Petty and the Heartbreakers	22,085,839

* November 17, 2004 to November 15, 2005

Source: "Billboard" magazine

Gold & Platinum Discs

⬆ Golden boys
The Rolling Stones, still touring after 44 years, have earned 21 gold albums.

the 10 first GOLD ALBUMS IN THE US

	ALBUM / ARTIST	CERTIFICATION DATE
1	Oklahoma!, Soundtrack	Jul 8, 1958
2	Hymns, Tennessee Ernie Ford	Feb 20, 1959
3	Johnny's Greatest Hits, Johnny Mathis	Jun 1, 1959
4 =	Sing Along with Mitch, Mitch Miller	Nov 16, 1959
=	The Music Man, Original Cast	Nov 16, 1959
6	South Pacific, Soundtrack	Dec 18, 1959
7	Peter Gunn, Henry Mancini	Dec 31, 1959
8	The Student Prince, Mario Lanza	Jan 19, 1960
9	Pat's Great Hits, Pat Boone	Feb 12, 1960
10 =	Elvis, Elvis Presley	Feb 17, 1960
=	60 Years of Music, Various Artists	Feb 17, 1960

Source: RIAA

Following the success of the 1943 original stage cast album, released as a set of 78-rpm discs, the soundtrack of the 1955 film musical *Oklahoma!* was still selling steadily when gold albums were launched three years later, staying in the US charts for an unprecedented five years.

top 10 GROUPS WITH THE MOST GOLD ALBUMS IN THE US

	GROUP	GOLD ALBUM AWARDS
1	The Beatles	42
2	The Rolling Stones	41
3	Aerosmith	25
4 =	Kiss	23
=	Rush	23
6 =	Alabama	22
=	Chicago	22
8	The Beach Boys	21
9	Jefferson Airplane/Starship	20
10 =	AC/DC	19
=	Queen	19

Source: RIAA

The RIAA's Gold Awards have been presented since 1958 to artists who have sold 500,000 units of a single, album, or multidisc set. The first single to be so honored was Perry Como's *Catch a Falling Star*, and the first album the soundtrack to *Oklahoma!*.

top 10 MALE ARTISTS WITH THE MOST PLATINUM ALBUM AWARDS IN THE US

	ARTIST	PLATINUM ALBUM AWARDS*
1	Garth Brooks	105
2	Elvis Presley	87
3	Billy Joel	75
4	Elton John	63
5 =	Michael Jackson	60
=	George Strait	60
7	Bruce Springsteen	50
8	Kenny G	46
9	Kenny Rogers	41#
10	Neil Diamond	40

* By number of album awards, rather than number of albums qualifying for awards
# Excluding one platinum album with Dottie West; one with Kim Carnes, Dottie West, and Sheena Easton; and a double platinum album with Dolly Parton

Source: RIAA

Platinum singles and albums are those that have sold over one million units. Since 1976, they have been awarded by the Recording Industry Association of America (RIAA), for escalating music sales. In 1984, Multiplatinum Awards were introduced for sales of 2 million or more units.

top 10 MALE SOLO ARTISTS WITH THE MOST GOLD ALBUM AWARDS IN THE US

	ARTIST	GOLD ALBUM AWARDS
1	Elvis Presley	79
2	Neil Diamond	38
3	Elton John	35
4	Bob Dylan	34*
5	Frank Sinatra	33
6	George Strait	32
7	Rod Stewart	24
8	Kenny Rogers	23#
9	Hank Williams Jr.	22
10	Eric Clapton	20†

* Excluding one gold album with Grateful Dead
# Excluding one gold album with Dolly Parton; two with Dottie West; and one with Kim Carnes, Dottie West, and Sheena Easton
† Excluding one gold album with B.B. King

Source: RIAA

top10 FEMALE SOLO ARTISTS WITH THE MOST GOLD ALBUMS IN THE US

	ARTIST	GOLD ALBUM AWARDS
1	Barbra Streisand	43*
2	Reba McEntire	23
3	Linda Ronstadt	17#
4	Madonna	15
5	= Aretha Franklin	14
	= Anne Murray	14
7	= Mariah Carey	12
	= Amy Grant	12
	= Olivia Newton-John	12†
	= Tanya Tucker	12

* Excluding one with Kris Kristofferson and Original Cast/Soundtrack recordings of "Funny Girl," "Funny Lady," and "The Mirror Has Two Faces"
# Excluding two with Dolly Parton and Emmylou Harris
† Excluding one with John Travolta and one with Electric Light Orchestra

Source: RIAA

top10 FEMALE ARTISTS WITH THE MOST PLATINUM ALBUMS IN THE US

	ARTIST	PLATINUM ALBUM AWARDS*
1	Madonna	60
2	Barbra Streisand	59#
3	= Mariah Carey	58
	= Whitney Houston	54
5	Celine Dion	46
6	Shania Twain	43
7	Reba McEntire	35
8	Britney Spears	30
9	Linda Ronstadt	28†
10	Janet Jackson	25

* By number of album awards, rather than number of albums qualifying for awards
# Excluding four with Kris Kristofferson and Original Cast/Soundtrack recordings of "Funny Girl" and "The Mirror Has Two Faces"
† Excluding one with Dolly Parton and Emmylou Harris

Source: RIAA

🔽 Platinum blonde
Madonna's 22-year US album career has seen her with 16 albums entering the Top 10, six of them reaching No.1. Her total album sales are almost 70 million in the US and 200 million worldwide.

top10 GROUPS WITH THE MOST PLATINUM ALBUMS IN THE US

	GROUP	PLATINUM ALBUM AWARDS*
1	The Beatles	164
2	Led Zeppelin	106
3	Eagles	89
4	Pink Floyd	70
5	AC/DC	64
6	Aerosmith	62
7	The Rolling Stones	58
8	Metallica	57
9	Van Halen	56
10	U2	50

* By number of album awards, rather than number of albums qualifying for awards; double/triple albums counted once

Source: RIAA

Music Awards

the10 LATEST GRAMMY
BEST ROCK PERFORMANCE*

YEAR	DUO/GROUP / SONG
2006	U2, Sometimes You Can't Make It on Your Own
2005	U2, Vertigo
2004	Bruce Springsteen & Warren Zevron, Disorder in the House
2003	Coldplay, In My Place
2002	U2, Elevation
2001	U2, Beautiful Day
2000	Everlast and Santana, Put Your Lights On
1999	Aerosmith, Pink
1998	The Wallflowers, One Headlight
1997	Dave Matthews Band, So Much to Say

* By a duo or group with vocal

the10 LATEST GRAMMY
POP VOCALISTS OF THE YEAR (MALE)

YEAR*	VOCALIST / SONG
2006	Stevie Wonder, From the Bottom of My Heart
2005	John Mayer, Daughters
2004	Justin Timberlake, Cry Me a River
2003	John Mayer, Your Body is a Wonderland
2002	James Taylor, Don't Let Me Be Lonely Tonight
2001	Sting, She Walks this Earth (Soberana Rosa)
2000	Sting, Brand New Day
1999	Eric Clapton, My Father's Eyes
1998	Elton John, Candle in the Wind (1997)
1997	Eric Clapton, Change the World

* Awards are for singles released during the previous year

the10 LATEST GRAMMY
POP VOCALISTS OF THE YEAR (FEMALE)

YEAR*	VOCALIST / SONG
2006	Kelly Clarkson, Since U Been Gone
2005	Norah Jones, Sunrise
2004	Christina Aguilera, Beautiful
2003	Norah Jones, Don't Know Why
2002	Nelly Furtado, I'm Like a Bird
2001	Macy Gray, I Try
2000	Sarah McLachlan, I Will Remember You
1999	Celine Dion, My Heart Will Go On
1998	Sarah McLachlan, Building a Mystery
1997	Toni Braxon, Un-Break My Heart

* Awards are for singles released during the previous year

the10 LATEST GRAMMY
RECORDS OF THE YEAR

YEAR*	ALBUM	PERFORMING ARTIST(S)
2006	Boulevard of Broken Dreams	Green Day
2005	Here We Go Again	Ray Charles & Norah Jones
2004	Clocks	Coldplay
2003	Don't Know Why	Norah Jones
2002	Walk On	U2
2001	Beautiful Day	U2
2000	Smooth	Rob Thomas & Santana
1999	My Heart Will Go On	Celine Dion
1998	Sunny Came Home	Shawn Colvin
1997	Change the World	Eric Clapton & Babyface/Wynonna

* Awards are for singles released during the previous year

the10 LATEST GRAMMY
BEST RAP PERFORMANCE*

YEAR	DUO/GROUP / SONG
2006	Black Eyed Peas, Don't Phunk With My Heart
2005	Black Eyed Peas, Let's Get It Started
2004	P. Diddy, Murphy Lee, and Nelly, Shake Ya Tailfeather
2003	OutKast and Killer Mike, The Whole World
2002	OutKast, Ms. Jackson
2001	Dr. Dre and Eminem, Forget About Dre
2000	The Roots and Erykah Badu, You Got Me
1999	Beastie Boys, Intergalactic
1998	Puff Daddy, Faith Evans and, and 112, I"ll Be Missing You
1997	Bone Thugs-N-Harmony, The Crossroads

* By a duo or group

the10 LATEST GRAMMY
NEW ARTISTS OF THE YEAR

YEAR*	ARTIST(S)
2006	John Legend
2005	Maroon 5
2004	Evanescence
2003	Norah Jones
2002	Alicia Keys
2001	Shelby Lynne
2000	Christina Aguilera
1999	Lauryn Hill
1998	Paula Cole
1997	LeeAnn Rimes

* Awards are for achievements during the previous year

The Best New Artist Grammy was first awarded at the second event in 1960 to Bobby Darin. Subsequent winners represent a catalog both of stars who went on to achieve greatness, such as The Beatles, and those who sank into obscurity (including Milli Vanilli, whose 1990 award was revoked when it was revealed that they had not actually sung on their records).

the10 LATEST GRAMMY **ALBUMS OF THE YEAR**

YEAR*	ALBUM	PERFORMING ARTIST(S)
2006	How to Dismantle an Atomic Bomb	U2
2005	Genius Loves Company	Ray Charles and various artists
2004	Speakerboxxx/The Love Below	OutKast
2003	Come Away with Me	Norah Jones
2002	O Brother, Where Art Thou? (Soundtrack)	Various artists
2001	Two Against Nature	Steely Dan
2000	Supernatural	Santana
1999	The Miseducation of Lauryn Hill	Lauryn Hill
1998	Time Out of Mind	Bob Dylan
1997	Falling into You	Celine Dion

* Awards are for albums released during the previous year

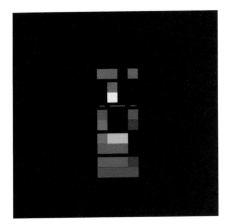

➲ Coldplay's code play
2004 Grammy-Award winners Coldplay and singer Chris Martin released their third album in 2006. Its cover depicts the title – X&Y – converted into an alphanumeric coding.

Classical Music

top10 CLASSICAL WORKS*

COMPOSER / TITLE

1 **Sergei Rachmaninov**, Piano Concerto No.2 in C minor
2 **Ralph Vaughan Williams**, The Lark Ascending
3 **Wolfgang Amadeus Mozart**, Clarinet Concerto in A
4 **Ludwig van Beethoven**, Piano Concerto No.5 in E flat major (The Emperor)
5 **Max Bruch**, Violin Concerto No.1 in G minor
6 **Ludwig van Beethoven**, Symphony No.6 Pastoral
7 **Edward Elgar**, Cello Concerto in E minor
8 **Edward Elgar**, Enigma Variations
9 **Karl Jenkins**, The Armed Man (A Mass for Peace)
10 **Edvard Grieg**, Piano Concerto in A minor

* Based on Classic FM Hall of Fame 2005

🔾 *Grand opera*
The restored Roman amphitheater of Verona, Italy, is the world's largest venue that regularly stages opera, especially during the city's annual festival.

top10 LATEST GRAMMY BEST CLASSICAL CONTEMPORARY COMPOSITION

YEAR   COMPOSER / WORK

2006 **William Bolcolm**, Songs of Innocence and of Experience
2005 **John Adams**, On the Transmigration of Souls
2004 **Dominick Argento**, Casa Guidi
2003 **John Tavener**, Lamentations and Praises
2002 **Christopher Rouse**, Concert de Gaudí for Guitar and Orchestra
2001 **George Crumb**, Star Child
2000 **Pierre Boulez**, Répons
1999 **Krzysztof Penderecki**, Violin Concerto No.2: Metamorphosen
1998 **John Adams**, El Dorado
1997 **John Corigliano**, String Quartet

top 10 LARGEST **OPERA THEATRES**

	THEATRE	LOCATION	CAPACITY*
1	Arena di Verona'	Verona, Italy	15,000
2	Metropolitan Opera House	New York, NY	3,800
3	NHK Hall	Tokyo, Japan	3,677
4	Civic Opera House	Chicago, IL	3,563
5	Music Hall	Cincinnati, OH	3,516
6	Music Hall	Dallas, TX	3,420
7	War Memorial Opera House	San Francisco, CA	3,176
8	The Hummingbird Centre	Toronto, Canada	3,167
9	Dorothy Chandler Pavilion	Los Angeles, CA	3,098
10	Civic Theatre	San Diego, CA	2,992

* Seating capacity only, excluding standing
' Open-air venue

Although there are many more venues in the world where opera is also performed, such as the 13,000-seat Municipal Opera Theater ("Muny") open-air auditorium, St. Louis, Missouri, this list is limited to those where the principal performances are opera.

top 10 MOST PROLIFIC **CLASSICAL COMPOSERS**

	COMPOSER / NATIONALITY / DATES	HOURS OF MUSIC
1	Joseph Haydn (Austrian; 1732–1809)	340
2	George Handel (German-English; 1685–1759)	303
3	Wolfgang Amadeus Mozart (Austrian; 1756–91)	202
4	Johann Sebastian Bach (German; 1685–1750)	175
5	Franz Schubert (German; 1797–1828)	134
6	Ludwig van Beethoven (German; 1770–1827)	120
7	Henry Purcell (English; 1659–95)	116
8	Giuseppe Verdi (Italian; 1813–1901)	87
9	Anton Dvorák (Czech; 1841–1904)	79
10 =	Franz Liszt (Hungarian; 1811–86)	76
=	Peter Tchaikovsky (Russian; 1840–93)	76

This list is based on a survey conducted by *Classical Music* magazine, which ranked classical composers by the total number of hours of music each composed. If the length of the composer's working life is brought into the calculation, Schubert wins: his 134 hours were composed in a career of 18 years, giving an average of 7 hours 27 minutes per annum. The same method would place Tchaikovsky ahead of Liszt: although both composed 76 hours of music, Tchaikovsky worked for 30 years and Liszt for 51, giving them annual averages of 2 hours 32 minutes and 1 hour 29 minutes, respectively.

top 10 **CLASSICAL ALBUMS** IN THE US

	TITLE	PERFORMER / ORCHESTRA	YEAR
1	The Three Tenors In Concert	José Carreras, Placido Domingo, Luciano Pavarotti	1990
2	Romanza	Andrea Bocelli	1997
3	Sogno	Andrea Bocelli	1999
4	Voice of an Angel	Charlotte Church	1999
5	Chant	Benedictine Monks of Santo Domingo De Silos	1994
6	The Three Tenors – In Concert 1994	José Carreras, Placido Domingo, Luciano Pavarotti	1994
7	Sacred Arias	Andrea Bocelli	1999
8	Tchaikovsky: Piano Concerto No.1	Van Cliburn	1958
9	Fantasia (50th Anniversary Edition)	Soundtrack (Philadelphia Orchestra)	1990
10	Perhaps Love	Placido Domingo	1981

Source: Music Information Database

top 10 OPERAS **MOST FREQUENTLY PERFORMED** AT THE METROPOLITAN OPERA HOUSE, NEW YORK, 1883–2006

	OPERA	COMPOSER	FIRST PERFORMANCE	TOTAL*
1	La Bohème	Giacomo Puccini	Dec 26, 1900	1,178
2	Aïda	Giuseppi Verdi	Nov 12, 1886	1,091
3	Carmen	Georges Bizet	Jan 9, 1884	936
4	La Traviata	Giuseppi Verdi	Nov 5, 1883	905
5	Tosca	Giacomo Puccini	Feb 4, 1901	873
6	Madama Butterfly	Giacomo Puccini	Feb 11, 1907	799
7	Rigoletto	Giuseppi Verdi	Nov 16, 1883	797
8	Faust	Charles Gounod	Oct 22, 1883	722
9	Pagliacci	Ruggero Leoncavallo	Dec 11, 1893	695
10	Cavalleria Rusticana	Pietro Mascagni	Dec 30, 1891	655

* As at Feb 9, 2006, including performances by company at other venues
Source: Metropolitan Opera

The most popular operas at the Met closely mirror those of the Royal Opera House, London, where *La Bohème*, *Aïda*, and *Carmen* similarly occupy the top three places. The only notable difference is the presence of Vincenzo Bellini's *Norma* in 10th position in London, in place of the Met's *Cavalleria Rusticana*.

Musicals

top10 MUSICAL **FILMS OF THE 1960s**

FILM	YEAR
1 The Sound of Music	1965
2 Mary Poppins	1964
3 My Fair Lady	1964
4 Funny Girl	1968
5 Let's Make Love	1960
6 West Side Story	1961
7 Oliver!	1968
8 Thoroughly Modern Millie	1967
9 Hello Dolly!	1969
10 Paint Your Wagon	1969

Improvements in color and sound technology prompted a wave of popular musicals in the 1960s. With the exception of *Mary Poppins*, the entire Top 10 were successful stage productions.

top10 ANDREW LLOYD WEBBER **MUSICALS ON BROADWAY**

SHOW / RUN	PERFORMANCES
1 The Phantom of the Opera (1988–)	7,517*
2 Cats (1982–2000)	7,485
3 Evita (1979–83)	1,567
4 Sunset Boulevard (1994–97)	977
5 Starlight Express (1987–89)	761
6 Joseph and the Amazing Technicolor Dreamcoat (1982–83)	747#
7 Jesus Christ Superstar (1971–73)	711†
8 Song and Dance (1985–86)	474
9 Aspects of Love (1990–91)	377
10 The Woman in White (2005–)	93*

* Still running, total as at February 5, 2006
# Plus 1993–94 revival (231 performances)
† Plus 1977–78 (96) and 2000 revivals (161)

top10 **MUSICAL** FILMS

FILM	YEAR
1 Grease	1978
2 Chicago	2002
3 Saturday Night Fever	1977
4 8 Mile	2002
5 Moulin Rouge!	2001
6 The Sound of Music	1965
7 The Phantom of the Opera	2004
8 Evita	1996
9 The Rocky Horror Picture Show	1975
10 Staying Alive	1983

Traditional musicals (films in which the cast actually sing) and films in which a musical soundtrack is a major component of the film are included here. With a few notable exceptions, in recent years animated films with an important musical content appear to have taken over from these, with *Beauty and the Beast, Aladdin, The Lion King*...

top10 LONGEST-RUNNING MUSICALS ON BROADWAY

	SHOW	RUN	PERFORMANCES
1	The Phantom of the Opera	Jan 26, 1988–	7,579*
2	Cats	Sep 23, 1982–Sep 10, 2000	7,485
3	Les Misérables	Mar 12, 1987–May 18, 2003	6,680
4	A Chorus Line	Jul 25, 1975–Apr 28, 1990	6,137
5	Beauty and the Beast	Mar 9, 1994–	4,909*
6	Miss Saigon	Apr 11, 1991–Jan 28, 2001	4,092
7	Rent	Apr 29, 1996–	4,141*
8	Chicago	Nov 14, 1996–	3,894*
9	The Lion King	Nov 13, 1997–	3,526*
10	42nd Street	Aug 18, 1980–Jan 8, 1989	3,486*

* Still running; total as at March 31, 2006

All the longest-running musicals date from the past 40 years. Prior to these record-breakers, the longest runner of the 1940s was *Oklahoma!*, which debuted in 1943 and ran for 2,212 performances up to 1948, and from the 1950s *My Fair Lady*, which opened in 1956 and closed in 1962 after 2,717 performances. With 3,388 performances, *Grease* – which opened in 1972 and closed in 1980 – just fails to enter the Top 10.

top10 LONGEST-RUNNING RODGERS & HAMMERSTEIN PRODUCTIONS ON BROADWAY

	SHOW / RUN	PERFORMANCES*
1	Oklahoma! (1943–1948)	2,212
2	South Pacific (1949–1954)	1,925
3	The Sound of Music (1959–1963)	1,443
4	The King and I (1951–1954)	1,246
5	Carousel (1945–1947)	890
6	The King and I (1996–1998)	780
7	The King and I (1977–1978)	695
8	The Flower Drum Song (1958–1960)	600
9	The Sound of Music (1998–1999)	533
10	Oklahoma! (2002–2003)	388

* Excluding previews

Oklahoma! was the first musical by the composer-lyricist partnership of Richard Rodgers and Oscar Hammerstein II. Its Broadway run was followed in 1955 by an Oscar-winning film version.

the10 LATEST TONY AWARDS FOR A MUSICAL

YEAR	MUSICAL
2005	Monty Python's Spamalot
2004	Avenue Q
2003	Hairspray
2002	Thoroughly Modern Millie
2001	The Producers
2000	Contact
1999	Fosse
1998	The Lion King
1997	Titanic
1996	Rent

Based on the 1975 film *Monty Python and the Holy Grail*, *Spamalot* by Python member Eric Idle received 14 Tony Award nominations, winning not only Best Musical but also in two other categories.

➲ Top Cats
Cats was the longest-running Broadway musical of all time – 7,485 performances over almost 18 years – until January 6, 2006, when it was finally overtaken by The Phantom of the Opera.

STAGE & SCREEN

Theater

Over half the longest-running nonmusical shows on Broadway began their runs before WWII; the others all date from the period up to the 1970s, before the long-running musical completely dominated the Broadway stage.

* Still running; total as at March 31, 2006

⊙ *Prince among actors*
American actor John Barrymore (1882–1942), the grandfather of film actress Drew Barrymore, was famed for his mastery of the demanding role of Hamlet, which he performed over 100 times in 1922–25.

top10 **LONGEST** SHAKESPEAREAN ROLES

	ROLE	PLAY	LINES
1	Hamlet	Hamlet	1,422
2	Falstaff	Henry IV, Parts I and II	1,178
3	Richard III	Richard III	1,124
4	Iago	Othello	1,097
5	Henry V	Henry V	1,025
6	Othello	Othello	860
7	Vincentio	Measure for Measure	820
8	Coriolanus	Coriolanus	809
9	Timon	Timon of Athens	795
10	Antony	Antony and Cleopatra	766

Hamlet's role comprises 11,610 words, but if multiple plays are considered, he is beaten by Falstaff who appears in *Henry IV*, Parts I and II, and in *The Merry Wives of Windsor*, his total of 1,614 lines making him the most talkative of all Shakespeare's characters. However, if more than one play (or parts of a play) are taken into account, others would increase their tallies, among them Richard III, who appears (as Richard, Duke of Gloucester) in *Henry VI*, Part III, and Henry V who appears (as Prince Hal) in *Henry IV*, where he speaks 117 lines, making his total 1,142. Rosalind's 668-line role in *As You Like It* is the longest female part in Shakespeare's works.

the10 LATEST **TONY AWARDS** FOR A PLAY

YEAR	PLAY	PLAYWRIGHT
2005	Doubt	John Patrick Shanley
2004	I Am My Own Wife	Doug Wright
2003	Take Me Out	Richard Greenberg
2002	The Goat or Who is Sylvia	Edward Albee
2001	Proof	David Auburn
2000	Copenhagen	Michael Frayn
1999	Side Man	Warren Leight
1998	Art	Yasmina Reza
1997	The Last Night of Ballyhoo	Alfred Uhry
1996	Master Class	Terrence McNally

The Tony Awards, established in 1947 by the American Theater Wing, honor outstanding Broadway plays and musicals, actors and actresses, music, costume, and other contributions. They are named for the actress and director Antoinette Perry (1888–1946), who headed the American Theater Wing during WWII.

the10 LATEST PULITZER **DRAMA AWARDS**

YEAR	PLAY / PLAYWRIGHT
2005	Doubt, John Patrick Shanley
2004	I Am My Own Wife, Doug Wright
2003	Anna in the Tropics, Nilo Cruz
2002	Topdog/Underdog, Suzan-Lori Parks
2001	Proof, David Auburn
2000	Dinner with Friends, Jhumpa Lahiri
1999	Wit, Margaret Edson
1998	How I Learned to Drive, Paula Vogel
1996	Rent, Jonathan Larson
1995	The Young Man from Atlanta, Horton Foote

The Pulitzer Drama Award is made for "An American play, preferably original and dealing with American life." It was first awarded in 1918. There were no awards in this category in both 1997 and 2006.

top10 **OLDEST** BROADWAY THEATERS

	THEATER	OPENING SHOW	OPENED
1	New Victory Theatre (originally Theatre Republic)	Sag Harbor	Sep 27, 1900
2 =	Lyceum Theatre	The Proud Prince	Nov 2, 1903
=	New Amsterdam Theatre	A Midsummer Night's Dream	Nov 2, 1903
4	Belasco Theatre (originally Stuyvesant)	A Grand Army Man	Oct 16, 1907
5	Lunt-Fontanne Theatre (originally Globe Theatre)	The Old Town	Jan 10, 1910
6	Winter Garden Theatre	La Belle Paree	Mar 20, 1911
7	Helen Hayes Theatre (originally Little Theatre)	The Pigeon	Mar 12, 1912
8	Cort Theatre	Peg o' My Heart	Dec 20, 1912
9	Palace Theatre	Vaudeville show	Mar 24, 1913
10	Longacre Theatre	Are You a Crook?	May 1, 1913

Unlike their London counterparts, several of which date back to the 17th century, no Broadway theater can claim an ancestry earlier than 1900. The oldest – the New Victory Theatre – was built by Oscar Hammerstein (1846–1919), the grandfather of the lyricist Oscar Hammerstein II, and underwent a radical makeover in 1995. Outside New York, the Walnut Street Theatre in Philadelphia, Pennsylvania, has operated continuously since it opened in 1809 and is claimed as America's oldest.

Movie Mosts

Except where otherwise stated, film lists are ranked on cumulative world box office income. In keeping with the industry standard, in order to compare on a like-for-like basis, these are gross totals and disregard production and marketing costs (which are unreliable and often either exaggerated or understated), earnings from subsequent DVD releases, and TV broadcasts. Inflation is also not taken into account. Unless they are meaningful (as with those comparing film opening weekends), the precise amounts are omitted.

top10 LONGEST FILMS EVER SCREENED

TITLE	DIRECTOR / COUNTRY / YEAR	DURATION HR	MIN
1 The Cure for Insomnia	John Henry Timmis IV, USA, 1987	87	0
2 The Longest and Most Meaningless Movie in the World	Vincent Patouillard, UK, 1970	48	0
3 The Burning of the Red Lotus Temple	Star Film Company, China, 1928–31	27	0
4 Die Zweite Heimat	Edgar Reitz, West Germany, 1992	25	32
5 **** (aka Four Stars)	Andy Warhol, USA, 1967	25	0
6 Heimat – Eine deutsche Chronik	Edgar Reitz, West Germany, 1984	15	40
7 Berlin Alexanderplatz	Rainer Werner Fassbinder, West Germany/Italy, 1980	15	21
8 Resan (The Journey)	Peter Watkins, Sweden, 1987	14	33
9 Comment Yukong déplaca les montagnes (How Yukong moved the mountains)	Joris Ivens and Marceline Lorigan, France, 1976	12	43
10 Out 1: Noli me Tangere	Jacques Rivette and Suzanne Schiffman, France, 1971	12	9

Although the list includes such "stunt" films as Andy Warhol's ****, all those listed have been screened commercially. *The Cure for Insomnia*, which depicts L.D. Groban reciting a 4,080-page poem, was shown in a cinema just once, in Chicago from January 31 to February 3, 1987. *The Longest and Most Meaningless Movie in the World* was later cut to a more manageable 1 hour 30 minutes, but remained just as meaningless.

⊕ A cast of thousands
The funeral sequence in Ghandhi *was filmed on the anniversary of the event. The final screen time lasted just 2 minutes 5 seconds, but featured the greatest-ever crowd of extras.*

top10 FILMS WITH THE MOST EXTRAS

FILM / COUNTRY / YEAR	EXTRAS
1 Gandhi*, UK, 1982	294,560
2 Kolberg, Germany, 1945	187,000
3 Monster Wangmagwi, South Korea, 1967	157,000
4 War and Peace, USSR, 1968	120,000
5 Ilya Muromets (The Sword and the Dragon)*, USSR, 1956	106,000
6 Dun-Huang (aka Ton ko), Japan, 1988	100,000
7 Razboiul independentei (The War of Independence), Romania, 1912	80,000
8 Around the World in 80 Days*, USA, 1956	68,894
9 =Intolerance, USA, 1916	60,000
=Dny Zrady (Days of Betrayal), Czechoslovakia, 1973	60,000

* Won Best Picture Oscar
\# Won Best Foreign Language Oscar

Unlike the enormous numbers of extras in these films, the vast crowd scenes in recent productions, such as *The Lord of the Rings* trilogy, were computer-generated.

top10 FILM-PRODUCING COUNTRIES

	COUNTRY	FEATURE FILMS PRODUCED, 2004
1	India	946
2	USA	611
3	Japan	310
4	China	212
5	France	203
6	Italy	134
7	Spain	133
8	UK	132
9	Germany	121
10	Russia	120

Source: Screen Digest

Based on the number of full-length feature films produced, Hollywood's "golden age" was the 1920s and 1930s, with a peak of 854 films made in 1921, and its nadir 1978 with just 354. Even the output of India's mighty film industry has dwindled since 2002, when some 1,200 films were made.

➲ Monster budget
The estimated production budget of King Kong set a new record – and was more than 300 times greater than the $670,000 of the 1933 original – but it is set to be eclipsed by ever more costly films.

top10 COUNTRIES WITH THE **MOST** CINEMA SCREENS

	COUNTRY	NUMBER OF CINEMA SCREENS, 2004
1	China	42,400
2	USA	36,594
3	India	11,000
4	France	5,295
5	Germany	4,870
6	Spain	4,388
7	Italy	3,566
8	UK	3,474
9	Mexico	3,197
10	Canada	2,974

Source: Film Distributors' Association

top10 FILM **BUDGETS**

	FILM	YEAR	BUDGET ($)
1 =	Spider-Man 3	2007*	250,000,000
=	Superman Returns	2006	250,000,000
3	King Kong	2005	207,000,000
4 =	Battle Angel	2007*	200,000,000
=	Spider-Man 2	2004	200,000,000
=	Titanic	1997	200,000,000
7 =	Waterworld	1995	175,000,000
=	Wild, Wild West	1999	175,000,000
9 =	The Polar Express	2004	170,000,000
=	Terminator 3: Rise of the Machines	2003	170,000,000
=	Van Helsing	2005	170,000,000

* Scheduled release

Film Hits

top10 FILMS OF ALL TIME

	FILM	YEAR	USA	GROSS INCOME ($) OVERSEAS	WORLD TOTAL
1	Titanic*	1997	600,788,188	1,244,246,000	1,845,034,188
2	The Lord of the Rings: The Return of the King*	2003	377,027,325	752,191,927	1,129,219,252
3	Harry Potter and the Sorcerer's Stone	2001	317,575,550	668,242,109	985,817,659
4	The Lord of the Rings: The Two Towers	2002	341,786,758	584,500,642	926,287,400
5	Star Wars: Episode I – The Phantom Menace	1999	431,088,297	493,229,257	924,317,554
6	Shrek 2#	2004	441,226,247	479,439,411	920,665,658
7	Jurassic Park	1993	357,067,947	562,636,053	919,700,000
8	Harry Potter and the Goblet of Fire	2005	289,908,213	602,000,000	891,908,213
9	Harry Potter and the Chamber of Secrets	2002	261,988,482	614,700,000	876,688,482
10	The Lord of the Rings: The Fellowship of the Ring	2001	314,776,170	556,592,194	871,368,364

* Won Best Picture Oscar
\# Animated

Prior to the release of *Star Wars* in 1977, no film had ever made over $500 million globally. Since then, some 43 films have done so. *Titanic* remains the only film to have made over this amount in the USA alone, and just 11 films have exceeded this total outside the USA. To date, those in the Top 10, together with *Finding Nemo* (2003), *Star Wars: Episode III – Revenge of the Sith* (2005), *Spider-Man* (2002), and *Independence Day* (1996), are the only films to have earned over $800 million worldwide.

top10 MOST PROFITABLE FILMS OF ALL TIME*

	FILM	YEAR	BUDGET ($)	WORLD GROSS ($)	PROFIT RATIO
1	The Blair Witch Project	1999	35,000	248,662,839	7,104.65
2	American Graffiti	1973	750,000	115,000,000	153.33
3	Snow White and the Seven Dwarfs#	1937	1,488,000	187,670,866	126.12
4	The Rocky Horror Picture Show	1975	1,200,000	139,876,417	116.56
5	Rocky†	1976	1,100,000	117,235,147	106.58
6	Gone With the Wind†	1939	3,900,000	400,176,459	102.61
7	E.T. The Extra-Terrestrial	1982	10,500,000	792,910,554	75.52
8	My Big Fat Greek Wedding	2002	5,000,000	368,744,044	73.75
9	The Full Monty	1997	3,500,000	257,850,122	73.67
10	Star Wars☆	1977	11,000,000	775,398,007	70.49

* Minimum entry $100 million world gross
\# Animated
† Won Best Picture Oscar
☆ Later retitled "Star Wars: Episode IV – A New Hope"

top10 FILMS WORLDWIDE, 2005

	FILM	WORLDWIDE GROSS ($)*
1	Harry Potter and the Goblet of Fire	891,908,213
2	Star Wars: Episode III – Revenge of the Sith	848,797,674
3	The Chronicles of Narnia: The Lion, the Witch, and the Wardrobe	718,262,636
4	War of the Worlds	591,413,316
5	King Kong	546,973,600
6	Madagascar#	527,952,324
7	Mr. and Mrs. Smith	477,671,954
8	Charlie and the Chocolate Factory	473,425,317
9	Batman Begins	371,853,783
10	Hitch	368,100,420

* Including income from ongoing US and overseas releases through 2006
\# Animated

top10 BLACK & WHITE FEATURE FILMS

	FILM	YEAR
1	Young Frankenstein	1974
2	Manhattan	1979
3	Good Night, and Good Luck.	2005
4	Psycho	1960
5	Mom and Dad	1944
6	Paper Moon	1973
7	From Here to Eternity	1953
8	Some Like It Hot	1959
9	The Best Years of Our Lives*	1946
10	Lenny	1974

* Won Best Picture Oscar

These are exclusively monochrome films, rather than combination black and white and color films (monochrome films with color sequences, or vice versa), a category that would be led by *Schindler's List* (1993). The Top 10 includes some recent examples where the director opted for black and white rather than color for aesthetic reasons, often to create the atmosphere of an earlier period.

⬆ Star turn
Star Wars: Episode III – Revenge of the Sith, *the world's top-earning film in 2005, completed the 28-year, six-episode* Star Wars *saga.*

top10 FILMS IN THE US BY **ATTENDANCE**

	FILM	YEAR	ATTENDANCE
1	Gone With the Wind	1939	283,100,000
2	Star Wars	1977	198,600,000
3	The Sound of Music	1965	170,600,000
4	E.T.: The Extraterrestrial	1982	151,600,000
5	The Ten Commandments	1956	132,800,000
6	The Jungle Book	1967	126,300,000
7	Titanic	1997	124,300,000
8	Jaws	1975	123,300,000
9	Doctor Zhivago	1965	122,700,000
10	101 Dalmatians	1961	119,600,000

This list is based on the actual number of people purchasing tickets at the US box office. Because it takes account of the relatively greater numbers of tickets sold to children and other discounted sales (such as matinées for certain popular films), it differs both from lists that present total box office receipts, which (as ticket prices increase) tend to feature more recent films, and those that are adjusted for inflation. However, it is interesting to observe that if inflation were factored in, *Gone With the Wind* would also top the all-time list, outearning even megablockbuster *Titanic*.

top10 FILMS IN THE **US**, 2005

	FILM	US GROSS ($)*
1	Star Wars: Episode III – Revenge of the Sith	380,270,577
2	The Chronicles of Narnia: The Lion, the Witch, and the Wardrobe	291,651,564
3	Harry Potter and the Goblet of Fire	290,013,036
4	War of the Worlds	234,280,354
5	King Kong	218,080,025
6	Wedding Crashers	209,255,921
7	Charlie and the Chocolate Factory	206,459,076
8	Batman Begins	205,343,774
9	Madagascar#	193,595,521
10	Mr. and Mrs. Smith	186,336,279

* Including income from ongoing US release through 2006
# Animated

Another Opening

top10 JANUARY OPENING WEEKENDS IN THE US

FILM / YEAR	$
1 Star Wars: Episode IV – A New Hope* (1997)	35,906,661
2 Black Hawk Down (2002)	28,611,736
3 Big Momma's House 2 (2006)	27,736,056
4 Along Came Polly (2004)	27,721,185
5 Underworld: Evolution (2006)	26,857,181
6 Coach Carter (2005)	24,182,961
7 White Noise (2005)	24,113,565
8 Save the Last Dance (2001)	23,444,930
9 Hide and Seek (2005)	21,959,233
10 Hostel (2006)	19,556,099

* Rerelease (Special Edition)

top10 FEBRUARY OPENING WEEKENDS IN THE US

FILM / YEAR	$
1 The Passion of The Christ (2004)	83,848,082
2 Hannibal (2001)	58,003,121
3 Hitch (2005)	43,142,214
4 Daredevil (2003)	40,310,419
5 50 First Dates (2004)	39,852,237
6 Scream 3 (2000)	34,713,342
7 Tyler Perry's Madea's Family Reunion (2006)	30,030,661
8 Constantine (2005)	29,769,098
9 Barbershop 2: Back in Business (2004)	24,241,612
10 How to Lose a Guy in 10 Days (2003)	23,774,850

top10 MARCH OPENING WEEKENDS IN THE US

FILM / YEAR	$
1 Ice Age: The Meltdown (2006)	68,033,544
2 Ice Age (2002)	46,312,454
3 Robots (2005)	36,045,301
4 The Ring Two (2005)	35,065,237
5 Blade II (2002)	32,528,016
6 Liar Liar (1997)	31,423,025
7 Bringing Down the House (2003)	31,101,026
8 The Pacifier (2005)	30,552,694
9 Panic Room (2002)	30,056,751
10 Scooby-Doo 2: Monsters Unleashed (2004)	29,438,331

top10 APRIL OPENING WEEKENDS IN THE US

FILM / YEAR	$
1 Anger Management (2003)	42,220,847
2 Scary Movie 4 (2006)	40,222,875
3 The Scorpion King (2002)	36,075,875
4 Sin City (2005)	29,120,273
5 The Matrix (1999)	27,788,331
6 Kill Bill Vol. 2 (2004)	25,104,949
7 Mean Girls (2004)	24,432,195
8 The Amityville Horror (2005)	23,507,007
9 Hellboy (2004)	23,172,440
10 The Interpreter (2005)	22,822,455

top10 MAY OPENING WEEKENDS IN THE US

FILM / YEAR	$
1 Spider-Man (2002)	114,844,116
2 Star Wars: Episode III – Revenge of the Sith (2005)	108,435,841
3 Shrek 2 (2004)	108,037,878
4 The Matrix Reloaded (2003)	91,774,413
5 X2: X-Men United (2003)	85,558,731
6 Star Wars: Episode II – Attack of the Clones (2002)	80,027,814
7 The Lost World: Jurassic Park (1997)	72,132,785
8 Finding Nemo (2003)	70,251,710
9 The Day After Tomorrow (2004)	68,743,584
10 The Mummy Returns (2001)	68,139,035

top10 JUNE OPENING WEEKENDS IN THE US

FILM / YEAR	$
1 Harry Potter and the Prisoner of Azkaban (2004)	93,687,367
2 Hulk (2003)	62,128,420
3 Austin Powers: The Spy Who Shagged Me (1999)	54,917,604
4 Scooby-Doo (2002)	54,155,312
5 Batman Forever (1995)	52,784,433
6 2 Fast 2 Furious (2003)	50,472,480
7 Mr. and Mrs. Smith (2005)	50,342,878
8 Batman Begins (2005)	48,745,440
9 Lara Croft: Tomb Raider (2001)	47,735,743
10 Jurassic Park (1993)	47,026,828

➲ *Battle Royal*
The Chronicles of Narnia: The Lion, the Witch, and the Wardrobe *achieved a creditable fourth place in its December box office fight against* The Lord of the Rings *trilogy.*

top10 JULY OPENING WEEKENDS IN THE US

	FILM / YEAR	$
1	Spider-Man 2 (2004)	88,156,227
2	Austin Powers in Goldmember (2002)	73,071,188
3	Planet of the Apes (2001)	68,532,960
4	War of the Worlds (2005)	64,878,725
5	Charlie and the Chocolate Factory (2005)	56,178,450
6	Fantastic Four (2005)	56,061,504
7	X-Men (2000)	54,471,475
8	The Bourne Supremacy (2004)	52,521,865
9	I, Robot (2004)	52,179,887
10	Men in Black II (2002)	52,148,751

top10 AUGUST OPENING WEEKENDS IN THE US

	FILM / YEAR	$
1	Rush Hour 2 (2001)	67,408,222
2	Signs (2002)	60,117,080
3	American Pie 2 (2001)	45,117,985
4	xXx (2002)	44,506,103
5	Alien vs. Predator (2004)	38,291,056
6	S.W.A.T. (2003)	37,062,535
7	Freddy vs. Jason (2003)	36,428,066
8	American Wedding (2003)	33,369,440
9	The Dukes of Hazard (2005)	30,675,314
10	The Sixth Sense (1999)	26,681,262

top10 SEPTEMBER OPENING WEEKENDS IN THE US

	FILM / YEAR	$
1	Sweet Home Alabama (2002)	35,648,740
2	Rush Hour (1998)	33,001,803
3	The Exorcism of Emily Rose (2005)	30,054,300
4	Flightplan (2005)	24,629,938
5	Once Upon a Time in Mexico (2003)	23,424,118
6	Double Jeopardy (1999)	23,162,542
7	Resident Evil: Apocalypse (2004)	23,036,273
8	Underworld (2003)	21,753,759
9	The Forgotten (2004)	21,022,111
10	Remember the Titans (2000)	20,905,831

top10 OCTOBER OPENING WEEKENDS IN THE US

	FILM / YEAR	$
1	Scary Movie 3 (2003)	48,113,770
2	Shark Tale (2004)	47,604,606
3	The Grudge (2004)	39,128,715
4	Red Dragon (2002)	36,540,945
5	Saw II (2005)	31,725,652
6	Meet the Parents (2000)	28,623,300
7	The Texas Chainsaw Massacre (2003)	28,094,014
8	Jackass: The Movie (2002)	22,763,437
9	Training Day (2001)	22,550,788
10	Kill Bill Vol. 1 (2003)	22,089,322

top10 NOVEMBER OPENING WEEKENDS IN THE US

	FILM / YEAR	$
1	Harry Potter and the Goblet of Fire (2005)	102,335,066
2	Harry Potter and the Sorcerer's Stone (2001)	90,294,621
3	Harry Potter and the Chamber of Secrets (2002)	88,357,488
4	The Incredibles (2004)	70,467,623
5	Monsters, Inc. (2001)	62,577,067
6	Toy Story 2 (1999)	57,388,839
7	How the Grinch Stole Christmas (2000)	55,082,330
8	8 Mile (2002)	51,240,555
9	The Matrix Revolutions (2003)	48,475,154
10	Die Another Day (2002)	47,072,040

top10 DECEMBER OPENING WEEKENDS IN THE US

	FILM / YEAR	$
1	The Lord of the Rings: The Return of the King (2003)	72,629,713
2	The Chronicles of Narnia: The Lion, the Witch and the Wardrobe (2005)	65,556,312
3	The Lord of the Rings: The Two Towers (2002)	62,007,528
4	King Kong (2005)	50,130,145
5	The Lord of the Rings: The Fellowship of the Ring (2001)	47,211,490
6	Meet the Fockers (2004)	46,120,980
7	Ocean's Twelve (2004)	39,153,380
8	Ocean's Eleven (2001)	38,107,822
9	What Women Want (2000)	33,614,543
10	Scream 2 (1997)	32,926,342

AMAZING FACT

Opening Weekends

Much of the promotional budget of a film is dedicated to the opening weekend, when it may earn between a quarter and a third of its total box office revenue. However, reviews and word-of-mouth criticism, competition from other films, and even bad weather may cause a decline in its subsequent audience. *Alien vs. Predator* (2004), for example, earned almost half its total US income during the first weekend, the rest in a lackluster 15 weeks. Conversely, *Titanic* (1997) made less than five percent of its record total during the first weekend.

Film Genres

top10 MAFIA FILMS

FILM	YEAR
1 The Firm	1993
2 The Godfather*	1972
3 The Untouchables	1987
4 Road to Perdition	2002
5 Analyze This	1999
6 The Specialist	1994
7 The Godfather, Part III	1990
8 L.A. Confidential	1997
9 Donnie Brasco	1997
10 The Client	1994

* Won Best Picture Oscar

Although *The Godfather* trilogy – with *The Godfather, Part II* (1974) falling just outside the Top 10 – represents the apogee of the Mafia movie, its history dates back to the silent era. In recent years, comedies in which organized crime and Mafia stereotypes are satirized have been especially popular, as exemplified by several entries in this Top 10 – which have all earned over $100 million worldwide.

top10 PIRATE FILMS

FILM	YEAR
1 Pirates of the Caribbean: The Curse of the Black Pearl	2003
2 Hook	1991
3 Peter Pan	2003
4 Peter Pan: Return to Never Land*	2002
5 Treasure Planet*	2002
6 Peter Pan*	1953
7 The Goonies	1985
8 Muppet Treasure Island	1996
9 Swiss Family Robinson	1960
10 The Island	1980

* Animated

After notable pirate film flops, such as *Pirates* (1986) and *Cutthroat Island* (1995), it seemed that the genre was finished, but then along came *Pirates of the Caribbean: The Curse of the Black Pearl*, which has earned so much worldwide that it is ranked as the 22nd highest-earning film of all time.

top10 COWBOY AND WESTERN FILMS

FILM	YEAR
1 Dances with Wolves*	1990
2 The Mask of Zorro	1998
3 Wild Wild West	1999
4 Maverick	1994
5 City Slickers	1991
6 Brokeback Mountain	2005
7 Legends of the Fall	1994
8 Unforgiven*	1992
9 The Legend of Zorro	2005
10 Blazing Saddles	1974

* Won Best Picture Oscar

Westerns have a history that dates back to the birth of cinema: *The Great Train Robbery* (1903), which is credited as the first narrative film ever made, was also the first-ever Western. The animated *Spirit: Stallion of the Cimarron* (2002) falls just outside the Top 10, each of which has earned upwards of $100 million.

top10 SUPERHERO FILMS

FILM	YEAR
1 Spider-Man	2002
2 Spider-Man 2	2004
3 The Incredibles*	2004
4 Batman	1989
5 X2: X-Men United	2003
6 Batman Begins	2005
7 The Mask	1994
8 Batman Forever	1995
9 Fantastic Four	2005
10 Superman	1978

* Animated

Superman makes a single showing in this Top 10, since it is in the unusual situation where the first film made a large amount (over $300 million) at the world box office, whereas each of its three sequels made progressively less.

top10 HORROR FILMS

FILM	YEAR
1 Jurassic Park	1993
2 The Sixth Sense	1999
3 The Lost World: Jurassic Park	1997
4 Jaws	1975
5 The Mummy Returns	2001
6 The Mummy	1999
7 Signs	2002
8 Godzilla	1998
9 Jurassic Park III	2001
10 Hannibal	2001

This list encompasses supernatural and science-fiction horror films featuring monster creatures, such as dinosaurs and oversized sharks, as well as serial killers. It has long been a successful genre: each of the films listed has earned $350 million or more at the world box office.

top10 COMEDY FILMS

FILM	YEAR
1 Forrest Gump*	1994
2 Pirates of the Caribbean: The Curse of the Black Pearl	2003
3 Men in Black	1997
4 Home Alone	1990
5 Meet the Fockers	2004
6 Ghost	1990
7 Bruce Almighty	2003
8 Mr. & Mrs. Smith	2005
9 Charlie and the Chocolate Factory	2005
10 Pretty Woman	1990

* Won Best Picture Oscar

Since the earliest days of Hollywood, comedy – including romantic comedies and other subgenres – has consistently performed well at the box office: all those in the Top 10 have earned over $450 million worldwide, while each of the first six has earned in excess of half a billion dollars globally.

top10 JAMES BOND FILMS

FILM / BOND ACTOR / YEAR

1
Die Another Day
Pierce Brosnan 2002

2
The World is Not Enough
Pierce Brosnan 1999

3
GoldenEye
Pierce Brosnan 1995

4
Tomorrow Never Dies
Pierce Brosnan 1997

5
Moonraker
Roger Moore 1979

6
For Your Eyes Only
Roger Moore 1981

7
The Living Daylights
Timothy Dalton 1987

8
The Spy Who Loved Me
Roger Moore 1977

9
Octopussy
Roger Moore 1983

10
Licence to Kill
Timothy Dalton 1990

Ian Fleming wrote 12 James Bond novels, only two of which, *Moonraker* (1955) and *The Spy Who Loved Me* (1962), figure in this Top 10. After his death in 1964, *For Your Eyes Only*, *Octopussy*, *The Living Daylights*, and *GoldenEye* were developed by other writers from his short stories, while subsequent releases were written without reference to Fleming's writings.

➔ *High-yield Bond*
Pierce Brosnan's four Bond films have made over $1.5 billion worldwide.

Animated Films

⬆ Wild things
Melman, Marty, Alex, and Gloria, stars of 2005 cartoon smash Madagascar.

top10 **ANIMATED** FILMS

	FILM	YEAR	WORLDWIDE TOTAL GROSS ($)
1	Shrek 2*	2004	920,665,658
2	Finding Nemo#	2003	864,625,978
3	The Lion King#	1994	783,841,776
4	The Incredibles#	2004	631,436,092
5	Monsters, Inc.#	2001	529,061,238
6	Madagascar*	2005	527,890,631
7	Ice Age: The Meltdown†	2006	512,794,142
8	Aladdin*	1992	504,050,219
9	Toy Story 2#	1999	485,015,179
10	Shrek*	2001	484,409,218

* DreamWorks
# Disney
† Fox Animation Studios

top10 ANIMATED FILMS **IN THE US**

	FILM	YEAR	US TOTAL GROSS ($)
1	Shrek 2*	2004	441,226,247
2	Finding Nemo#	2003	339,714,978
3	The Lion King#	1994	328,541,776
4	Shrek*	2001	267,665,011
5	The Incredibles#	2004	261,441,092
6	Monsters, Inc.#	2001	255,873,250
7	Toy Story 2#	1999	245,852,179
8	Aladdin*	1992	217,350,219
9	Madagascar*	2005	193,595,521
10	Toy Story#	1995	191,796,233

* DreamWorks
# Disney

top10 ANIMATED **FILM BUDGETS**

	FILM	YEAR	BUDGET ($)
1	The Polar Express	2004	170,000,000
2	Tarzan	1999	145,000,000
3	Treasure Planet	2002	140,000,000
4	Final Fantasy: The Spirits Within	2001	137,000,000
5	Dinosaur	2000	128,000,000
6	Monsters, Inc.	2001	115,000,000
7	Home on the Range	2004	110,000,000
8	The Emperor's New Groove	2000	100,000,000
9	The Road to El Dorado	2000	95,000,000
10	Finding Nemo	2003	94,000,000

Snow White and the Seven Dwarfs (1937) established a record budget of $1.49 million. The $2.6-million budget for *Pinocchio* (1940) and $2.28 million for the original *Fantasia* (1940) were the two biggest of the 1940s, while *Sleeping Beauty* (1959) at $6 million was the highest of the 1950s. Since the 1990s, budgets of $50 million or more have become commonplace: *The Lion King* (1994) cost $79.3 million, while *Tarzan* has become the first to break through $100 million.

top10 ANIMATED FILMS BASED ON **TV SERIES**

	FILM	TV SERIES*	FILM YEAR
1	Pokémon: The First Movie	1997	1999
2	The Rugrats Movie	1991	1998
3	The SpongeBob SquarePants Movie	1999	2004
4	Pokémon: The Movie 2000	1997	2000
5	Rugrats in Paris: The Movie – Rugrats II	1991	2000
6	South Park: Bigger, Longer & Uncut	1997	1999
7	Beavis and Butt-head Do America	1993	1996
8	Pokémon 3: The Movie	1997	2001
9	The Wild Thornberrys Movie	1998	2002
10	Rugrats Go Wild	1991	2003

* Launched on TV in USA

Such is the fan following of many TV animated series that when they reach the big screen they attract huge audiences: the first five films in this list each earned in excess of $100 million, and the others have all made over $50 million each.

top10 ANIMATED **OPENING WEEKENDS** IN THE US

	FILM	YEAR	OPENING WEEKEND GROSS ($)
1	Shrek 2	2004	108,037,878
2	The Incredibles	2004	70,467,623
3	Finding Nemo	2003	70,251,710
4	Ice Age: The Meltdown	2006	68,033,544
5	Monsters, Inc.	2001	62,577,067
6	Toy Story 2*	1999	57,388,839
7	Shark Tale	2004	47,604,606
8	Madagascar	2005	47,224,594
9	Ice Age	2002	46,312,454
10	Shrek	2001	42,347,760

* Second weekend; opening weekend release in limited number of cinemas only

➲ Baby boom
Tommy Pickles, voiced, like many other animated characters, by Elizabeth Daily, appeared in the popular Rugrats films.

Film Actors

top10 HIGHEST-EARNING FILM ACTORS

ACTOR	2005 INCOME ($)
1 Mel Gibson	185,000,000
2 Johnny Depp	37,000,000
3 Will Smith	35,000,000
4 Tobey Maguire	32,000,000
5 Tom Cruise	31,000,000
6 Denzel Washington	30,000,000
7 Adam Sandler	28,000,000
8 Matt Damon	27,000,000
9 Brad Pitt	25,000,000
10 Frankie Muniz	8,000,000

Source: Forbes magazine

top10 MEL GIBSON FILMS

FILM	YEAR
1 Signs	2002
2 What Women Want	2000
3 Lethal Weapon 3	1992
4 Ransom	1996
5 Lethal Weapon 4	1998
6 Lethal Weapon 2	1989
7 The Patriot	2000
8 Braveheart*	1995
9 Maverick	1994
10 Payback	1999

* Won Best Picture Oscar

top10 SAMUEL L. JACKSON FILMS

FILM	YEAR
1 Star Wars: Episode I – The Phantom Menace	1999
2 Jurassic Park	1993
3 Star Wars: Episode III – Revenge of the Sith	2005
4 Star Wars: Episode II - Attack of the Clones	2002
5 Die Hard: With a Vengeance	1995
6 Coming to America	1988
7 xXx	2002
8 Unbreakable	2000
9 Pulp Fiction	1994
10 S.W.A.T.	2003

top10 TOM CRUISE FILMS

FILM	YEAR
1 War of the Worlds	2005
2 Mission: Impossible II	2000
3 The Last Samurai	2003
4 Mission: Impossible	1996
5 Rain Man	1988
6 Minority Report	2002
7 Top Gun	1986
8 Jerry Maguire	1996
9 The Firm	1993
10 A Few Good Men	1992

top10 AL PACINO FILMS

FILM	YEAR
1 The Godfather*	1972
2 Heat	1995
3 Dick Tracy	1990
4 The Devil's Advocate	1997
5 The Godfather: Part III	1990
6 Scent of a Woman*	1992
7 Donnie Brasco	1997
8 Insomnia	2002
9 Sea of Love	1989
10 The Godfather: Part II	1974

* Won Best Picture Oscar
# Won Best Actor Oscar

top10 ROBERT DE NIRO FILMS

FILM	YEAR
1 Meet the Fockers	2004
2 Meet the Parents	2000
3 Heat	1995
4 The Untouchables	1987
5 Cape Fear	1991
6 Analyze This	1999
7 Sleepers	1996
8 Backdraft	1991
9 Hide and Seek	2005
10 Casino	1995

Here's Johnny!
Johnny Depp as Willy Wonka in Charlie and the Chocolate Factory, *his second chocolate-based film, and his fifth film since* Edward Scissorhands *under the direction of Tim Burton.*

top10 **JOHNNY DEPP** FILMS

	FILM	YEAR
1	Pirates of the Caribbean: The Curse of the Black Pearl	2003
2	Charlie and the Chocolate Factory	2004
3	Sleepy Hollow	1999
4	Platoon	1986
5	Chocolat	2000
6	Donnie Brasco	1997
7	Finding Neverland	2004
8	Desperado II: Once Upon a Time in Mexico	2003
9	Secret Window	2004
10	Edward Scissorhands	1990

Seven of Johnny Depp's Top 10 films have earned over $100 million, his run of successes led – by a considerable margin – by *Pirates of the Caribbean*.

top10 **GEORGE CLOONEY** FILMS

	FILM	YEAR
1	Ocean's Eleven	2001
2	Ocean's Twelve	2004
3	The Perfect Storm	2000
4	Batman & Robin	1997
5	Spy Kids	2001
6	Intolerable Cruelty	2003
7	The Peacemaker	1997
8	Three Kings	1999
9	One Fine Day	1996
10	The Thin Red Line	1998

Already well-known as Dr Doug Ross in TV series *ER* – as well as some best-forgotten early film parts, such as *Return of the Killer Tomatoes!* (1988) – George Clooney has appeared in a run of successful films during the past 10 years. He also provided voices for the animated *South Park: Bigger, Longer & Uncut* (1999).

top10 **BRAD PITT** FILMS

	FILM	YEAR
1	Troy	2004
2	Mr. & Mrs. Smith	2005
3	Ocean's Eleven	2001
4	Ocean's Twelve	2004
5	Se7en	1995
6	Interview with the Vampire: The Vampire Chronicles	1994
7	Twelve Monkeys	1995
8	Sleepers	1996
9	Legends of the Fall	1994
10	The Mexican	2001

Although *Troy* earned almost $500 million worldwide, Brad Pitt's action comedies have been among his most successful films. Including the four films in his Top 10, he has appeared in 10 films or TV series with a number in the title.

Film Actresses

top10 HIGHEST-EARNING FILM ACTRESSES

	ACTRESS	2005 INCOME ($)
1	Bette Midler	31,000,000
2	Drew Barrymore	22,000,000
3	Jennifer Aniston	18,500,000
4	Jennifer Lopez	17,000,000
5	Nicole Kidman	14,500,000
6	Jennifer Garner	14,000,000
7	Cameron Diaz	13,000,000
8	Naomi Watts	11,500,000
9	Lindsay Lohan	11,000,000
10	Sandra Bullock	10,500,000

Source: Forbes magazine

top10 CAMERON DIAZ FILMS

	FILM	YEAR
1	There's Something About Mary	1998
2	The Mask	1994
3	My Best Friend's Wedding	1997
4	Charlie's Angels	2000
5	Charlie's Angels: Full Throttle	2003
6	Vanilla Sky	2001
7	Gangs of New York	2002
8	Any Given Sunday	1999
9	In Her Shoes	2005
10	The Sweetest Thing	2002

Cameron Diaz's Top 10 films include some of the highest earning of recent years. She also provided the voice of Princess Fiona in *Shrek* (2001) and *Shrek 2* (2004) – which have outearned all of them.

Pay acceleration
Cameron Diaz earned $20 million for her role in Charlie's Angels: Full Throttle *(2003) – 10 times the amount she received for* There's Something About Mary *(1998).*

top10 NICOLE KIDMAN FILMS

	FILM	YEAR
1	Batman Forever	1995
2	The Others	2001
3	Moulin Rouge!	2001
4	Cold Mountain	2003
5	Days of Thunder	1990
6	The Interpreter	2005
7	Eyes Wide Shut	1999
8	Far and Away	1992
9	Bewitched	2005
10	The Peacemaker	1997

top10 SANDRA BULLOCK FILMS

	FILM	YEAR
1	Speed	1994
2	Miss Congeniality	2000
3	Two Weeks Notice	2002
4	While You Were Sleeping	1995
5	Speed 2: Cruise Control	1997
6	A Time to Kill	1996
7	The Net	1995
8	Miss Congeniality 2: Armed and Fabulous	2005
9	Forces of Nature	1999
10	Crash	2005

top10 JUDI DENCH FILMS

	FILM	YEAR
1	Die Another Day	2002
2	The World is Not Enough	1999
3	GoldenEye	1995
4	Tomorrow Never Dies	1997
5	Shakespeare in Love	1998
6	Chocolat	2000
7	The Chronicles of Riddick	2004
8	Pride and Prejudice	2005
9	The Shipping News	2001
10	Tea with Mussolini	1999

top10 CATHERINE ZETA-JONES FILMS

	FILM	YEAR
1	Ocean's Twelve	2004
2	Chicago*	2002
3	The Mask of Zorro	1998
4	Entrapment	1999
5	Traffic	2000
6	The Terminal	2004
7	The Haunting	1999
8	America's Sweethearts	2001
9	The Legend of Zorro	2005
10	Intolerable Cruelty	2003

* Won Best Picture Oscar

In little over 12 years, Catherine Zeta-Jones has graduated from British TV series *The Darling Buds of May* (1991–93), in which she appeared as Mariette Larkin, to starring roles in major Hollywood blockbusters, all of which have grossed over $100 million worldwide.

➔ Strong poison
Uma Thurman received $5 million for her Batman and Robin *role as Poison Ivy – and $12 million for each of the* Kill Bill *films.*

top10 UMA THURMAN FILMS

	FILM	YEAR
1	Batman & Robin	1997
2	Pulp Fiction	1994
3	Kill Bill: Vol. 1	2003
4	Kill Bill: Vol. 2	2004
5	Paycheck	2003
6	Be Cool	2005
7	The Truth About Cats & Dogs	1996
8	The Avengers	1998
9	Final Analysis	1992
10	Dangerous Liaisons	1988

top10 CATE BLANCHETT FILMS

	FILM	YEAR
1	The Lord of the Rings: The Return of the King	2003
2	The Lord of the Rings: The Two Towers	2002
3	The Lord of the Rings: The Fellowship of the Ring	2001
4	The Aviator	2004
5	The Talented Mr. Ripley	1999
6	Bandits	2001
7	Elizabeth	1998
8	The Gift	2000
9	The Missing	2003
10	The Life Aquatic With Steve Zissou	2004

top10 SCARLETT JOHANSSON FILMS

	FILM	YEAR
1	The Horse Whisperer	1998
2	The Island	2005
3	Lost in Translation	2003
4	Home Alone 3	1997
5	Match Point	2005
6	Just Cause	1995
7	In Good Company	2004
8	Eight Legged Freaks	2002
9	Girl with a Pearl Earring	2003
10	The Man Who Wasn't There	2001

Film Directors

⬆ **Glowing report** Minority Report, *Spielberg's first blockbuster of the 21st century, earned over $350 million worldwide.*

top10 **HIGHEST-EARNING** DIRECTORS

	DIRECTOR	FILMS	HIGHEST-EARNING FILM	TOTAL US GROSS OF ALL FILMS ($)
1	Steven Spielberg	24	E.T.: the Extra-Terrestrial	3,505,000,223
2	Robert Zemeckis	13	Forrest Gump	1,715,281,884
3	George Lucas	6	Star Wars: Episode IV – A New Hope	1,700,470,625
4	Chris Columbus	12	Harry Potter and the Sorcerer's Stone	1,567,938,485
5	Ron Howard	16	Dr Seuss's How the Grinch Stole Christmas	1,388,746,933
6	Peter Jackson	8	The Lord of the Rings: The Return of the King	1,270,962,886
7	Tim Burton	13	Batman	1,247,173,343
8	Richard Donner	17	Lethal Weapon 2	1,217,512,205
9	James Cameron	8	Titanic	1,150,831,308
10	Andrew Adamson	3	Shrek 2	998,070,204

While the cumulative total US box office income of all the films of these directors provides a comparative view of the overall earning power of the group, the most impressive representative is George Lucas, with relatively few but extremely high-grossing releases, an unrivaled per-picture average of over $283 million.

top10 FILMS DIRECTED BY **STEVEN SPIELBERG**

	FILM	YEAR
1	Jurassic Park	1993
2	E.T.: the Extra-Terrestrial	1982
3	The Lost World: Jurassic Park	1997
4	War of the Worlds	2005
5	Indiana Jones and the Last Crusade	1989
6	Saving Private Ryan	1998
7	Jaws	1975
8	Raiders of the Lost Ark	1981
9	Minority Report	2002
10	Catch Me if You Can	2002

Steven Spielberg has directed some of the most successful films of all time: the top six in this list appear among the 50 highest-earning films of all time worldwide, while the cumulative world box-office gross of his Top 10 alone amounts to an unrivaled $5.5 billion.

top10 DIRECTORS, 2005

	DIRECTOR	FILM(S) OF YEAR	WORLD TOTAL (US$)
1	Mike Newell	Harry Potter and the Goblet of Fire	891,338,639
2	George Lucas	Star Wars: Episode III – Revenge of the Sith	848,797,674
3	Andrew Adamson	The Chronicles of Narnia: The Lion, the Witch and the Wardrobe	677,522,946
4	Steven Spielberg	War of the Worlds	591,416,316
5	Tim Burton	Charlie and the Chocolate Factory/Corpse Bride*	590,520,433
6	Peter Jackson	King Kong	544,456,306
7	Eric Darnell	Madagascar*	527,890,631
8	Jay Roach	Meet the Fockers#	515,291,929
9	Doug Liman	Mr. & Mrs. Smith	477,671,954
10	Christopher Nolan	Batman Begins	371,853,783

* Animated
# Late 2004 release

top10 FILMS DIRECTED BY WOMEN

	FILM	DIRECTOR	YEAR
1	Shrek*	Victoria Jenson#	2001
2	What Women Want	Nancy Meyers	2000
3	Deep Impact	Mimi Leder	1998
4	Look Who's Talking	Amy Heckerling	1989
5	Doctor Dolittle	Betty Thomas	1998
6	Bridget Jones's Diary	Sharon Maguire	2001
7	Something's Gotta Give	Nancy Meyers	2003
8	You've Got M@il	Nora Ephron	1998
9	Sleepless in Seattle	Nora Ephron	1993
10	The Prince of Egypt*	Brenda Chapman†	1998

* Animated
# Codirector with Andrew Adamson
† Codirector with Steve Hickner and Simon Wells

top10 FILMS DIRECTED BY RIDLEY SCOTT

	FILM	YEAR
1	Gladiator	2000
2	Hannibal	2001
3	Kingdom of Heaven	2005
4	Black Hawk Down	2001
5	Black Rain	1989
6	Alien	1979
7	G.I. Jane	1997
8	Matchstick Men	2003
9	Thelma & Louise	1991
10	Blade Runner	1982

British director Sir Ridley Scott (b.1937) began his career in television and as a maker of such celebrated TV commercials as the Hovis bread advertisement (1974), but has been directing films since the late 1970s with *The Duellists* (1977) and especially *Alien*, launching a run of box office hits – although *1492: Conquest of Paradise*, with an estimated budget of $47 million and a US gross of just over $7 million, may be regarded as a notable "flop." He is credited with relaunching the epic "sword-and-sandal" genre with the enormously successful *Gladiator* ($458 million worldwide) and *Kingdom of Heaven*. He was knighted in 2003.

top10 FILMS DIRECTED BY CHRIS COLUMBUS

	FILM	YEAR
1	Harry Potter and the Sorcerer's Stone	2001
2	Harry Potter and the Chamber of Secrets	2002
3	Home Alone	1990
4	Mrs. Doubtfire	1993
5	Home Alone 2: Lost in New York	1992
6	Stepmom	1998
7	Nine Months	1995
8	Bicentennial Man	1999
9	Adventures in Babysitting	1987
10	Only the Lonely	1991

➲ Heaven-sent
Ridley Scott on the set of Kingdom of Heaven. *His Top 10 films have earned almost $1.7 billion worldwide.*

top10 FILMS DIRECTED BY TIM BURTON

	FILM	YEAR
1	Charlie and the Chocolate Factory	2005
2	Batman	1989
3	Planet of the Apes	2001
4	Batman Returns	1992
5	Sleepy Hollow	1999
6	Big Fish	2003
7	Tim Burton's Corpse Bride*	2005
8	Mars Attacks!	1996
9	Edward Scissorhands	1990
10	Beetlejuice	1988

* Animated; codirected with Mike Johnson

Film Studios

The Studios

A small group of studios once controlled the entire film industry, owning production facilities and acting as producers, distributors, and, before the 1950s through their ownership of cinema chains, exhibitors. The definition of a "studio" is no longer clear-cut: some of the original studios no longer exist, while as a result of mergers and takeovers, most of the leading names are now components of large global media conglomerates operating alongside some newer independent studios, such as Artisan and Dimension, the specialist studio within Miramax. Studios are primarily financial and distribution organizations with the actual production undertaken by independent production companies – often more than one may be involved in a coproduction. The films listed here represent the Top 10 productions distributed by each of the major studios within the US, but based on total global revenue – although in many instances different companies may have acted as distributors outside the US.

top10 **STUDIOS**, 2005

	STUDIO	FILMS RELEASED	TOTAL US GROSS, 2005 ($)
1	Warner Bros	25	1,377,106,137
2	Fox	21	1,353,871,333
3	Universal	24	1,010,193,093
4	Buena Vista	23	921,523,769
5	Sony	26	917,764,099
6	Paramount	17	832,177,664
7	Dreamworks SKG	10	501,837,191
8	New Line	13	420,532,445
9	Lions Gate	20	283,992,663
10	Dimension	7	185,149,258

top10 **SONY** (+ COLUMBIA/TRISTAR) FILMS

	FILM	YEAR
1	Spider-Man	2002
2	Spider-Man 2	2004
3	Men in Black	1997
4	Terminator 2: Judgment Day	1991
5	Men in Black II	2002
6	Terminator 3: Rise of the Machines	2003
7	Hitch	2005
8	Air Force One	1997
9	As Good as It Gets	1997
10	Close Encounters of the Third Kind	1977/80

top10 **PARAMOUNT** FILMS

	FILM	YEAR
1	Titanic*	1997
2	Forrest Gump*	1994
3	War of the Worlds	2005
4	Mission: Impossible II	2000
5	Ghost	1990
6	Indiana Jones and the Last Crusade	1989
7	Saving Private Ryan	1998
8	Mission: Impossible	1996
9	Grease	1978
10	Raiders of the Lost Ark	1981

* Won Best Picture Oscar

top10 **UNIVERSAL** FILMS

	FILM	YEAR
1	E.T. the Extra-Terrestrial	1982
2	Jurassic Park	1993
3	The Lost World: Jurassic Park	1997
4	King Kong	2005
5	Meet the Fockers	2004
6	Bruce Almighty	2003
7	Jaws	1975
8	The Mummy Returns	2001
9	The Mummy	1999
10	Back to the Future	1985

top10 **NEW LINE** FILMS

	FILM	YEAR
1	The Lord of the Rings: The Return of the King*	2003
2	Lord of the Rings: The Two Towers	2002
3	Lord of the Rings: The Fellowship of the Ring	2001
4	The Mask	1994
5	Rush Hour 2	2001
6	Se7en	1995
7	Austin Powers: The Spy who Shagged Me	1999
8	Austin Powers in Goldmember	2002
9	Wedding Crashers	2005
10	Rush Hour	1998

* Won Best Picture Oscar

top10 20TH CENTURY FOX FILMS

FILM	YEAR
1 Star Wars: Episode I – The Phantom Menace	1999
2 Star Wars: Episode III – Revenge of the Sith	2005
3 Independence Day	1996
4 Star Wars: Episode IV – A New Hope	1977
5 Star Wars: Episode II – Attack of the Clones	2002
6 Star Wars: Episode VI – Return of the Jedi	1983
7 The Day After Tomorrow	2004
8 Star Wars: Episode V – The Empire Strikes Back	1980
9 Home Alone	1990
10 Mr. & Mrs. Smith	2005

William Fox founded a film production company in 1912. It was merged with 20th Century Pictures in 1935 and achieved some of its greatest successes, especially a series of musicals starring Betty Grable, in the 1940s. Despite the box office success of *The Sound of Music* (1965) the studio suffered a number of setbacks, including the failure of the colossally expensive *Cleopatra* (1963). Its return to prosperity began in the 1970s with *The French Connection* (1971) and was consolidated by the outstanding achievement of *Star Wars* (1977) and its successors.

⊕ *Fire power*
Daniel Radcliffe as the eponymous hero of Harry Potter and the Goblet of Fire, *the latest blockbuster in this highly successful series.*

top10 WARNER BROS FILMS

FILM	YEAR
1 Harry Potter and the Sorcerer's Stone	2001
2 Harry Potter and the Goblet of Fire	2005
3 Harry Potter and the Chamber of Secrets	2002
4 Harry Potter and the Prisoner of Azkaban	2004
5 The Matrix Reloaded	2003
6 Troy	2004
7 Twister	1996
8 Charlie and the Chocolate Factory	2005
9 The Matrix	1999
10 Ocean's Eleven	2001

The coming of sound launched Warner Bros into its important place in cinema history, with *The Jazz Singer* (1927). In the 1960s its feature films took a lesser role as the company focused on TV production, although a handful, among them *Bonnie and Clyde* (1967), were notable box office draws. In the 1970s Warner Bros embarked on an era of notable success that began with *The Exorcist* (1973). *Batman* (1989) became one of the then highest-earning films ever – though now far eclipsed by the enormous global success of the *Harry Potter* series.

Oscar-winning Films

top10 FILMS TO WIN THE **MOST OSCARS***

	FILM	YEAR	NOMINATIONS	AWARDS
1	= Ben-Hur	1959	12	11
	= Titanic	1997	14	11
	= The Lord of the Rings: The Return of the King	2003	11	11
4	West Side Story	1961	11	10
5	= Gigi	1958	9	9
	= The Last Emperor	1987	9	9
	= The English Patient	1996	12	9
8	= Gone With the Wind	1939	13	8#
	= From Here to Eternity	1953	13	8
	= On the Waterfront	1954	12	8
	= My Fair Lady	1964	12	8
	= Cabaret†	1972	10	8
	= Gandhi	1982	11	8
	= Amadeus	1984	11	8

* Oscar® is a Registered Trade Mark
# Plus two special awards
† Did not win Best Picture Oscar

Ten other films have won seven Oscars each: *Going My Way* (1944), *The Best Years of Our Lives* (1946), *The Bridge on the River Kwai* (1957), *Lawrence of Arabia* (1962), *Patton* (1970), *The Sting* (1973), *Out of Africa* (1985), *Dances With Wolves* (1991), *Schindler's List* (1993), and *Shakespeare in Love* (1998). A further nine films have each won six Oscars, most recently *Chicago* (2002), including the award for Best Picture.

top10 FILMS TO WIN THE **MOST OSCARS** WITHOUT WINNING BEST PICTURE

	FILM	YEAR	WINS
1	Cabaret	1972	8
2	= A Place in the Sun	1951	6
	= Star Wars	1977	6
4	= Wilson	1944	5
	= The Bad and the Beautiful	1952	5
	= The King and I	1956	5
	= Mary Poppins	1964	5
	= Doctor Zhivago	1965	5
	= Who's Afraid of Virginia Woolf?	1966	5
	= Saving Private Ryan	1998	5
	= The Aviator	2004	5

top10 FILMS **NOMINATED** FOR THE MOST OSCARS

	FILM	YEAR	AWARDS	NOMINATIONS
1	= All About Eve	1950	6	14
	= Titanic	1997	11	14
3	= Gone With the Wind	1939	8*	13
	= From Here to Eternity	1953	8	13
	= Mary Poppins#	1964	5	13
	= Who's Afraid of Virginia Woolf?#	1966	5	13
	= Forrest Gump	1994	6	13
	= Shakespeare in Love	1998	7	13
	= The Lord of the Rings: The Fellowship of the Ring#	2001	4	13
	= Chicago	2002	6	13

* Plus two special awards
# Did not win Best Picture Oscar

Thirteen is not an unlucky number where Oscar nominations are concerned, no fewer than eight films having received that total. They and the two with 14 are those that received the greatest share of votes from Academy members (over 5,800, including previous nominees and winners), using a system that creates a shortlist of five nominees in each of 24 categories.

the10 FILMS WITH THE **MOST NOMINATIONS** WITHOUT A SINGLE WIN

	FILM	YEAR	NOMINATIONS
1	= The Turning Point	1977	11
	= The Color Purple	1985	11
3	Gangs of New York	2002	10
4	= The Little Foxes	1941	9
	= Peyton Place	1957	9
6	= Quo Vadis	1951	8
	= The Nun's Story	1959	8
	= The Sand Pebbles	1966	8
	= The Elephant Man	1980	8
	= Ragtime	1981	8
	= The Remains of the Day	1993	8

Gangs of New York is the latest of a number of films that have received an impressive tally of nominations, but no wins in any category. *The Broadway Melody* (1928–29), *Grand Hotel* (1931–32), and *Mutiny on the Bounty* (1935) are the only films to win Best Picture but to receive no other awards in any category.

⬆ Crash drama
Thandie Newton and Matt Dillon in Crash, *winner of three Oscars including Best Picture.*

top10 HIGHEST-EARNING BEST PICTURE OSCAR WINNERS

FILM	YEAR*	WORLD BOX OFFICE ($)
1 Titanic	1997	1,845,000,000
2 The Lord of the Rings: The Return of the King	2003	1,118,900,000
3 Forrest Gump	1994	677,400,000
4 Gladiator	2000	457,600,000
5 Dances With Wolves	1990	424,200,000
6 Rain Man	1988	416,000,000
7 Gone With the Wind	1939	400,200,000
8 American Beauty	1999	356,300,000
9 Schindler's List	1993	321,300,000
10 A Beautiful Mind	2001	313,500,000

* Of release; Academy Awards are made the following year

the10 LATEST BEST PICTURE OSCAR WINNERS

YEAR	FILM	DIRECTOR
2005	Crash	Paul Haggis*
2004	Million Dollar Baby	Clint Eastwood
2003	The Lord of the Rings: The Return of the King	Peter Jackson
2002	Chicago	Rob Marshall*
2001	A Beautiful Mind	Ron Howard
2000	Gladiator	Ridley Scott*
1999	American Beauty	Sam Mendes
1998	Shakespeare in Love	John Madden*
1997	Titanic	James Cameron
1996	The English Patient	Anthony Minghella

* Did not also win Best Director Oscar

Oscar-winning Actors

the 10 LATEST **BEST ACTOR** OSCAR WINNERS

YEAR	ACTOR / FILM
2005	Philip Seymour Hoffman, Capote
2004	Jamie Foxx, Ray
2003	Sean Penn, Mystic River
2002	Adrien Brody, The Pianist
2001	Denzel Washington, Training Day
2000	Russell Crowe, Gladiator*
1999	Kevin Spacey, American Beauty*
1998	Roberto Benigni, Life is Beautiful
1997	Jack Nicholson, As Good As It Gets
1996	Geoffrey Rush, Shine

* Won Best Picture Oscar

top 10 ACTORS WITH THE MOST NOMINATIONS **WITHOUT A WIN***

	ACTOR	NOMINATIONS
1 =	Richard Burton	7
=	Peter O'Toole	7
2 =	Albert Finney	5
=	Arthur Kennedy	5
4 =	Warren Beatty	4
=	Charles Boyer	4
=	Jeff Bridges	4
=	Montgomery Clift	4
=	Ed Harris	4
=	Claude Rains	4
=	Mickey Rooney	4

* In any acting categories

top 10 **YOUNGEST** OSCAR-WINNING ACTORS

	ACTOR	AWARD / FILM	YEAR	AGE* YRS	MTHS	DAYS
1	Vincent Winter	Special Award: Outstanding Performance (The Little Kidnappers)	1954	7	3	1
2	Jon Whiteley	Special Award: Outstanding Juvenile Performance (The Little Kidnappers)	1954	10	1	11
3	Ivan Jandl	Special Award: Outstanding Juvenile Performance of 1948 (The Search)	1948	12	2	0
4	Claude Jarman Jr.	Special Award: Outstanding Child Actor of 1946 (The Yearling)	1946	12	5	14
5	Bobby Driscoll	Special Award: Outstanding Juvenile Actor of 1949 (The Window)	1949	13	0	20
6	Mickey Rooney	Special Award for juvenile players setting a high standard of ability and achievement#	1938	18	5	0
7	Timothy Hutton	Best Supporting Actor (Ordinary People)	1980	20	7	15
8	George Chakiris	Best Supporting Actor (West Side Story)	1961	26	7	1
9	Cuba Gooding Jr.	Best Supporting Actor (Jerry Maguire)	1996	29	3	22
10	Adrien Brody	Best Actor (The Pianist)	2002	29	11	9

* As at date of award ceremony
# Shared with fellow teen star Deanna Durbin

Jackie Cooper was nine at the time of his nomination as Best Actor for his part in *Skippy* (1930–31 Academy Awards), while eight-year-old Justin Henry is the youngest-ever Oscar nominee for Best Supporting Actor, for his role in *Kramer vs. Kramer* (1979).

top 10 **OLDEST** OSCAR-WINNING ACTORS

	ACTOR	FILM	YEAR	YRS	AGE* MTHS	DAYS
1	George Burns	The Sunshine Boys	1975	80	2	9
2	Melvyn Douglas	Being There	1979	79	0	9
3	John Gielgud	Arthur	1981	77	11	15
4	Don Ameche	Cocoon	1985	77	9	24
5	Henry Fonda	On Golden Pond	1981	76	10	13
6	Edmund Gwenn	Miracle on 34th Street	1947	72	5	24
7	Jack Palance	City Slickers	1991	72	0	1
8	John Houseman	The Paperchase	1973	71	6	0
9	Morgan Freeman	Million Dollar Baby#	2004	67	8	27
10	Charles Coburn	The More the Merrier	1943	66	8	13

* As at date of award ceremony
# Won Best Picture Oscar

All of the Academy Awards listed above are for Best Supporting Actor, apart from Henry Fonda's Best Actor award for *On Golden Pond*. The oldest person to win the Best Actor award prior to Fonda was John Wayne, who was 62 when he received his 1969 award for *True Grit*. Richard Farnsworth was 80 when nominated for *The Straight Story* (1999).

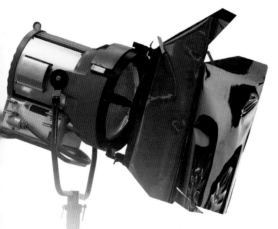

← *Mr. Cool*
Paul Newman in Cool Hand Luke *(1967). As well as his nine acting nominations, he received one as a director and has won both an Honorary Oscar and the prestigious Jean Hersholt Humanitarian Award.*

top10 ACTORS WITH THE MOST NOMINATIONS*

	ACTOR	WINS SUPPORTING	WINS BEST	NOMS.
1	Jack Nicholson	1	2	12
2	Laurence Olivier	0	1	10
3	= Paul Newman	0	1	9
	= Spencer Tracy	0	2	9
5	= Marlon Brando	0	2	8
	= Jack Lemmon	1	1	8
	= Al Pacino	0	1	8
8	= Richard Burton	0	0	7
	= Dustin Hoffman	0	2	7
	= Peter O'Toole	0	0	7

* In all acting categories

Oscar-winning Actresses

top10 ACTRESSES WITH THE **MOST OSCAR NOMINATIONS** *

	ACTOR	WINS SUPPORTING	WINS BEST	NOMS.
1	Meryl Streep	1	1	13
2	Katharine Hepburn	0	4	12
3	Bette Davis	0	2	10
4	Geraldine Page	0	1	8
5 =	Ingrid Bergman	1	2	7
=	Jane Fonda	0	2	7
=	Greer Garson	0	1	7
8 =	Ellen Burstyn	0	1	6
=	Deborah Kerr	0	0	6
=	Jessica Lange	1	1	6
=	Vanessa Redgrave	1	0	6
=	Thelma Ritter	0	0	6
=	Norma Shearer	0	0	6
=	Maggie Smith	1	1	6
=	Sissy Spacek	0	1	6

* In all acting categories

top10 **YOUNGEST** OSCAR-WINNING ACTRESSES

	ACTRESS	AWARD/FILM (WHERE SPECIFIED)	YEAR	AGE* YRS	MTHS	DAYS
1	Shirley Temple	Special Award – Outstanding Contribution during 1934	1934	6	10	4
2	Margaret O'Brien	Special Award – Outstanding Child Actress of 1944 (Meet Me in St. Louis)	1944	8	2	0
3	Tatum O'Neal	Best Supporting Actress (Paper Moon)	1973	10	4	28
4	Anna Paquin	Best Supporting Actress (The Piano)	1993	11	7	25
5	Hayley Mills	Special Award: Outstanding Juvenile Performance of 1960 (Pollyanna)	1960	13	11	30
6	Peggy Ann Garner	Special Award: Outstanding Child Performer of 1945 (A Tree Grows in Brooklyn)	1945	14	4	18
7	Patty Duke	Best Supporting Actress (The Miracle Worker)	1962	16	3	25
8	Deanna Durbin	Special Award for juvenile players setting a high standard of ability and achievement#	1938	17	2	19
9	Judy Garland	Special Award (The Wizard of Oz)	1939	17	8	19
10	Marlee Matlin	Best Actress (Children of a Lesser God)	1986	21	7	6

* Age at time of award ceremony
# Shared with fellow teen star Mickey Rooney

British actress Hayley Mills, the 12th and last winner of the Special Award miniature Oscar, won her award precisely one day before her 14th birthday. Subsequent winners have had to compete on the same basis as adult actors and actresses for the major acting awards. Tatum O'Neal is thus the youngest winner of – as well as the youngest-ever nominee for – an "adult" Oscar. The youngest Best Actress nominee is Keisha Castle-Hughes (Australia), who was 13 in 2004 when she was nominated for her role in *Whale Rider*.

AMAZING FACT

Why Oscar?

The Academy Awards or "Oscars" have been presented since 1929. The actual award is a gold-plated statuette made of antimony, copper, and tin, standing 13.5 in (34.3 cm) high and weighing 8 lb 8 oz (3.85 kg). According to legend, Academy librarian Margaret Herrick named it when she commented, "It looks just like my Uncle Oscar!" The name stuck as a universally recognized symbol of excellence in filmmaking.

the10 LATEST ACTRESSES TO WIN **TWO BEST ACTRESS OSCARS**

	ACTRESS	FIRST WIN	YEAR	SECOND WIN	YEAR
1	Hilary Swank	Boys Don't Cry	1999	Million Dollar Baby*	2004
2	Jodie Foster	The Accused	1988	The Silence of the Lambs*	1991
3	Sally Field	Norma Rae	1979	Places in the Heart	1984
4	Jane Fonda	Klute	1971	Coming Home	1978
5	Glenda Jackson	Women in Love	1970	A Touch of Class	1973
6	Katharine Hepburn	The Lion in Winter	1968	On Golden Pond	1981
7	Katharine Hepburn	Morning Glory	1932–33	Guess Who's Coming to Dinner?	1967
8	Elizabeth Taylor	Butterfield 8	1960	Who's Afraid of Virginia Woolf	1966
9	Ingrid Bergman	Gaslight	1944	Anastasia	1956
10	Vivien Leigh	Gone With the Wind*	1939	A Streetcar Named Desire	1951

* Won Best Picture Oscar

Katharine Hepburn is the only actress to win a third and a fourth Best Actress Oscar. Other double winners were Olivia de Havilland for *To Each His Own* (1946) and *The Heiress* (1949), and Louise Rainer for *The Great Ziegfeld* (1936) and *The Good Earth* (1937). The only actors with doubles are Marlon Brando, Gary Cooper, Tom Hanks, Dustin Hoffman, Fredric March, Jack Nicholson, and Spencer Tracy.

the10 LATEST ACTRESSES TO RECEIVE THREE OR MORE **CONSECUTIVE OSCAR NOMINATIONS**

	ACTRESS	NOMINATIONS*	YEARS
1	Renée Zellweger	3	2001–03
2	Glenn Close	3	1982–84
3	Meryl Streep	3	1981–83
4	Jane Fonda	3	1977–79
5	Elizabeth Taylor	4	1957–60
6	Deborah Kerr	3	1956–58
7	Thelma Ritter	4	1950–53
8	Jennifer Jones	4	1943–46
9	Ingrid Bergman	3	1943–45
10	Greer Garson	5	1941–45

* In Best Actress or Best Supporting Actress categories

top10 **OLDEST** OSCAR-WINNING ACTRESSES

	ACTRESS	FILM	YEAR	YRS	AGE* MTHS	DAYS
1	Jessica Tandy	Driving Miss Daisy#	1989	80	9	21
2	Peggy Ashcroft	A Passage to India	1984	77	3	3
3	Katharine Hepburn	On Golden Pond	1981	74	4	11
4	Ruth Gordon	Rosemary's Baby	1968	72	5	15
5	Margaret Rutherford	The VIPs	1963	71	11	2
6	Helen Hayes	Airport	1970	70	5	25
7	Ethel Barrymore	None But the Lonely Heart	1944	65	7	0
8	Josephine Hull	Harvey	1950	65	1	26
9	Judi Dench	Shakespeare in Love#	1998	64	3	12
10	Beatrice Straight	Network	1976	62	7	26

* Age at time of award ceremony
# Won Best Picture Oscar

All of the Academy Awards listed here are for Best Supporting Actress, apart from Katharine Hepburn, whose win was in the Best Actress category (as were all 12 of the nominations she received from 1933 to 1981).

Jessica Tandy is the oldest nominee and oldest winner of a Best Actor/Actress Academy Award ever. Among the female seniors who received nominations but did not win are May Robson, 75 when she was nominated as Best Actress in *Lady for a Day* (1933), and Gloria Stuart (87) for Best Supporting Actress in *Titanic* (1997).

the10 LATEST **BEST ACTRESS** OSCAR WINNERS

YEAR	ACTRESS	FILM
2005	Reese Witherspoon	Walk the Line
2004	Hilary Swank	Million Dollar Baby*
2003	Charlize Theron	Monster
2002	Nicole Kidman	The Hours
2001	Halle Berry	Monster's Ball
2000	Julia Roberts	Erin Brockovich
1999	Hilary Swank	Boys Don't Cry
1998	Gwyneth Paltrow	Shakespeare in Love*
1997	Helen Hunt	As Good As It Gets
1996	Frances McDormand	Fargo

* Won Best Picture Oscar

⬅ ***Something to smile about***
Following her Best Actress Oscar win for Walk the Line, *Reese Witherspoon is reported to be receiving $29 million for her role in* Our Family Trouble *(2007), beating Julia Roberts's $24 million for* Mona Lisa Smile *(2003) and making her Hollywood's highest-paid female star.*

DVD & Video

top10 BESTSELLING **DVDS AND VIDEOS** IN THE US, 2005

	DVD/VIDEO	COMBINED SALES ($)
1	The Incredibles	289,000,000
2	Madagascar	190,000,000
3	Star Wars: Revenge of the Sith	175,000,000
4	Shark Tale	171,000,000
5	The Polar Express	163,000,000
6	National Treasure	146,000,000
7	Meet the Fockers	134,000,000
8	Batman Begins	125,000,000
9 =	Ray	122,000,000
=	War of the Worlds	122,000,000

Source: Video Business

Four of the Top 10 are animated films. Their success on DVD and video closely follows that of the original film releases, *The Incredibles* having already earned over $250 million at the US box office and $630 worldwide. It sold in a DVD to VHS ratio of 87:13, pointing to the inexorable decline of the latter format.

top10 **BESTSELLING DVDS** IN THE US

	FILM / YEAR OF RELEASE*	REVENUE ($)#
1	Finding Nemo, 2003	320,400,000
2	Shrek 2, 2004	316,000,000
3	The Incredibles, 2005	285,000,000
4	The Lord of the Rings: The Two Towers, 2003	280,500,000
5	The Lord of the Rings: The Fellowship of the Ring, 2002	257,300,000
6	The Lord of the Rings: The Return of the King, 2004	257,000,000
7	Pirates of the Caribbean: The Curse of the Black Pearl, 2003	235,300,000
8	Spider-Man, 2002	215,300,000
9	Star Wars trilogy, 2004	215,000,000
10	Monsters, Inc., 2002	202,000,000

* Of DVD release
\# In release year

top10 **MOST-RENTED TV SHOWS** IN THE US ON DVD AND VHS, 2005

	SHOW	REVENUE ($)
1	Chappelle's Show – Season 2	60,100,000
2	Lost – Season 1	43,300,000
3	Family Guy – Season 4	30,100,000
4	Oprah: 20th Anniversary	29,800,000
5	The Sopranos – Season 5	29,100,000
6	Sex and the City – Complete series	28,400,000
7	Seinfeld – Season 4	28,200,000
8	Band of Brothers	27,300,000
9	Family Guy – Seasons 1 & 2	26,900,000
10	Desperate Housewives – Season 1	23,500,000

Source: Video Business

Dave Chapelle's comedy show debuted on Comedy Central in 2003 and has since become the second highest-rated (after *South Park*) on the network, with the Season 1 DVD ranked as the bestselling TV show DVD of all time. *Lost* is notable in being a success not only on TV and video, but also among the first shows to be made available for digital download.

top10 **VIDEO GAMES** IN THE US, 2005

	TITLE / PLATFORM	PUBLISHER
1	Madden NFL 06 (PS2)	Electronic Arts
2	Pokémon Emerald (GBA)	Nintendo
3	Gran Turismo 4 (PS2)	Sony Computer Entertainment
4	Madden NFL 06 (Xbox)	Electronic Arts
5	NCAA Football 06 (PS2)	Electronic Arts
6	Star Wars: Battlefront II (PS2)	LucasArts
7	MVP Baseball 2005 (PS2)	Electronic Arts
8	Star Wars: Episode III – Revenge of the Sith (PS2)	LucasArts
9	NBA Live 06 (PS2)	Electronic Arts
10	Lego Star Wars: The Video Game (PS2)	Eidos Interactive

Source: The NPD Group

Madden NFL 06 was the 2005 release of a game with a long pedigree, having been first released for PCs in 1989 as *John Madden Football*. In addition to the success of its PlayStation 2 version, it is available for most other popular platforms. In 2004, its makers secured a five-year exclusive licence with the NFL, ensuring the likelihood of its annual releases being among America's bestselling computer games until at least 2009.

top10 VIDEO PIRACY COUNTRIES

	COUNTRY	EST. LOSSES, 2005* ($)
1	Mexico	483,000,000
2	Russia	266,000,000
3	China	244,000,000
4	Italy	161,000,000
5	Thailand	149,000,000
6	Brazil	120,000,000
7	Canada	118,000,000
8 =	Hungary	102,000,000
=	Poland	102,000,000
10	Taiwan	98,000,000

* Or latest year for which data available, including illicit broadcasts

Source: International Intellectual Property Alliance (IIPA)

The Washington, DC-based International Intellectual Property Alliance estimates the losses to the business and entertainment software, movie, music, and publishing industries as a result of piracy. Those affecting the motion picture business – primarily through illicit DVDs – totaled almost $2 billion in 2005.

⬆ Incredible success
The DVD and video of The Incredibles *earned over $50 million in rentals within four months of its March 2005 release in the US, its retail version becoming the biggest seller of the year.*

top10 BESTSELLING DVDS IN THE US, 2005

	DVD	UNITS	REVENUE ($)
1	The Incredibles	15,600,000	285,000,000
2	Madagascar	10,400,000	186,000,000
3	Star Wars: Episode III – Revenge of the Sith	9,600,000	175,000,000
4	Shark Tale	9,400,000	160,000,000
5	The Polar Express	8,600,000	157,000,000
6	National Treasure	7,800,000	143,000,000
7	Meet the Fockers	7,800,000	130,000,000
8	Batman Begins	6,800,000	125,000,000
9	Ray	6,600,000	119,000,000
10	War of the Worlds	6,400,000	113,000,000

Source: Video Business

top10 MOST-RENTED DVDS IN THE USA, 2005

	DVD	REVENUE ($)
1	National Treasure	64,850,000
2	Hitch	64,470,000
3	Meet the Fockers	60,650,000
4	Ladder 49	52,510,000
5	The Longest Yard	51,580,000
6	Guess Who	50,610,000
7	The Notebook	49,350,000
8	Without a Paddle	48,680,000
9	Monster-in-Law	48,540,000
10	The Pacifier	48,100,000

Source: Video Business

TV & Radio

top10 TV COUNTRIES

	COUNTRY	TV HOUSEHOLDS*
1	China	186,679,720
2	USA	112,884,190
3	India	83,512,900
4	Japan	48,842,920
5	Brazil	48,390,910
6	Russia	40,822,010
7	Germany	38,715,850
8	Indonesia	34,334,330
9	UK	25,269,160
10	France	24,369,170
	World total	*1,176,019,000*

* Households with color TVs, 2007 forecast

Source: Euromonitor

Both local and national television in China is state controlled. CCTV (China Central Television), the principal broadcaster, offers 16 channels with a wide range of programs.

top10 LONGEST-RUNNING TV SERIES IN THE US*

	PROGRAM / BROADCAST	EPISODES
1	Gunsmoke, 1955–75	633
2	Lassie, 1954–73	588
3	Death Valley Days, 1952–72	452
4	Ozzie and Harriet, 1952–66	435
5	Bonanza, 1959–72	430
6	My Three Sons, 1960–72	369
7	The Simpsons, 1989–	365
8	Alfred Hitchcock Presents, 1955–65	361
9	Law and Order, 1990–	360
10	Dallas, 1978–1991	357

* To January 7, 2006

In *Gunsmoke*, James Arness played the same character, Marshal Matt Dillon, for the entire 20-year run, a record until overtaken in 2004 by Kelsey Grammer as Dr. Frasier Crane.

the10 LATEST WINNERS OF THE PRIMETIME EMMY "OUTSTANDING LEAD ACTRESS IN A COMEDY SERIES" AWARD

SEASON ENDING	ACTRESS / PROGRAM
2005	Felicity Huffman, Desperate Housewives
2004	Sarah Jessica Parker, Sex and the City
2003	Debra Messing, Will & Grace
2002	Jennifer Aniston, Friends
2001	Patricia Heaton, Everybody Loves Raymond
2000	Patricia Heaton, Everybody Loves Raymond
1999	Helen Hunt, Mad About You
1998	Helen Hunt, Mad About You
1997	Helen Hunt, Mad About You
1996	Helen Hunt, Mad About You

This Emmy has been awarded since 1974, when it was first won by Mary Tyler Moore for her eponymous show.

the10 LATEST WINNERS OF THE PRIMETIME EMMY "OUTSTANDING LEAD ACTOR IN A COMEDY SERIES" AWARD

SEASON ENDING	ACTOR / PROGRAM
2005	Tony Shalhoub, Monk
2004	Kelsey Grammer, Frasier
2003	Tony Shalhoub, Monk
2002	Ray Romano, Everybody Loves Raymond
2001	Eric McCormack, Will & Grace
2000	Michael J. Fox, Spin City
1999	John Lithgow, 3rd Rock from the Sun
1998	Kelsey Grammer, Frasier
1997	John Lithgow, 3rd Rock from the Sun
1996	John Lithgow, 3rd Rock from the Sun

Alan Alda won the first Emmy in this category for his role as Hawkeye Pierce in the long-running series *M*A*S*H*.

top10 TV AUDIENCES IN THE US

	PROGRAM	DATE	TOTAL	VIEWERS %
1	M*A*S*H Special	Feb 28, 1983	50,150,000	60.2
2	Dallas	Nov 21, 1980	41,470,000	53.3
3	Roots Part 8	Jan 30, 1977	36,380,000	51.1
4	Super Bowl XVI	Jan 24, 1982	40,020,000	49.1
5	Super Bowl XVII	Jan 30, 1983	40,480,000	48.6
6	XVII Winter Olympics	Feb 23, 1994	45,690,000	48.5
7	Super Bowl XX	Jan 26, 1986	41,490,000	48.3
8	Gone With the Wind Pt.1	Nov 7, 1976	33,960,000	47.7
9	Gone With the Wind Pt.2	Nov 8, 1976	33,750,000	47.4
10	Super Bowl XII	Jan 15, 1978	34,410,000	47.2

Source: Nielsen Media Research

In 2006, there are an estimated 110.2 million television households in the USA, so a single ratings point would represent one percent, or 1,102,000 households, and so on. Historically, as more households acquired television sets, audiences generally increased, but the rise in channel choice and use of recording has checked this trend, and it is unlikely that such high percentages will ever again be attained.

top10 LONGEST-RUNNING PROGRAMS ON NATIONAL PUBLIC RADIO

	PROGRAM	FIRST BROADCAST
1	All Things Considered	1971
2	Weekend All Things Considered	1974
3	Fresh Air with Terry Gross	1977
4	Marian McPartland's Piano Jazz	1978
5	Morning Edition	1979
6	Weekend Edition/Saturday with Scott Simon	1985
7	Performance Today	1987
8	Weekend Edition/Sunday with Liane Hansen	1987
9	Car Talk	1987
10	Talk of the Nation	1991

Source: National Public Radio

All Things Considered, the longest-running National Public Radio program, was first broadcast on May 3, 1971.

top10 COUNTRIES WITH THE MOST TV STATIONS

	COUNTRY	TELEVISION STATIONS
1	Russia	7,306
2	China	3,240
3	USA	2,218
4	Serbia and Montenegro	771
5	Turkey	635
6	France	584
7	India	562
8	South Africa	556
9	Germany	373
10	Norway	360

Source: Central Intelligence Agency, "The World Factbook 2006"

In addition to these, some countries have numerous "repeater stations" that relay signals: Germany has 8,042, the UK 3,523, Norway 2,729, and Turkey 2,394.

top10 RADIO-OWNING COUNTRIES

	COUNTRY	RADIOS PER 1,000 POPULATION, 2003*
1	Norway	3,324
2	Sweden	2,811
3	USA	2,109
4	Australia	1,999
5	Finland	1,624
6	UK	1,445
7	Denmark	1,400
8	Estonia	1,136
9	Canada	1,047
10	South Korea	1,034
	World average	*419*

* Or latest year for which data available

Source: World Bank, "World Development Indicators 2005"

These figures stand in sharp contrast to those of developing countries, such as Malawi, where the ratio is four radios per 1,000, or 250 people to every radio.

top10 CABLE TELEVISION COUNTRIES

	COUNTRY	CABLE TV SUBSCRIBERS, 2004
1	China	96,380,000
2	USA	66,100,200
3	Japan	24,683,900
4	Germany	19,350,000
5	South Korea	14,200,000
6	Canada	7,608,300
7	Russia	6,396,400
8	Netherlands	6,390,000
9	Argentina	5,900,000
10	Taiwan	4,856,000
	World	*317,047,500*

Source: International Telecommunication Union, "World Telecommunication/ICT Development Report 2006"

At present, over 30 percent of TV households in China receive TV via cable, and in the lead-up to the 2008 Beijing Olympic Games, the country is developing its digital cable TV network.

COMMERCIAL WORLD

8

Workers of the World

COMPANIES WITH THE **MOST EMPLOYEES**

COMPANY / COUNTRY	INDUSTRY	EMPLOYEES
1 Wal-Mart Stores, USA	Retail	1,400,000
2 McDonald's, USA	Fast food restaurants	438,000
3 Siemens, Germany	Electronics	430,000
4 Carrefour, France	Food markets	419,040
5 PetroChina, China	Oil and gas	417,229
6 China Petroleum and Chemical, China	Oil and gas	400,513
7 DaimlerChrysler, Germany	Automotive	384,723
8 United Parcel Service, USA	Package delivery	355,000
9 Deutsche Post, Germany	Post and courier	348,781
10 Volkswagen Group, Germany	Automotive	334,873

Source: Forbes 2000

TYPES OF JOB IN THE US 100 YEARS AGO*

JOB SECTOR	EMPLOYEES
1 Farmers and farm managers	5,763,000
2 Farm laborers and foremen	5,125,000
3 Operatives and kindred workers (miners, etc.)	3,720,000
4 Laborers (except farm and mine)	3,620,000
5 Craftsmen and foremen	3,062,000
6 Private household workers	1,579,000
7 Salesworkers	1,307,000
8 Professional and technical workers	1,234,000
9 Service workers (except private household)	1,047,000
10 Clerical workers	877,000
Total labor force	*29,030,000*

* From 1900 Census

Source: US Bureau of the Census

COUNTRIES WITH THE HIGHEST PROPORTION OF **CHILD WORKERS**

	COUNTRY	PERCENTAGE OF 5–14-YEAR-OLDS AT WORK, 1999–2004		
		MALE	FEMALE	TOTAL
1	= Niger	69	64	66
	= Nigeria	69	64	66
3	Togo	62	59	60
4	= Burkina Faso	n/a	n/a	57
	= Chad	60	55	57
	= Ghana	57	57	57
	= Sierra Leone	57	57	57
8	Central African Rep.	54	57	56
9	Guinea-Bissau	54	54	54
10	= Cameroon	52	50	51
	= Costa Rica	71	29	51
	World average	*18*	*17*	*18*

Source: UNICEF, "The State of the World's Children 2006"

Despite the efforts of bodies such as the International Labor Organization's International Program on the Elimination of Child Labor to combat the exploitation of children in often dangerous work, over half the children in these countries work. According to UNICEF's definitions, this may be a combination of economic activity (paid labor) and of domestic work (in the case of those aged 12 to 14), totaling at least 14 hours of economic activity or a combination of 42 hours of economic activity and domestic work per week.

OCCUPATIONS IN THE US

OCCUPATION	EMPLOYEES, 2004
1 Retail salespersons	4,260,150
2 Cashiers	3,451,100
3 Office clerks, general	2,943,750
4 Laborers and freight, stock, and material movers	2,388,930
5 Registered nurses	2,338,530
6 Waiters and waitresses	2,228,950
7 Combined food preparation and serving workers, including fast food	2,223,820
8 Janitors and cleaners (except maids and housekeeping cleaners)	2,119,800
9 Customer service representatives	2,036,090
10 Bookkeeping, accounting, and auditing clerks	1,777,320
All occupations	*129,146,700*

Source: Bureau of Labor Statistics

In the past century, the US labor force has more than quadrupled. At the same time, it has undergone a seismic shift away from being dominantly agriculture-based (with over one-third of the entire population engaged in farming) to a service economy, while manufacturing industries have declined, become automated, or shifted overseas.

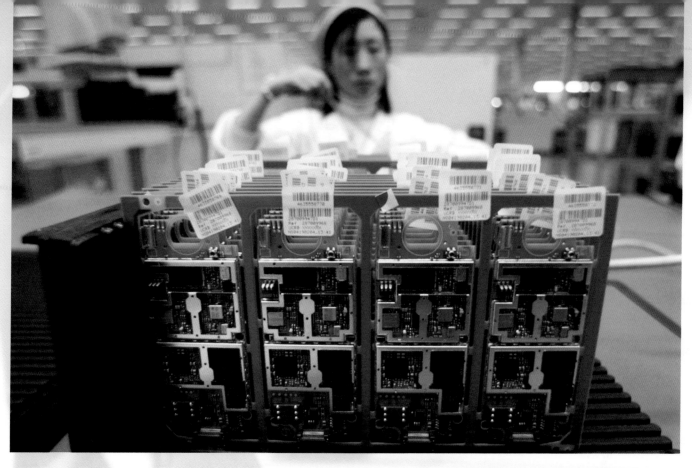

↑ Flying start
With China's vast labor force at its disposal, Ningbo Bird has become the country's largest manufacturer of mobile phones.

top10 COUNTRIES WITH THE **MOST WORKERS**

	COUNTRY	WORKERS*
1	China	778,100,000
2	India	472,000,000
3	USA	147,401,000
4	Indonesia	105,700,000
5	Brazil	82,590,000
6	Russia	71,680,000
7	Japan	66,660,000
8	Bangladesh	64,020,000
9	Nigeria	54,360,000
10	Vietnam	45,740,000

* 2004 or latest year available; based on people aged 15–64, currently employed; exclude unpaid groups

Source: Central Intelligence Agency/International Labor Organization

Labor statistics include employed and unemployed people aged 15 to 64, but exclude unpaid groups, such as students, housewives, and retired people. In some countries, those involved in subsistence agriculture or informal work activities often go unrecorded.

top10 COUNTRIES WORKING THE **LONGEST HOURS**

	COUNTRY	AVERAGE ANNUAL HOURS PER PERSON*
1	Korea	2,380
2	Czech Republic	1,986
3	Poland	1,983
4	Slovakia	1,958
5	Greece	1,925
6	Mexico	1,848
7	New Zealand	1,826
8	USA	1,824
9	Australia	1,816
10	Hungary	1,806

* In employment, 2004 – total (employed and self-employed) or employed only, depending on source; OECD countries only

Source: Organization for Economic Cooperation and Development (OECD)

Historical assessments of hours worked suggest that in the mid19th century, the average US employee worked up to 3,650 hours a year, equivalent to 10 hours a day.

the10 COUNTRIES WITH **HIGHEST UNEMPLOYMENT**

	COUNTRY	EST. % LABOUR FORCE UNEMPLOYED, 2005*
1	Nauru	90
2	Liberia	85
3	=Turkmenistan	60
	=Zimbabwe	60
5	=Djibouti	50
	=East Timor	50
	=Tajikistan	50
	=Zambia	50
9	Senegal	48
10	Nepal	47
	USA	5.1

* Or latest year; in those countries for which data available

Source: CIA, "World Factbook, 2005"

The Global Economy

top10 COUNTRIES BY GROSS NATIONAL INCOME

COUNTRY / % OF WORLD TOTAL / GNI, 2004 ($)

1 USA 30.5 $12,150,931,000,000

2 Japan 11.9 $4,749,910,000,000

3 Germany 6.2 $2,488,974,000,000

4 UK 5.1 $2,016,393,000,000

5 France 4.7 $1,858,731,000,000

6 China 4.2 $1,676,846,000,000

7 Italy 3.8 $1,503,562,000,000

8 Canada 2.3 $905,629,000,000

World total 100.0
$39,833,561,000,000

Source: World Bank

9 Spain 2.2 $875,817,000,000

10 Mexico 1.8 $703,080,000,000

top10 SOURCES OF US GOVERNMENT INCOME

	SOURCE	EST. FEDERAL RECEIPTS, 2007 ($)
1	Individual income tax	1,071,169,000,000
2	Old-age and survivors' insurance	537,849,000,000
3	Corporation income tax	229,817,000,000
4	Hospital insurance	182,412,000,000
5	Disability insurance	91,333,000,000
6	Unemployment insurance	46,159,000,000
7	Highway trust funds	41,027,000,000
8	Airport and airway trust funds	11,996,000,000
9	Alcohol excise taxes	8,171,000,000
10	Tobacco excise taxes	7,590,000,000

top10 AREAS OF FEDERAL GOVERNMENT EXPENDITURE

	AREA OF EXPENDITURE	EST. EXPENDITURE, 2007 ($)
1	Social security	571,219,000,000
2	National defense	448,878,000,000
3	Medicare	386,355,000,000
4	Income security	361,854,000,000
5	Health	282,654,000,000
6	Interest payments	244,955,000,000
7	Education, training, employment, and social services	86,323,000,000
8	Veterans/benefits and services	72,484,000,000
9	Transportation	71,159,000,000
10	Administration of justice	42,286,000,000

AMAZING FACT

Tax Return
Total US Government income 100 years ago stood at $666 million. By 1957, it had escalated to $79.99 billion, and in 2007 it is projected to reach $2.3 trillion, or $7,784 for every US inhabitant – over 3,500 times its level in 1907.

top10 RICHEST COUNTRIES

	COUNTRY	GDP* PER CAPITA, 2004 ($)
1	Luxembourg	69,737
2	Norway	54,600
3	Switzerland	49,300
4	Ireland	45,675
5	Denmark	44,808
6	Iceland	41,804
7	USA	39,935
8	Sweden	38,493
9	Qatar	37,610
10	Netherlands	37,326
	World average	*6,411*

* Gross Domestic Product

Source: International Monetary Fund

the10 POOREST COUNTRIES

	COUNTRY	GDP* PER CAPITA, 2004 ($)
1	Burundi	90
2	Dem. Rep. of the Congo	111
3	Ethiopia	113
4	Myanmar	127
5	Eritrea	139
6	Malawi	152
7	Guinea-Bissau	177
8	Sierra Leone	202
9	Rwanda	214
10	Afghanistan	228

Source: International Monetary Fund

the10 COUNTRIES MOST IN DEBT

	COUNTRY	EXTERNAL DEBT*, 2004–05 ($)
1	USA	8,837,000,000,000
2	UK	7,107,000,000,000
3	Germany	3,626,000,000,000
4	France	2,826,000,000,000
5	Italy	1,682,000,000,000
6	Netherlands	1,645,000,000,000
7	Japan	1,545,000,000,000
8	Spain	1,249,000,000,000
9	Ireland	1,049,000,000,000
10	Belgium	980,000,000,000

*External debt is total public and private debt owed to nonresidents repayable in foreign currency, goods, or services.

Source: World Bank

top10 MOST EXPENSIVE COUNTRIES IN WHICH TO BUY A BIG MAC

COUNTRY / COST OF A BIG MAC* ($)

A regular feature of the magazine since 1986, *The Economist*'s Big Mac index is based on the concept of "Purchasing Power Parity," which assumes that an identical amount of goods and services should cost the same in all countries, comparing the value of countries' currencies against the standard US price of a Big Mac. The cheapest in the survey was China at $1.30, with Malaysia at $1.47.

1 Switzerland $4.93

2 Denmark $4.49

3 Sweden $4.15

4 UK $3.32

5 USA $3.15

6 New Zealand $3.08

7 Turkey $3.07

8 Canada $3.01

9 Chile $2.98

10 Brazil $2.74

* As at Jan 9, 2006; of those countries surveyed

Source: "The Economist"/McDonald's price data

Personal Wealth

top10 RICHEST MEN*

NAME / COUNTRY (CITIZEN / RESIDENCE)	SOURCE	NET WORTH ($)
1 William H. Gates III, USA	Microsoft (software)	50,000,000,000
2 Warren Edward Buffett, USA	Berkshire Hathaway (investments)	42,000,000,000
3 Carlos Slim Helu, Mexico	Communications	30,000,000,000
4 Ingvar Kamprad, Sweden/ Switzerland	Ikea (home furnishings)	28,000,000,000
5 Lakshmi Mittal, India/UK	Mittal Steel	25,500,000,000
6 Paul Gardner Allen, USA	Microsoft (software)	22,000,000,000
7 Bernard Arnault, France	Louis Vuitton (luxury goods)	21,500,000,000
8 Prince Alwaleed Bin Talal Alsaud, Saudi Arabia	Investments	20,000,000,000
9 Li Ka-shing, China	Diverse investments	18,800,000,000
10 Roman Abramovich, Russia	Oil	18,200,000,000

* Excluding rulers and family fortunes

Source: Forbes magazine, "The World's Richest People," 2006

⊙ *World's wealthiest*
Bill Gates has devoted a large share of his vast fortune to research, to rid the world of killer diseases.

top10 RICHEST WOMEN*

NAME / COUNTRY	SOURCE	NET WORTH ($)
1 Liliane Bettencourt, France	L'Oréal	16,000,000,000
2 Alice L. Walton, USA	Wal-Mart	15,700,000,000
3 Helen R. Walton, USA	Wal-Mart	15,600,000,000
4 Abigail Johnson, USA	Finance	12,500,000,000
5 =Anne Cox Chambers, USA	Media/entertainment	12,400,000,000
=Barbara Cox Anthony, USA	Media/entertainment	12,400,000,000
7 Jacqueline Mars, USA	Candy	10,000,000,000
8 Susanne Klatten, Germany	Pharmaceuticals	8,100,000,000
9 Johanna Quandt, Germany	BMW cars	6,100,000,000
10 Shari Arison, Israel	Carnival cruise line	5,200,000,000

* Excluding rulers and family fortunes

Source: Forbes magazine, "The World's Richest People," 2006

top10 HIGHEST-EARNING **CELEBRITIES**

CELEBRITY*	PROFESSION	EARNINGS# ($)
1 George Lucas	Film producer/director	290,000,000
2 Oprah Winfrey	Talk show host/producer	225,000,000
3 Mel Gibson	Film producer/director/actor	185,000,000
4 Tiger Woods	Golfer	87,000,000
5 Steven Spielberg	Film producer/director	80,000,000
6 Dan Brown	Author	76,500,000
7 Jerry Bruckheimer	Film and TV producer	66,000,000
8 Michael Schumacher, Germany	Racing driver	60,000,000
9 J.K. Rowling, UK	Author	59,100,000
10 David Copperfield	Magician	57,000,000

* All USA, unless otherwise stated
# June 2004–June 2005

Source: Forbes magazine, "The Celebrity 100," 2005

top10 HIGHEST-EARNING **DEAD CELEBRITIES**

CELEBRITY	PROFESSION	DEATH	EARNINGS, 2005 ($)
1 Elvis Presley	Rock star	Aug 16, 1977	37,000,000
2 Charles Schultz	"Peanuts" cartoonist	Feb 12, 2000	35,000,000
3 John Lennon	Rock star	Dec 8, 1980	22,000,000
4 Andy Warhol	Artist	Feb 22, 1987	16,000,000
5 Theodor "Dr Seuss" Geisel	Author	Sep 24, 1991	10,000,000
6 Marlon Brando	Actor	Jul 1, 2004	9,000,000
7 = Marilyn Monroe	Actress	Aug 5, 1962	8,000,000
= J.R.R. Tolkien	Author	Sep 2, 1973	8,000,000
9 = Irving Berlin	Songwriter	Sep 22, 1989	7,000,000
= Johnny Cash	Musician	Sep 12, 2003	7,000,000
= George Harrison	Rock star	Nov 29, 2001	7,000,000

Source: Forbes magazine, "Top-Earning Dead Celebrities," 2005

➔ By George!
George Lucas's success as the writer and producer of the Star Wars series and other blockbusters places him first among the world's richest celebrities.

Brand Image

top10 MOST-ADVERTISED PRODUCTS*

	CATEGORY	WORLD ADVERTISING SPENDING, 2004 ($)
1	Automotive	22,693,000,000
2	Personal care	17,163,000,000
3	Entertainment and media	10,459,000,000
4	Pharmaceuticals	8,197,000,000
5	Food	8,015,000,000
6	Soft drinks	3,331,000,000
7	Electronics	3,186,000,000
8	Restaurants	3,148,000,000
9	Cleaning products	2,982,000,000
10	Computers	2,973,000,000

* Based on total worldwide spend by Top 100 companies

Source: "Advertising Age Global Marketing Report 2005"

World spending on advertising in all media in 2004 totaled $94 billion, with that for 2005 forecast to top $100 billion. Falling outside the Top 10, but with spending in excess of $2 billion each, are telecommunications, retailers, alcohol, and financial services.

top10 GLOBAL RETAILERS

	COMPANY / COUNTRY	RETAIL SALES, 2004 ($)*
1	Wal-Mart, USA	285,222,000,000
2	Carrefour, France	89,568,000,000
3	Home Depot, USA	73,094,000,000
4	Metro, Germany	69,781,000,000
5	Tesco, UK	62,505,000,000
6	Kroger, USA	56,434,000,000
7	Costco, USA	47,146,000,000
8	Target, USA	45,682,000,000
9	Koninklijke, Netherlands	44,793,000,000
10	Aldi, Germany	42,906,000,000

* Financial year

Source: Deloitte/Stores "2006 Global Powers of Retailing"

In 2004 the total sales of the Top 250 global retailers was $2.84 trillion – almost one-third of the estimated world total of $9 trillion. Even those at the bottom of this extended list sold over $2.3 billion-worth of goods.

top10 MOST VALUABLE GLOBAL BRANDS

	BRAND NAME*	INDUSTRY	BRAND VALUE, 2005 ($)
1	Coca-Cola	Beverages	67,525,000,000
2	Microsoft	Technology	59,941,000,000
3	IBM	Technology	53,376,000,000
4	General Electric	Diversified	46,996,000,000
5	Intel	Technology	35,588,000,000
6	Nokia, Finland	Technology	26,452,000,000
7	Disney	Leisure	26,441,000,000
8	McDonald's	Food retail	26,014,000,000
9	Toyota, Japan	Automobiles	24,837,000,000
10	Marlboro	Tobacco	21,189,000,000

* All US-owned unless otherwise stated

Source: Interbrand/BusinessWeek

Brand consultants Interbrand use a method of estimating value that takes account of the profitability of individual brands within a business (rather than the companies that own them), as well as such factors as their potential for growth.

top10 OLDEST FAMILY BUSINESSES IN THE WORLD

	BUSINESS	LOCATION	FOUNDED
1	Kongo Gumi (construction)	Osaka, Japan	578
2	Hoshi Ryokan (hotel)	Komatsu, Japan	718
3	= Château de Goulaine (vineyard)	Haute Goulaine, France	1000
	= Fonderia Pontificia Marinelli (bell foundry)	Agnone, Italy	1000
5	Barone Ricasoli (wine and olive oil)	Siena, Italy	1141
6	Barovier & Tos (glassmaking)	Venice, Italy	1295
7	Pilgrim Haus (hotel)	Soest, Germany	1304
8	Richard de Bas (papermaking)	Ambert d'Auvergne, France	1326
9	Torrini Firenze (goldsmiths)	Florence, Italy	1369
10	Antinori (winemakers)	Florence, Italy	1385

Source: "Family Business Magazine"

⬆ *Great Wal-Mart of China*
The world's largest retailer Wal-Mart opened its first store in China in 1996. It now operates 47 units in 22 cities, employing over 25,000 people.

top10 **OLDEST ESTABLISHED** BUSINESSES IN THE US

	COMPANY* / LOCATION	BUSINESS	FOUNDED
1	White Horse Tavern, Newport, RI	Dining	1673
2	J.E. Rhoads & Sons, Branchburg, NJ	Conveyor belts	1702
3	Wayside Inn, Sudbury, MA	Inn	1716
4	Elkridge Furnace Inn, Elkridge, MD	Inn	1744
5	Moravian Book Shop, Bethlehem, PA	Retail, books	1745
6	Pennsylvania Hospital, Philadelphia, PA	Hospital	1751
7	Philadelphia Contributorship, Philadelphia, PA	Insurance	1752
8	New Hampshire Gazette, Portsmouth, NH	Newspaper	1756
9	Hartford Courant, Hartford, CT	Newspaper	1764
10	Bachman Funeral Home, Strasburg, PA	Funeral home	1769

* Excluding mergers and transplanted companies

Source: Institute for Family Enterprise, Bryant College

top10 **GLOBAL** INDUSTRIAL COMPANIES

	COMPANY / LOCATION	SECTOR	ANNUAL REVENUE ($)
1	Exxon Mobil, USA	Oil, gas	328,213,000,000
2	Wal-Mart Stores, Inc., USA	Retailing	312,427,000,000
3	Royal Dutch/Shell Group, Netherlands/UK	Oil, gas, chemicals	306,731,000,000
4	BP plc, UK	Oil, gas	249,465,000,000
5	General Motors Corp., USA	Motor vehicles	192,604,000,000
6	Chevron Corp., USA	Oil, gas	184,922,000,000
7	Ford Motor Co., USA	Motor vehicles	178,101,000,000
8	DaimlerChrysler AG, Germany	Motor vehicles	177,040,000,000
9	Toyota Motor, Japan	Motor vehicles	173,086,000,000
10	ConcoPhillips Company, USA	Oil, gas	162,405,000,000

Source: Forbes, 2,000 Largest Companies, April 17, 2006

Food Business

top10 GLOBAL CONFECTIONERY BRANDS

	BRAND	COMPANY	% OF GLOBAL MARKET
1	M&Ms	Mars Inc.	2.13
2	Snickers	Mars Inc.	2.10
3	Reese's	Hershey Foods Corp.	1.35
4	Milka	Kraft Foods Inc.	1.08
5	Orbit	William Wrigley Jr. Co.	0.97
6 =	Extra	William Wrigley Jr. Co.	0.94
=	Mars	Mars Inc.	0.94
8	Trident	Cadbury Schweppes plc	0.86
9	Lindt	Chocoladefabriken Lindt & Sprüngli AG	0.83
10	Artisanal	Artisanal	0.81

Source: Euromonitor, "The World Market for Packaged Food, 2005"

top10 FAST FOOD COMPANIES

	COMPANY	GLOBAL SALES ($)
1	McDonald's Corp.	45,933,000,000
2	Yum! Brands Inc. (KFC, Taco Bell, Pizza Hut)	24,418,000,000
3	Burger King Corp.	11,100,000,000
4	Wendy's International Inc.	10,200,000,000
5	Doctor's Associates Inc. (Subway)	6,523,000,000
6	Darden Restaurants Inc.	4,655,000,000
7	Domino's Pizza Inc.	4,193,000,000
8	Brinker International Inc.	3,807,000,000
9	Applebee's International Inc.	3,593,000,000
10	Starbucks Corp.	3,450,000,000

Source: Euromonitor, "The World Market for Consumer Foodservice, 2004"

top10 RESTAURANT CHAINS IN THE US

	CHAIN	OUTLETS
1	Subway	17,918
2	McDonald's	13,578
3	Burger King	7,596
4	Pizza Hut	7,500
5	Taco Bell	5,982
6	Starbucks	5,827
7	Wendy's	5,779
8 =	KFC	5,450
=	7-Eleven	5,297
10	Domino's Pizza	5,008

Source: Euromonitor, "Consumer Foodservice in the US, 2005"

top10 FAST FOOD COUNTRIES

COUNTRY / GLOBAL SALES ($)

1 USA 148,612,900,000

2 Japan 13,875,100,000

3 Canada 12,709,900,000

4 UK 12,062,400,000

5 China 9,765,000,000

6 South Korea 9,249,100,000

7 Germany 7,376,900,000

8 Australia 5,685,300,000

9 Brazil 4,967,300,000

10 India 4,914,700,000

Source: Euromonitor, "The World Market for Consumer Foodservice, 2004"

top10 FAST FOOD OUTLETS IN THE US

TYPE*	OUTLETS	SALES ($)
1 Burgers	76,066	85,130,200,000
2 Bakery products	66,303	29,715,700,000
3 Chicken	17,105	14,400,600,000
4 Latin American	14,670	10,881,500,000
5 Convenience stores	23,122	6,764,300,000
6 Asian	6,125	3,795,700,000
7 Pizza	6,004	2,593,300,000
8 Ice cream	14,208	2,525,500,000
9 Fish	3,772	2,129,300,000
10 Middle Eastern	555	214,800,000

* Excluding nonspecific categories

Source: Euromonitor, "Consumer Foodservice in the US, 2005"

⊙ Exotic eating
The first Chinese restaurant in the US was the Macao and Woosung, which opened in San Francisco, California, during the 1849 Gold Rush. The first pizzeria, Lombardi's, was established in New York in 1905.

top10 COUNTRIES THAT SPEND THE MOST EATING OUT

COUNTRY	GLOBAL SALES ($)
1 USA	175,946,100,000
2 China	100,310,000,000
3 Japan	89,197,700,000
4 India	87,167,200,000
5 Italy	36,233,400,000
6 France	31,740,400,000
7 South Korea	15,297,100,000
8 Germany	14,514,100,000
9 Spain	14,013,300,000
10 Mexico	11,725,500,000

Source: Euromonitor, "The World Market for Consumer Foodservice, 2004"

top10 COUNTRIES WITH MOST CAFÉS AND BARS

COUNTRY	GLOBAL SALES ($)
1 Japan	55,222,900,000
2 Italy	24,094,200,000
3 USA	13,951,100,000
4 UK	12,398,500,000
5 South Korea	11,273,800,000
6 Spain	11,059,500,000
7 Brazil	7,436,100,000
8 Canada	3,618,200,000
9 Thailand	3,307,100,000
10 India	2,787,700,000

Source: Euromonitor, "The World Market for Consumer Foodservice, 2004"

top10 STREET FOOD SALES COUNTRIES*

COUNTRY	GLOBAL SALES ($)
1 USA	9,357,200,000
2 Thailand	4,699,000,000
3 Venezuela	3,541,200,000
4 India	3,295,000,000
5 UK	2,064,500,000
6 Brazil	1,411,200,000
7 Germany	1,313,700,000
8 France	855,600,000
9 Russia	824,600,000
10 Indonesia	817,900,000

* Sales from stalls and kiosks

Source: Euromonitor, "The World Market for Consumer Foodservice, 2004"

Drinks Industry

top10 WINE-PRODUCING COUNTRIES

	COUNTRY	ANNUAL PRODUCTION PINTS	ANNUAL PRODUCTION LITERS
1	France	11,283,230,000	5,338,900,000
2	Italy	10,586,650,000	5,009,300,000
3	Spain	6,445,870,000	3,050,000,000
4	USA	4,057,730,000	1,920,000,000
5	Argentina	3,346,570,000	1,583,500,000
6	China	2,282,470,000	1,080,000,000
7	Australia	2,147,850,000	1,016,300,000
8	Germany	1,879,020,000	889,100,000
9	Portugal	1,646,130,000	778,900,000
10	South Africa	1,367,580,000	647,100,000
	World total	55,948,040,000	26,473,000,000

Source: Commission for Distilled Spirits

The rise of New World and Southern Hemisphere wine-producing countries is the most notable recent development, ending the industry's centuries-old domination by European vineyards – since 1980, Australia's production has increased by over 200 percent.

top10 BEER-PRODUCING COUNTRIES

	COUNTRY	ANNUAL PRODUCTION PINTS	ANNUAL PRODUCTION LITERS
1	China	49,833,970,000	23,580,000,000
2	USA	49,572,330,000	23,456,200,000
3	Germany	22,895,730,000	10,833,600,000
4	Brazil	18,175,240,000	8,600,000,000
5	Russia	15,216,480,000	7,200,000,000
6	Japan	14,646,700,000	6,930,400,000
7	Mexico	13,462,360,000	6,370,000,000
8	UK	11,977,060,000	5,667,200,000
9	Spain	5,887,930,000	2,786,000,000
10	Poland	5,515,970,000	2,610,000,000
	World total	305,011,170,000	144,322,500,000

Source: Commission for Distilled Spirits

top10 BREWERS

	BREWERY / COUNTRY	PRODUCTION, 2004 PINTS	PRODUCTION, 2004 LITERS
1	InBev (Belgium)	38,823,160,000	18,370,000,000
2	SABMiller (USA)	36,984,500,000	17,500,000,000
3	Anheuser-Busch (USA)	30,475,230,000	14,420,000,000
4	Heineken (Netherlands)	23,585,540,000	11,160,000,000
5	Carlsberg (Denmark)	14,159,780,000	6,700,000,000
6	Molson Coors (USA)	12,173,180,000	5,760,000,000
7	Scottish & Newcastle (UK)	10,884,010,000	5,150,000,000
8	Modelo (Mexico)	9,045,350,000	4,280,000,000
9	Tsingtao (China)	7,840,710,000	3,710,000,000
10	Kirin (Japan)	7,608,240,000	3,600,000,000

top10 CHAMPAGNE-IMPORTING COUNTRIES

	COUNTRY	BOTTLES IMPORTED, 2003
1	UK	34,465,159
2	USA	18,957,031
3	Germany	12,053,665
4	Belgium	9,143,810
5	Italy	8,506,287
6	Switzerland	5,596,549
7	Japan	5,013,705
8	Netherlands	2,575,838
9	Spain	2,158,056
10	Australia	1,659,441

Source: Comité Interprofessionnel du Vin de Champagne (CIVC)

top10 CARBONATED SOFT DRINK CONSUMERS

	COUNTRY	ANNUAL CONSUMPTION PER CAPITA	
		PINTS	LITERS
1	USA	413.8	195.8
2	Mexico	266.3	126.0
3	Norway	257.8	122.0
4	Ireland	256.6	121.4
5	Canada	247.5	117.1
6	Belgium	231.0	109.3
7	Australia	218.1	103.2
8	Netherlands	210.9	99.8
9	Chile	210.7	99.7
10	Spain	207.7	98.3
	World average	*60.2*	*28.5*

Source: Euromonitor

In marked contrast to the countries in the Top 10, India (4.2 pints/2 liters per capita), Indonesia (6.8 pints/3.2 liters), and many African nations are among the lowest consumers in a world market that in 2003 drank 379.1 billion pints (179.4 billion liters) – equivalent to almost 60,000 Olympic swimming pools full!

top10 BOTTLED WATER DRINKERS

	COUNTRY	CONSUMPTION PER CAPITA, 2003	
		PINTS	LITERS
1	Italy	374.3	177.1
2	Spain	331.2	156.7
3	France	322.3	152.5
4	Mexico	321.4	152.1
5	Belgium	275.0	130.1
6	Germany	250.6	118.6
7	Switzerland	236.7	112.0
8	Austria	207.1	98.0
9	Portugal	204.6	96.8
10	Argentina	172.0	81.4
	World average	*48.4*	*22.9*
	USA	*151.3*	*71.6*

Source: Euromonitor

Worldwide consumption of bottled mineral water has more than doubled in the past decade, hitting a 2003 total of 305.4 billion pints (144.5 billion liters).  Although its total consumption of 38.7 billion pints (18.3 billion liters) makes it the world's leading overall consumer, on a per capita basis the USA remains unusually absent from the Top 10.

top10 COFFEE-PRODUCING COUNTRIES

	COUNTRY	PRODUCTION, 2005 (TONNES)
1	Brazil	2,179,270
2	Vietnam	990,000
3	Indonesia	762,006
4	Colombia	682,580
5	Mexico	310,861
6	India	275,400
7	Ethiopia	260,000
8	Guatemala	216,600
9	Honduras	190,640
10	Uganda	186,000
	World total	*7,718,531*

Source: Food and Agriculture Organization of the United Nations

top10 TEA-PRODUCING COUNTRIES

	COUNTRY	PRODUCTION, 2005 (TONNES)
1	China	900,500
2	India	852,800
3	Sri Lanka	308,090
4	Kenya	295,000
5	Turkey	202,000
6	Indonesia	171,410
7	Vietnam	110,000
8	Japan	100,000
9	Argentina	64,000
10	Bangladesh	55,627
	World total	*3,200,877*

Source: Food and Agriculture Organization of the United Nations

Farming

top10 COUNTRIES WITH THE MOST FARMLAND

COUNTRY	AGRICULTURAL LAND, 2003 (ACRES)
1 China	13,710,645,000
2 Australia	10,860,264,000
3 USA	10,114,007,000
4 Brazil	651,369,000
5 Russia	534,431,000
6 Kazakhstan	513,445,000
7 India	446,776,000
8 Saudi Arabia	429,464,000
9 Sudan	332,603,000
10 Mongolia	322,472,000
World total	12,289,534,000

Source: Food and Agriculture Organization of the United Nations

top10 WHEAT-PRODUCING COUNTRIES

COUNTRY	PRODUCTION, 2005 (TONNES)
1 China	96,160,250
2 India	72,000,000
3 USA	57,105,552
4 Russia	45,500,000
5 France	36,922,000
6 Canada	25,546,900
7 Australia	24,067,000
8 Germany	23,578,000
9 Pakistan	21,591,400
10 Turkey	21,000,000
World total	626,466,585

Source: Food and Agriculture Organization of the United Nations

top10 CATTLE COUNTRIES

COUNTRY	CATTLE, 2005
1 Brazil	192,000,000
2 India	185,000,000
3 China	115,229,500
4 USA	95,848,000
5 Argentina	50,768,000
6 Ethiopia	38,500,000
7 Sudan	38,325,000
8 Mexico	31,476,600
9 Australia	26,900,000
10 Colombia	25,000,000
World	1,355,187,580

Source: Food and Agriculture Organization of the United Nations

top10 COUNTRIES WHERE SHEEP MOST OUTNUMBER PEOPLE

COUNTRY	SHEEP POPULATION, 2005	HUMAN POPULATION, 2005	SHEEP PER PERSON
1 New Zealand	40,009,000	4,035,461	9.91
2 Australia	106,000,000	20,090,437	5.27
3 Mongolia	11,686,400	2,791,272	4.18
4 Mauritania	8,850,000	3,086,859	2.86
5 Uruguay	9,712,000	3,415,920	2.84
6 Turkmenistan	13,000,000	4,952,081	2.62
7 Iceland	454,000	296,737	1.52
8 Namibia	2,900,000	2,030,692	1.42
9 Sudan	48,000,000	40,187,486	1.19
10 Ireland	4,556,700	4,015,676	1.13
World average	1,079,735,160	6,451,058,790	0.16
USA	6,090,000	295,734,134	0.02

Source: Food and Agriculture Organization of the United Nations/ US Census Bureau

➲ You say "tomato"...
The tomato – botanically a fruit – is celebrated in the annual Tomatina festival in Buñol, Valencia, Spain, during which some 30,000 people do battle with over 220,000 lb (100,000 kg) of tomatoes.

top10 **FRUIT** CROPS

CROP	PRODUCTION, 2005 (TONNES)
1 Tomatoes	124,748,292
2 Watermelons	95,292,051
3 Bananas	72,464,562
4 Grapes	66,533,393
5 Apples	63,488,907
6 Oranges	59,858,474
7 Coconuts	55,037,524
8 Plantains	33,407,921
9 Cantaloupes and other melons	28,321,159
10 Mangoes	27,966,749

Source: Food and Agriculture Organization of the United Nations

top10 **VEGETABLE** CROPS

CROP*	PRODUCTION, 2005 (TONNES)
1 Sugar cane	1,293,220,050
2 Potatoes	321,974,152
3 Sugar beets	241,985,317
4 Soybeans	209,531,558
5 Sweet potatoes	129,888,827
6 Cabbages	69,480,505
7 Onions (dry)	57,594,350
8 Cucumbers and pickles	41,743,840
9 Yams	39,897,327
10 Eggplants	30,517,767

* Excluding cereals

Source: Food and Agriculture Organization of the United Nations

This includes only vegetables grown for human and annual consumption. Among nonfood vegetable crops, cotton is the most important, with a total annual production of over 70 million tonnes, while rubber, tobacco, jute, and other fibers are also economically significant.

top10 **RICE*-PRODUCING** COUNTRIES

COUNTRY	PRODUCTION, 2005 (TONNES)
1 China	184,254,000
2 India	129,000,000
3 Indonesia	53,984,592
4 Bangladesh	40,054,000
5 Vietnam	36,341,000
6 Thailand	27,000,000
7 Myanmar	22,000,000
8 Philippines	14,800,000
9 Brazil	13,140,900
10 Japan	10,989,000
World total	*614,654,895*

* Paddy rice only

Source: Food and Agriculture Organization of the United Nations

top10 COUNTRIES WITH THE **MOST AGRICULTURAL WORKERS**

COUNTRY	% OF TOTAL WORKFORCE	AGRICULTURAL WORKERS, 2003
1 China	65	510,573,000
2 India	58	273,515,000
3 Indonesia	46	50,254,000
4 Bangladesh	53	39,466,000
5 Vietnam	66	28,582,000
6 Pakistan	46	26,173,000
7 Ethiopia	81	25,056,000
8 Myanmar	69	18,671,000
9 Nigeria	31	15,178,000
10 Turkey	44	14,779,000
World	*43*	*1,340,460,000*
USA	*1.9*	*2,848,000*

Source: Food and Agriculture Organization of the United Nations

Rich Resources

top10 COUNTRIES WITH THE MOST GOLD

	COUNTRY	GOLD RESERVES* (TROY OUNCES)	(TONNES)
1	USA	261,497,718	8,133.5
2	Germany	110,206,169	3,427.8
3	France	90,681,049	2,820.5
4	Italy	78,827,086	2,451.8
5	Switzerland	41,477,618	1,290.1
6	Japan	24,601,715	765.2
7	Netherlands	22,341,521	694.9
8	China	19,290,420	600.0
9	Spain	14,715,375	457.7
10	Taiwan	13,609,391	423.3

* As at Mar 2006

Source: World Gold Council

Gold reserves are the government holdings of gold in each country – which are often far greater than the gold owned by private individuals. In the days of the "Gold Standard," this provided a tangible measure of a country's wealth, guaranteeing the convertibility of its currency, and determined such factors as exchange rates. Though less significant today, gold reserves remain a component in calculating a country's international reserves, alongside its holdings of foreign exchange and SDRs (Special Drawing Rights).

AMAZING FACT

Gold Record

The world's total gold reserves are estimated at 30,836.8 tonnes, worth about $583 billion. However, these account for only one-fifth of all the gold ever mined, estimated at some 150,000 tonnes, the rest having been made into jewellery and coins, or used in dentistry and industrial processes. The total – worth $2.84 trillion at today's price – could be stretched into a wire that would circle the Earth 9 million times, but if made into a sphere would be only 82 ft (25 m) in diameter.

top10 GOLD-PRODUCING COUNTRIES

	COUNTRY	% OF WORLD TOTAL	2004 PRODUCTION (TONNES)
1	South Africa	13.9	342.7
2	USA	10.6	261.8
3	Australia	10.5	258.4
4	China	8.8	217.3
5	Russia	7.4	181.6
6	Peru	7.0	173.2
7	Canada	5.2	128.5
8	Indonesia	4.6	114.2
9	Uzbekistan	3.4	83.7
10	Ghana	2.3	57.6
	World total	*100.0*	*2,464.4*

Source: Gold Fields Mineral Services Ltd, "Gold Survey 2004"

Since hitting an all-time high of 619.5 tonnes in 1993, the output by South Africa, the world's dominant gold producer, has steadily declined, as has that of Australia, which peaked at 313.2 tonnes in 1997.

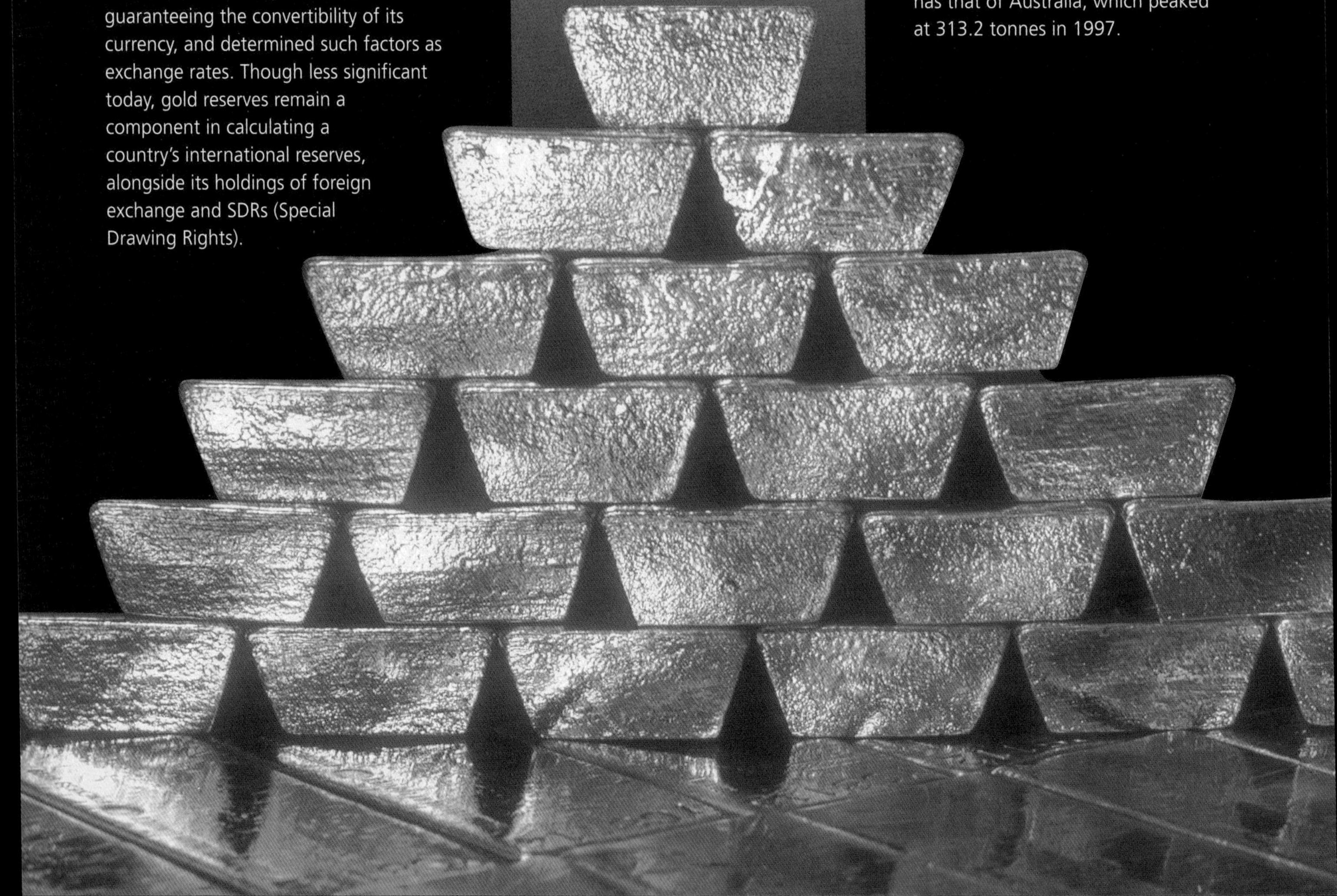

top10 **SILVER** PRODUCERS

	COUNTRY	PRODUCTION, 2004 (TONNES)
1	Peru	3,060
2	Mexico	2,700
3	China*	2,450
4	Australia	2,237
5	Chile	1,360
6	Canada	1,336
7	Russia*	1,277
8	= Poland	1,250
	= USA	1,250
10	Kazakhstan	733
	World total	*19,700*

* Estimated

Source: US Geological Survey, "Minerals Yearbook"

top10 **PLATINUM** PRODUCERS

	COUNTRY	PRODUCTION, 2004 (LBS)	(KILOS)
1	South Africa	352,767	160,013
2	Russia*	79,366	36,000
3	Canada	15,432	7,000
4	Zimbabwe	9,784	4,438
5	USA	8,906	4,040
6	Colombia	3,086	1,400
7	Japan	1,719	780
8	Finland	1,102	500
9	Poland	44	20
10	Serbia & Montenegro	11	5
	World total	*471,788*	*214,000*

* Estimated

Source: US Geological Survey, "Minerals Yearbook"

top10 **URANIUM-PRODUCING** COUNTRIES

	COUNTRY	PRODUCTION, 2004 (TONNES)
1	Canada	11,597
2	Australia	8,982
3	Kazakhstan	3,719
4	Niger	3,282
5	Russia*	3,200
6	Namibia	3,038
7	Uzbekistan	2,016
8	USA	846
9	Ukraine*	800
10	South Africa	755
	World total	*40,219*

* Estimated

Source: World Nuclear Association

In 2004 some 7,200 tonnes, or 18 percent of the world's uranium output, came from a single mine: McArthur River in Canada.

top10 **DIAMOND** PRODUCERS (BY VOLUME)

COUNTRY
VALUE, 2004 ($) / VOLUME, 2004 (CARATS)

1 Russia
$1,989,000,000 / 35,000,000

2 Botswana
$2,940,000,000 / 31,125,000

3 Dem. Rep. of Congo
$790,000,000 / 29,000,000

4 Australia
$343,000,000 / 20,673,000

5 South Africa
$1,458,000,000 / 14,233,000

6 Canada
$1,646,000,000 / 12,618,000

7 Angola
$1,300,000,000 / 7,500,000

8 Namibia
$698,000,000 / 2,011,000

9 Ghana
$26,000,000 / 900,000

10 Brazil
$35,000,000 / 700,000

Source: Diamond Facts 2005

Oil Essentials

top10 COUNTRIES WITH THE **GREATEST** OIL-REFINING CAPACITY

	COUNTRY	BARRELS PER DAY, 2005*
1	USA	17,042,000
2	China	5,818,000
3	Russia	5,412,000
4	Japan	4,531,000
5	South Korea	2,598,000
6	India	2,513,000
7	Germany	2,314,000
8	Italy	2,294,000
9	Saudi Arabia	2,061,000
10	France	1,977,000

* One barrel = 159 liters

Source: BP Statistical Review of World Energy 2005

In 2005, the refining capacity of the USA was reduced by the effects of Hurricane Katrina. In September 2005, British entrepreneur Sir Richard Branson announced he was considering building an oil refinery in Newfoundland to counteract the escalating fuel costs borne by his Virgin Atlantic airline.

top10 **OIL-CONSUMING** COUNTRIES

	COUNTRY	CONSUMPTION, 2004 (TONNES)
1	USA	937,600,000
2	China	308,600,000
3	Japan	241,500,000
4	Russia	128,500,000
5	Germany	123,600,000
6	India	119,300,000
7	South Korea	104,800,000
8	Canada	99,600,000
9	France	94,000,000
10	Italy	89,500,000
	World total	*3,767,100,000*

Source: BP Statistical Review of World Energy 2005

the10 COUNTRIES WITH **LONGEST** OIL PIPELINES

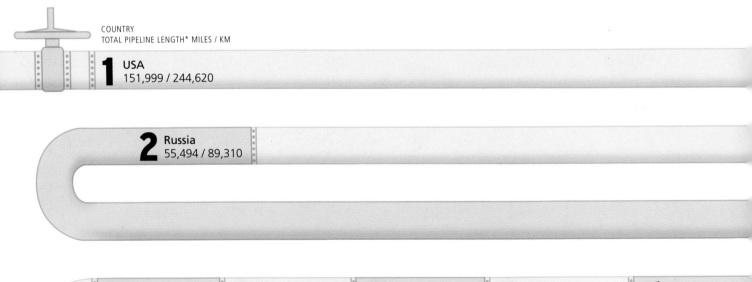

COUNTRY
TOTAL PIPELINE LENGTH* MILES / KM

1 USA
151,999 / 244,620

2 Russia
55,494 / 89,310

10 Kazakhstan
6,311 / 10,158

9 Brazil
6,405 / 10,308

8 UK
6,769 / 10,894

7 India
6,946 / 11,180

6 Iran
9,981 / 16,064

* Oil + petroleum products   Source: Central Intelligence Agency, "The World Factbook 2005"

↑ **Strategic supply** *The pipeline from the Iraq oilfield of Kirkuk carries oil to Ceyhan, Turkey.*

top10 COUNTRIES WITH THE GREATEST OIL RESERVES

COUNTRY	2004 RESERVES (TONNES)
1 Saudi Arabia	36,100,000,000
2 Iran	18,200,000,000
3 Iraq	15,500,000,000
4 Kuwait	13,600,000,000
5 United Arab Emirates	13,000,000,000
6 Venezuela	11,100,000,000
7 Russia	9,900,000,000
8 Kazakhstan	5,400,000,000
9 Libya	5,100,000,000
10 Nigeria	4,800,000,000
USA	*3,600,000,000*

Source: BP Statistical Review of World Energy 2005

top10 OIL-PRODUCING COUNTRIES

COUNTRY	PRODUCTION, 2004 (TONNES)
1 Saudi Arabia	505,900,000
2 Russia	458,700,000
3 USA	329,800,000
4 Iran	202,600,000
5 Mexico	190,700,000
6 China	174,500,000
7 Venezuela	153,500,000
8 Norway	149,900,000
9 Canada	147,600,000
10 United Arab Emirates	125,800,000
World total	*3,867,900,000*

Source: BP Statistical Review of World Energy 2005

top10 OIL IMPORTERS, 2004

COUNTRY	NET OIL IMPORTS (MILLION BARRELS PER DAY)*
1 USA	12.1
2 Japan	5.3
3 China	2.9
4 Germany	2.4
5 South Korea	2.2
6 France	1.9
7 Italy	1.7
8 Spain	1.6
9 India	1.5
10 Taiwan	1.0

* One barrel = 159 liters; weight depends on oil type

3 Mexico 23,829 / 38,350

5 China 11,034 / 17,758

4 Canada 14,641 / 23,564

Energy & the Environment

top10 MOST ENVIRONMENTALLY FRIENDLY COUNTRIES

	COUNTRY	ESI RANKING*
1	Finland	75.1
2	Norway	73.4
3	Uruguay	71.8
4	Sweden	71.7
5	Iceland	70.8
6	Canada	64.4
7	Switzerland	63.7
8	Guyana	62.9
9	= Argentina	62.7
	= Austria	62.7
	USA	*52.9*

* Based on calculations of 20 key indicators in five categories: environmental systems, environmental stresses, human vulnerability to environmental risks, a society's institutional capacity to respond to environmental threats, and a nation's stewardship of the shared resources of the global commons

Source: World Economic Forum, "2005 Environmental Sustainability Index"

⊛ Burning issue
The industrial and domestic output of greenhouse gases is one of the most important items on the world's agenda for a sustainable future.

the10 LEAST ENVIRONMENTALLY FRIENDLY COUNTRIES

	COUNTRY	ESI RANKING
1	North Korea	29.2
2	Taiwan	32.7
3	Turkmenistan	33.1
4	Iraq	33.6
5	Uzbekistan	34.4
6	Haiti	34.8
7	Sudan	35.9
8	Trinidad and Tobago	36.3
9	Kuwait	36.6
10	Yemen	37.3

Source: World Economic Forum, "2005 Environmental Sustainability Index"

top10 COUNTRIES WITH MOST NUCLEAR REACTORS

	COUNTRY	REACTORS
1	USA	104
2	France	59
3	Japan	54
4	Russia	30
5	UK	27
6	Germany	19
7	South Korea	18
8	Canada	16
9	India	14
10	Ukraine	13

Source: International Atomic Energy Agency

top10 CARBON DIOXIDE-EMITTING COUNTRIES

	COUNTRY	CO_2 EMISSIONS PER CAPITA, 2003 (TONNES OF CO_2)
1	Qatar	45.73
2	United Arab Emirates	44.11
3	Bahrain	30.89
4	Singapore	27.89
5	Trinidad and Tobago	24.92
6	Luxembourg	24.28
7	Kuwait	23.17
8	USA	19.95
9	Australia	19.10
10	Canada	19.05
	World average	*3.98*

Source: Energy Information Administration

CO_2 emissions derive from three principal sources – fossil fuel burning, cement manufacturing, and gas flaring – as well as various industrial processes. In the past 60 years, increasing industrialization in many countries has resulted in huge increases in carbon output, a trend that most countries are now actively attempting to reverse, with some degree of success among the former leaders in this Top 10, although the USA remains the worst offender in total, with over 5.9 billion tonnes released in 2003.

top10 ELECTRICITY-CONSUMING COUNTRIES

	COUNTRY	CONSUMPTION KW/HR, 2003
1	USA	4,054,000,000,000
2	China	1,907,000,000,000
3	Japan	1,038,000,000,000
4	Russia	914,000,000,000
5	India	633,000,000,000
6	Germany	594,000,000,000
7	Canada	587,000,000,000
8	France	562,000,000,000
9	UK	396,000,000,000
10	Brazil	365,000,000,000
	World total	*16,661,000,000,000*

top10 COAL-CONSUMING COUNTRIES

	COUNTRY	CONSUMPTION, 2004 (TONNES OF OIL EQUIVALENT)
1	China	956,900,000
2	USA	564,300,000
3	India	204,800,000
4	Japan	120,800,000
5	Russia	105,900,000
6	South Africa	94,500,000
7	Germany	85,700,000
8	Poland	57,700,000
9	Australia	54,400,000
10	South Korea	53,100,000
	World total	*2,778,200,000*

Source: "BP Statistical Review of World Energy 2005"

top10 ALTERNATIVE POWER*-PRODUCING COUNTRIES

	COUNTRY	PRODUCTION KW/HR, 2003
1	USA	93,530,000,000
2	Germany	31,400,000,000
3	Japan	27,850,000,000
4	Spain	16,270,000,000
5	Brazil	16,240,000,000
6	Italy	11,330,000,000
7	Finland	10,120,000,000
8	Philippines	9,420,000,000
9	Canada	8,540,000,000
10	Denmark	7,950,000,000
	World	*310,100,000,000*

* Includes biomass, geothermal, solar, and wind electric power

Source: Energy Information Administration

the10 MOST COMMON TYPES OF WASTE IN THE US

	MATERIAL	TONS, 2003
1	Paper and paperboard	83,100,000
2	Yard wastes	28,600,000
3	Food wastes	27,550,000
4	Plastics	26,650,000
5	Metals	18,820,000
6	Wood	13,630,000
7	Glass	12,470,000
8	Textiles	10,590,000
9	Rubber and leather	6,820,000
10	Other wastes	4,320,000
	Total (including materials not in Top 10)	*236,170,000*

Source: Franklin Associates Ltd/Environmental Protection Agency

This annual survey of solid waste accounts for materials disposed of by residents and commercial organizations, but excludes mining, agriculture, industrial processes, demolition, sewage, and junked automobiles. It is equivalent to 4.4 lb (2 kg) a day for every US citizen.

Communications

top10 COUNTRIES SENDING AND RECEIVING THE **MOST LETTERS** (DOMESTIC)

COUNTRY	ITEMS OF MAIL HANDLED, 2004
1 USA	194,000,000,000
2 Japan	24,923,245,000
3 Germany	21,744,000,000
4 UK	21,030,000,000
5 France	17,571,000,000
6 Canada	10,714,615,000*
7 India	8,747,400,000#
8 China	8,235,030,000
9 Brazil	7,957,580,000
10 Italy	6,574,465,610
World total	*429,869,376,225*

* Estimate
# 2003

Source: Universal Postal Union

top10 COUNTRIES WITH THE **MOST POSTAL STAFF**

COUNTRY	FULL-TIME POSTAL STAFF, 2004
1 USA	707,485
2 China	401,000
3 Germany	379,828
4 Russia	309,962
5 India*	262,752
6 France	230,046
7 Great Britain	150,370
8 Italy	147,354
9 Japan	114,158
10 Brazil	107,836
World total	*3,964,642*

* 2003

Source: Universal Postal Union

the10 FIRST CITIES AND COUNTRIES TO ISSUE **POSTAGE STAMPS**

CITY / COUNTRY	STAMPS ISSUED
1 Great Britain	May 1840
2 New York City, USA	Feb 1842
3 Zurich, Switzerland	Mar 1843
4 Brazil	Aug 1843
5 Geneva, Switzerland	Oct 1843
6 Basle, Switzerland	Jul 1845
7 USA	Jul 1847
8 Mauritius	Sep 1847
9 Bermuda	Unknown 1848
10 France	Jan 1849

The first adhesive postage stamps issued in the UK were the Penny Blacks that went on sale on May 1, 1840. The first issued in the US were designed for local delivery (as authorized by an 1836 Act of Congress) and produced by the City Despatch Post, New York City, inaugurated on February 15, 1842, and later that year incorporated into the US Post Office Department. After a further Act in 1847, the rest of the United States followed suit and the Post Office Department issued its first national stamps: a 5-cent Benjamin Franklin stamp and a 10-cent George Washington stamp, both of which first went on sale in New York City on July 1, 1847. By the time they were withdrawn, 3,712,200 and 891,000, respectively, had been issued.

AMAZING FACT

The First Airmail

The first-ever airmail letter was sent on January 7, 1785 by William Franklin, the son of US statesman Benjamin Franklin, to his son William Temple Franklin. It was carried in a balloon piloted by French balloonist Jean-Piere Blanchard and American doctor John Jeffries, from Dover, UK to the Felmores Forest, France. The letter is now in the collection of the American Philosophical Society.

top10 COMPUTER COUNTRIES

	COUNTRY	COMPUTERS, 2004
1	USA	223,810,000
2	Japan	69,200,000
3	China	52,990,000
4	Germany	46,300,000
5	UK	35,890,000
6	France	29,410,000
7	South Korea	26,200,000
8	Italy	22,650,000
9	Canada	22,390,000
10	Brazil	19,350,000
	World total	*822,150,000*

Source: Computer Industry Almanac Inc.

top10 COUNTRIES WITH THE MOST INTERNET USERS

	COUNTRY	EST. NO. OF INTERNET USERS, 2005
1	USA	203,576,811
2	China	103,000,000
3	Japan	78,050,000
4	Germany	47,127,725
5	India	39,200,000
6	UK	37,800,000
7	South Korea	32,570,000
8	Italy	28,870,000
9	France	25,614,899
10	Brazil	22,320,000
	World total	*972,828,001*

Source: Internet World Stats

top10 CELL PHONE COUNTRIES

	COUNTRY	MOBILE SUBSCRIBERS PER 100
1	Luxembourg	138.17
2	Hong Kong	118.77
3	Sweden	108.47
4	Italy	108.19
5	Czech Republic	105.64
6	Israel	105.25
7	Norway	103.60
8	UK	102.16
9	Slovenia	100.51
10	Taiwan	100.31
	World average	*27.61*

Source: International Telecommunications Union, "World Telecommunication/ICT Development Report 2006"

This is the ratio of cell phone subscriptions to population – Taiwan, for example, has just over 100 phones per 100 people. For countries showing an even higher average "teledensity," these figures may include people who have taken out new subscriptions but have not canceled their old ones, so the original numbers are still counted in the statistics.

top10 COUNTRIES WITH THE MOST TELEPHONES

	COUNTRY	TELEPHONE LINES PER 100	TOTAL, 2004
1	China	23.98	311,756,000
2	USA	60.60	177,947,000
3	Japan	46.00	58,788,000
4	Germany	66.15	54,574,000
5	India	4.07	43,960,000
6	Brazil	23.46	42,382,000
7	Russia	27.47	36,616,000
8	France	56.04	33,870,200
9	UK	56.35	33,700,000
10	South Korea	55.31	26,595,100
	World	*18.89*	*1,203,247,200*

Source: International Telecommunications Union, "World Telecommunication/ICT Development Report 2006"

Of the world's telephone lines, Asia has 538,981,500, Europe 327,580,000, the Americas 295,306,500, Africa 25,925,000, and Oceania 13,773,000. In developing countries, cell phones have replaced non-existent, defunct, or inefficent fixed lines, enabling their telephone systems rapidly to adopt 21st-century technology.

TRANSPORTATION & TOURISM

9

Land Speed

DRIVER / CAR	LOCATION	DATE	SPEED MPH	SPEED KM/H
1 Gaston de Chasseloup-Laubat, Jeantaud	Achères, France	Dec 18, 1898	39.24	62.78
2 Camille Jenatzy, Jenatzy	Achères, France	Jan 17, 1899	41.42	66.27
3 Gaston de Chasseloup-Laubat, Jeantaud	Achères, France	Jan 17, 1899	43.69	69.90
4 Camille Jenatzy, Jenatzy	Achères, France	Jan 27, 1899	49.92	79.37
5 Gaston de Chasseloup-Laubat, Jeantaud	Achères, France	Mar 4, 1899	57.60	92.16
6 Camille Jenatzy, Jenatzy	Achères, France	Apr 29, 1899	65.79	105.26
7 Leon Serpollet, Serpollet	Nice, France	Apr 13, 1902	75.06	120.09
8 William Vanderbilt, Mors	Albis, France	Aug 5, 1902	76.08	121.72
9 Henri Fournier, Mors	Dourdan, France	Nov 5, 1902	76.60	122.56
10 M. Augières, Mors	Dourdan, France	Nov 17, 1902	77.13	123.40

The official Land Speed Record was set and broken five times within a year. The first six holders were rival racers Comte Gaston de Chasseloup-Laubat (France) and Camille Jenatzy (Belgium). The trial, held under the aegis of the Automobile Club de France over a 1.2-mile (2-km) course at Achères, near Paris, was open to any vehicle – both the Jeantaud and the Jenatzy (nicknamed La Jamais Contente/"Never Satisfied") were electrically powered. Leon Serpollet, the first driver to beat them, drove a steam-powered car. US millionaire William Vanderbilt was the first to hold the record driving a petrol-engined vehicle.

the10 **LATEST HOLDERS** OF THE LAND SPEED RECORD

DRIVER / CAR	DATE	SPEED MPH	SPEED KM/H
1 Andy Green (UK), ThrustSSC*	Oct 15, 1997	763.04	1,227.99
2 Richard Noble (UK), Thrust2*	Oct 4, 1983	633.47	1,013.47
3 Gary Gabelich (USA), The Blue Flame	Oct 23, 1970	622.41	995.85
4 Craig Breedlove (USA), Spirit of America – Sonic 1	Nov 15, 1965	600.60	960.96
5 Art Arfons (USA), Green Monster	Nov 7, 1965	576.55	922.48
6 Craig Breedlove (USA), Spirit of America – Sonic 1	Nov 2, 1965	555.48	888.76
7 Art Arfons (USA), Green Monster	Oct 27, 1964	536.71	858.73
8 Craig Breedlove (USA), Spirit of America	Oct 15, 1964	526.28	842.04
9 Craig Breedlove (USA), Spirit of America	Oct 13, 1964	468.72	749.95
10 Art Arfons (USA), Green Monster	Oct 5, 1964	434.02	694.43

* Location: Black Rock Desert, Nevada; all other speeds were achieved at Bonneville Salt Flats, Utah

Having gained the Land Speed Record on August 23, 1939, British driver John Cobb broke it again on September 16, 1947, when he achieved a land speed of 394.20 mph (630.72 km/h) in his Railton Mobil Special, at Bonneville Salt Flats, Utah. Cobb was killed in 1952 in an attempt on the water speed record, but his land record stood until 1963, since when it has been successively broken and now stands at over double its prewar figure.

⬆ *The speed of sound*
RAF pilot Andy Green (b.1962) smashed the Land Speed Record in ThrustSSC, to become the first to break the sound barrier on land, achieving Mach 1.016.

The first ton
Belgian racer Camille Jenatzy
(1868–1913) celebrates breaking
the Land Speed Record. He did so
on three occasions, becoming the
first driver to exceed 62 mph (100
km/h) in his bullet-shaped electric
vehicle La Jamais Contente.

Water & Air Speed

← Water power
With Dave Villwock at the controls, hydroplane Miss Budweiser established a new water speed record for a propeller-driven craft.

Since 1928 water speed records have been under the control of the Union Internationale du Yachting Automobile (later Union Internationale Motonautique) and take place over a kilometre course, averaging the speed of runs in both directions. All these record-holders were propeller-driven craft, but since the 1950s, jet-powered boats, which skim over the surface of the water, have achieved consistently faster speeds, with Ken Warby's Spirit of Australia setting the jet record of 317.58 mph (511.11 km/h) on Blowering Dam, New South Wales, Australia, on October 8, 1978.

the10 FIRST HOLDERS OF THE WATER SPEED RECORD

DRIVER / BOAT / LOCATION	DATE	SPEED MPH	SPEED KM/H
1 George Wood (USA), Miss America VII, Detroit River, Michigan	Sep 4, 1928	92.838	149.408
2 Gar Wood (USA), Miss America VII, Indian Creek, Florida	Mar 23, 1929	93.123	149.867
3 Henry Segrave (UK), Miss England II, Lake Windermere, UK	Jun 13, 1930	98.760	158.938
4 Gar Wood, Miss America IX, Indian Creek, Florida	Mar 20, 1931	102.256	164.565
5 Kaye Don (UK), Miss England II, Tigre, Parana River, Argentina	Apr 2, 1931	103.490	166.551
6 Kaye Don, Miss England II, Lake Garda, Italy	Jul 9, 1931	110.223	177.387
7 Gar Wood, Miss America IX, Indian Creek, Florida	Feb 5, 1932	111.712	179.783
8 Kaye Don, Miss England III, Loch Lomond, Scotland	Jul 18, 1932	119.810	192.816
9 Gar Wood, Miss America X, Revier Canal, Detroit, Michigan	Sep 20, 1932	124.910	201.023
10 Malcolm Campbell (UK), Blue Bird K3, Lake Maggiore, Switzerland	Sep 1, 1937	126.320	203.292

the10 LATEST HOLDERS OF THE WATER SPEED RECORD

DRIVER / BOAT / LOCATION	DATE	SPEED MPH	SPEED KM/H
1 Dave Villwock, Miss Budweiser, Lake Oroville, California	Mar 13, 2004	220.493	354.849
2 Russ Wicks, Miss Freei, Lake Washington	Jun 15, 2000	205.494	330.711
3 Roy Duby, Miss US1, Lake Guntersville, Alabama	Apr 17, 1962	200.419	322.543
4 Bill Muncey, Miss Thriftaway, Lake Washington	Feb 16, 1960	192.001	308.996
5 Jack Regas, Hawaii Kai III, Lake Washington	Nov 30, 1957	187.627	301.956
6 Art Asbury, Miss Supertest II, Lake Ontario, Canada	Nov 1, 1957	184.540	296.988
7 Stanley Sayres, Slo-Mo-Shun IV, Lake Washington	Jul 7, 1952	178.497	287.263
8 Stanley Sayres, Slo-Mo-Shun IV, Lake Washington	Jun 26, 1950	160.323	258.015
9 Malcolm Campbell, Bluebird K4, Coniston Water, UK	Aug 19, 1939	141.740	228.108
10 Malcolm Campbell, Bluebird K3, Hallwiler See, Switzerland	Aug 17, 1938	130.910	210.679

↑ Fastest flight
An X-15 traveling faster than a bullet.

top10 **FASTEST** X-15 FLIGHTS

	PILOT	FLIGHT NO.	DATE	MACH*	MPH	KM/H
1	William J. Knight	188	Oct 3, 1967	6.70	4,520	7,274
2	William J. Knight	175	Nov 18, 1966	6.33	4,261	6,857
3	Joseph A. Walker	59	Jun 27, 1962	5.92	4,105	6,606
4	Robert M. White	45	Nov 9, 1961	6.04	4,094	6,589
5	Robert A. Rushworth	97	Dec 5, 1963	6.06	4,018	6,466
6	Neil A. Armstrong	64	Jul 26, 1962	5.74	3,989	6,420
7	John B. McKay	137	Jun 22, 1965	5.64	3,938	6,388
8	Robert A. Rushworth	89	Jul 18, 1963	5.63	3,925	6,317
9	Joseph A. Walker	86	Jun 25, 1963	5.51	3,911	6,294
10	William H. Dana	189	Oct 4, 1967	5.53	3,910	6,293

The columns MPH and KM/H fall under the **SPEED** heading.

* Mach No. varies with altitude – the list is ranked on actual speed

↑ *Pilot William J. Knight and X-15A-2.*

Although some were achieved almost 50 years ago, the speeds attained by the rocket-powered X-15 and X-15A-2 aircraft in a program of 199 flights in the period 1959–68 remain the greatest ever attained by piloted vehicles in the Earth's atmosphere. They were air-launched by being released from B-52 bombers, and thus do not qualify for the official air speed record, for which aircraft must take off and land under their own power. The X-15s attained progressively greater speeds, ultimately more than double that of the now long-standing conventional air speed record, and set an unofficial altitude record (during Flight No. 91 on August 22, 1963, when Joseph A. Walker piloted an X-15 to 354,200 ft/107,960 m – some 67 miles/108 km high).

top10 FASTEST **PRE-JET AIR SPEED** RECORDS

	PILOT / COUNTRY	LOCATION	AIRCRAFT	DATE	MPH	KM/H
1	Fritz Wendel, Germany	Augsburg, Germany	Messerschmitt Me209 V1	Apr 26, 1939	469.221	755.138
2	Hans Dieterle, Germany	Orianenburg, Germany	Heinkel He100 V8	Mar 30, 1939	463.919	746.606
3	Francesco Agello, Italy	Desenzano, Italy	Macchi MC72	Oct 23, 1934	440.682	709.209
4	Francesco Agello, Italy	Desenzano, Italy	Macchi MC72	Apr 10, 1933	423.824	682.078
5	George H. Stainforth, UK	Lee-on-Solent, UK	Supermarine S6B	Sep 29, 1931	407.494	665.798
6	Mario de Bernardi, Italy	Venice, Italy	Macchi M52bis	Mar 30, 1928	318.624	512.776
7	Mario de Bernardi, Italy	Venice, Italy	Macchi M52	Nov 4, 1927	297.817	479.290
8	Florentin Bonnet, France	Istres, France	Bernard V2	Dec 11, 1924	278.457	448.133
9	Alford J. Williams, USA	Mineola, New York	Curtiss R2C-1	Nov 4, 1923	266.584	429.025
10	Harold J. Brow, USA	Mineola, New York	Curtiss R2C-1	Nov 2, 1923	259.478	417.590

The columns MPH and KM/H fall under the **SPEED** heading.

All these aircraft were powered by conventional internal combustion engines. No.1 was the last piston-driven aircraft to gain the official air speed record (approved by the Féderation Aéronautique Internationale), all subsequent record-holders being jets.

Road Works

top10 BESTSELLING CARS OF ALL TIME

	MANUFACTURER / MODEL	YEARS IN PRODUCTION	EST. NO. MADE*
1	Toyota Corolla	1966–	29,000,000
3	Volkswagen Golf	1974–	>22,000,000
2	Volkswagen Beetle	1937–2003#	21,529,464
4	Lada Riva	1972–97	19,000,000
5	Ford Model T	1908–27	16,536,075
6	Honda Civic	1972–	14,920,000
7	Nissan Sunny/Pulsar	1966–94	13,571,100
8	Honda Accord	1976–	12,520,000
9	Ford Escort/Orion	1967–2000	12,000,000
10	Chevy Impala/Caprice	1959–	11,509,165

* To January 1, 2003, except where otherwise indicated
\# Produced in Mexico 1978–2003

top10 MOTOR VEHICLE-OWNING COUNTRIES

	COUNTRY	CARS	COMMERCIAL VEHICLES	TOTAL
1	USA	128,714,022	87,968,915	216,682,937
2	Japan	53,300,000	19,985,000	73,285,000
3	Germany	44,383,323	3,592,054	47,975,377
4	Italy	33,239,029	3,755,552	36,994,581
5	France	28,700,000	5,897,000	34,597,000
6	UK	27,790,025	3,412,086	31,202,111
7	Russia	21,200,000	5,063,000	26,263,000
8	Spain	18,150,880	4,161,104	22,311,984
9	Brazil	15,800,000	4,045,000	19,845,000
10	Canada	17,964,798	728,545	17,783,343
	World total	*561,686,927*	*202,218,380*	*767,905,307*

Source: "Ward's Motor Vehicle Facts & Figures 2003"

As the total number of vehicles on the world's roads has increased, the average ratio of people to cars has fallen from 23 in 1960 to 10.6 per car. In the US there are 2.2 and in the UK 2.1 people per car, but in some countries the ratio is very high: in China it stands as 294 per car and in Myanmar 6,780 people for every car! About two-thirds of the world's vehicles are in the Top 10 countries.

⊕ Beetlemania
The bodies of Beetles on the Volkswagen production line, 1960. Launched in prewar Germany and a byword for reliability, the Beetle became one of the bestselling and most iconic cars of all time. Its distinctive shape was little altered during its unrivaled 66-year manufacturing lifespan.

top10 CAR **PRODUCERS**

COUNTRY	CAR PRODUCTION, 2004*
1 Japan	8,720,385
2 Germany	5,192,101
3 USA	4,229,625
4 France	3,220,329
5 South Korea	3,122,600
6 Spain	2,402,103
7 China	2,316,262
8 Brazil	1,756,166
9 UK	1,646,881
10 Canada	1,335,464

* Provisional figures

Source: OICA Correspondents Survey

top10 CARS **IN THE US**, 2005

CAR	SALES, 2005
1 Ford F-Series	901,463
2 Chevrolet Silverado	705,891
3 Toyota Camry	433,703
4 Dodge Ram	400,543
5 Honda Accord	369,293
6 Honda Civic	308,415
7 Nissam Altima	255,371
8 Chevrolet Impala	246,481
9 Chevrolet Malibu	245,861
10 Chevrolet TrailBlazer	244,150

Source: J.D. Power and Associates, Automotive News Data Center

top10 CAR **MANUFACTURERS**

COMPANY / COUNTRY	CAR PRODUCTION, 2004*
1 General Motors (USA)	8,112,000
2 Ford (USA)	6,526,000
3 Toyota (Japan)	6,241,000
4 Renault-Nissan (France/Japan)	5,328,000
5 Volkswagen group (Germany)	5,024,000
6 DaimlerChrysler (Germany)	4,238,000
7 PSA Peugeot Citröen (France)	3,310,000
8 Honda (Japan)	2,923,000
9 Hyundai (South Korea)	2,697,000
10 Fiat (Italy)	2,078,000

* Including light commercial vehicles

top10 LONGEST **ROAD TUNNELS**

TUNNEL / LOCATION	YEAR COMPLETED	LENGTH FT	LENGTH M
1 Laerdal, Norway	2000	80,413	24,510
2 Zhongnanshan, China	2007*	59,186	18,040
3 St Gotthard, Switzerland	1980	55,505	16,918
4 Arlberg, Austria	1978	45,850	13,972
5 Hsuehshan, Taiwan	2005	42,323	12,900
6 Fréjus, France/Italy	1980	42,306	12,895
7 Mont-Blanc, France/Italy	1965	38,094	11,611
8 Gudvangen, Norway	1991	37,493	11,428
9 Folgefonn, Norway	2001	36,417	11,100
10 Kan-Etsu II (southbound), Japan	1990	36,122	11,010

* Under construction – scheduled completion date

Nos. 1, 3, 4, and 7 have all held the record as "world's longest road tunnel." Previous record-holders include the 19,206-ft (5,854-m) Grand San Bernardo (Italy-Switzerland, 1964), the 16,841-ft (5,133-m) Alfonos XIII or Viella (Spain, 1948), the 10,620-ft (3,237-m) Queensway (Mersey) Tunnel (Liverpool to Birkenhead, UK, 1934), and the 10,453-ft (3,186-m) Col de Tende (France-Italy, 1882), originally built as a rail tunnel and converted in 1928.

Track Records

top10 FASTEST RAILROAD JOURNEYS

JOURNEY* / COUNTRY	TRAIN	DISTANCE		SPEED	
		MILES	KM	MPH	KM/H
1 Lyon-St Exupéry to Aix-en-Provence, France	TGV 6171	179.9	289.6	163.6	263.3
2 Hiroshima to Kokura, Japan	15 Nozomi	119.3	192.0	162.7	261.8
3 Frankfurt Flughafen to Siegburg/Bonn, Germany	17 ICE trains	89.5	144.0	145.1	233.5
4 Brussels Midi to Marseilles-St Charles, Belgium/France	ThalysSoleil	654.9	1,054.0	145.0	233.4
5 Madrid Atocha to Cuidad Atocha, Spain	6 AVE trains	106.1	170.7	127.3	204.8
6 Falköping to Katrineholm, Sweden	X2000 438	130.3	209.7	118.4	190.6
7 Seoul to Taejeon, South Korea	5 KTX trains	96.3	155.0	117.9	189.8
8 Stevenage to Grantham, UK	1 IC255	77.9	125.3	112.5	181.1
9 Roma (Rome) Termini to Firenze (Florence) SMN, Italy	Eurostar 9458	162.2	261.0	103.5	166.6
10 Wilmington to Baltimore, USA	13 Acela Expresses	68.4	110.1	102.6	165.1

* Fastest journey for each country; all those in the Top 10 have other equally or similarly fast services

Source: "Railway Gazette International," 2005 World Speed Survey

> **Bullet train**
> Japan's Shinkansen bullet trains have been in service for over 40 years. Capable of speeds of up to 300 km/h (186 mph), they have consistently maintained the world record for the fastest scheduled rail service.

the10 FIRST COUNTRIES WITH RAILROADS

	COUNTRY	FIRST RAILROAD ESTABLISHED
1	UK	Sep 27, 1825
2	France	Nov 7, 1829
3	USA	May 24, 1830
4	Ireland	Dec 17, 1834
5	Belgium	May 5, 1835
6	Germany	Dec 7, 1835
7	Canada	Jul 21, 1836
8	Russia	Oct 30, 1837
9	Austria	Jan 6, 1838
10	Netherlands	Sep 24, 1839

The Stockton & Darlington Railway in the UK inaugurated the world's first steam railway service. In their early years some of the countries listed here offered only limited services over short distances, but their opening dates mark the generally accepted beginning of each country's steam railroad system.

top10 LONGEST RAILROAD NETWORKS

	COUNTRY	TOTAL RAIL LENGTH	
		MILES	KM
1	USA	141,508	227,736
2	Russia	54,156	87,157
3	China	44,675	71,898
4	India	39,280	63,230
5	Australia	33,826	54,439
6	Canada	30,250	48,683
7	Germany	28,671	46,142
8	Argentina	21,183	34,091
9	France	18,342	29,519
10	Brazil	18,275	29,412
	World	*1,115,205*	*692,956*

Source: Central Intelligence Agency, "The World Factbook 2005"

The US's railroad mileage has declined considerably since its 1916 peak of 254,000 miles (408,773 km).

top10 OLDEST UNDERGROUND RAILROAD NETWORKS

	CITY / COUNTRY/STATE	OPENED
1	London, UK	1863
2	Budapest, Hungary	1896
3	Glasgow, UK	1896
4	Boston, Massachusetts	1897
5	Paris, France	1900
6	Berlin, Germany	1902
7	New York, NY	1904
8	Philadelphia, Pennsylvania	1907
9	Hamburg, Germany	1912
10	Buenos Aires, Argentina	1913

Source: Tony Pattison, Centre for Environmental Initiatives Researcher

London and the world's first underground network, a section of the Metropolitan Railway from Paddington to Farringdon Street, with specially adapted steam trains, was opened on January 10, 1863.

top10 LONGEST **UNDERGROUND RAILROAD** NETWORKS

CITY / COUNTRY/STATE	OPENED	STATIONS	TOTAL TRACK LENGTH MILES	KM
1 London, UK	1863	267	244	392
2 New York, NY	1904	468	231	371
3 Moscow, Russia	1935	160	163	262
4 Tokyo, Japan*	1927	241	160	256
5 Paris, France#	1900	297	126	202
6 Mexico City, Mexico	1969	175	125	201
7 San Francisco, California	1972	42	124	200
8 Chicago, Illinois	1943	140	107	173
9 Madrid, Spain	1919	201	106	171
10 Washington, DC	1976	83	104	166

* Includes Toei, Eidan lines
# Metro and RER

Source: Tony Pattison, Centre for Environmental Initiatives Researcher

When its current expansion program is completed, the Seoul Metropolitan Subway, South Korea, one of the world's busiest, will also be the third longest.

top10 LONGEST **RAILROAD TUNNELS**

TUNNEL / COUNTRY	YEAR COMPLETED	LENGTH FT	M
1 AlpTransit Gotthard, Switzerland	2010*	187,244	57,072
2 Seikan, Japan	1988	176,673	53,850
3 Channel Tunnel, France/England	1994	165,518	50,450
4 Moscow Metro (Serpukhovsko-Timiryazevskaya line), Russia	1983	127,625	38,900
5 Guadarrama, Spain	2007*	97,100	28,377
6 London Underground (East Finchley-Morden, Northern Line), UK	1939	91,339	27,840
7 Hakkouda, Japan	2013*	86,795	26,455
8 Iwate, Japan	2013*	84,678	25,810
9 Iiyama, Japan	2013*	72,917	22,225
10 Dai-Shimizu, Japan	1982	72,904	22,221

* Under construction – scheduled completion date

The AlpTransit Gotthard, proposed in 1947 and begun in 1998 following a referendum of the Swiss electorate, will be the world's longest, as the original 49,213-ft (15,000-m) Gotthard tunnel was when completed in 1882. Trains will travel at 155 mph (250 km/h).

Waterways

⬆ **Slow boats in China**
Barge traffic makes its leisurely progress on China's ancient Grand Canal.

top10 COUNTRIES WITH THE **LONGEST** INLAND WATERWAY NETWORKS*

COUNTRY	LENGTH	
	MILES	KM
1 China	75,532	121,557
2 Russia	59,651	96,000
3 Brazil	31,068	50,000
4 USA#	25,481	41,009
5 Indonesia	13,408	21,579
6 Vietnam	11,000	17,702
7 Dem. Rep. of Congo	9,320	15,000
8 India	9,009	14,500
9 Myanmar	7,953	12,800
10 Argentina	6,835	11,000
World total†	*417,490*	*671,886*

* Canals and navigable rivers
# Excluding Great Lakes
† Of all countries for which data available

Source: Central Intelligence Agency, "The World Factbook 2005"

top10 **LONGEST** SHIP CANALS

CANAL / COUNTRY	OPENED	LENGTH	
		MILES	KM
1 Grand Canal, China	AD 283*	1,114	1,795
2 Erie Canal, USA	1825	363	584
3 Göta Canal, Sweden	1832	240	386
4 St. Lawrence Seaway, Canada/USA	1959	180	290
5 Canal du Midi, France	1692	149	240
6 Main-Danube, Germany	1992	106	171
7 Suez, Egypt	1869	101	162
8 Albert, Belgium	1939	81	130
9 Moscow (formerly Moscow-Volga), Russia	1937	80	129
10 Volga-Don, Russia	1952	63	101

* Extended from 605–10 and rebuilt between 1958–72

Connecting Hang Zhou in the south to Beijing in the north, China's Grand Canal was largely built by manual labor alone, long before the invention of the mechanized digging used in the construction of the other major artificial waterways. The Panama Canal, opened in 1914 (51 miles/82 km), just fails to find a place in the Top 10.

top10 **LARGEST** OIL TANKERS*

TANKER	YEAR BUILT	OPERATOR'S COUNTRY	DEAD-WEIGHT TONNAGE#
1 =TI Africa	2002	Belgium	441,893
=TI Asia	2002	USA	441,893
=TI Europe	2002	Belgium	441,893
4 TI Oceania	2003	USA	441,585
5 Marine Pacific	1979	USA	404,536
6 Enterprise	1981	Hong Kong	360,700
7 Nisa	1983	Saudia Arabia	322,912
8 Settebello	1983	Brazil	322,446
9 Aries Voyager	2006	Greece	320,870
10 Andromeda Voyager	2005	Greece	320,472

* As at Apr 2006
# Total weight of the vessel, including its cargo, crew, passengers, and supplies

Source: Lloyd's Register-Fairplay Ltd.

Once the world's largest tanker, the 1,504-ft (485.45-m), 564,764-ton *Knock Nevis* (formerly *Happy Giant*, *Seawise Giant*, and *Jahre Viking*) was damaged during the Iran-Iraq War. In 2004, it was adapted for use in Qatar as a floating storage and offloading unit.

Queen of the oceans
At her launch the Queen Mary 2 became the largest passenger ship of all time. In 2006 she lost her crown to the Freedom of the Seas.

top10 **BUSIEST** PORTS

PORT / COUNTRY	CONTAINER TRAFFIC, 2003 TEU*
1 Hong Kong, China	20,499,000
2 Singapore, Singapore	18,411,000
3 Shanghai, China	11,280,000
4 Shenzhen, China	10,615,000
5 Busan, South Korea	10,408,000
6 Kaohsiung, Taiwan	8,843,000
7 Los Angeles, USA	7,149,000
8 Rotterdam, Netherlands	7,107,000
9 Hamburg, Germany	6,138,000
10 Antwerp, Belgium	5,445,000

* Twenty-foot Equivalent Units

Source: American Association of Port Authorities

A "Twenty-Foot Equivalent Unit" (a container measuring 20 ft long x 8 ft wide x 8.5 ft high) is a standard measurement used in quantifying container traffic, in which Hong Kong is the world leader – although Singapore is the largest in terms of total weight handled, with over 347 million tonnes in 2003, compared with Hong Kong's 207 million.

top10 **LARGEST** CRUISE SHIPS

SHIP	ENTERED SERVICE	COUNTRY BUILT	PASSENGER CAPACITY	GROSS TONNAGE
1 Freedom of the Seas	2006	Finland	4,370	158,000
2 Queen Mary 2	2004	France	3,090	148,528
3 = Mariner of the Seas	2004	Finland	3,840	138,279
= Navigator of the Seas	2003	Finland	3,840	138,279
5 Explorer of the Seas	2000	Finland	3,840	137,308
6 = Adventure of the Seas	2001	Finland	3,838	137,276
= Voyager of the Seas	1999	Finland	3,838	137,276
8 Crown Princess	2006	Italy	3,800	117,477
9 = Diamond Princess	2004	Japan	3,100	115,875
= Sapphire Princess	2004	Japan	3,100	115,875

Source: Lloyd's Register-Fairplay Ltd

top10 **LARGEST** YACHTS

YACHT	OWNER / COUNTRY	BUILT/ REFITTED	FT	IN	LENGTH M
1 Al Salamah	King Fahd, Saudi Arabia	1999	456	10	139.8
2 Rising Sun	Larry Ellison, USA	2004	452	8	138.4
3 Octopus	Paul Allen, USA	2003	414	0	126.1
4 Savarona	Kahraman Sadikoglu, Turkey (charter)	1931/1992	408	0	124.3
5 Alexander	Latsis family, Greece	1976/1986	400	2	122.0
6 Turama	Latsis family, Greece	1990/2004	381	9	116.9
7 Atlantis II	Niarchos family, Greece	1981	379	7	115.6
8 Pelorus	Roman Abramovich, Russia	2003	377	3	114.9
9 Le Grand Bleu	Roman Abramovich, Russia	2000	370	0	112.7
10 Lady Moura	Nasser al-Rashid, Saudi Arabia	1990	344	0	104.8

Source: "Power & Motoryacht, 2005"

Marine Transport Disasters

the 10 LARGEST PASSENGER SHIPS EVER SUNK

SHIP / LOCATION	DATE	TONNAGE
1 Titanic* Off Newfoundland	Apr 14, 1912	46,328
2 Lusitania Off Ireland	May 7, 1915	31,550
3 Andrea Doria Off US coast	Jul 25, 1956	29,083
4 Angelina Pacific	Sep 24, 1979	24,377
5 Lakonia Atlantic	Dec 23, 1963	20,314
6 Mikhail Lermontov Off New Zealand	Feb 16, 1986	20,027
7 Rasa Sayang Kynosoura, Greece	Aug 27, 1980	18,739
8 Bianca C. Off Grenada	Oct 22, 1961	18,427
9 Georges Philppar* Off Cape Guardafui	May 19, 1931	17,539
10 Admiral Nakhimov Odessa/Batumi	Aug 31, 1986	17,053

* Sunk on maiden voyage

This list excludes liners used as troop carriers and lost as a result of military conflict and vessels that were damaged or keeled over, but did not actually sink, such as the 83,763-ton *Seawise University* (formerly *Queen Elizabeth*), which caught fire and partly sank in Hong Kong harbor on January 9, 1972.

① *Sinking the unsinkable*
The tragic circumstances surrounding the sinking of the supposedly unsinkable Titanic *on her maiden voyage, the then worst-ever loss of life and the retelling of the story in many books and films, have made it the most famous of all marine disasters.*

the 10 WORST PASSENGER FERRY DISASTERS

FERRY / LOCATION / DATE	APPROX. NO.KILLED
1 Doña Paz, Philippines, Dec 21, 1987	up to 3,000
2 MV Joola, Gambia, Sep 26, 2003	over 1,863
3 Neptune, Haiti, Feb 17, 1992	1,800
4 Toya Maru, Japan, Sep 26, 1954	1,172
5 Al Salaam Boccaccio 98, Red Sea, Feb 2, 2006	1,018
6 Don Juan, Philippines, Apr 22, 1980	over 1,000
7 Estonia, Baltic Sea, Sep 28, 1994	909
8 Samia, Bangladesh, May 25, 1986	600
9 Tampomas II, Indonesia, Jan 27, 1981	580
10 MV Bukoba, Lake Victoria, Tanzania, May 21, 1996	549

The *Doña Paz* sank in the Tabias Strait, Philippines, after the ferry was struck by the oil tanker MV *Vector*. The loss of life may have been much higher than the official figure (some authorities suggested figures between 4,341 and 4,386) due to overcrowding, but there was no accurate record of the numbers who actually boarded. Chaotic scenes often follow such incidents – as when the families of passengers on the *Al Salaam Boccaccio 98* rioted in Safaga, Egypt, further confusing the reporting of the disaster.

the10 WORST **MARINE DISASTERS**

LOCATION / DATE / INCIDENT	APPROX. NO. KILLED
1 Off Gdansk, Poland, Jan 30, 1945	up to 7,800

The German liner *Wilhelm Gustloff*, laden with refugees, was torpedoed by a Soviet submarine, S-13. The precise death toll remains uncertain, but with recent research suggesting a total of 10,582 on board, it could be over the estimated figure of 7,800.

2 Off Cape Rixhöft (Rozeewie), Poland, Apr 16, 1945	6,800

A German ship *Goya*, carrying evacuees from Gdansk, was torpedoed in the Baltic.

3 Off Yingkow, China, Dec 3, 1948	over 6,000

The boilers of an unidentified Chinese troopship carrying Nationalist soldiers from Manchuria exploded, detonating its ammunition.

4 Off Sumatra, Sep 18, 1944	5,620

The Japanese ship *Junyo Maru*, carying Dutch, British, American, and Australian prisoners of war and Javanese slave laborers, was torpedoed by British submarine HMS *Tradewind*.

5 En route for Okinawa, Jun 29, 1944	5,400

Japanese troop transport *Toyama Maru* was torpedoed by American submarine USS *Sturgeon*, with just 600 survivors of the 6,000 on board.

6 Lübeck, Germany, May 3, 1945	5,000

The German ship *Cap Arcona*, carrying concentration camp survivors, was bombed and sunk by British Typhoon fighter-bombers.

7 Off British coast, Aug to Oct 1588	4,000

Military conflict and storms combined to destroy the Spanish Armada.

8 Off Stolpmünde (Ustka), Poland, Feb 10, 1945	3,500

German war-wounded and refugees were lost when the *General Steuben* was torpedoed by the same Russian submarine that had sunk the *Wilhelm Gustloff* 10 days earlier.

9 Off St Nazaire, France, Jun 17, 1940	over 3,000

The British ship *Lancastria*, carrying troops and French refugees, sank after a dive-bombing attack by Luftwaffe aircraft.

10 Tabias Strait, Philippines, Dec 21, 1987	up to 3,000

The ferry *Doña Paz* was struck by oil tanker MV *Vector*. The *Doña Paz* was so overcrowded that a death toll of 4,341, claimed by some sources, may be possible.

Recent reassessments of the death tolls in some of the World War II marine disasters means that the most famous marine disaster of all – the *Titanic* – no longer ranks in the Top 10. However, the *Titanic* tragedy remains one of the worst-ever peacetime disasters, along with such notable incidents as that involving the *General Slocum*, an excursion liner that caught fire in the port of New York on June 15, 1904, with the loss of 1,021 lives.

the10 WORST **SUBMARINE DISASTERS***

SUBMARINE / LOCATION / DATE / INCIDENT	NO. KILLED
1 Surcourf, Gulf of Mexico, Feb 18, 1942	159

A French submarine, accidentally rammed by a US merchant ship, the USS *Thomson Lykes*.

2 Thresher, North Atlantic, Apr 10, 1963	129

A three-year-old US nuclear submarine, worth $45,000,000, sank.

3 Kursk (K-141), Barents Sea, Aug 12, 2000	118

A Russian nuclear submarine sank following an unspecified accident during a military exercise, with the loss of all hands. It was raised on Oct 8, 2001.

4 I-12, Central Pacific, c.Jan 15, 1945	114

A Japanese submarine, sank in unknown circumstances.

5 I-174, Central Pacific, c.Apr 12, 1944	107

A Japanese submarine, sank in unknown circumstances.

6 I-26, Off Leyte, Philippines, Oct 1944	105

A Japanese submarine, sank, possibly as a result of US depth-bombing.

7 I-169, Truk, Micronesia, Apr 4, 1944	103

A Japanese submarine flooded and sank while under attack in harbor.

8 I-22, off the Solomon Islands, c.Oct 4, 1942	100

A Japanese submarine sank.

9 =Thetis, Liverpool Bay, UK, Jun 1, 1939	99

A British submarine sank during trials, with civilians on board. (*Thetis* was later salvaged and renamed *Thunderbolt*; on March 13, 1943 she was sunk by an Italian ship with the loss of 63 lives.)

=Seawolf, off Morotai, Indonesia, Oct 3, 1944	99

A US submarine, sunk in error by USS *Rowell*.

= Scorpion, Southwest of the Azores, North Atlantic, May 21, 1968	99

A US nuclear submarine, sank after being struck by one of its own torpedos; the wreck was located on October 31, 1968.

* Excluding those as a result of military action

The loss of the *Thresher* is the worst-ever accident involving a nuclear submarine. It sank while undertaking tests off the US coast, and after an exhaustive search was eventually located by the bathyscaphe *Trieste*. It found the remains of the submarine scattered over the ocean floor at a depth of 8,400 ft (2,560 m). The cause of the disaster, if it was ever established, remains a military secret. The loss of the *Kursk* is the most recent of several tragedies affecting the former Soviet fleet: an unidentified vessel was lost with some 90 hands in 1968 and another with a similar number in 1983.

High Fliers

top10 COUNTRIES WITH THE MOST AIRPORTS

COUNTRY	AIRPORTS (2005 EST.)
1 USA	14,857
2 Brazil	4,136
3 Russia	2,586
4 Mexico	1,833
5 Argentina	1,334
6 Canada	1,326
7 Bolivia	1,065
8 Colombia	980
9 Paraguay	878
10 South Africa	728
World total	*49,973*

Source: CIA, "The World Factbook 2005"

top10 AIRLINES WITH THE MOST PASSENGERS

AIRLINE / COUNTRY	PASSENGERS CARRIED, 2004*
1 American Airlines, USA	91,570,000
2 Delta Air Lines, USA	86,783,000
3 United Airlines, USA	71,236,000
4 Northwest Airlines, USA	56,429,000
5 Japan Airlines, Japan	51,736,000
6 Lufthansa, Germany	48,268,000
7 All Nippon Airways, Japan	46,450,000
8 Air France, France	45,393,000
9 US Airways, USA	42,400,000
10 Continental Airlines, USA	40,548,000

* Total of international and domestic

Source: International Air Transport Association

top10 LARGEST AIRSHIPS EVER BUILT

	AIRSHIP	COUNTRY	YEAR	VOLUME CU FT	VOLUME CU M	LENGTH FT	LENGTH M
1	= Hindenburg	Germany	1936	7,062,934	200,000	804	245
	= Graf Zeppelin II	Germany	1938	7,062,934	200,000	804	245
3	= Akron	USA	1931	6,500,000	184,060	785	239
	= Macon	USA	1933	6,500,000	184,060	785	239
5	R101	UK	1930	5,500,000	155,744	777	237
6	Graf Zeppelin	Germany	1928	3,708,040	105,000	776	237
7	L72	Germany	1920	2,419,055	68,500	743	226
8	R100	UK	1929	5,500,000	155,744	709	216
9	R38	UK*	1921	2,724,000	77,136	699	213
10	L70 and L71	Germany	1918	2,418,700	62,200	694	212

* UK-built, but sold to US Navy

the10 FIRST PEOPLE TO PILOT HEAVIER-THAN-AIR AIRCRAFT

PILOT / DATES / NATIONALITY	AIRCRAFT	APPROX. DISTANCE (M)	DATE*
1 Orville Wright (1871–1948, USA)	Wright Flyer I	37	Dec 17, 1903
2 Wilbur Wright (1867–1912, USA)	Wright Flyer I	53	Dec 17, 1903
3 Jacob Christian Hansen Ellehammer (1871–1946, Denmark)	Ellehammer	42	Sep 12, 1906
4 Alberto Santos-Dumont (1873–1932, Brazil)	No.14-bis	60	Oct 23, 1906
5 Charles Voisin (1882–1912, France)	Voisin-Delagrange I	60	Mar 30, 1907
6 Robert Esnault-Pelterie (1881–1957, France)	REP No.1	100	Oct 10, 1907
7 Henri Farman (1874–1958, UK, later France)	Voisin-Farman I-bis	712	Oct 26, 1907
8 Ferdinand Léon Delagrange (1873–1910, France)	Voisin-Delagrange I	100	Nov 5, 1907
9 Comte Henri de La Vaulx (1870–1930, France)	Antoinette	70	Nov 19, 1907
10 Alfred de Pischoff (1882–1922, Hungary)	Anzani	50–100	Dec 12, 1907

* Of first flight only: most fliers listed flew on subsequent occasions and broke their first-time records

⬇ The Wright stuff
Wilbur Wright watches as his brother Orville becomes the first to fly a powered aircraft. The flight lasted 12 seconds, covering 37 m (120 ft).

↑ Giant of the skies
Fully laden, the Russian Antonov An-225 Mriya, the world's largest powered aircraft, weighs 600 tonnes.

the10 FIRST COUNTRIES TO HAVE BALLOON FLIGHTS*

COUNTRY DATE

1 France Nov 21, 1783
The Montgolfier brothers, Joseph and Etienne, tested their first unmanned hot-air balloon in the French town of Annonay on June 5, 1783. On November 21, 1783, François Laurent, Marquis d'Arlandes, and Jean-François Pilâtre de Rozier took off from the Bois de Boulogne, Paris, in a Montgolfier hot-air balloon. This first-ever manned flight covered a distance of about 5.5 miles (9 km) in 23 minutes, landing safely near Gentilly.

2 Italy Feb 25, 1784
The Chevalier Paolo Andreani and the brothers Augustino and Carlo Giuseppe Gerli (the builders of the balloon) made the first-ever flight outside France, at Moncucco, near Milan, Italy.

3 Austria Jul 6, 1784
Johann Georg Stuwer made the first Austrian flight from the Prater, Vienna.

4 Scotland Aug 27, 1784
James Tytler (known as "Balloon Tytler"), a doctor and newspaper editor, took off from Comely Gardens, Edinburgh, in a hot-air balloon, achieving an altitude of 350 ft (107 m) in a 1/2-mile (0.8-km) hop in a homemade balloon.

5 England Sep 15, 1784
Watched by a crowd of 200,000, Italian balloonist Vincenzo Lunardi ascended from the Artillery Company Ground, Moorfields, London, flying to Standon near Ware in Hertfordshire. On October 4, 1784 James Sadler flew a Montgolfier balloon at Oxford, thereby becoming the first English-born pilot.

6 Ireland Jan 19, 1785
Although there are earlier claims, it is likely that Richard Crosbie's hydrogen balloon flight from Ranelagh Gardens, Dublin, was the first in Ireland.

7 Holland Jul 11, 1785
French balloon pioneer Jean-Pierre Blanchard took off from The Hague in a hydrogen balloon.

8 Germany Oct 3, 1785
Blanchard made the first flight in Germany from Frankfurt.

9 Belgium Oct 20, 1785
Blanchard flew his hydrogen balloon from Ghent.

10 Switzerland May 5, 1788
Blanchard flew from Basel. As well as flights from other European cities, Blanchard made the first in the USA, from Philadelphia, on January 9, 1793. He was watched by George Washington, as well as future Presidents John Adams, Thomas Jefferson, and James Monroe.

* Several of the balloonists also made subsequent flights, but in each instance only their first flights are included

⊙ The first to fly
With Pilâtre de Rozier and the Marquis d'Arlandes on board, the Montgolfier hot-air balloon takes off, launching France as the pioneer of world aviation.

top10 LONGEST WINGSPAN AIRCRAFT

	AIRCRAFT	WINGSPAN		
		FT	IN	M
1	H-4 Hercules "Spruce Goose"	320	0	97.5
2	Antonov An-225 Cossack	290	0	88.4
3	Airbus A380F	261	8	79.8
4	Antonov An-124 Condor	240	6	73.3
5	Convair B-36 Peacemaker	230	0	70.1
6	Lockheed C-5 Galaxy	222	9	67.3
7	Boeing 777-300ER	212	7	64.8
8	Boeing 747	211	5	64.4
9	Airbus A340-600	208	2	63.5
10	Boeing 777	199	11	60.9

Air Transport Disasters

the10 FIRST AIRCRAFT **FATALITIES**

VICTIM / NATIONALITY / LOCATION	DATE
1 Lt. Thomas Etholen Selfridge, American, Fort Myer, USA	Sep 17, 1908
2 Eugène Lefèbvre, French, Juvisy, France	Sep 7, 1909
3 Ferdinand Ferber, French, Boulogne, France	Sep 22, 1909
4 Antonio Fernandez, Spanish, Nice, France	Dec 6, 1909
5 Aindan de Zoseley, Hungarian, Budapest, Hungary	Jan 2, 1910
6 Léon Delagrange, French, Croix d'Hins, France	Jan 4, 1910
7 Hubert Le Blon, French, San Sebastián, Spain	Apr 2, 1910
8 Hauvette Michelin, French, Lyons, France	May 13, 1910
9 Thaddeus Robl, German, Stettin, Germany	Jun 18, 1910
10 Charles Louis Wachter, French, Rheims, France	Jul 3, 1910

Following the Wright Brothers' first flights in 1903, the first four years of powered flying remained surprisingly accident-free, and it was not until 1908 that anyone was killed in an airplane. On September 17 at Fort Myer, Virginia, Orville Wright was demonstrating his *Flyer* to the US Army with Lt. Thomas Etholen Selfridge as a passenger when it crash-landed (from a height of just 75 ft/23 m), injuring Wright and killing Lt. Selfridge. On July 12, 1910, the 11th fatal accident and the first involving a British citizen occurred when the Hon. Charles Stewart Rolls (the Rolls of Rolls-Royce) crashed a Wright *Flyer* during an air show at Bournemouth.

the10 **WORST US** AIR DISASTERS

LOCATION / DATE / INCIDENT	NO. KILLED
1 New York, Sep 11, 2001 See World's Worst No.1	c.1,622
2 New York, Sep 11, 2001 See World's Worst No.2	c.677
3 Chicago, Illinois, May 25, 1979 The worst air disaster in the US occurred when an engine fell off an American Airlines DC-10 as it took off from Chicago O'Hare airport; the plane plunged out of control, killing all 271 on board and two on the ground.	273
4 Belle Harbor, New York, Nov 12, 2001 An American Airlines Airbus A300 crashed soon after takeoff from New York-JFK, killing all 260 passengers and crew and five people on the ground.	265
5 Off Long Island, New York, Jul 17, 1996 Soon after takeoff from JFK, a TWA Boeing 747 en route for Paris exploded in midair and crashed into the Atlantic Ocean nine miles south of Moriches Inlet, Long Island, killing all on board.	230
6 Nantucket Sound, Massachusetts, Oct 31, 1999 Soon after reaching its cruising altitude, an EgyptAir Boeing 767 went out of control, broke up, and crashed into the sea, killing all 203 passengers and 14 crew.	217
7 Washington, DC, Sep 11, 2001 As part of the 9/11 terrorist attacks, a Boeing 757 was hijacked and deliberately crashed into the Pentagon, killing all 64 on board and a further 125 on the ground.	189
8 Romulus, Michigan, Aug 16, 1987 A Northwest Airlines McDonnell Douglas DC-9 crashed onto a road following an engine fire after takeoff from Detroit. A girl aged four was the only survivor.	156
9 Kenner, Louisiana, Jul 9, 1982 A PanAm Boeing 727 crashed after takeoff from New Orleans for Las Vegas, killing all on board (137 passengers and the crew of eight) and eight on the ground.	153
10 San Diego, California, Sep 25, 1978 A Pacific Southwest Airline Boeing 727 collided in the air with a Cessna 172 light aircraft, killing 135 in the airliner, two in the Cessna, and seven on the ground.	144

the 10 WORST **AIR DISASTERS**

LOCATION / DATE / INCIDENT   NO. KILLED

1 New York, USA, Sep 11, 2001   c.1,622
Following a hijacking by terrorists, an American Airlines Boeing 767 was deliberately flown into the North Tower of the World Trade Center, killing all 81 passengers (including five hijackers) and 11 crew on board, and an estimated 1,530 on the ground, both as a direct result of the crash and the subsequent fire and collapse of the building, which also killed 479 rescue workers.

2 New York, USA, Sep 11, 2001   c.677
As part of the coordinated attack, hijackers commandeered a second Boeing 747 and crashed it into the South Tower of the World Trade Center, killing all 56 passengers and 9 crew on board and approximately 612 on the ground.

3 Tenerife, Canary Islands, Mar 27, 1977   583
Two Boeing 747s (PanAm and KLM, carrying 380 passengers and 16 crew, and 234 passengers and 14 crew, respectively) collided and caught fire on the runway of Los Rodeos airport after the pilots received incorrect control-tower instructions. A total of 61 escaped.

4 Mt. Ogura, Japan, Aug 12, 1985   520
A JAL Boeing 747 on an internal flight from Tokyo to Osaka crashed, killing all but four of the 509 passengers and all 15 crew on board.

5 Charkhi Dadri, India, Nov 12, 1996   349
Soon after taking off from New Delhi's Indira Gandhi International Airport, a Saudi Arabian Airlines Boeing 747 collided with a Kazakh Airlines Ilyushin IL-76 cargo aircraft on its descent and exploded, killing all 312 (289 passengers and 23 crew) on the Boeing and all 37 (27 passengers and 10 crew) on the Ilyushin, in the world's worst midair crash.

LOCATION / DATE / INCIDENT   NO. KILLED

6 Paris, France, Mar 3, 1974   346
Immediately after takeoff for London, a Turkish Airlines DC-10 suffered an explosive decompression when a door burst open and crashed at Ermenonville, north of Paris, killing all 335 passengers, including many England rugby supporters, and its crew of 11.

7 Off the Irish coast, Jun 23, 1985   329
An Air India Boeing 747 on a flight from Vancouver to Delhi exploded in midair, probably as a result of a terrorist bomb, killing all 307 passengers and 22 crew.

8 Riyadh, Saudi Arabia, Aug 19, 1980   301
Following an emergency landing a Saudia (Saudi Arabian) Airlines Lockheed TriStar caught fire. The crew were unable to open the doors, and all 287 passengers and 14 crew died from smoke inhalation.

9 Off the Iranian coast, Jul 3, 1988   290
An Iran Air A300 airbus was shot down in error by a missile fired by the USS *Vincennes*, which mistook it for an Iranian fighter aircraft. All 274 passengers and 16 crew were killed.

10 Sirach Mountain, Iran, Feb 19, 2003   275
An Ilyushin 76 flying from Zahedan to Kerman crashed into the mountain in poor weather. It was carrying 257 Revolutionary Guards and a crew of 18, none of whom survived.

↻ *Collision course*
The aftermath of the worst-ever midair collision at Charkhi Dadri, India. There were no survivors after a cargo aircraft mistakenly descended into the path of an airliner. Both crashed in flames onto uninhabited farmland.

World Tourism

top10 DESTINATIONS FOR US TOURISTS

DESTINATION COUNTRY	US VISITORS, 2004
1 Mexico	19,360,000
2 Canada	15,056,000
3 UK	3,692,000
4 France	2,407,000
5 Italy	1,915,000
6 China	1,805,000
7 Germany	1,750,000
8 Jamaica	1,258,000
9 Japan	1,067,000
10 Bahamas	1,012,000

Source: US Department of Commerce, International Trade Administration, Office of Travel and Tourism Industries

top10 TOURIST DESTINATIONS

COUNTRY	INTERNATIONAL VISITORS, 2004
1 France	75,100,000
2 Spain	53,600,000
3 USA	46,100,000
4 China*	41,800,000
5 Italy	37,100,000
6 UK	27,800,000
7 Mexico	20,600,000
8 Germany	20,100,000
9 Austria	19,400,000
10 Canada	19,200,000
World total	763,000,000

* Hong Kong separately enumerated: 21.8 million visitors in 2004

Source: World Tourism Organization

top10 TOURIST EARNING COUNTRIES*

COUNTRY	INTERNATIONAL TOURISM RECEIPTS, 2004 ($)
1 USA	74,500,000,000
2 Spain	45,200,000,000
3 France	40,800,000,000
4 Italy	35,700,000,000
5 Germany	27,700,000,000
6 UK	27,300,000,000
7 China	25,700,000,000
8 Turkey	15,900,000,000
9 Austria	15,400,000,000
10 Australia	13,000,000,000
World total	623,000,000,000

* Countries earning the most from tourism

Source: World Tourism Organization

top10 OLDEST AMUSEMENT PARKS*

PARK / LOCATION	YEAR FOUNDED
1 Bakken, Klampenborg, Denmark	1583
2 The Prater, Vienna, Austria	1766
3 Blackgang Chine Cliff Top Theme Park, Ventnor, Isle of Wight, UK	1842
4 Tivoli Gardens, Copenhagen, Denmark	1843
5 Lake Compounce Amusement Park, Bristol, Connecticut	1846
6 Hanayashiki, Tokyo, Japan	1853
7 Grand Pier, Teignmouth, UK	1865
8 Blackpool Central Pier, Blackpool, UK	1868
9 Cedar Point, Sandusky, Ohio	1870
10 Clacton Pier, Clacton, UK	1871

* In same location

Source: National Amusement Park Historical Association

top10 MOST VISITED NATIONAL PARKS IN THE US

PARK / LOCATION	RECREATION VISITS, 2004
1 Great Smoky Mountains National Park, North Carolina/Tennessee	9,167,046
2 Grand Canyon National Park, Arizona	4,326,234
3 Cuyahoga Valley National Park, near Cleveland and Akron, Ohio	3,306,175
4 Yosemite National Park, California	3,280,911
5 Olympic National Park, Washington	3,073,722
6 Yellowstone National Park, Wyoming	2,868,317
7 Rocky Mountain National Park, Colorado	2,781,899
8 Zion National Park, Utah	2,677,342
9 Grand Teton National Park, Wyoming	2,360,373
10 Acadia National Park, Maine	2,207,847

The total number of recreation visits to the US National Park System in 2004 was 276,908,337 – similar to the entire population of the US. This includes visitors to National Recreation Areas, National Monuments, and other areas under the management of the National Park Service not included in this list, which is exclusively of National Parks.

top10 TOURISM **SPENDING COUNTRIES** *

COUNTRY	INTERNATIONAL TOURISM EXPENDITURE, 2004 ($)
1 Germany	71,000,000,000
2 USA	65,600,000,000
3 UK	55,900,000,000
4 Japan	38,100,000,000
5 France	28,600,000,000
6 Italy	20,500,000,000
7 Netherlands	16,500,000,000
8 Canada	16,000,000,000
9 Russia	15,700,000,000
10 China	15,200,000,000#
World total	*623,000,000,000*

* Countries spending the most on tourism
# 2003 data

Source: World Tourism Organization

top10 COUNTRIES WITH THE **BIGGEST INCREASE** IN TOURISM

COUNTRY	% INCREASE, 2003–04
1 Malaysia	48.5
2 Taiwan	31.2
3 Kenya	30.7
4 Guam	27.5
5 China	26.7
6 Turkey	26.1
7 Lebanon	25.8
8 Ukraine	24.9
9 Uruguay	23.7
10 India	23.6
USA	*11.8*

Source: World Tourism Organization

top10 COUNTRIES OF **ORIGIN OF OVERSEAS VISITORS** TO THE US

COUNTRY	OVERSEAS VISITORS TO THE US, 2004
1 Canada	13,849,000
2 Mexico	11,906,000
3 UK	4,302,737
4 Japan	3,747,620
5 Germany	1,319,904
6 France	775,274
7 South Korea	626,595
8 Australia	519,955
9 Italy	470,805
10 Netherlands	424,872
Total all countries	*46,077,257*

Source: US Department of Commerce, International Trade Administration, Office of Travel and Tourism Industries

⊙ East meets West
The Tivoli Taj Mahal opened on August 15, 1843. One of many attractions in Tivoli Gardens, Copenhagen, Denmark, it is also one of the world's oldest amusement parks.

⊙ Head of the list
The USA easily tops the world list for receipts from tourism, but its own nationals are outspent by Germans.

SPORTS

Summer Olympics

top10 SPORTS CONTESTED AT THE MOST OLYMPIC GAMES*

	SPORT	YEARS	APPEARANCES
1	=Fencing	1896–2004	26
	=Gymnastics	1896–2004	26
	=Swimming	1896–2004	26
	=Track & Field	1896–2004	26
5	=Cycling	1896–1900, 1906–2004	25
	=Wrestling	1896, 1904–2004	25
	=Rowing	1900–2004	25
8	=Shooting	1896–1900, 1906–24, 1932–2004	24
	=Sailing#	1900, 1906–2004	24
	=Soccer	1900–28, 1936–2004	24

* Summer Olympics 1896–2004, including the 1906 Intercalated Games
\# Formerly Yachting

Other than wartime interruptions in 1916, 1940, and 1944, the Summer Games have been held every four years since 1896. The Intercalated Games were held in 1906. It was intended that they would take place in Athens midway between those in other countries (in this instance, St. Louis in 1904 and Rome in 1908), but the 1906 event was never repeated and records set and medals awarded in it are often disregarded.

top10 MOST MEDALS WON AT ONE OLYMPIC GAMES*

	NATION	YEAR	MEDALS GOLD	SILVER	BRONZE	TOTAL
1	USA	1904	79	84	82	245
2	USSR	1980	80	69	46	195
3	USA	1984	83	61	30	174
4	UK	1908	54	46	38	138
5	USSR	1988	55	31	46	132
6	East Germany#	1980	47	37	42	126
7	USSR	1976	49	41	35	125
8	Unified Team	1992	45	38	29	112
9	USA#	1992	37	34	37	108
10	USA	1968	45	28	34	107

* Summer Olympics 1896–2004, including the 1906 Intercalated Games
\# Not the leading medal-winning nation at that Games

Following the collapse of the Soviet Union, the Unified Team (or "EUN" – Equipe Unifée) was a short-lived confederation of athletes from the old USSR member countries other than the Baltic states. Some competed under this banner at the 1992 Winter Olympic Games in Albertville and all participated at the 1992 Summer Games at Barcelona, where it led the medals table. Since then, the respective countries have competed separately.

top10 GOLD MEDAL-WINNING COUNTRIES AT THE SUMMER OLYMPICS*

	COUNTRY	GOLDS
1	USA	907
2	USSR/Russia/Unified Team	525
3	Germany/West Germany	228
4	France	199
5	= Italy	189
	= UK	189
7	East Germany	159
8	Hungary	158
9	Sweden	140
10	Australia	119

* Summer Olympics 1896–2004, including the 1906 Intercalated Games

top10 MOST OLYMPIC MEDALS (WOMEN)*

	ATHLETE / COUNTRY	SPORT	YEARS	MEDALS GOLD	SILVER	BRONZE	TOTAL
1	**Larissa Latynina**, USSR	Gymnastics	1956–64	9	5	4	18
2	=**Birgit Fischer**, Germany/East Germany	Canoeing/ Kayaking	1980–2004	8	4	0	12
	=**Jenny Thompson**, USA	Swimming	1992–2004	8	3	1	12
4	**Vera Cáslavská**, Czechoslovakia	Gymnastics	1960–68	7	4	0	11
5	=**Agnes Keleti**, Hungary	Gymnastics	1952–56	5	3	2	10
	=**Polina Astakhova**, USSR	Gymnastics	1956–64	5	2	3	10
7	=**Lyudmila Tourischeva**, USSR	Gymnastics	1968–76	4	3	2	9
	=**Nadia Comaneci**, Romania	Gymnastics	1976–80	5	3	1	9
	=**Dara Torres**, USA	Swimming	1984–2000	4	1	4	9
10	=**Sofia Muratova**, USSR	Gymnastics	1956–60	2	2	4	8
	=**Dawn Fraser**, Australia	Swimming	1956–64	4	4	0	8
	=**Shirley Babashoff**, USA	Swimming	1972–76	2	6	0	8
	=**Kornelia Ender**, East Germany	Swimming	1972–76	4	4	0	8
	=**Inge de Bruijn**, Netherlands	Swimming	2000–04	4	2	2	8

* Up to and including 2004 Games

top10 US **OLYMPIC** MEDALISTS*

	ATHLETE / SPORT	MEDALS TOTAL
1	Jenny Thompson, Swimming	12
2 =	Carl Osburn, Shooting	11
=	Mark Spitz, Swimming	11
=	Matt Biondi#, Swimming	11
5 =	Ray Ewry, Track & Field	10
=	Carl Lewis, Track & Field	10
7 =	Martin Sheridan, Track & Field	9
=	Dara Torres, Swimming	9
=	Gary Hall Jr, Swimming	9
10 =	Charles Daniels, Swimming	8
=	Shirley Babashoff, Swimming	8
=	Michael Phelps#, Swimming	8

* At the Summer Olympics 1896–2004, including the 2006 Intercalated Games
# Biondi and Phelps totals include one gold medal as preliminary members of gold medal-winning relay teams

◐ *Vaulting to victory*
Russian gymnast Alexei Nemov (b.1976) has won a total of 12 Olympic medals, including four golds, in every gymnastics event except rings.

top10 **MOST OLYMPIC MEDALS** (MEN)*

	ATHLETE / COUNTRY	SPORT	YEARS	GOLD	SILVER	BRONZE	TOTAL
1	Nikolai Andrianov, USSR	Gymnastics	1972–80	7	5	3	15
2 =	Edoardo Mangiarotti, Italy	Fencing	1936–60	6	5	2	13
=	Takashi Ono, Japan	Gymnastics	1952–64	5	4	4	13
=	Boris Shakhlin, USSR	Gymnastics	1956–64	7	4	2	13
5 =	Paavo Nurmi, Finland	Track & Field	1920–28	9	3	0	12
=	Sawao Kato, Japan	Gymnastics	1968–76	8	3	1	12
=	Alexei Nemov, Russia	Gymnastics	1996–2000	4	2	6	12
8 =	Carl Osburn, USA	Shooting	1912–24	5	4	2	11
=	Viktor Chukarin, USSR	Gymnastics	1952–56	7	3	1	11
=	Mark Spitz, USA	Swimming	1968–72	9	1	1	11
=	Matt Biondi#, USA	Swimming	1984–92	8	2	1	11

* Up to and including 2004 Games
# Biondi's total includes one gold medal as preliminary member of a gold medal-winning relay team

top10 **MEDAL-WINNING COUNTRIES** NEVER TO HAVE WON A GOLD MEDAL*

	COUNTRY	GOLD	SILVER	BRONZE	TOTAL
1	Mongolia	0	5	10	15
2	Philippines	0	2	7	9
3 =	Bohemia	0	1	5	6
=	Puerto Rico	0	1	5	6
5 =	Ghana	0	1	3	4
=	Lebanon	0	2	2	4
=	Moldova	0	2	2	4
=	Namibia	0	4	0	4
9 =	Iceland	0	1	2	3
=	Malaysia	0	1	2	3

* Summer Olympics 1896–2004, including the 1906 Intercalated Games

Winter Olympics

top10 **MEDAL-WINNING** COUNTRIES AT THE WINTER OLYMPICS*

	COUNTRY	GOLD	MEDALS SILVER	BRONZE	TOTAL
1	USSR/Unified Team/Russia	122	89	86	297
2	Norway	96	102	84	282
3	USA	78	81	59	218
4	Germany/West Germany	76	78	57	211
5	Austria	50	64	71	185
6	Finland	42	57	52	151
7	Sweden	46	32	44	122
8	East Germany	39	37	35	118
9	Switzerland	37	37	43	117
10	Canada	38	38	44	111

* Up to and including the 2006 Turin Games; includes medals won at figure skating and ice hockey included in the Summer Games prior to the launch of the Winter Olympics in 1924

top10 **MEDAL-WINNING COUNTRIES** AT THE 2006 TURIN WINTER OLYMPICS

	COUNTRY	GOLD	MEDALS SILVER	BRONZE	TOTAL
1	Germany	11	12	6	29
2	USA	9	9	7	25
3	Canada	7	10	7	24
4	Austria	9	7	7	23
5	Russia	8	6	8	22
6	Norway	2	8	9	19
7	=Sweden	7	2	5	14
	=Switzerland	5	4	5	14
9	=China	2	4	5	11
	=Italy	5	0	6	11
	=Korea	6	3	2	11

top10 OLYMPIC **ICE-HOCKEY** COUNTRIES*

	COUNTRY	GOLD	MEDALS SILVER	BRONZE	TOTAL
1	Canada	9	5	2	16
2	USA	3	8	2	13
3	Soviet Union/Unified Team/Russia	8	2	2	12
4	Sweden	2	3	5	10
5	Czechoslovakia	0	4	4	8
6	Finland	0	2	3	5
7	=Czech Republic	1	0	1	2
	=Germany/West Germany	0	0	2	2
	=Switzerland	0	0	2	2
	=UK	1	0	1	2

* Up to and including the 2006 Turin Games

➲ Olympic victory
Italian cross-country skier Stefania Belmondo won medals at four consecutive Winter Olympics, with golds in the 30-km event in 1992 and 15 km in 2002. As a local Olympian, she was chosen to light the Olympic flame at the 2006 Games in Turin.

top10 **MEN'S MEDAL WINNERS** AT THE WINTER OLYMPICS*

| ATHLETE / COUNTRY | EVENT | MEDALS | | | |
		GOLD	SILVER	BRONZE	TOTAL
1 Bjorn Dählie, Norway	Cross Country	8	4	0	12
2 = Ole Einar Bjoerndalen, Norway	Biathlon	5	3	1	9
= Sixten Jernberg, Sweden	Cross Country	4	3	2	9
4 = Kjetil André Aamodt, Norway	Alpine Skiing	4	2	2	8
= Sven Fischer, Germany	Biathlon	4	2	2	8
= Ricco Gross, Germany	Biathlon	4	3	1	8
7 = Ivar Ballangrud, Norway	Speed Skating	4	2	1	7
= Veikko Hakulinen, Finland	Cross Country	3	3	1	7
= Eero Mäntyranta, Finland	Cross Country	3	2	2	7
= Bogdan Musiol, Germany/East Germany	Bobsled	1	5	1	7
= Clas Thunberg, Finland	Speed Skating	5	1	1	7

* All events up to and including the 2006 Turin Games

top10 **WOMEN'S MEDAL WINNERS** AT THE WINTER OLYMPICS*

| ATHLETE / COUNTRY | EVENT | MEDALS | | | |
		GOLD	SILVER	BRONZE	TOTAL
1 = Stefania Belmondo, Italy	Cross Country	2	3	5	10
= Raisa Smetanina, USSR/Unified Team	Cross Country	4	5	1	10
3 = Uschi Disl, Germany	Biathlon	2	4	3	9
= Lyubov Egorova, Unified Team/Russia	Cross Country	6	3	0	9
= Claudia Pechstein, Germany	Speed Skating	5	2	2	9
6 = Karin Kania (née Enke), East Germany	Speed Skating	3	4	1	8
= Galina Kulakova, USSR	Cross Country	4	2	2	8
= Gunda Neimann-Stirnemann, Germany	Speed Skating	3	4	1	8
9 = Andrea Ehrig (née Mitscherlich, formerly Schöne), East Germany	Speed Skating	1	5	1	7
= Marja-Liisa Kirvesniemi (née Hämäläinen), Finland	Cross Country	3	0	4	7
= Larissa Lazutina, Unified Team/Russia	Cross Country	5	1	1	7
= Elena Valbe, Unified Team/Russia	Cross Country	3	0	4	7

* All events up to and including the 2006 Turin Gamesy

Until Stefania Belmondo equaled her tally in 2002, Russian Nordic skier Raisa Smetanina (b.1952) stood alone as the only woman ever to win 10 Winter Olympic medals. All were gained in five consecutive Games – from 1976, when she won her first gold, to 1992, when she achieved her last, at the age of 40 (becoming the oldest woman ever to win a Winter Olympic gold medal).

⊙ Downhill champion
Kjetil André Aamodt is the leading Alpine skiing medal-winner, with victories in the Winter Olympic Games of 1992, 1994, 2002, and 2006, including four golds – a record for any Alpine competitor.

Track & Field

	RUNNER / COUNTRY	YEAR	TIME HR/MIN/SEC
1	Margaret Okayo, Kenya	2003	2:22.31
2	Paula Radcliffe, UK	2004	2:23.10
3	Margaret Okayo, Kenya	2001	2:24.21
4	Lisa Ondieki, Australia	1992	2:24.40
5	Jelena Prokopcuka, Latvia	2005	2:24.41
6	Adriana Fernandez, Mexico	1999	2:25.06
7	Franca Fiacconi, Italy	1998	2:25.17
8	Allison Roe, New Zealand	1981	2:25.29
9	Ingrid Kristiansen, Norway	1989	2:25.30
10	Grete Waitz, Norway	1980	2:25.41

* Up to and including 2005

top10 FASTEST WINNING TIMES IN THE **NEW YORK CITY MARATHON (MEN)**

	RUNNER / COUNTRY	YEAR	TIME HR/MIN/SEC
1	Tesfaye Jifar, Ethiopia	2001	2:07.43
2	Juma Ikangaa, Tanzania	1989	2:08.01
3	Rodgers Rop, Kenya	2002	2:08.07
4	John Kagwe, Kenya	1997	2:08.12
5	Alberto Salazar, USA	1981	2:08.13
6	Steve Jones, UK	1988	2:08.20
7	John Kagwe, Kenya	1998	2:08.45
8	Rod Dixon, New Zealand	1983	2:08.59
9	Joseph Chebet, Kenya	1999	2:09.14
10 =	Salvador Garcia, Mexico	1991	2:09.28
=	Hendrik Ramaala, South Africa	2004	2:09.28

* Up to and including 2005

← **In the long run** Marathons have been run worldwide since they were introduced in the first modern Olympics in 1896.

top10 **LONGEST-STANDING WOMEN'S** OUTDOOR ATHLETICS WORLD RECORDS*

	EVENT	TIME/DISTANCE	SET BY / COUNTRY#	DATE
1	800 metres	1 min 53.28 secs	Jarmila Kratochvílová, Czechoslovakia	Jul 26, 1983
2 =	400 metres	47.60 secs	Marita Koch, East Germany	Oct 6, 1985
=	4x100 metres relay	41.37 secs	East Germany	Oct 6, 1985
4	Shot	22.63 metres	Natalya Lisovskay, USSR	Jun 7, 1987
5	High jump	2.09 metres	Stefka Kostadinova, Bulgaria	Aug 30, 1987
6	Long jump	7.52 metres	Galina Chistyakova, USSR	Jun 11, 1988
7	Discus	76.80 metres	Gabriele Reinsch, East Germany	Jul 9, 1988
8	100 metres	10.49 secs	Florence Griffith Joyner, USA	Jul 16, 1988
9	100 metres hurdles	12.21 secs	Yordanka Donkova, Bulgaria	Aug 20, 1988
10	Heptathlon	7,291 points	Jackie Joyner-Kersee, USA	Sep 24, 1988

* In recognized Olympic events only; as at December 17, 2005
# At the time of setting the record

Source: International Association of Athletics Federations (IAAF)

top10 **FASTEST MEN** OVER 100 METRES

	ATHLETE / COUNTRY	YEAR	TIME (SECS)
1	Asafa Powell, Jamaica	2005	9.77
2	Maurice Greene, USA	1999	9.79
3	=Donovan Bailey, Canada	1999	9.84
	=Bruny Surin, Canada	1999	9.84
5	=Leroy Burrell, USA	1994	9.85
	=Justin Gatlin, USA	2004	9.85
7	=Carl Lewis, USA	1991	9.86
	=Frank Fredericks, Namibia	1996	9.86
	=Ato Boldon, Trinidad	1998	9.86
	=Francis Obikwelu, Portugal	2004	9.86

Source: IAAF

A special prestige attaches to the holder of the men's 100-metre record, since he is considered the "fastest man in the world," but the race has been beset by controversy in recent years: records of 9.79 and 9.83 seconds set by Ben Johnson (Canada) were disallowed after he was found guilty of using banned substances and, on December 13, 2005, US athlete Tim Montgomery's record of 9.78 seconds, set in Paris on September 14, 2002, was deleted from the record books for the same reason.

top10 **LONGEST-STANDING MEN'S** OUTDOOR ATHLETICS WORLD RECORDS*

	EVENT	TIME/DISTANCE	SET BY / COUNTRY#	DATE
1	Discus	74.08 metres	Jürgen Schult, East Germany	Jun 6, 1986
2	Hammer	86.74 metres	Yuriy Sedykh, USSR	Aug 30, 1986
3	Shot	23.12 metres	Randy Barnes, USA	May 20, 1990
4	Long jump	8.95 metres	Mike Powell, USA	Aug 30, 1991
5	400 metres hurdles	46.78 secs	Kevin Young, USA	Aug 6, 1992
6	4x100 metres relay	37.40 secs	United States[†]	Aug 8, 1992
7	High jump	2.45 metres	Javier Sotomayor, Cuba	Jul 27, 1993
8	110 metres hurdles	12.91 secs	Colin Jackson, UK☆	Aug 20, 1993
9	20 kilometre walk	1 hour 17 mins 25 secs	Bernardo Segura, Mexico	May 7, 1994
10	Pole vault	6.14 metres	Sergey Bubka, Ukraine	Jul 31, 1994

* In recognized Olympic events only; as at Dec 17, 2005
# At the time of setting the record
† Record equaled, again by USA, on Aug 21, 1993
☆ Record equaled by Liu Xiang, China, in 2004

Source: IAAF

The longest-standing of all athletics records as recognized by the IAAF is the 4x1,500 metres relay (although not often run) by the West German team in Cologne on August 17, 1977, when they set a new best time of 14 minutes 38.8 seconds.

➔ *Fastest man on earth*
Asafa Powell set a new 100-m record in Athens on June 14, 2005.

Boxing

the10 FIRST MEN TO WIN WORLD TITLES AT THREE DIFFERENT WEIGHTS

	BOXER / COUNTRY	WEIGHTS / YEARS
1	Bob Fitzsimmons, UK	Middle 1891, Heavy 1897, Light-heavy 1903
2	Tony Canzoneri, USA	Feather* 1927, Light 1930, Junior-welter 1931
3	Barney Ross, USA	Light 1933, Junior-welter 1933, Welter 1934
4	Henry Armstrong, USA	Feather 1937, Welter 1938, Light 1938
5	Wilfred Benitez, USA	Junior-welter 1976, Welter 1979, Junior-middle 1981
6	Alexis Arguello, Nicaragua	Feather 1974, Junior-light 1978, Light 1981
7	Roberto Duran, Panama	Light 1972, Welter 1980, Junior-middle 1983
8	Wilfredo Gomez, Puerto Rico	Junior-feather 1977, Feather 1984, Junior-light 1985
9	Thomas Hearns, USA	Welter 1980, Junior-middle 1982, Light-heavy 1987
10	Sugar Ray Leonard, USA	Welter 1979, Junior-middle 1981, Middle 1987

* New York version of the title

Emile Griffith (b.1938; US Virgin Islands) and Terry McGovern (1880–1918; USA) were claimants to the junior-middle and lightweight crowns, respectively, and would have appeared in this list, but most records do not accept the claims as being for the world title. On October 29, 1987, Thomas Hearns beat Juan Roldan of Argentina in Las Vegas for the WBC middleweight crown, to become the first man to win titles at four different weights. In 1988, Sugar Ray Leonard went on to win both his fourth and fifth world titles.

top10 MOST WINS IN WORLD HEAVYWEIGHT TITLE FIGHTS*

	BOXER / COUNTRY#	BOUTS	WINS
1	Joe Louis	27	26
2	Muhammad Ali/ Cassius Clay	25	22
3	Larry Holmes	25	21
4	Lennox Lewis, UK	22	17
5	= Tommy Burns, Canada	13	12
	= Mike Tyson	16	12
7	= Joe Frazier	11	10
	= Evander Holyfield	16	10
	= Jack Johnson	11	10
10	Ezzard Charles	13	9

* As at January 1, 2006
# All USA, unless otherwise stated

This list also represents the *Top 10 Most World Heavyweight Title Bouts* with the exception of Floyd Patterson (USA), who would be in at 9th with 12 fights.

top10 HEAVIEST CHAMPIONSHIP FIGHTS*

	FIGHTERS# / WEIGHT (LB)	DATE	COMBINED WEIGHT LB	KG
1	Nikolai Valuev (324) vs. John Ruiz (237³/4)	Dec 17, 2005	562	254.8
2	Vitaly Klitschko (250) vs. Danny Williams (270)	Dec 11, 2004	520	235.9
3	Lennox Lewis (256¹/2) vs. Vitaly Klitschko (248)	Jun 21, 2003	505	228.8
4	Lennox Lewis (247) vs. Michael Grant (250)	Apr 29, 2000	497	225.4
5	Lennox Lewis (249) vs. David Tua (245)	Nov 11, 2000	494	224.1
6	Hasim Rahman (238) vs. Lennox Lewis (253¹/2)	Apr 22, 2001	492	222.9
7	Primo Carnera (259¹/2) vs. Paulino Uzcudun (229¹/4)	Oct 22, 1933	489	221.7
8	= Lennox Lewis (251) vs. Oliver McCall (237)	Jul 2, 1997	488	221.4
	= Lennox Lewis (244) vs. Andrew Golota (244)	Oct 14, 1997	488	221.4
10	= Riddick Bowe (243) vs. Michael Dokes (244)	Feb 6, 1993	487	220.9
	= Lennox Lewis (250) vs. Francois Botha (237)	Jul 15, 2000	487	220.9
	= John Ruiz (241) vs. Hasim Rahman (246)	Dec 13, 2003	487	220.9

* As at January 1, 2006
# Winner first

Known as "The Beast from The East," Russian Nikolai Valuev is not only the heaviest world heavyweight champion but, at 7 ft (2.13 m), is also the tallest. He is unbeaten in 44 fights.

⬅ *Russian giant*
WBA heavyweight champion Nikolai Valuev (b.1972) won his title from John Ruiz, despite fighting with one hand, his other having been injured.

↑ Tyson vs. Lewis
In his 2002 defence of his world title, British heavyweight Lennox Lewis (right) won with a knockout in the 8th round.

the10 LATEST
UNDISPUTED* WORLD HEAVYWEIGHT CHAMPIONS#

	BOXER†	DATE LAST HELD UNIFIED TITLE
1	Lennox Lewis, UK	Apr 29, 2000
2	Riddick Bowe	Dec 14, 1992
3	Evander Holyfield	Nov 13, 1992
4	James "Buster" Douglas	Oct 25, 1990
5	Mike Tyson	Feb 10, 1990
6	Leon Spinks	Mar 18, 1978
7	Muhammad Ali	Feb 15, 1978
8	George Foreman	Oct 30, 1974
9	Joe Frazier	Jan 22, 1973
10	Muhammad Ali	Apr 29, 1967

* The term "undisputed" refers to a boxer who has won all three recognized titles (WBA, WBC, IBF) in his weight class
# As at January 1, 2006, as recognized by the three main bodies at the time: WBA – World Boxing Association, WBC – World Boxing Council, IBF – International Boxing Federation; with the exception of Lennox Lewis, all those listed are from the USA
† All USA, unless otherwise stated

the10 FIRST AMERICAN-BORN **WORLD CHAMPIONS***

	BOXER	BIRTHPLACE	WEIGHT AT WHICH FIRST TITLE WON	FIRST TITLE WON
1	Paddy Duffy	Boston, Massachusetts	Welterweight	Oct 30, 1888
2	James J. Corbett	San Francisco, California	Heavyweight	Sep 7, 1892
3	Tommy Ryan	Redwood, New York	Welterweight	Jul 26, 1894
4	Charles "Kid" McCoy	Rush County, Indiana	Welterweight	Mar 2, 1896
5	George "Kid" Lavigne	Bay City, Michigan	Lightweight	Jun 1, 1896
6	Solly Smith	Los Angeles, California	Featherweight	Oct 4, 1897
7	Jimmy Barry	Chicago, Illinois	Bantamweight	Dec 6, 1897
8	James J. Jeffries	Carroll, Ohio	Heavyweight	Jun 9, 1899
9	Terry McGovern	Johnstown, Pennsylvania	Bantamweight	Sep 12, 1899
10	Rube Ferns	Pittsburg, Kansas	Welterweight	Jan 15, 1900

* Under Queensberry Rules

The first recognized world champion under Queensberry Rules was middleweight Jack "Nonpareil" Dempsey, who captured the title in 1884. However, although he represented America, Dempsey was in fact born in County Kildare in the Republic of Ireland.

Basketball

top10 POINTS SCORERS IN THE NBA*

	PLAYER	POINTS
1	Kareem Abdul-Jabbar	38,387
2	Karl Malone	36,928
3	Michael Jordan	32,292
4	Wilt Chamberlain	31,419
5	Moses Malone	27,409
6	Elvin Hayes	27,313
7	Hakeem Olajuwon	26,946
8	Oscar Robertson	26,710
9	Dominique Wilkins	26,668
10	John Havlicek	26,395

* As at the end of the 2004–05 season

top10 MOST FIELD GOALS MADE IN THE NBA*

	PLAYER	FIELD GOALS ATTEMPTED	FIELD GOALS MADE
1	Kareem Abdul-Jabbar	28,307	15,837
2	Karl Malone	26,210	13,528
3	Wilt Chamberlain	23,497	12,681
4	Michael Jordan	24,537	12,192
5	Elvin Hayes	24,272	10,976
6	Hakeem Olajuwon	20,991	10,749
7	Alex English	21,036	10,659
8	John Havlicek	23,930	10,513
9	Dominique Wilkins	21,589	9,963
10	Patrick Ewing	19,241	9,702

* As at the end of the 2004–05 season

Source: National Basketball Association

top10 MOST POINTS IN A SINGLE NBA GAME*

	PLAYER	MATCH	DATE	POINTS
1	Wilt Chamberlain	Philadelphia Warriors vs. New York Knicks	Mar 2, 1962	100
2	Kobe Bryant	Los Angeles Lakers vs. Toronto Raptors	Jan 22, 2006	81
3	Wilt Chamberlain	Philadelphia Warriors vs. Los Angeles Lakers#	Dec 8, 1961	78
4 =	Wilt Chamberlain	Philadelphia Warriors vs. Chicago Packers	Jan 13, 1962	73
=	Wilt Chamberlain	San Francisco Warriors vs. New York Knicks	Nov 16, 1962	73
=	David Thompson	Denver Nuggets vs. Detroit Pistons	Apr 9, 1978	73
7	Wilt Chamberlain	San Francisco Warriors vs. Los Angeles Lakers	Nov 3, 1962	72
8 =	Elgin Baylor	Los Angeles Lakers vs. New York Knicks	Nov 15, 1960	71
=	David Robinson	San Antonio Spurs vs. Los Angeles Clippers	Apr 24, 1994	71
10	Wilt Chamberlain	San Francisco Warriors vs. Syracuse Nationals	Mar 10, 1963	70

* As at the end of the 2004–05 season
# Triple overtime game

top10 MOST GAMES PLAYED IN THE NBA*

	PLAYER	MATCHES
1	Robert Parish	1,611
2	Kareem Abdul-Jabbar	1,560
3	John Stockton	1,504
4	Karl Malone	1,476
5	Kevin Willis	1,419
6	Reggie Miller	1,389
7	Moses Malone	1,329
8	Buck Williams	1,307
9	Elvin Hayes	1,303
10	Mark Jackson	1,296

* As at the end of the 2004–05 season

If American Basketball Association appearances were included, Moses Malone's two seasons with the ABA would move him up to fifth place with 1,455 games played, while Artis Gilmore would be in eighth place with 1,329 games.

the10 LATEST **NBA CHAMPIONS**

	WINNERS	SCORE	SEASON
1	San Antonio Spurs	4–3	2004–05
2	Detroit Pistons	4–1	2003–04
3	San Antonio Spurs	4–2	2002–03
4	Los Angeles Lakers	4–0	2001–02
5	Los Angeles Lakers	4–1	2000–01
6	Los Angeles Lakers	4–2	1999–00
7	San Antonio Spurs	4–1	1998–99
8	Chicago Bulls	4–2	1997–98
9	Chicago Bulls	4–2	1996–97
10	Chicago Bulls	4–2	1995–96

Source: National Basketball Association

➜ NBA champions
Bolton Celtics enter their 60th season as the holders of the most NBA championship titles, with 16 from 1957 to 1986.

top10 **SCORING AVERAGES** IN AN NBA CAREER*

	PLAYER	AVERAGE POINTS PER GAME
1	Michael Jordan	30.12
2	Wilt Chamberlain	30.07
3	Allen Iverson#	27.44
4	Elgin Baylor	27.36
5	Jerry West	27.03
6	Shaquille O'Neal	26.74
7	Bob Pettit	26.36
8	George Gervin	26.18
9	Oscar Robertson	25.68
10	Karl Malone	25.02

* As at the end of the 2004–05 season
# Active in 2004–05

top10 TEAMS WITH THE **MOST NBA TITLES***

	TEAM	TITLES
1	Boston Celtics	16
2	Minneapolis/ Los Angeles Lakers#	14
3	Chicago Bulls	6
4	=Detroit Pistons	3
	=Philadelphia/ Golden State Warriors#	3
	=San Antonio Spurs	3
	=Syracuse Nationals/ Philadelphia 76ers#	3
8	=Baltimore/Washington Bullets#	2
	=Houston Rockets	2
	=New York Knicks	2

* As at the end of 2004–05 season
# Teams separated by / indicate change of franchise and have won the championship under both names

Source: National Basketball Association

the10 COACHES WITH THE **MOST WINS** IN THE NBA*

	COACH	YEARS	REGULAR SEASON WINS
1	Lenny Wilkens	31	1,315
2	Don Nelson#	26	1,190
3	Pat Riley	21	1,110
4	Larry Brown#	22	987
5	Bill Fitch	25	944
6	Jerry Sloan#	20	943
7	Red Auerbach	20	938
8	Dick Motta	25	935
9	Jack Ramsay	21	864
10	Phil Jackson#	14	832

* As at the end of the 2004–05 season
# Active in 2004–05

American Football

❶ *Football stars* The Dallas Cowboys are one of the most successful teams in the National Football League.

top10 **MOST SUCCESSFUL** SUPER BOWL TEAMS*

	TEAM	WINS	LOSSES	APPEARANCES
1	Dallas Cowboys	5	3	8
2	= Denver Broncos	2	4	6
	= Pittsburgh Steelers	5	1	6
4	= Miami Dolphins	2	3	5
	= New England Patriots	3	2	5
	= Oakland/Los Angeles Raiders	3	2	5
	= San Francisco 49ers	5	0	5
	= Washington Redskins	3	2	5
9	= Buffalo Bills	0	4	4
	= Green Bay Packers	3	1	4
	= Minnesota Vikings	0	4	4

* Based on appearances up to and including Superbowl XL, 2006

top10 **MOST POINTS** IN A REGULAR NFL SEASON*

	PLAYER / TEAM	SEASON	POINTS
1	Paul Hornung, Green Bay Packers	1960	176
2	Shaun Alexander, Seattle Seahawks	2005	169
3	Gary Anderson, Minnesota Vikings	1998	164
4	Jeff Wilkins, St. Louis Rams	2003	163
5	Priest Holmes, Kansas City Chiefs	2003	162
6	Mark Moseley, Washington Redskins	1983	161
7	Marshall Faulk, St. Louis Rams	2000	160
8	Mike Vanderjagt, Indianapolis Colts	2003	157
9	Gino Cappelletti, Boston Patriots	1964	155
10	Emmitt Smith, Dallas Cowboys	1995	150

* Up to and including 2005

top10 BIGGEST WINNING MARGINS IN THE SUPER BOWL

	WINNERS	RUNNERS-UP	YEAR	SCORE	MARGIN
1	San Francisco 49ers	Denver Broncos	1990	55–10	45
2	Chicago Bears	New England Patriots	1986	46–10	36
3	Dallas Cowboys	Buffalo Bills	1993	52–17	35
4	Washington Redskins	Denver Broncos	1988	42–10	32
5	Los Angeles Raiders	Washington Redskins	1984	38–9	29
6	= Baltimore Ravens	New York Giants	2001	34–7	27
	= Tampa Bay Buccaneers	Oakland Raiders	2003	48–21	27
8	Green Bay Packers	Kansas City Chiefs	1967	35–10	25
9	San Francisco 49ers	San Diego Chargers	1995	49–26	23
10	San Francisco 49ers	Miami Dolphins	1985	38–16	22

Source: National Football League

The closest Super Bowl was in 1991 when the New York Giants beat the Buffalo Bills 20–19. Scott Norwood missed a 47-yard field goal eight seconds from the end of time to deprive the Bills of their first-ever Super Bowl win. It was the Giants' second win.

top10 MOST TOUCHDOWNS IN AN NFL CAREER*

	PLAYER	YEARS	TOUCHDOWNS
1	Jerry Rice	1985–2004	208
2	Emmitt Smith	1995–2004	175
3	Marcus Allen	1982–97	145
4	Marshall Faulk#	1994–	136
5	Cris Carter	1987–2002	131
6	Jim Brown	1957–65	126
7	Walter Payton	1975–87	125
8	John Riggins	1971–85	116
9	Lenny Moore	1956–67	113
10	Marvin Harrison#	1996–	110

* Regular seasons only, up to and including 2005
# Active in 2005

top10 PLAYERS WITH THE MOST NFL CAREER POINTS*

	PLAYER	POINTS
1	Gary Anderson	2,434
2	Morten Andersen	2,358
3	George Blanda	2,002
4	Norm Johnson	1,736
5	Nick Lowery	1,711
6	Jan Stenerud	1,699
7	John Carney#	1,634
8	= Eddie Murray	1,594
	= Matt Stover#	1,594
10	Al Del Greco	1,584

* Regular season only, up to and including the 2005 season
# Still active during 2005–06 season

Source: National Football League

Born in 1959, Gary Anderson started his career with the Steelers in 1982 before two seasons with Philadelphia in 1995–96. He had a year with the 49ers in 1997, moving on to the Minnesota Vikings in 1998, and then to the Tennessee Titans in 2003. He broke George Blanda's points record in 2000. Anderson came out of retirement in 2003 and again in 2004.

top10 AVERAGE HOME ATTENDANCES IN THE NFL, 2005*

	TEAM / AGGREGATE	AVERAGE
1	Washington Redskins 716,999	89,624
2	New York Giants 628,519	78,564
3	Kansas City Chiefs 623,325	77,915
4	New York Jets 619,958	77,494
5	Denver Broncos 608,790	76,098
6	Carolina Panthers 587,700	73,462
7	Cleveland Browns 578,330	72,291
8	Miami Dolphins 575,256	71,907
9	Buffalo Bills 575,248	71,906
10	Atlanta Falcons 565,106	70,638

* Regular season only

top10 NFL COACHES WITH THE MOST WINS*

	COACH	GAMES WON
1	Don Shula	347
2	George Halas	324
3	Tom Landry	270
4	Curly Lambeau	229
5	Chuck Noll	209
6	Dan Reeves	201
7	Chuck Knox	193
8	Marty Schottenheimer#	191
9	Bill Parcells#	174
10	Paul Brown	170

* Regular and postseason games, up to and including the 2005–06 season
# Active in the 2005–06 season

Source: National Football League

International Soccer

CLUB / COUNTRY	CHAMPIONS' LEAGUE	UEFA CUP	CUP-WINNERS CUP	TOTAL
1 Real Madrid, Spain	9	2	0	11
2 = Barcelona, Spain	1	3	4	8
= Liverpool, England	5	3	0	8
= AC Milan, Italy	6	0	2	8
5 = Ajax, Netherlands	4	1	1	6
= Bayern Munich, Germany	4	1	1	6
= Juventus, Italy	2	3	1	6
8 Inter Milan, Italy	2	3	0	5
9 Valencia, Spain	0	3	1	4
10 = Anderlecht, Belgium	0	1	2	3
= Manchester United, England	2	0	1	3
= Parma, Italy	0	2	1	3
= Porto, Portugal	2	1	0	3
= Tottenham Hotspur, England	0	2	1	3

* Based on wins in the Champions League/Cup, UEFA Cup/Fairs Cup, and Cup-winners Cup, up to and including 2004–05

top10 **MOST DOMESTIC** LEAGUE TITLES*

CLUB	COUNTRY	TITLES
1 Glasgow Rangers	Scotland	51
2 Linfield	Northern Ireland	45
3 Glasgow Celtic	Scotland	39
4 Olympiakos	Greece	33
5 Rapid Vienna#	Austria	32
6 Benfica	Portugal	31
7 CSKA Sofia	Bulgaria	30
8 = Ajax Amsterdam	Netherlands	29
= Real Madrid	Spain	29
10 = Ferencvaros	Hungary	28
= Juventus	Italy	28

* Amongst UEFA affiliated countries as at the end of the 2004–05 season
# Total includes one wartime German League title

The best totals for the other leading European nations are: England – Liverpool, 18; Germany – Bayern Munich, 19; France – Saint Etienne, 10; and Belgium – Anderlecht, 27.

⊙ Top transfer for Zidane
Three times winner of the FIFA World Player of the Year title, Zinedine Zidane (b.1972) became the world's most expensive player when he moved to his present club, Real Madrid, in 2001.

top10 WORLD TRANSFERS*

PLAYER / NATIONALITY	FROM	TO	YEAR	FEE ($)
1 Zinedine Zidane, France	Juventus, Italy	Real Madrid, Spain	2001	64,200,000
2 Luis Figo, Portugal	Barcelona, Spain	Real Madrid, Spain	2000	56,200,000
3 Hernan Crespo, Italy	Parma, Italy	Lazio, Italy	2000	51,300,000
4 Christian Vieri, Italy	Lazio, Italy	Inter Milan, Italy	1999	49,600,000
5 Gianluigi Buffon, Italy	Parma, Italy	Juventus, Italy	2001	46,200,000
6 Rio Ferdinand, England	Leeds United, England	Manchester United, England	2002	45,200,000
7 Ronaldo, Brazil	Inter Milan, Italy	Real Madrid, Spain	2002	43,700,000
8 Gaizka Mendieta, Spain	Valencia, Spain	Lazio, Italy	2001	40,700,000
9 Juan Sebastian Veron, Argentina	Lazio, Italy	Manchester United, England	2001	39,600,000
10 Rui Costa, Portugal	Fiorentina, Italy	AC Milan, Italy	2001	39,400,000

* As at January 1, 2006

Zinedine Zidane played a major part in putting French football on the world soccer map at the end of the 20th century. He helped the French team to victory over Brazil in the 1998 FIFA World Cup Final with two first-half goals that set up a 3–0 victory. Two years later, he scored the extra-time winner against Portugal in the semifinal before going on to beat Italy in the finals, also after extra time. His pivotal role in France's rise to world supremacy led Real Madrid to pay a world record sum for him in 2001.

top10 BIGGEST WINS IN MAJOR INTERNATIONAL TOURNAMENTS*

WINNERS / LOSERS	TOURNAMENT	SCORE
1 Australia vs. American Samoa	2002 World Cup Qualifier	31–0
2 Australia vs. Tonga	2002 World Cup Qualifier	22–0
3 Kuwait vs. Bhutan	2000 Asian Championship Qualifier	20–0
4 =China vs. Guam	2000 Asian Championship Qualifier	19–0
=Iran vs. Guam	2002 World Cup Qualifier	19–0
6 Tahiti vs. American Samoa	2000 Oceania Championship Qualifier	18–0
7 =China vs. Maldives	1992 Olympic Games Qualifier	17–0
=Iran vs. Maldives	1998 World Cup Qualifier	17–0
=Australia vs. Cook Islands	2000 Oceania Championship	17–0
10 =Denmark vs. France	1908 Olympic Games	17–1
=Australia vs. Cook Islands	1998 Oceania Championship	16–0
=Tajikistan vs. Guam	2002 World Cup Qualifier	16–0
=South Korea vs. Nepal	2004 Asian Championship Qualifier	16–0

* As at January 1, 2006

The record wins for other major tournaments are: Copa America: Argentina vs. Ecuador, 1942, 12–0; European Championship: Spain vs. Malta, 1984, 12–1; and British Championship: England vs. Ireland, 1899, 13–2. The record for women's football is 21–0 achieved on four occasions, all in World Cup qualifying matches: 1997 Japan vs. Guam; 1998 Canada vs. Puerto Rico; 1998 New Zealand vs. Samoa; and 1998 Australia vs. Western Samoa. These last two matches were on the same date: October 9, 1998.

top10 MOST MATCHES PLAYED IN THE FINAL STAGES OF THE WORLD CUP*

COUNTRY	TOURNAMENTS	MATCHES
1 Brazil	17	87
2 Germany/West Germany	15	85
3 Italy	15	70
4 Argentina	13	60
5 England	11	50
6 Spain	11	45
7 France	11	44
8 Mexico	12	41
9 Uruguay	10	40
10 Sweden	9	39

* Up to and including the 2002 event

Ice Hockey

top10 MOST POINTS IN AN NHL SEASON*

	PLAYER / TEAM	SEASON	GOALS	ASSISTS	POINTS
1	Wayne Gretzky, Edmonton Oilers	1985–86	52	163	215
2	Wayne Gretzky, Edmonton Oilers	1981–82	92	120	212
3	Wayne Gretzky, Edmonton Oilers	1984–85	73	135	208
4	Wayne Gretzky, Edmonton Oilers	1983–84	87	118	205
5	Mario Lemieux, Pittsburgh Penguins	1988–89	85	114	199
6	Wayne Gretzky, Edmonton Oilers	1982–83	71	125	196
7	Wayne Gretzky, Edmonton Oilers	1986–87	62	121	183
8 =	Mario Lemieux, Pittsburgh Penguins	1987–88	70	98	168
=	Wayne Gretzky, Los Angeles Kings	1988–89	54	114	168
10	Wayne Gretzky, Edmonton Oilers	1980–81	55	109	164

* As at the end of the 2003–04 season

Wayne Gretzky (b.1961) has set more NHL records than any other man. The game's top goalscorer and points scorer, his first goal was past goalkeeper Glen Hanlon of Vancouver on October 14, 1979. During his 20-year career, he played for Edmonton, Los Angeles, St. Louis, and the New York Rangers. He played in four winning Stanley Cup teams and was the NHL top scorer on 10 occasions. Gretzky won the Hart Trophy a record nine times and was inducted into the Hockey Hall of Fame in 1999.

top10 LATEST STANLEY CUP WINNERS

	YEAR	WINNERS
1	Tampa Bay Lightning	2004
2	New Jersey Devils	2003
3	Detroit Red Wings	2002
4	Colorado Avalanche	2001
5	New Jersey Devils	2000
6	Dallas Stars	1999
7	Detroit Red Wings	1998
8	Detroit Red Wings	1997
9	Colorado Avalanche	1996
10	New Jersey Devils	1995

The Stanley Cup was not held in 2005 due to the NHL dispute.

top10 NHL COACHES*

	COACH	YEARS	WINS	PERCENTAGE
1	Scott Bowman	1967–2002	1,244	.654
2	Toe Blake	1955–68	500	.634
3	Ken Hitchcock	1995–2004	362	.613
4	Fred Shero	1971–81	390	.612
5	Glen Sather	1979–2004	497	.600
6	Emile Francis	1965–83	388	.574
7 =	Billy Reay	1957–77	542	.571
=	Marc Crawford	1994–2004	369	.571
9	Pat Burns	1988–2004	501	.570
10	Al Arbour	1970–94	781	.564

* As at the start of the 2005–06 season based on best win percentage in regular season matches

top10 TEAMS WITH THE MOST STANLEY CUP WINS*

	TEAM	YEARS#	WINS
1	Montreal Canadiens	1916–93	24
2	Toronto Maple Leafs	1918–67	13
3	Detroit Red Wings	1936–2002	10
4 =	Boston Bruins	1929–72	5
=	Edmonton Oilers	1984–90	5
6 =	Ottawa Senators	1920–27	4
=	New York Rangers	1933–94	4
=	New York Islanders	1980–83	4
9 =	Chicago Black Hawks	1934–61	3
=	New Jersey Devils	1995–2003	3

* Since 1910 when the NHA (National Hockey Association) took over the running of the tournament
# Up to and including the 2004 Stanley Cup; no winner in 2005 due to NHL dispute

The Montreal Canadiens' first Stanley Cup win was in 1916, when they beat Portland 3–2 in the best-of-5 series. They were coached and managed by George Kennedy. The Canadiens have enjoyed two great periods of Stanley Cup success. The first was 1956–60 when they won the trophy five years in succession under coach Toe Blake, and again in the 1970s when they won four consecutive titles in the 1976–79 season under Scott Bowman.

top10 **MOST GOALS** IN AN NHL CAREER*

PLAYER	YEARS	GOALS
1 Wayne Gretzky	1979–99	894
2 Gordie Howe	1946–80	801
3 Brett Hull	1985–2004	741
4 Marcel Dionne	1971–89	731
5 Phil Esposito	1963–81	717
6 Mike Gartner	1979–98	708
7 Mark Messier	1979–2004	694
8 Mario Lemieux#	1984–2004	683
9 Steve Yzerman#	1983–2004	678
10 Luc Robitaille#	1986–2004	653

* As at the end of the 2003–04 season
# Active in the 2005–06 season

Gordie Howe (b.1928), who holds the record for the most seasons (26) and games played (1,767) in the NHL, retired in 1971, but then returned to play alongside his sons Mark and Marty for Houston in the newly formed World Hockey Association. He finally retired in 1980 with 801 goals and 1,049 assists to his credit, having – uniquely – played hockey across five decades.

top10 **MOST GAMES PLAYED** IN THE NHL*

PLAYER	YEARS	MATCHES
1 Gordie Howe	1946–80	1,767
2 Mark Messier	1979–2004	1,756
3 Ron Francis	1981–2004	1,731
4 Scott Stevens	1982–2004	1,635
5 Larry Murphy	1980–2001	1,615
6 Ray Bourque	1979–2001	1,612
7 Dave Andreychuk#	1982–2004	1,597
8 Alex Delvecchio	1950–74	1,550
9 Johnny Bucyk	1955–78	1,540
10 Phil Housley	1982–2003	1,495

* As at the end of the 2003–04 season
# Active in the 2005–06 season

top10 **GOALKEEPERS** IN AN NHL CAREER*

PLAYER / CAREER	WINS
1 Patrick Roy (1984–2003)	551
2 Terry Sawchuk (1949–70)	447
3 Ed Belfour# (1988–)	435
4 Jacques Plante (1952–73)	434
5 Tony Esposito (1968–84)	423
6 Glenn Hall (1952–71)	407
7 =Grant Fuhr (1981–2000)	403
=Martin Brodeur# (1991–)	403
9 Curtis Joseph# (1989–)	396
10 Mike Vernon (1982–2002)	385

* As at the start of the 2005–06 season
# Active in the 2005–06 season

The first of Patrick Roy's career wins was in the 1984–85 season when he came on for one period for the Montreal Canadiens against Winnipeg Jets. He faced just two shots but received credit for the win. He was traded to Colorado Avalanche, staying with them until he retired in 2003. He won four Stanley Cups in 1986, 1993, 1996, and 2001 and was a three-times winner of the Conn Smythe Trophy.

Baseball Teams

the10 LATEST WINNERS OF THE WORLD SERIES

	WINNING TEAM	SCORE	RUNNER-UP	YEAR
1	Chicago White Sox	4–0	Houston Astros	2005
2	Boston Red Sox	4–0	St. Louis Cardinals	2004
3	Florida Marlins	4–2	New York Yankees	2003
4	Anaheim Angels	4–3	San Francisco Giants	2002
5	Arizona Diamondbacks	4–3	New York Yankees	2001
6	New York Yankees	4–1	New York Mets	2000
7	New York Yankees	4–0	Atlanta Braves	1999
8	New York Yankees	4–0	San Diego Padres	1998
9	Florida Marlins	4–2	Cleveland Indians	1997
10	New York Yankees	4–2	Atlanta Braves	1996

Major League baseball started with the National League in 1876. The rival American League was started in 1901, and two years later Pittsburgh, champions of the National League, invited American League champions Boston to take part in a best-of-nine games series to establish the "real" champions. Boston won 5–3. It has been a best-of-seven games series since 1905, with the exception of 1919–21, when it reverted to a nine-game series.

top10 TEAMS WITH THE MOST WINS IN A MAJOR LEAGUE BASEBALL SEASON*

	TEAM	SEASON	PLAYED	WON
1 =	Chicago Cubs	1906	152	116
=	Seattle Mariners	2001	162	116
3	New York Yankees	1998	162	114
4	Cleveland Indians	1954	154	111
5 =	Pittsburgh Pirates	1909	152	110
=	New York Yankees	1927	154	110
7 =	New York Yankees	1961	162	109
=	Baltimore Orioles	1969	162	109
9 =	Baltimore Orioles	1970	162	108
=	Cincinnati Reds	1975	162	108
=	New York Mets	1986	162	108

* Regular season only; up to and including the 2005 season

top10 TEAMS WITH THE BEST BATTING AVERAGES IN 2005

	TEAM	LEAGUE	AVERAGE
1	Boston Red Sox	AL	.281
2	New York Yankees	AL	.276
3	Tampa Bay Devil Rays	AL	.274
4 =	Detroit Tigers	AL	.272
=	Florida Marlins	NL	.272
6	Cleveland Indians	AL	.271
7 =	Chicago Cubs	NL	.270
=	Los Angeles Angels	NL	.270
=	Philadelphia Phillies	NL	270
=	St. Louis Cardinals	NL	.270

AL – American League; NL = National League

Perhaps surprisingly, the inventor of the batting average was an English statistician, Henry Chadwick (1824–1908). He adapted the batting average used in his own country's national game, cricket, to baseball, and organized the first baseball tour (*see* below). Chadwick's Brooklyn grave bears the inscription "The Father of Baseball." He was elected to the Baseball Hall of Fame in 1938.

The Cubs' 1906 record was set during a 154-game season, whereas the Mariners equaled it 95 years later in one of 162 games. If the Cubs' result were extrapolated across the higher number, it would represent a remarkable 123 wins.

AMAZING FACT

Away Games

In 1874, two baseball teams – the Boston Red Stockings and the Philadelphia Athletics – traveled to England and Ireland for the first-ever demonstrations of baseball outside the US. Led by Boston pitcher Albert Spaulding, their manager Harry Wright, and baseball writer Henry Chadwick, the teams played matches in London and four other cities. Although they failed in their intention of introducing the sport to the English, they did take on several home teams at their national sport of cricket – and defeated them!

top10 TEAMS WITH **MOST APPEARANCES** IN THE WORLD SERIES*

	TEAM	WINS	LOSSES	APPS.
1	New York Yankees	26	13	39
2	Brooklyn/Los Angeles Dodgers	6	12	18
3	New York/San Francisco Giants	5	12	17
4	St. Louis Cardinals	9	7	16
5	Philadelphia/Kansas City/ Oakland Athletics	9	5	14
6	= Boston Red Sox	6	4	10
	= Chicago Cubs	2	8	10
8	= Boston/Milwaukee/Atlanta Braves	3	6	9
	= Cincinnati Reds	5	4	9
	= Detroit Tigers	4	5	9

* Up to and including 2005

The Yankees appeared in 15 of the 18 World Series held between 1947 and 1964, winning 10 and losing five. That streak included a record five straight wins 1949–53. On October 2, 1936, they achieved the biggest-ever win in the World Series, scoring 18 to the New York Giants' 4.

the10 **NEWEST** MAJOR LEAGUE BASEBALL TEAMS

	TEAM	CURRENT BALLPARK	YEAR
1	= Arizona Diamondbacks	Chase Field	1998
	= Tampa Bay Devil Rays	Tropicana Field	1998
3	= Colorado Rockies	Coors Field	1993
	= Florida Marlins	Dolphin Stadium	1993
5	= Seattle Mariners	Safeco Field	1977
	= Toronto Blue Jays	Rogers Centre	1977
7	= Kansas City Royals	Kauffman Stadium	1969
	= Milwaukee Brewers*	Miller Park	1969
	= San Diego Padres	PETCO Park	1969
	= Washington Nationals#	RFK Stadium	1969

* Milwaukee Brewers were known as the Seattle Pilots in their first season
# Washington Nationals were known as the Montreal Expos 1969–2004

The Arizona Diamondbacks expanded the National League to 15 franchises. The Milwaukee Brewers moved from the American League to the National to bring it up to its current 16 teams, six of which appear in this list of the most recently founded teams.

top10 TEAMS WITH THE **MOST WINS** IN MAJOR LEAGUE BASEBALL*

	TEAM#	FIRST YEAR	WINS
1	New York Yankees	1901	9,192
2	San Francisco Giants	1883	8,763
3	Los Angeles Dodgers	1890	8,492
4	St. Louis Cardinals	1892	8,431
5	Boston Red Sox	1901	8,359
6	Pittsburgh Pirates	1887	8,343
7	Cleveland Indians	1901	8,302
8	Detroit Tigers	1901	8,221
9	Chicago Cubs	1876	8,214
10	Cincinnati Reds	1876	8,180

* Regular season only; up to and including the 2005 season
# Including franchise changes

The New York Yankees was founded as the Baltimore Orioles in 1901, became the New York Highlanders in 1903–12, and the New York Yankees since 1913, establishing their status with the aid of megastars of the caliber of Babe Ruth, Lou Gehrig, and Joe DiMaggio.

top10 TEAMS PLAYING THE **MOST MATCHES** IN MAJOR LEAGUE BASEBALL*

	TEAM#	FIRST YEAR	PLAYED
1	Chicago Cubs	1876	16,366
2	Detroit Tigers	1901	16,364
3	Cincinnati Reds	1876	16,361
4	St. Louis Cardinals	1892	16,359
5	San Francisco Giants	1883	16,348
6	= Los Angeles Dodgers	1890	16,347
	= Pittsburgh Pirates	1887	16,347
8	Minnesota Twins	1901	16,345
9	Cleveland Indians	1901	16,339
10	Baltimore Orioles	1901	16,338

* Regular season only; up to and including the 2005 season
# Including franchise changes

The Chicago Cubs existed as the Chicago White Stockings, before the founding of the National League in 1876, recovering from the loss of their ballpark in the Great Chicago Fire of 1871, to become a major team under the ownership of chewing gum magnate William Wrigley Jr.

Baseball Stars

top10 MOST **GAMES** PLAYED IN **MAJOR LEAGUE BASEBALL***

	PLAYER	GAMES
1	Peter Rose	3,562
2	Carl Yastrzemski	3,308
3	Hank Aaron	3,298
4	Rickey Henderson	3,081
5	Ty Cobb	3,035
6 =	Eddie Murray	3,026
=	Stan Musial	3,026
8	Cal Ripken	3,001
9	Willie Mays	2,992
10	Dave Winfield	2,973

* As at end of 2005 season

top10 **PITCHERS** WITH THE MOST WINS IN A **MAJOR LEAGUE BASEBALL CAREER***

	PLAYER	WINS
1	Cy Young	511
2	Walter Johnson	417
3 =	Grover Alexander	373
=	Christy Mathewson	373
5	Pud Galvin	365
6	Warren Spahn	363
7	Kid Nichols	361
8	Tim Keefe	342
9	Roger Clemens#	341
10	Steve Carlton	329

* As at the end of the 2005 season
# Active in 2005

top10 MOST **HOME RUNS** IN A **MAJOR LEAGUE BASEBALL CAREER***

	PLAYER	HOMERS
1	Hank Aaron	755
2	Babe Ruth	714
3	Barry Bonds#	708
4	Willie Mays	660
5	Sammy Sosa#	588
6	Frank Robinson	586
7	Mark McGwire	583
8	Harmon Killebrew	573
9	Rafael Palmeiro#	569
10	Reggie Jackson	563

* As at the end of the 2005 season
# Active in 2005

top10 **PLAYERS** WITH THE **MOST HITS** IN A CAREER

	PLAYER	HITS
1	Peter Rose	4,256
2	Ty Cobb	4,189
3	Hank Aaron	3,771
4	Stan Musial	3,630
5	Tris Speaker	3,514
6	Carl Yastrzemski	3,419
7	Honus Wagner	3,418
8	Paul Molitor	3,319
9	Eddie Collins	3,315
10	Willie Mays	3,283

While he is only fifth on this list, Tris Speaker is the all-time leader in outfield assists (449) and doubles (792). His record of 50 steals and 50 doubles in a year (1912) was not equaled until 1998, by Craig Biggio of the Houston Astros.

top10 MOST **HOME RUNS** IN A **MAJOR LEAGUE BASEBALL SEASON***

	PLAYER	YEAR	HOMERS
1	Barry Bonds#	2001	73
2	Mark McGwire	1998	70
3	Sammy Sosa#	1998	66
4	Mark McGwire	1999	65
5	Sammy Sosa#	2001	64
6	Sammy Sosa#	1999	63
7	Roger Maris	1961	61
8	Babe Ruth	1927	60
9	Babe Ruth	1921	59
10	= Jimmie Foxx	1932	58
	= Hank Greenberg	1938	58
	= Mark McGwire	1997	58

* As at the end of the 2005 season
# Active in 2005

top10 MOST **HOME RUNS** IN THE **WORLD SERIES**

	PLAYER	HOMERS
1	Mickey Mantle	18
2	Babe Ruth	15
3	Yogi Berra	12
4	Duke Snider	11
5	= Lou Gehrig	10
	= Reggie Jackson	10
7	= Joe DiMaggio	8
	= Frank Robinson	8
	= Bill Skowron	8
10	= Hank Bauer	7
	= Goose Goslin	7
	= Gil McDougald	7

* Up to and including the 2005 World Series

top10 MOST **RUNS** IN **MAJOR LEAGUE BASEBALL***

	PLAYER	RUNS
1	Rickey Henderson	2,295
2	Ty Cobb	2,246
3	= Hank Aaron	2,174
	= Babe Ruth	2,174
5	Pete Rose	2,165
6	Barry Bonds#	2,078
7	Willie Mays	2,062
8	Cap Anson	1,996
9	Stan Musial	1,949
10	Lou Gehrig	1,888

* As at the end of the 2005 season
# Active in 2005

top10 PITCHERS WITH THE **LOWEST ERA** IN A **MAJOR LEAGUE BASEBALL CAREER***

	PLAYER	ERA
1	Ed Walsh	1.816
2	Addie Joss	1.887
3	Jack Pfiester	2.024
4	Joe Wood	2.030
5	Jim Devlin	2.050
6	Mordecai Brown	2.057
7	John Ward	2.102
8	Christy Mathewson	2.133
9	Al Spalding	2.136
10	Rube Waddell	2.161

* As at the end of the 2005 season; minimum 1,000 innings

On the all-time list, the highest placed active player from the 2005 season was Pedro Martinez in joint 78th place. The all-time five best ERA among players active in 2005 were:

1	Pedro Martinez	2.718
2	John Franco	2.890
3	Greg Maddux	3.015
4	Randy Johnson	3.113
5	Roger Clemens	3.122

top10 PITCHERS WITH THE **MOST STRIKEOUTS** IN A **MAJOR LEAGUE BASEBALL CAREER***

	PLAYER	STRIKEOUTS
1	Nolan Ryan	5,714
2	Roger Clemens#	4,502
3	Randy Johnson#	4,372
4	Steve Carlton	4,136
5	Bert Blyleven	3,701
6	Tom Seaver	3,640
7	Don Sutton	3,574
8	Gaylord Perry	3,534
9	Walter Johnson	3,508
10	Phil Niekro	3,342

* As at the end of the 2005 season
# Active in 2005

Randy Johnson and Steve Carlton are the only two pitchers in the above list who throw left-handed. Nolan Ryan was known as the "Babe Ruth of strikeout pitchers," pitching faster – a record 101 mph (162.5 km/h) – and longer (27 seasons: 1966 and 1968–93) than any previous player.

top10 BASEBALL **MANAGERS***

	MANAGER / YEARS	WINS
1	Connie Mack 1894–1950	3,731
2	John McGraw 1899–1932	2,784
3	Tony LaRussa 1979–2005	2,214
4	Sparky Anderson 1970–95	2,194
5	Bucky Harris 1924–56	2,157
6	Joe McCarthy 1926–50	2,125
7	Bobby Cox 1978–2005	2,092
8	Walter Alston 1954–76	2,040
9	Leo Durocher 1939–73	2,008
10	Casey Stengel 1934–65	1,905

* Based on the number of regular season wins to the end of the 2005 season

Tennis

top10 MOST CAREER TOURNAMENT WINS – MEN

	PLAYER / COUNTRY	WINS*
1	Jimmy Connors, USA	109
2	Ivan Lendl, Czechoslovakia/USA	94
3	John McEnroe, USA	77
4	Pete Sampras, USA	64
5	= Bjorn Borg, Sweden	62
	= Guillermo Vilas, Argentina	62
7	Andre Agassi, USA	60
8	Ilie Nastase, Romania	57
9	Boris Becker, Germany	49
10	Rod Laver, Australia	47

* As at January 1, 2006

➊ Singles-minded
In a 20-year career span Martina Navratilova competed in 380 singles tournaments, winning 167 titles. This record and her nine Wimbledon wins remain unbeaten.

top10 MOST CAREER TOURNAMENT WINS – WOMEN

	PLAYER / COUNTRY	WINS*
1	Martina Navratilova, Czechoslovakia/USA	167
2	Chris Evert-Lloyd, USA	154
3	Steffi Graf, Germany	107
4	Margaret Court (née Smith), Australia	92
5	Evonne Cawley (née Goolagong), Australia	68
6	Billie Jean King (née Moffitt), USA	67
7	Virginia Wade, UK	55
8	Monica Seles, Yugoslavia/USA	53
9	Lindsay Davenport, USA	51
10	Martina Hingis, Switzerland	40

* As at January 1, 2006

top10 MOST MEN'S GRAND SLAM SINGLES TITLES*

	PLAYER / COUNTRY	A	F	W	US	TOTAL
1	Pete Sampras, USA	2	0	7	5	14
2	Roy Emerson, Australia	6	2	2	2	12
3	= Bjorn Borg, Sweden	0	6	5	0	11
	= Rod Laver, Australia	3	2	4	2	11
5	Bill Tilden, USA	0	0	3	7	10
6	= Andre Agassi, USA	4	1	1	2	8
	= Jimmy Connors, USA	1	0	2	5	8
	= Ivan Lendl, Czechoslovakia/USA	2	3	0	3	8
	= Fred Perry, UK	1	1	3	3	8
	= Ken Rosewall, Australia	4	2	0	2	8

A – Australian Open, F – French Open, W – Wimbledon, US – US Open

* Up to and including 2005

top10 MOST WOMEN'S GRAND SLAM SINGLES TITLES

	PLAYER / COUNTRY	YEARS	A	F	W	US	TOTAL
1	Margaret Court (née Smith), Australia	1960–73	11	5	3	5	24
2	Steffi Graf, Germany	1987–99	4	6	7	5	22
3	Helen Wills-Moody, USA	1923–38	0	4	8	7	19
4	= Chris Evert-Lloyd, USA	1974–86	2	7	3	6	18
	= Martina Navratilova, Czechoslovakia/USA	1978–90	3	2	9	4	18
6	Billie Jean King (née Moffitt), USA	1966–75	1	1	6	4	12
7	= Maureen Connolly, USA	1951–54	1	2	3	3	9
	= Monica Seles, Yugoslavia/USA	1990–96	4	3	0	2	9
9	= Molla Mallory (née Bjurstedt), USA	1915–26	0	0	0	8	8
	= Suzanne Lenglen, France	1919–26	0	2	6	0	8

A – Australian Open, F – French Open, W – Wimbledon, US – US Open

* Up to and including 2005

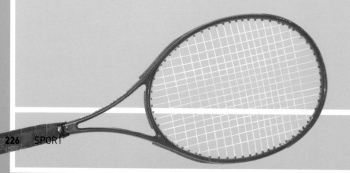

top10 MOST **WOMEN'S GRAND SLAM TITLES***

	PLAYER / COUNTRY#	YEARS	SINGLES	DOUBLES	MIXED	TOTAL
1	Margaret Court (née Smith), Australia)	1960–75	24	19	19	62
2	Martina Navratilova, Czechoslovakia/USA	1974–2003	18	32	9	59
3	Bille Jean King (née Moffitt), USA	1961–80	12	16	11	39
4	Margaret Du Pont, USA	1941–62	6	21	10	37
5	=Louise Brough, USA	1942–57	6	21	8	35
	=Doris Hart, USA	1948–55	6	14	15	35
7	Helen Wills-Moody, USA	1922–38	19	9	3	31
8	Elizabeth Ryan, USA	1914–34	0	17	9	26
9	Suzanne Lenglen, France	1919–26	12	8	5	25
10	=Pam Shriver, USA	1981–91	0	22	1	23
	=Steffi Graf, Germany	1987–99	22	1	0	23

* Up to and including 2005

top10 MOST **US OPEN MEN'S SINGLES** TITLES

	PLAYER*	YEARS"	TITLES
1	=Richard Sears	1881–87	7
	=Bill Larned	1901–11	7
	=Bill Tilden	1920–29	7
4	=Jimmy Connors	1974–83	5
	=Pete Sampras	1990–2002	5
6	=Robert Wrenn	1893–97	4
	=John McEnroe	1979–84	4
8	=Oliver Campbell	1890–92	3
	=Malcolm Whitman	1898–1900	3
	=Fred Perry, UK	1933–36	3
	=Ivan Lendl, Czechoslovakia	1985–87	3

* All USA, unless otherwise stated

" Of first and last win; up to and including 2005

top10 MOST MEN'S **GRAND SLAM TITLES***

	PLAYER / COUNTRY#	YEARS	SINGLES	DOUBLES	MIXED	TOTAL
1	Roy Emerson	1959–71	12	16	0	28
2	John Newcombe	1964–76	7	17	1	25
3	Todd Woodbridge	1990–2004	0	16	7	23
4	Frank Sedgman	1948–52	5	9	8	22
5	Bill Tilden, USA	1913–30	10	6	5	21
6	Rod Laver	1959–71	11	6	3	20
7	=John Bromwich	1938–50	2	13	4	19
	=Neale Fraser	1957–62	3	11	5	19
9	=Jean Borotra, France	1925–36	4	9	5	18
	=Ken Rosewall	1953–72	8	9	1	18

* Up to and including 2005
" Australia unless otherwise stated

top10 MOST **US OPEN WOMEN'S SINGLES** TITLES

	PLAYER / COUNTRY*	YEARS"	TITLES
1	Molla Mallory (née Bjurstedt)	1915–24	8
2	=Helen Wills-Moody	1923–31	7
	=Margaret Court (née Smith)†, Australia	1962–70	7
4	Chris Evert-Lloyd	1975–82	6
5	Steffi Graf, Germany	1988–96	5
6	=Elisabeth Moore	1896–1905	4
	=Hazel Wightman (née Hotchkiss)	1909–19	4
	=Helen Jacobs	1932–35	4
	=Alice Marble	1936–40	4
	=Pauline Betz	1942–46	4
	=Mario Bueno, Brazil	1959–66	4
	=Billie Jean King	1967–74	4
	=Martina Navratilova	1983–87	4

* All USA, unless otherwise stated
" Of first and last wins; up to and including 2005
† Includes two wins in Amateur Championships of 1968 and 1969, which were held alongside the Open Championship

Golf

⬆ Tiger economy
The career earnings of Tiger Woods are unmatched in the history of professional golf.

	PLAYER / COUNTRY#	WINNINGS ($)
1	Tiger Woods	57,940,144
2	Vijay Singh, Fiji	46,407,643
3	Phil Mickelson	36,167,360
4	Davis Love III	32,817,075
5	Ernie Els, South Africa	26,552,751
6	Jim Furyk	25,175,800
7	David Toms	24,953,728
8	Justin Leonard	20,720,563
9	Nick Price, Zimbabwe	20,395,519
10	Kenny Perry	19,766,233

* On the US PGA Tour as at March 26, 2006
# All USA, unless otherwise stated

Source: PGA Tour

top10 CAREER **MONEY WINNERS (WOMEN)***

	PLAYER / COUNTRY#	WINNINGS ($)
1	Annika Sörenstam, Sweden	18,512,764
2	Karrie Webb, Australia	10,748,665
3	Juli Inkster	9,954,470
4	Meg Mallon	8,767,439
5	Beth Daniel	8,503,533
6	Rosie Jones	8,306,013
7	Se Ri Pak, Korea	8,087,834
8	Betsy King	7,637,621
9	Laura Davies, UK	7,352,195
10	Dottie Pepper	6,827,284

* On the LPGA Tour, as at March 20, 2006
# All USA, unless otherwise stated

Source: LPGA

top10 **BIGGEST WINNING MARGINS** IN MEN'S MAJORS

	PLAYER / COUNTRY	YEAR	TOURNAMENT	VENUE	WINNING MARGIN
1	Tiger Woods, USA	2000	US Open	Pebble Beach	15
2	Tom Morris Sr, UK	1862	British Open	Prestwick	13
3 =	Tom Morris Jr, UK	1870	British Open	Prestwick	12
=	Tiger Woods, USA	1997	US Masters	Augusta	12
5	Willie Smith, USA	1899	US Open	Baltimore	11
6 =	Jim Barnes, USA	1921	US Open	Columbia	9
=	Jack Nicklaus, USA	1965	US Masters	Augusta	9
8 =	J.H. Taylor, UK	1900	British Open	St. Andrews	8
=	James Braid, UK	1908	British Open	Prestwick	8
=	J.H.Taylor, UK	1913	British Open	Hoylake	8
=	Ray Floyd, USA	1976	US Masters	Augusta	8
=	Tiger Woods, USA	2000	British Open	St. Andrews	8

The biggest winning margin in the other Major – the US PGA Championship – was in 1980, when Jack Nicklaus won by seven strokes from Andy Bean at Oak Hill.

top10 **LOWEST 4-ROUND** WINNING TOTALS IN MEN'S MAJORS

	PLAYER / COUNTRY / VENUE	YEAR	TOURNAMENT	SCORE
1	David Toms, USA Atlanta	2001	US PGA	265
2 =	Greg Norman, Australia Royal St George's	1993	British Open	267
=	Steve Elkington, Australia Riviera	1995	US PGA	267
4 =	Tom Watson, USA Turnberry	1977	British Open	268
=	Nick Price, Zimbabwe Turnberry	1994	British Open	268
6 =	Nick Price, Zimbabwe Southern Hills	1994	US PGA	269
=	Davis Love III, USA Winged Foot	1997	US PGA	269
=	Tiger Woods, USA St. Andrews	2000	British Open	269
9 =	Nick Faldo, UK St. Andrews	1990	British Open	270
=	Tiger Woods, USA Augusta	1997	Masters	270
=	Tiger Woods, USA Valhalla	2000	US PGA	270

David Toms' record-breaking total – 15 under par – at Atlanta was made up with rounds of 66-65-65-69. In addition to this win, he has won 12 events on the PGA Tour.

⬆ ***World No.1***
In 2006, Sweden's Annika Sörenstam was ranked first among women golfers.

top10 PLAYERS TO WIN THE **MOST PROFESSIONAL MAJORS** IN A CAREER*

	PLAYER / COUNTRY#	YEARS	BRITISH OPEN	US OPEN	MASTERS	PGA	TOTAL
1	Jack Nicklaus	1962–86	3	4	6	5	18
2	Walter Hagen	1924–29	4	2	0	5	11
3	Tiger Woods	1997–2005	2	2	4	2	10
4 =	Ben Hogan	1946–53	1	4	2	2	9
=	Gary Player, South Africa	1959–78	3	1	3	2	9
6	Tom Watson	1975–83	5	1	2	0	8
7 =	Harry Vardon, UK	1896–1914	6	1	0	0	7
=	Gene Sarazen	1922–35	1	2	1	3	7
=	Bobby Jones	1923–30	3	4	0	0	7
=	Sam Snead	1942–54	1	0	3	3	7
=	Arnold Palmer	1958–64	2	1	4	0	7

* Up to and including 2005
# All USA, unless otherwise indicated

top10 MOST **WOMEN'S MAJORS**

	PLAYER / COUNTRY*	YEARS#	MAJORS
1	Patty Berg	1937–58	15
2	Mickey Wright	1958–66	13
3	Louise Suggs	1946–59	11
4 =	Babe Zaharias	1940–54	9
=	Annika Sörenstam, Sweden	1999–2005	9
6	Betsy Rawls	1951–69	8
7	Juli Inkster	1984–2002	7
8 =	Kathy Whitworth	1965–75	6
=	Pat Bradley	1980–86	6
=	Patty Sheehan	1983–96	6
=	Betsy King	1987–97	6
=	Karrie Webb, Australia	1999–2002	6

* All USA, unless otherwise stated
# Of first and last wins

Water Sports

top10 OLYMPIC SAILING* COUNTRIES#

	COUNTRY	GOLD	MEDALS SILVER	BRONZE	TOTAL
1	USA	18	22	18	58
2	UK	23	14	10	47
3	France	16	11	14	41
4	Sweden	9	12	11	32
5	Norway	17	11	3	31
6	= Denmark	11	8	6	25
	= Netherlands	7	9	9	25
8	Germany/West Germany	6	6	7	19
9	Australia	5	3	8	16
10	= New Zealand	6	4	5	15
	= Spain	10	4	1	15
	= USSR/Unified Team/Russia	4	6	5	15

* Previously Olympic yachting
# Up to and including the 2004 Games

⊕ **Sailing to victory**

The success of 2003 America's Cup-winning yacht Alinghi was all the more remarkable as it was owned by a group from Switzerland, a landlocked country, although its crew was multinational – and was skippered by Russell Couts, previously a member of the winning New Zealand crew.

the10 LATEST WINNERS OF THE AMERICA'S CUP

	WINNER	SKIPPER	COUNTRY	YEAR
1	Alinghi	Russell Couts	Switzerland	2003
2	New Zealand	Russell Couts	New Zealand	2000
3	Black Magic I	Russell Couts	New Zealand	1995
4	America[3]	Bill Koch	USA	1992
5	Stars and Stripes	Dennis Conner	USA	1988
6	Stars and Stripes	Dennis Conner	USA	1987
7	Australia II*	John Bertrand	Australia	1983
8	Freedom	Dennis Conner	USA	1980
9	Courageous	Ted Turner	USA	1977
10	Courageous	Ted Hood	USA	1974

* The first nonAmerican winner of the race since it was inaugurated in 1851

top10 OLYMPIC ROWING COUNTRIES*

	COUNTRY	GOLD	MEDALS SILVER	BRONZE	TOTAL
1	United States	30	30	21	81
2	Germany/West Germany	27	19	20	66
3	East Germany	33	7	8	48
4	UK	21	18	8	47
5	USSR/Unified Team/Russia	13	20	13	46
6	Italy	14	13	10	37
7	Canada	8	13	13	34
8	France	6	14	13	33
9	Romania	15	10	7	32
10	Australia	8	9	12	29

* Men and women, up to and including 2004

top10 FASTEST WINNING TIMES IN THE OXFORD-CAMBRIDGE BOAT RACE*

	WINNER	YEAR	TIME MIN:SEC
1	Cambridge	1998	16:19
2	Cambridge	1999	16:41
3	Oxford	2005	16:42
4	Oxford	1984	16:45
5	Oxford	1976	16:50
6	Oxford	2002	16:54
7	Cambridge	1996	16:58
8	Oxford	1991	16:59
9	Cambridge	1993	17:00
10	Oxford	1985	17:11

* Putney to Mortlake course, up to and including 2005

The University Boat Race has been held annually since 1829. Crews have included many Olympic medalists and nonBritish oarsmen, including many Americans and Canadians. In the 2006 event, both crews had American rowers.

top10 WATERSKIERS WITH THE MOST WORLD CUP WINS*

	SKIER / COUNTRY	M/F#	SLALOM	JUMP	TOTAL
1	Andy Mapple, UK	M	31	–	31
2	= Jaret Llewellyn, Canada	M	–	18	18
	= Emma Sheers, Australia	F	2	16	18
4	= Kristi Johnson (née Overton), USA	F	13	–	13
	= Toni Neville, Australia	F	3	10	13
6	= Wade Cox, USA	M	10	–	10
	= Freddy Krueger, USA	M	–	10	10
8	Bruce Neville, Australia	M	–	9	9
9	Scot Ellis, USA	M	–	7	7
10	= Susi Graham, Canada	F	6	–	6
	= Carl Roberge, USA	M	1	5	6

* Up to and including 2005
# Male/female

Waterskiing was invented in 1922 by 18-year-old Ralph W. Samuelson of Lake City, Minnesota. The first international governing body, the World Water Ski Union, was established in 1946 in Geneva, Switzerland. Its successor, the International Water Ski Federation, organized the Water Ski World Cup, from 1996.

top10 LONGEST STANDING SWIMMING WORLD RECORDS*

	SWIMMER / COUNTRY / EVENT	TIME MIN:SEC	DATE SET
1	Janet Evans, USA 1500 metres freestyle (W)	15:52.10	Mar 26, 1988
2	Janet Evans, USA 400 metres freestyle (W)	4:03.85	Sep 22, 1988
3	Janet Evans, USA 800 metres freestyle (W)	8:16.22	Aug 20, 1989
4	Kristini Egerszegi, Hungary 200 metres backstroke (W)	2:06.62	Aug 25, 1991
5	Yanyan Wu, China 200 metres individual medley (W)	2:09.72	Oct 17, 1997
6	Alexsandr Popov, Russia 50 metres freestyle (M)	0:21.64	Jun 16, 2000
7	Anna-Karin Kammerling, Sweden 50 metres butterfly (W)	0:25.57	Jul 30, 2000
8	Yana Klochkova, Ukraine 400 metres individual medley (W)	4:33.59	Sep 16, 2000
9	Inge de Bruijn, Netherlands 100 metres butterfly (W)	0:56.61	Sep 17, 2000
10	Pieter van den Hoogenband, Netherlands, 100 metres freestyle (M)	0:47.84	Sep 19, 2000

* Long course records as at January 1, 2006; (W) = women (M) = men

Winter Sports

top10 SNOWBOARDERS WITH THE MOST FIS WORLD CHAMPIONSHIP MEDALS

	SNOWBOARDER / COUNTRY	YEARS	GOLD	MEDALS SILVER	BRONZE	TOTAL
1	Nicolas Huet, France	1999–2005	2	1	2	5
2	= Mike Jacoby, USA	1996–97	1	2	–	3
	= Helmut Pramstaller, Austria	1996–97	1	–	2	3
	= Jasey-Jay Anderson, Canada	2001–05	3	–	–	3
	= Antti Autti, Finland	2003–05	2	–	1	3
6	= Bernd Kroschewski, Germany	1997	1	–	1	2
	= Markus Hurme, Finland	1997–2001	–	1	1	2
	= Anton Pogue, USA	1997–2001	–	–	2	2
	= Markus Ebner, Germany	1999–2001	1	1	–	2
	= Stefan Kaltschuetz, Austria	1999–2001	–	1	1	2
	= Mathieu Bozzetto, France	1999–2003	–	2	–	2
	= Dejan Kosir, Slovenia	2001–03	1	1	–	2
	= Kim Christiansen, Norway	2001–05	1	–	1	2
	= Simon Schoch, Switzerland	2003	–	1	1	2
	= Seth Wescott, USA	2003–05	1	1	–	2

Source: Fédération Internationale de Ski (FIS)

top10 MOST WORLD FIGURE-SKATING TITLES*

	SKATER / COUNTRY	MEN	TITLES WOMEN	PAIRS	DANCE	TOTAL
1	= Sonja Henie, Norway	0	10	0	0	10
	= Irina Rodnina, USSR	0	0	10	0	10
	= Ulrich Salchow, Sweden	10	0	0	0	10
4	= Herma Planck (née Szabo), Austria	0	5	2	0	7
	= Karl Schafer, Austria	7	0	0	0	7
6	= Aleksandr Gorshkov, USSR	0	0	6	0	6
	= Lyudmila Pakhomova, USSR	0	0	0	6	6
	= Aleksandr Zaitsev, USSR	0	0	6	0	6
9	= Dick Button, USA	5	0	0	0	5
	= Carol Heiss, USA	0	5	0	0	5
	= Michelle Kwan, USA	0	5	0	0	5

* Up to and including the 2005 World Championships

⬤ Canadian snowman
Snowboarder Jasey-Jay Anderson was first in the Parallel GS and Parallel Slalom events at the 2005 FIS Snowboarding Championship at Whistler in his native Canada.

top10 WOMEN'S ALPINE SKIING WORLD CUP TITLES

SKIER / COUNTRY	O	D	GS	SG	S	C	TOTAL
1 Annemarie Moser-Pröll, Austria	6	7	3	0	0	1	17
2 Vreni Schneider, Switzerland	3	0	5	0	6	0	14
3 Katja Seizinger, Germany	2	4	0	5	0	0	11
4 Renate Götschl, Austria	1	4	0	2	0	3	10
5 Erika Hess, Switzerland	2	0	1	0	5	1	9
6 =Michela Figini, Switzerland	2	4	1	1	0	0	8
=Hanni Wenzel, Liechtenstein	2	0	2	0	1	3	8
8 Maria Walliser, Switzerland	2	2	1	1	0	1	7
9 =Janika Kostelic, Croatia	2	0	0	0	2	2	6
=Carole Merle, France	0	0	2	4	0	0	6
=Lisa-Marie Morerord, Switzerland	1	0	3	0	2	0	6
=Anita Wachter, Austria	1	0	2	0	0	3	6

* Up to and including the 2004–05 season

O = Overall; D = Downhill; GS = Giant Slalom; SG = Super Giant Slalom; S = Slalom; C = Combined

Annemarie Moser-Pröll (b.1953) gained her tally of titles at the Alpine skiing World Championship events during the 1970s. She also won silver medals at the 1972 Winter Olympics and gold at the 1980 Games.

top10 MEN'S ALPINE SKIING WORLD CUP TITLES*

SKIER / COUNTRY	O	D	GS	SG	S	C	TOTAL
1 Ingemar Stenmark, Sweden	3	0	8	0	8	0	19
2 =Marc Girardelli, Luxembourg	5	2	1	0	3	4	15
=Pirmin Zurbriggen, Switzerland	4	2	3	4	0	2	15
4 Hermann Maier, Austria	4	2	3	5	0	0	14
5 =Phil Mahre, USA	3	0	2	0	1	3	9
=Alberto Tomba, Italy	1	0	4	0	4	0	9
7 Gustavo Thoeni, Italy	4	0	2	0	2	0	8
8 =Kjetil André Aamodt, Norway	1	0	1	1	1	3	7
=Stephan Ebergarter, Austria	2	3	0	2	0	0	7
10 Jean-Claude Killy, France	2	1	2	0	1	0	6

* Up to and including the 2004–05 season

O = Overall; D = Downhill; GS = Giant Slalom; SG = Super Giant Slalom; S = Slalom; C = Combined

The World Cup was launched in the 1966–67 season, under the auspices of the Fédération Internationale de Ski (FIS), and is a winter-long series of races with champions in five categories, as well as an overall champion.

Motor Sports

top10 DRIVERS WITH THE MOST FORMULA ONE WINS*

	DRIVER / COUNTRY	YEARS	WINS
1	Michael Schumacher, Germany	1992–2005	84
2	Alain Prost, France	1981–93	51
3	Ayrton Senna, Brazil	1985–93	41
4	Nigel Mansell, UK	1985–94	31
5	Jackie Stewart, UK	1965–73	27
6 =	Jim Clark, UK	1962–68	25
=	Niki Lauda, Austria	1974–85	25
8	Juan Manuel Fangio, Argentina	1950–57	24
9	Nelson Piquet, Brazil	1980–91	23
10	Damon Hill, UK	1993–98	22

* Up to and including the 2005 season

top10 MANUFACTURERS WITH THE MOST FORMULA ONE WINS*

	MANUFACTURER	FIRST WIN / DRIVER	WINS
1	Ferrari#	1951 British GP (José Froilán González)	183
2	McLaren#	1968 Belgian GP (Bruce McLaren)	148
3	Williams#	1977 British GP (Clay Regazzoni)	113
4	Lotus	1960 Monaco GP (Stirling Moss)	79
5	Brabham	1964 French GP (Dan Gurney)	35
6	Benetton	1986 Mexican GP (Gerhard Berger)	27
7	Renault#	1979 French GP (Jean-Pierre Jabouille)	25
8	Tyrrell	1971 Spanish GP (Jackie Stewart)	23
9	BRM	1959 Dutch GP (Jo Bonnier)	17
10	Cooper	1958 Argentina GP (Stirling Moss)	16

* Up to and including the 2005 season
# Raced in 2005

top10 MOST RALLY WINS*

	DRIVER / COUNTRY	WINS
1	Carlos Sainz, Spain#	26
2	Colin McRae, UK#	25
3	Tommi Makinen, Finland	24
4	Juha Kankkunen, Finland	23
5 =	Didier Auriol, France	20
=	Sebastien Loeb, France#	20
7	Markku Alen, Finland	19
8 =	Marcus Gronholm, Finland#	18
=	Hannu Mikkola, Finland	18
10	Massimo Biasion, Italy	17

* Up to and including the 2005 season
# Active in 2005

Source: FIM World Rally Championship

Winning formula
His remarkable tally of 84 Formula One Grand Prix wins places third youngest World Champion Michael Schumacher (b.1969) far ahead of his closest rivals.

top10 YOUNGEST FORMULA ONE WORLD CHAMPIONS

			AGE	
	DRIVER / COUNTRY	YEAR	YEARS	DAYS
1	Fernando Alonso, Spain	2005	24	59
2	Emerson Fittipaldi, Brazil	1972	25	273
3	Michael Schumacher, Germany	1994	25	315
4	Jacques Villeneuve, Canada	1997	26	200
5	Niki Lauda, Austria	1975	26	201
6	Jim Clark, UK	1963	27	187
7	Jochen Rindt, Austria	1970	28	168
8	Ayrton Senna, Brazil	1988	28	223
9	James Hunt, UK	1976	29	55
10	Nelson Piquet, Brazil	1981	29	60

top10 INDIANAPOLIS 500 WINS*

	DRIVER / COUNTRY#	YEARS	WINS
1	= A. J. Foyt	1961, 1964, 1967, 1977,	4
	= Al Unser	1970–71, 1978, 1987	4
	= Rick Mears	1979, 1984, 1988, 1991,	4
4	= Louie Meyer	1928, 1933, 1936	3
	= Wilbur Shaw	1937, 1939–40	3
	= Mauri Rose	1941†, 1947–48	3
	= Bobby Unser	1968, 1975, 1981	3
	= Johnny Rutherford	1974, 1976, 1980	3
9	= Tommy Milton	1921, 1923	2
	= Bill Vukovich	1953–54	2
	= Rodger Ward	1959, 1962	2
	= Gordon Johncock	1973, 1982	2
	= Emerson Fittipaldi (Brazil)	1989, 1993	2
	= Arie Luyendyk (Holland)	1990, 1997	2
	= Al Unser Jr.	1992, 1994	2
	= Hélio Castroneves (Brazil)	2001, 2002	2

* Up to and including the 2005 race
# All from the USA unless otherwise stated
† Shared drive with Floyd Davis

top10 MOST CART RACE WINS*

	DRIVER	COUNTRY	YEARS	WINS
1	Michael Andretti	USA	1986–2002	42
2	Al Unser Jr.	USA	1984–95	31
3	Paul Tracy	Canada	1993–2005	30
4	Rick Mears	USA	1979–91	26
5	Bobby Rahal	USA	1982–92	24
6	Emerson Fittipaldi	Brazil	1985–95	22
7	Mario Andretti	USA	1980–93	19
8	Danny Sullivan	USA	1984–93	17
9	Alessandro Zanardi	Italy	1996–98	15
10	Sébastien Bourdais	France	2003–05	13

* Since the formation of the CART series in 1979

the10 LEAST SUCCESSFUL FORMULA ONE DRIVERS*

	DRIVER / COUNTRY	YEARS	STARTS
1	Andrea De Cesaris, Italy	1980–94	208
2	Martin Brundle, UK	1984–96	158
3	Derek Warwick, UK	1981–93	147
4	Jean Pierre Jarier, France	1971–83	134
5	Eddie Cheever, USA	1978–89	132
6	Pierluigi Martini, Italy	1985–95	118
7	Philippe Alliot, France	1984–94	110
8	Mika Salo, Finland	1994–2002	109
9	Jos Verstappen, Netherlands	1994–2003	107
10	Jenson Button, UK	2000–05	100

* Based on number of starts without a win up to and including the 2005 season

Motorcycling

	COUNTRY	TITLES
1	Italy	72
2	UK	43
3	Spain	28
4 =	Germany/West Germany	16
=	USA	16
6	Australia	9
7 =	Southern Rhodesia	8
=	Switzerland	8
9	Japan	7
10	South Africa	5

* As at the end of the 2005 season

⬅ Winner's flag
*Italian rider Valentino Rossi (b.1979) won
seven World Championships between
1997 and 2005, five of them consecutive.*

top10 RIDERS WITH THE MOST **SOLO** MOTORCYCLING WORLD TITLES*

	RIDER / COUNTRY	500/MOTOGP	350CC	250CC	125CC	80/50CC	TOTAL
1	Giacomo Agostini, Italy	8	7	–	–	–	15
2	Angel Nieto, Spain	–	–	–	7	6	13
3 =	Mike Hailwood, UK	4	2	3	–	–	9
=	Carlo Ubbiali, Italy	–	–	3	6	–	9
5 =	Phil Read, UK	2	–	4	1	–	7
=	Valentino Rossi, Italy	5	–	1	1	–	7
=	John Surtees, UK	4	3	–	–	–	7
8 =	Geoff Duke, UK	4	2	–	–	–	6
=	Jim Redman, Southern Rhodesia	–	4	2	–	–	6
10 =	Mick Doohan, Australia	5	–	–	–	–	5
=	Anton Mang, West Germany	–	2	3	–	–	5

* As at the end of the 2005 season

top10 RIDERS WITH THE MOST **MOTO CROSS WORLD TITLES**

	RIDER / COUNTRY	500CC	250CC	125CC	TOTAL
1	Stefan Everts, Belgium	2	6	1	9
2	Joel Robert, Belgium	–	6	–	6
3 =	Roger de Coster, Belgium	5	–	–	5
=	Eric Geboers, Belgium	2	1	2	5
=	Georges Jobe, Belgium	3	2	–	5
=	Joel Smets, Belgium	5	–	–	5
7 =	Harry Everts, Belgium	–	1	3	4
=	Torsten Hallman, Sweden	–	4	–	4
=	Heikki Mikkola, Finland	3	1	–	4
10 =	Greg Albertyn, South Africa	–	2	1	3
=	Alessio Chiodi, Italy	–	–	3	3
=	Paul Friedrich, East Germany	3	–	–	3
=	Andre Malherbe, Belgium	3	–	–	3
=	Guennady Moisseev, USSR	–	3	–	3
=	Gaston Rahier, Belgium	–	–	3	3
=	David Thorpe, UK	3	–	–	3

* FIM World titles 1957–2005

top10 RIDERS WITH THE MOST **SUPERBIKE RACE WINS***

	RIDER / COUNTRY	WINS
1	Carl Fogarty, UK	59
2	= Troy Corser, Australia	31
	= Colin Edwards, USA	31
4	Doug Polen, USA	27
5	Raymand Roche, France	23
6	Troy Bayliss, Australia	22
7	Noriyuki Haga, Japan	19
8	Pier Francesco Chili, Italy	17
9	= Giancarlo Falappa, Italy	16
	= Neil Hodgson, UK	16

* Since the start of Superbike racing in 1988 to the end of the 2005 season

➡ **Fogarty's firsts**
Up to his retirement in 2000, British rider Carl Fogarty (b.1966) established a commanding lead with 59 Superbike victories.

top10 RIDERS WITH THE MOST **SPEEDWAY WORLD TITLES***

	RIDER / COUNTRY	YEARS	TITLES
1	Ivan Mauger, New Zealand	1968–79	6
2	= Ove Fundin, Sweden	1956–67	5
	= Tony Rickardsson, Sweden	1994–2002	5
4	= Barry Briggs, New Zealand	1957–66	4
	= Hans Nielsen, Denmark	1986–95	4
6	= Ole Olsen, Denmark	1971–78	3
	= Erik Gundersen, Denmark	1984–88	3
8	= Fred Williams, UK	1950–53	2
	= Jack Young, Australia	1951–52	2
	= Ronnie Moore, New Zealand	1954–59	2
	= Peter Craven, UK	1955–62	2
	= Bruce Penhall, USA	1981–82	2
	= Greg Hancock, USA	1992–97	2

* Up to and including 2005

Up to 1995 the world title was decided by a series of qualifying heats with the final being a single-night event. Since 1995 it has been a season-long series of Grand Prix events with points tallied up throughout the season ultimately deciding the champion.

top10 RIDERS WITH MOST **AMA SUPERCROSS RACE WINS***

	RIDER[#]	250CC	125CC	TOTAL WINS
1	Jeremy McGrath[†]	72	13	85
2	Ricky Carmichael[†]	40	11	51
3	Chad Reed[†] (Australia)	23	6	29
4	Ricky Johnson	28	–	28
5	Bob Hannah	27	–	27
6	Damon Bradshaw	19	6	25
7	Kevin Windham[†]	12	11	23
8	James Stewart Jr.[†]	3	18	21
9	Jeff Ward	20	–	20
10	Ezra Lusk[†]	12	7	19

* 1974–2005
[#] All riders from the US unless otherwise stated
[†] Active during 2005 season

Cycling

top10 MOST WINS IN THE **TOUR DE FRANCE***

	RIDER / COUNTRY	YEARS	WINS
1	Lance Armstrong, USA	1999–2005	7
2	=Jacques Anquetil, France	1957–64	5
	=Eddy Merckx, Belgium	1969–74	5
	=Bernard Hinault, France	1978–85	5
	=Miguel Induráin, Spain	1991–95	5
6	=Philippe Thys, Belgium	1913–20	3
	=Louison Bobet, France	1953–55	3
	=Greg LeMond, USA	1986–90	3
9	=Lucien Petit-Breton, France	1907–08	2
	=Firmin Lambot, Belgium	1919–22	2
	=Ottavio Bottecchia, Italy	1924–25	2
	=Nicolas Frantz, Luxembourg	1927–28	2
	=André Leducq, France	1930–32	2
	=Antonin Magne, France	1931–34	2
	=Sylvère Maes, Belgium	1936–39	2
	=Gino Bartali, Italy	1938–48	2
	=Fausto Coppi, Italy	1949–52	2
	=Bernard Thévenet, France	1975–77	2
	=Laurent Fignon, France	1983–84	2

* Up to and including 2005

top10 RIDERS WITH MOST WINS IN THE **THREE MAJOR TOURS***

	NAME / COUNTRY	TOUR	GIRO	VUELTA	YEARS	TOTAL
1	Eddy Merckx, Belguim	5	5	1	1968–74	11
2	Bernard Hinault, France	5	3	2	1978–85	10
3	Jacques Anquetil, France	5	2	1	1957–64	8
4	=Fausto Coppi, Italy	2	5	0	1940–53	7
	=Miguel Induráin, Spain	5	2	0	1991–95	7
	=Lance Armstrong, USA	7	0	0	1999–2005	7
7	=Alfredo Binda, Italy	0	5	0	1925–33	5
	=Gino Bartali, Italy	2	3	0	1938–48	5
	=Felice Gimondi, Italy	1	3	1	1965–76	5
10	=Tony Rominger, Switzerland	0	1	3	1992–95	4
	=Roberto Heras, Spain	0	0	4	2000–05	4

* Up to and including 2005

The three major tours are: Tour de France, launched in 1903, won by Maurice Garin, France; Tour of Italy (Giro d'Italia) first contested in 1909, won by Luigi Ganna, Italy; and Tour of Spain (Vuelta de España), first held in 1935, won by Gustave Deloor, Belgium.

⊙ Seven wonders

American cyclist Lance Armstrong (b.1971) overcame serious illness to become the most successful Tour de France competitor of all time, with seven consecutive victories between 1999 and 2005.

top10 COUNTRIES WITH MOST **TOUR DE FRANCE WINNERS**

	COUNTRY	WINS
1	France	36
2	Belgium	18
3	USA	10
4	Italy	9
5	Spain	8
6	Luxembourg	4
7 =	Netherlands	2
=	Switzerland	2
9 =	Denmark	1
=	Germany	1
=	Ireland	1

* Up to and including 2005

top10 **OLYMPIC CYCLING** NATIONS*

	COUNTRY	GOLD MEDALS
1	France	39
2	Italy	36
3	Germany/West Germany	16
4	USSR/Russia	15
5	Holland	14
6 =	Australia	13
=	USA	13
8	UK	12
9 =	Belgium	6
=	Denmark	6
=	East Germany	6

* All events up to and including the 2004 Athens Games, including discontinued events and the 1906 Intercalated Games

AMAZING FACT

A Bicycle Race for Two

Now discontinued as an Olympic event, a men's 6,560-ft (2,000-m) tandem race was competed from 1906 to 1972. British riders John Matthews and Arthur Rushen won gold in 1906, with German brothers Bruno and Max Götz gaining silver.

top10 WINNERS OF **CYCLING CLASSICS***

	RIDER / NATIONALITY	YEARS	MSR	TL	TF	LBL	PR	TOTAL
1	Eddy Merckx, Belgium	1966–76	7	2	2	5	3	19
2	Roger de Vlaeminck, Belgium	1970–79	3	2	1	1	4	11
3 =	Constante Girardengo, Italy	1918–26	6	3	–	–	–	9
=	Fausto Coppi, Italy	1946–54	3	5	–	–	1	9
=	Sean Kelly, Ireland	1984–92	2	3	–	2	2	9
6	Rik Van Looy, Belgium	1958–65	1	1	2	1	3	8
7	Gino Bartalli, Italy	1939–50	4	3	–	–	–	7
8 =	Henri Pelissier, France	1911–21	1	3	–	–	2	6
=	Alfredo Binda, Italy	1925–31	2	4	–	–	–	6
=	Francesco Moser, Italy	1975–84	1	2	–	–	3	6
=	Moreno Argentin, Italy	1985–91	–	1	1	4	–	6
=	Johan Museeuw, Belgium	1993–2002	–	–	3	–	3	6

* Up to and including 2005

After the three major Tours, the Classics are the most prestigious of all cycling races. All Classics are single day races and since 2005 have formed part of the UCI (Union Cycliste Internationale) Pro Tour. The top five, often regarded as the toughest of the Classics, are known as the Monuments. They are:

(i) Milan-San Remo (MSR) – raced each spring, it was first held in 1907 and is the longest of all Classics at nearly 186 miles (300 km).

(ii) Tour of Lombardy (TL) – held in October and first raced as the Milan-Milan race in 1905.

(iii) Tour of Flanders (TF) – held early April each year, it was first staged in 1913.

(iv) Liége-Bastogne-Liége (LBL) – is the oldest of all current Classics, first held for amateurs in 1892 and since 1894 for professionals.

(v) Paris-Roubaix (PR) – held since 1896 and known as the Hell of the North.

Only three riders have won all five Monuments: Roger De Vlaeminck, Rik Van Looy, and Eddy Merckx, all of whom were Belgian.

top10 **OLDEST** CYCLING CLASSIC RACES AND TOUR

	RACE	FIRST HELD
1	Liège-Bastogne-Liège	1892
2	Paris-Brussels	1893
3	Paris-Roubaix	1896
4	Paris-Tours	1896
5	Tour de France	1903
6	Tour of Lombardy	1905
7	Milan-San Remo	1907
8	Tour of Italy	1909
9	Tour of Flanders	1913
10	Championship of Zurich	1914

The Bordeaux-Paris race was the first of the major cycling races and was, until its demise in 1988, the oldest of all Classics. Regarded as the "Derby of Road Racing," the Bordeaux-Paris race lasted for around 16 hours, starting in darkness in the early hours of the morning. The first race in 1891 was won by Britain's George Pilkington Mills. Originally for amateurs, it became a professional race and remained so until its last staging in 1988.

Skateboarding

top10 **SKATEBOARDERS** WITH THE MOST GOLD MEDALS IN THE X GAMES

	SKATER / COUNTRY	YEARS	BIG AIR	STREET/PARK	VERT	TOTAL*
1	Tony Hawk, USA	1995–2003	–	–	9	9
2	Andy Macdonald, USA	1996–2002	–	–	8	8
3	Bucky Lasek, USA	1999–2004	–	–	6	6
4	Rodil de Araujo Jr., Brazil	1996–2002	–	5	–	5
5	Bob Burnquist, Brazil	2000–05	–	–	4	4
6 =	Chris Senn, USA	1995–99	–	3	–	3
=	Eric Koston, Thailand	2000–03	–	–	3	3
=	Pierre-Luc Gagnon, Canada	2002–05	–	–	3	3
9	Paul Rodriguez, USA	2004–05	–	2	–	2
10 =	Matt Dove, USA	2001	–	–	1	1
=	Kerry Getz, USA	2001	–	1	–	1
=	Ryan Sheckler, USA	2003	–	1	–	1
=	Sandro Dias, Brazil	2004	–	–	1	1
=	Chad Muska, USA	2004	–	1	–	1
=	Danny Way, USA	2005	1	–	–	1

* Medals won in X Games 1–11 and 2003 X Games Global; includes doubles and best trick

◀ *Flyin' Ryan*
Ryan Sheckler became the world's youngest professional skateboarder at 13, going on to win numerous competitions.

top10 **VERT SKATEBOARDERS** WITH THE MOST MEDALS IN THE X GAMES

	SKATER / COUNTRY	YEARS	BRONZE	MEDALS SILVER	GOLD	TOTAL*
1	Tony Hawk, USA	1995–2003	3	2	9	14#
2	Andy Macdonald, USA	1996–2003	2	3	8	13†
3 =	Bucky Lasek, USA	1998–2004	–	4	6	10
=	Bob Burnquist, Brazil	1998–2005	3	3	4	10
5 =	Rune Glifberg, Denmark	1995–2004	6	2	–	8
=	Pierre-Luc Gagnon, Canada	2002–05	1	4	3	8
7 =	Neal Hendrix, USA	1995–2003	2	2	–	4
=	Mike Crum, USA	1999–2003	2	2	–	4
=	Sandro Dias, Brazil	2002–05	1	2	1	4
10	Colin McKay, Canada	2000–05	1	2	–	3

* Includes doubles and best trick
# Also won a silver medal for Street in 1995
† Also won two silver medals for Street 1997–98

the10 LATEST **STREET/PARK SKATEBOARDING** CHAMPIONS AT THE X GAMES

YEAR	SKATER / COUNTRY
2005	Paul Rodriguez, USA
2004	Paul Rodriguez, USA
2003	Eric Koston (street), USA
2003	Ryan Sheckler (park), USA
2002	Rodil de Araujo Jr. (street), Brazil
2002	Rodil de Araujo Jr. (park), Brazil
2001	Kerry Getz, USA
2000	Eric Koston, USA
1999	Chris Senn, USA
1998	Rodil de Araujo Jr., Brazil

top10 STREET SKATERS, 2005 (MALE)

	SKATER / COUNTRY	WCS WORLD RANKING POINTS, 2005
1	Ryan Sheckler, USA	3,725
2	Ronnie Creager, USA	3,650
3	Jereme Rogers, USA	3,100
4	Greg Lutzka, USA	2,650
5	Austen Seaholm, USA	1,750
6	Dayne Brummet, USA	1,700
7	Daisuke Mochizuki, Japan	1,675
8	Rick McCrank, Canada	1,450
9	Mike Peterson, USA	1,400
10	Kyle Berard, USA	1,165

Source: World Cup Skateboarding (WCS)

Ranking is arrived at by adding the points from a skater's four best results at North American WCS Points Events (Lake Forest, Toronto, Vancouver, Philadelphia) together with their best three results from WCS Points Events in Europe, Australia, South America, and Asia. Skaters must take part in the World Championships in Münster, Germany, to win the No.1 ranking.

➲ P-Rod's double X
Paul Rodriguez (nickname "P-Rod") won consecutive victories in the X Games.

top10 STREET SKATERS, 2005 (FEMALE)

	SKATER / COUNTRY	WCS WORLD RANKING POINTS, 2005*
1	Vanessa Torres, USA	3,350
2	Lauren Perkins, USA	3,200
3	Lyn-Z Adams Hawkins, USA	2,200
4	Lacey Baker, USA	2,150
5	=Amy Caron, USA	2,000
	=Elissa Steamer, USA	2,000
7	Sophie Poppe, Belgium	1,550
8	Elizabeth Nitu, USA	1,350
9	Georgina Matthews, New Zealand	1,250
10	Anne-Sophie Julien, France	1,100

* Total of points won in the Gallaz Skate Jam, World Championships Germany, Slam City Jam, and West 49 Canadian Open

Source: World Cup Skateboarding (WCS)

top10 VERT SKATERS, 2005 (MALE)

	SKATER / COUNTRY	WCS WORLD RANKING POINTS, 2005
1	Sandro Dias, Brazil	4,600
2	Rodrigo Menezes, Brazil	3,200
3	Neal Hendrix, USA	3,175
4	Bob Burnquist, Brazil	2,650
5	Trevor Ward, Australia	2,325
6	Otavio Neto, Brazil	2,100
7	Macelo Kosake, Brazil	1,750
8	Mathias Ringstrom, Sweden	1,600
9	Lincoln Ueda, Brazil	1,425
10	Max Dufour, Canada	1,300

Source: World Cup Skateboarding (WCS)

top10 VERT SKATERS, 2005 (FEMALE)

	SKATER / COUNTRY	WCS WORLD RANKING POINTS, 2005*
1	Cara-Beth Burnside, USA	3,000
2	Mimi Knoop, USA	2,400
3	Karen Jones, Brazil	1,700
4	Jen O'Brien, USA	1,650
5	=Tina Neff, Germany	1,550
	=Apryl Woodcock, USA	1,550
7	Holly Lyons, USA	1,450
8	Rebecca Aimee Davis, UK	1,400
9	Nicole Zuck, USA	650
10	Mandy Esch, USA	600

* Total of points won in the Slam City Jam, World Championships Germany, X Games, and West Beach Games Soul Bowl

Source: World Cup Skateboarding (WCS)

Horse Sports

top10 MOST OLYMPIC DRESSAGE MEDALS*

	COUNTRY	GOLD	SILVER	BRONZE	TOTAL
1	Germany/West Germany	18	9	8	35
2	Sweden	7	5	7	19
3	Switzerland	3	6	4	13
4	= France	3	5	2	10
	= USSR/Russia	4	3	3	10
6	= Netherlands	2	4	2	8
	= USA	0	1	7	8
8	Denmark	0	3	0	3
9	= Austria	1	0	1	2
	= Spain	0	1	1	2

* Up to and including the 2004 Olympics

top10 JOCKEYS IN THE BREEDERS' CUP*

	JOCKEY	YEARS	WINS
1	Jerry Bailey	1991–2005	15
2	Pat Day	1984–2001	12
3	Mike Smith	1992–2002	10
4	Chris McCarron	1985–2001	9
5	Gary Stevens	1990–2000	8
6	= Eddie Delahoussaye	1984–93	7
	= Laffit Pincay Jr	1985–93	7
	= José Santos	1986–2002	7
	= Pat Valenzuela	1986–2003	7
10	= Corey Nakatani	1996–2004	6
	= John Velazquez	1998–2004	6

* Up to and including 2005

Source: The Breeders' Cup

top10 COUNTRIES WITH THE MOST OLYMPIC SHOW-JUMPING MEDALS*

	COUNTRY	GOLD	SILVER	BRONZE	TOTAL
1	Germany/West Germany	13	3	7	23
2	USA	4	8	3	15
3	France	5	4	5	14
4	Italy	3	5	5	13
5	UK	1	3	5	9
6	Sweden	3	1	3	7
7	= Belgium	1	2	3	6
	= Switzerland	1	3	2	6
9	= Mexico	2	1	2	5
	= Netherlands	2	3	0	5

* Up to and including the 2004 Olympics

top10 JOCKEYS IN THE US TRIPLE CROWN RACES

	JOCKEY	YEARS	KENTUCKY	PREAKNESS	BELMONT	TOTAL
1	Eddie Arcaro	1938–57	5	6	6	17
2	Bill Shoemaker	1955–75	4	2	5	11
3	= Earle Sande	1921–30	3	1	5	9
	= Bill Hartack	1956–69	5	3	1	9
	= Pat Day	1985–2000	1	5	3	9
6	= Jimmy McLaughlin	1881–88	1	6	8
	= Gary Stevens	1988–2001	3	2	3	8
8	= Chas Kurtsinger	1931–37	2	2	2	6
	= Ron Turcotte	1965–73	2	2	2	6
	= Angel Cordero Jr.	1974–85	3	2	1	6
	= Chris McCarron	1986–97	2	2	2	6
	= Jerry Bailey	1991–2003	2	2	2	6

* Up to and including the 2005 races

top10 MONEY-WINNING JOCKEYS IN THOROUGHBRED RACING, 2005

	JOCKEY	WINS	PRIZEMONEY ($)
1	John Velazquez	249	20,770,272
2	Edgar Prado	298	18,603,171
3	Jerry Bailey	169	18,297,384
4	Rafael Bejarano	261	14,295,761
5	Garrett Gomez	239	13,889,511
6	Javier Castellano	205	12,487,797
7	Pat Valenzuela	196	11,531,152
8	Cornelio Velasquez	205	11,256,836
9	Victor Espinoza	186	11,044,604
10	Ramon Dominguez	309	10,664,218

the10 FASTEST WINNING TIMES OF THE PRIX DE L'ARC DE TRIOMPHE*

	HORSE	JOCKEY	YEAR	TIME MIN/SEC
1	Peintre Célèbre	Olivier Peslier	1997	2:24.60
2	Bago	Thierry Gillet	2004	2:25.00
3	Sinndar	Johnny Murtagh	2000	2:25.80
4	Trempolino	Pat Eddery	1987	2:26.30
5	Marienbard	Frankie Dettori	2002	2:26.70
6	Tony Bin	John Reid	1988	2:27.30
7	Hurricane Run	Kieren Fallon	2005	2:27.40
8	Dancing Brave	Pat Eddery	1986	2:27.70
9	Detroit	Pat Eddery	1980	2:28.00
10	All Along	Walter Swinburn	1983	2:28.10

* Up to and including 2005

Held every October at the Longchamp racecourse in the Bois de Boulogne, Paris. The first Prix de l'Arc de Triomphe was in 1920, to celebrate the Allies' victory in World War I. Raced over about 1 mile 4 furlongs (2,400 metres), the race is for horses of three years of age and upward.

top10 US JOCKEYS*

	JOCKEY	CAREER WINS*
1	Laffit Pincay Jr.	9,530
2	Russell Baze#	9,169
3	Willie Shoemaker	8,833
4	Pat Day	8,803
5	David Gall	7,396
6	Chris McCarron	7,141
7	Angel Cordero Jr.	7,057
8	Jorge Velasquez	6,795
9	Sandy Hawley	6,449
10	Larry Snyder	6,388

* As at December 19, 2005
# Active in 2005

Laffit Pincay Jr. (b.1946, Panama) began racing in the US in 1966. On December 10, 1999, he broke Bill Shoemaker's then record with his 8,834th win, going on to achieve a further 696 victories before his retirement in 2003.

⊙ *In the pink*
US jockey Jerry Bailey gallops to his record 15th Breeders' Cup victory.

Stadium Stats

top10 BIGGEST STADIUMS*

	STADIUM	LOCATION	YEAR OPENED	OFFICIAL CAPACITY
1	Strahov Stadium	Prague, Czech Republic	1926	250,000
2	May Day Stadium	Pyöngyang, North Korea	1989	150,000
3	Saltlake Stadium	Calcutta, India	1984	120,000
4	Estádio Azteca	Mexico City, Mexico	1966	114,465
5	Michigan Stadium	Ann Arbor, Michigan	1927	107,501
6	Beaver Stadium	Penn State University, Pennsylvania	1960	107,282
7	Neyland Stadium	Knoxville, Tennessee	1921	104,079
8	Jornalista Mário Filho#	Rio de Janeiro, Brazil	1950	103,045
9	Ohio Stadium	Colombus, Ohio	1922	101,568
10	National Stadium Bukit Jalil	Kuala Lumpur, Malaysia	1998	100,200

* Excluding speedway and motor racing circuits and horse racing tracks
# Formerly the Maracana Stadium

The Strahov Stadium, a wooden structure built in 1926 and since much modified, covers a total area of 2.4 sq miles (6.3 sq km).

⬇ Political arena
The 16-arched May Day Stadium, North Korea, has a floor area of 2,228,125 sq ft (207,000 sq m). It is used for both sporting events and political parades in which there can be as many as 100,000 people on the pitch.

top10 BIGGEST BALL PARKS IN MAJOR LEAGUE BASEBALL

	STADIUM / HOME TEAM	OFFICIAL CAPACITY
1	Yankee Stadium — New York Yankees	57,546
2	H.H.H. Metrodome — Minnesota Twins	56,144
3	Dodger Stadium — Los Angeles Dodgers	56,000
4	Shea Stadium — New York Mets	55,601
5	Rogers Centre — Toronto Blue Jays	50,516
6	Coors Field — Colorado Rockies	50,381
7	Busch Stadium — St. Louis Cardinals	49,676
8	Turner Field — Atlanta Braves	49,381
9	Ameriquest Field — Texas Rangers	49,166
10	Camden Yards — Baltimore Orioles	48,876

top10 BIGGEST STADIUMS IN THE NFL

STADIUM / HOME TEAM	OFFICIAL CAPACITY
1 FedExField Washington Redskins	80,000
2 Giants Stadium New York Giants/Jets	79,469
3 Arrowhead Stadium Kansas City Chiefs	79,409
4 Invesco Field Denver Broncos	76,125
5 Ralph Wilson Stadium Buffalo Bills	75,339
6 Dolphins Stadium Miami Dolphins	75,000
7 Bank of America Stadium Carolina Panthers	73,250
8 Sun Devil Stadium Arizona Cardinals	73,234
9 Alltel Stadium Jacksonville Jaguars	73,000
10 Lambeau Field Green Bay Packers	72,515

The official capacity of FedExField in Landover, Maryland, has been exceeded, most notably on December 18, 2005, when the Redskins defeated the Dallas Cowboys 35–7 in front of a crowd of 90,558. The stadium was opened on September 14, 1996, as the Jack Kent Cooke Stadium, changing its name to that of its sponsor in 1999.

the10 BIGGEST STADIUMS TO HOST MATCHES IN WORLD CUP 2006

STADIUM	LOCATION	HOME TEAM	OFFICIAL CAPACITY
1 Olympic Stadium	Berlin	Hertha Berlin	74,220
2 Alliaqnz Arena	Munich	Bayern Munich	66,016
3 Westfaloenstadion	Dortmund	Borussia Dortmund	65,982
4 Arena Aufschalke	Gelsenkirkchen	Schalke 04	53,804
5 Gottlieb-Daimler Stadion	Stuttgart	Vfb Stuttgart	53,200
6 AOL Arena	Hamburg	Hamburg SV	51,055
7 Waldstadion	Frankfurt	Intracht Frankfurt	48,132
8 Rhine Energy Stadium	Cologne	1.FC Cologne	46,120
9 AWD Arena	Hannover	Hannover 96	44,652
10 Zentralstadion	Leipzig	FC Sachsen Leipzig	44,199

top10 MOST WATCHED PROFESSIONAL SPORTING LEAGUES

LEAGUE	SPORT	COUNTRY	SEASON	AVERAGE*
1 National Football League	American Football	USA	2005	67,463
2 Bundesliga 1	Soccer	Germany	2004–05	37,771
3 Australian Football League	Australian Rules	Australia	2004	35,703
4 FA Premier League	Soccer	England	2004–05	33,893
5 Major League Baseball	Baseball	USA/Canada	2005	30,970
6 La Liga	Soccer	Spain	2004–05	28,401
7 Canadian Football League	Canadian Football	Canada	2004	27,303
8 Serie A	Soccer	Italy	2004–05	25,805
9 Ligue 1	Soccer	France	2004–05	21,392
10 = J-League 1	Soccer	Japan	2004	18,965
= NFL Europe	American Football	Europe	2005	18,965

* Average attendance during latest season

Further Information

THE UNIVERSE & THE EARTH

Asteroids
http://neo.jpl.nasa.gov/
NASA's Near Earth Object Program

Astronautics
http://www.astronautix.com/
Spaceflight news and reference

Comets
http://www.cometography.com/
Comet catalog and descriptions

Islands
http://islands.unep.ch/isldir.htm
Information on the world's islands

Mountains
http://peaklist.org/
Lists of the world's tallest mountains

NASA
http://www.nasa.gov/home/index.html
The main website for the US space program

Oceans
http://www.oceansatlas.org/index.jsp
The UN's resource on oceanographic issues

Planets
http://www.nineplanets.org/
A multimedia tour of the Solar System

Space
http://www.space.com/
Reports on events in space exploration

Waterfalls
http://www.world-waterfalls.com/
Data on the world's tallest and largest
waterfalls

LIFE ON EARTH

Animals
http://animaldiversity.ummz.umich.edu/site/
index.html
A wealth of animal data

Birds
http://www.bsc-eoc.org/avibase/avibase.jsp
A database on the world's birds

Conservation
http://iucn.org/
The leading nature conservation site

Endangered
http://www.cites.org/
Lists of endangered species of flora and fauna

Environment
http://www.unep.ch/
The UN's Earthwatch and other programs

Fish
http://www.fishbase.org/home.htm
Global information on fish

Food and Agriculture Organization
http://www.fao.org/
Statistics from the UN's FAO website

Forests
http://www.americanforests.org/
Information on the nation's trees and forests

Insects
http://ufbir.ifas.ufl.edu/
The University of Florida Book of Insect Records

Sharks
http://www.flmnh.ufl.edu/fish/Sharks/sharks.htm
Extensive shark research and attack reports

THE HUMAN WORLD

Death penalty
http://www.deathpenaltyinfo.org/
Facts ands statistics from the Death Penalty
Information Center

Health
http://www.cdc.gov/nchs
Information and links on health for US citizens

Leaders
http://www.terra.es/personal2/monolith/home.
htm
Facts about world leaders since 1945

Names
http://www.ssa.gov/OACT/babynames/index.
html
Most common names from the Social Security
Administration

Parliaments
http://www.ipu.org/
Women in parliaments, etc. from the Inter-
Parliamentary Union

Prisons
http://www.bop.gov
Public information on all aspects of the US
prison system

Religions
http://www.worldchristiandatabase.org/wcd/
World religion data

Rulers
http://rulers.org/
Database of rulers and political leaders

US Presidents
http://www.whitehouse.gov/history/presidents/
The White House's biographies of every
president

World Health Organization
http://www.who.int/en/
World health information and advice

TOWN & COUNTRY

Countries
http://www.theodora.com/wfb/
Country data, rankings, etc.

Country and city populations
http://www.citypopulation.de/cities.html
A searchable guide to the world's countries
and major cities

Country data
http://www.odci.gov/cia/publications/factbook/
The CIA World Factbook

Country population
http://www.un.org/esa/population/unpop.htm
The UN's worldwide data on population issues

Population
http://www.census.gov/
US and international population statistics

Population issues
http://www.un.org/esa/population/unpop.htm
The UN's Population Division

Refugees
http://www.refugees.org/
Global facts and figures from the US
Committee for Refugees and Immigrants

Skyscrapers
http://www.emporis.com/en/bu/sk/
The Emporis database of high-rise buildings

Tunnels
http://home.no.net/lotsberg/
A database of the world's longest tunnels

US geography
http://www.usgs.gov
National and regional geographical information

CULTURE

The Art Newspaper
http://www.theartnewspaper.com/
News and views on the art world

Books
http://www.publishersweekly.com
Publisher's Weekly, the trade journal of
American publishers

Education
http://nces.ed.gov
The home of federal education data

Languages of the world
http://www.ethnologue.com/
The world's 6,912 living languages

Languages online
http://global-reach.biz/globstats/index.php3
Facts and figures on online languages

Libraries
http://www.ala.org
US library information and book awards from
the American Library Association

The Library of Congress
http://www.loc.gov
An online gateway to one of the world's
greatest collections of words and pictures

The New York Public Library
http://www.nypl.org
One of the country's foremost libraries, with
an online catalog

The Pulitzer Prizes
http://www.pulitzer.org
A searchable guide to the prestigious US
literary prize

UNESCO
http://www.unesco.org/
Comparative international statistics on
education and culture

MUSIC

All Music Guide
http://www.allmusic.com/
A comprehensive guide to all genres of music

American Society of Composers, Authors, and Publishers
http://www.ascap.com
ASCAP songwriter and other awards

Billboard
http://www.billboard.com/
US music news and charts data

Classical Music
http://www.classicalusa.com
Online guide to classical music in the US

Country Music Hall of Fame and Museum
http://www.countrymusichalloffame.com/site/
The history of and information about country music

Grammy Awards
http://www.naras.org/
The official site for the famous US music awards

MTV
http://www.mtv.com/
The online site for the MTV music channel

Recording Industry Association of America
http://www.riaa.org
Searchable data on gold and platinum disc award winners

Rock and Roll Hall of Fame
http://www.rockhall.com
The museum of the history of rock

Rolling Stone magazine
http://www.rollingstone.com
Features on popular music since 1967

STAGE & SCREEN

Academy Awards
http://www.oscars.org/academyawards/
The official "Oscars" website

Emmy Awards
http://www.emmyonline.org/
Emmy TV awards from the National Television Academy site

Golden Globe Awards
http://www.hfpa.org/
Hollywood Foreign Press Association's Golden Globe site

Hollywood
http://www.hollywood.com/
US cinema site with details on all the new releases

Internet Broadway Database
http://www.ibdb.com/
Broadway theater information

Internet Movie Database
http://www.imdb.com/
The best of the publicly accessible film websites; IMDbPro is available to subscribers

Internet Theater Database
http://www.theatredb.com/
A Broadway-focused searchable stage site

Tony Awards
http://www.tonyawards.com/
Official website of the American Theater Wing's Tonys

Variety
http://www.variety.com/
Extensive entertainment information (extra features available to subscribers)

Yahoo! Movies
http://movies.yahoo.com/
Charts plus features and links to the latest film releases

COMMERCIAL WORLD

The Economist
http://www.economist.com/
Global economic and political news

Energy
http://www.eia.doe.gov/
Official US energy statistics

Environmental Sustainability Index
http://sedac.ciesin.columbia.edu/es/esi/
Data on the planet's future

Forbes magazine
http://www.forbes.com/
"Rich lists" and other rankings

Gold
http://www.gold.org/
The website of the World Gold Council

Labor, US
http://www.bls.gov
US Department of Labor statistics

Organization for Economic Cooperation and Development
http://www.oecd.org/home/
World economic and social statistics

Telecommunications
http://www.itu.int
Worldwide telecommunications statistics

United Nations Development Program
http://www.undp.org/
Country GDPs and other development data

The World Bank
http://www.worldbank.org/
World trade and labor statistics

TRANSPORTATION & TOURISM

Air disasters
http://www.airdisaster.com/
Reports on aviation disasters

Airports
http://www.airports.org/
Airports Council International's world coverage

Aviation
http://www.aerofiles.com
Information on a century of American aviation

Car manufacture
http://www.oica.net/
The International Organization of Motor Vehicle Manufacturers' website

Metros
http://www.lrta.org/world/worldind.html
The world's light railways and tram systems

Railroads
http://www.railwaygazette.com/
The world's railroad business in depth

Shipwrecks
http://www.shipwreckregistry.com/
A database of the world's lost ships

Tourism Offices Worldwide Directory
http://www.towd.com/
Tourism offices around the world

Travel industry
http://www.tia.org
Stats on travel to and within the US

World Tourism Organization
http://www.world-tourism.org/
The world's top tourism organization

SPORTS

Baseball
www.mlb.com
The official website of Major League Baseball

Basketball
http://www.nba.com
The official website of the NBA

Football
http://www.nhl.com
The official website of the NFL

Golf
http://www.pgatour.com
The Professional Golfers' Association (PGA) Tour

Ice Hockey
http://www.nhl.com
The official website of the NHL

Olympics
www.olympic.org/uk/games/index_uk.asp
The official Olympics website

Skateboarding
http://www.wcsk8.com/
Results, biographies, etc. from World Cup Skateboarding

Skiing
http://www.fis-ski.com/
Fédération Internationale de Ski, the world governing body of skiing and snowboarding

Sports Illustrated
http://www.sportsillustrated.cnn.com
Comprehensive coverage of all major sports

Track & Field
http://wwwiaaf.org
Statistics and rankings of the world's top athletes

Index

Acknowledgments

Special research: Ian Morrison (sport); Dafydd Rees (US); Louise Reip

Alexander Ash
Caroline Ash
Nicholas Ash
Jodie Benson
Peter Bond
Richard Braddish
Thomas Brinkhoff
Richard Chapman
Stanley Coren
Luke Crampton
Christopher Forbes
Russell E. Gough
Robert Grant
Brad Hackley
Richard Hurley
Larry Kilman
Aylla Macphail
Chris Mead
Roberto Ortiz de Zarate
Tony Pattison
Christiaan Rees
Robert Senior
Lucy T. Verma

Academy of Motion Picture Arts and Sciences – Oscar statuette is the registered trademark and copyrighted property of the Academy of Motion Picture Arts and Sciences
Advertising Age
Airports Council International
American Association of Botanical Gardens and Arboreta
American Association of Port Authorities
American Forests
American Kennel Club
American Pet Classics
Amnesty International
Amusement Business
The Art Newspaper
Art Sales Index
Audit Bureau of Circulations
Automotive News Data Center
Billboard
Box Office Mojo
BP Statistical Review of World Energy 2005
The Breeders' Cup
British Library
British Museum
Bureau of Labor Statistics
Business Week
Canada Geological Survey
Cat Fancier's Association
Central Intelligence Agency
Christie's
Classic FM
Commission for Distilled Spirits
Comité Interprofessionnel du Vin de Champagne
Computer Industry Almanac
Consumer Healthcare Products Association
Cremation Society of Great Britain
Death Penalty Information Center
De Beers

Deloitte
Department of Agriculture
Department of Commerce
Earth Impact Database
The Economist
Editor and Publisher Year Book
Energy Information Administration
Environmental Protection Agency
Ethnologue
Euromonitor
Family Business Magazine
FBI Uniform Crime Reports
Fédération Internationale de Football Association
Fédération International de Ski
Film Distributors' Association
Food and Agriculture Organization of the United Nations
Forbes
Franklin Associates Ltd.
Gold Fields Mineral Services Ltd.
Home Office (UK)
Institute for Family Enterprises, Bryant College
Interbrand
International Air Transport Association
International Atomic Energy Agency
International Centre for Prison Studies (UK)
International Civil Aviation Organization
International Game Fish Association
The International Institute for Strategic Studies, *The Military Balance 2005–2006*
International Intellectual Property Alliance
International Labor Organization
International Monetary Fund
International Obesity Task Force
International Olympic Committee
International Shark Attack File/American Elasmobranch Society/Florida Museum of Natural History
International Telecommunication Union
International Union for Conservation of Nature and Natural Resources
Internet Movie Database
Internet World Stats
Inter-Parliamentary Union
Joint United Nations Programme on HIV/AIDS (UNAIDS)
Ladies Professional Golf Association
League of American Theaters and Producers
Library of Congress
Lloyds Register-Fairplay Ltd.
TTB Gordonsart/Art Sales Index
Magazine Publishers of America
Major League Baseball
Metropolitan Opera
MRIB
Music Information Database
National Academy of Recording Arts and Sciences (Grammy Awards)
National Academy of Television Arts & Sciences (Emmy Awards)
National Aeronautics and Space Administration (NASA)
National Amusement Park Historical Association
National Basketball Association
National Center for Chronic Disease Prevention and Health Promotion

National Center for Education Statistics
National Center for Health Statistics
National Climatic Data Center
National Directory of Magazines
National Football League
National Hockey League
National Public Radio
Newspaper Association of America
AC Nielsen
Nielsen Bookscan
Nielsen Media Research
Nielsen Soundscan
NK Lawns & Gardens Co.
The NPD Group
Office of Immigration Statistics
Official Museums Directory
Organisation for Economic Co-operation and Development (OECD)
Organisation Internationale des Constructeurs d'Automobiles
Power & Motoryacht
J.D. Power & Associates
Population Reference Bureau
Professional Golfers' Association
Publishers Weekly
Railway Gazette International
Recording Industry Association of America (RIAA)
Royal Astronomical Society (UK)
Screen Digest
Screen International
Social Security Administration
Sotheby's
Sport England (formerly Sports Council)
Statistical Abstract of the United States
Stockholm International Peace Research Institute
Stores
Tony Awards
Tour de France
United Nations
United Nations Children's Fund
United Nations Educational, Scientific and Cultural Organization (UNESCO)
United Nations Population Division
Universal Postal Union
US Census Bureau
US Committee for Refugees and Immigrants
US Fish & Wildlife Service
US Geological Survey
US Lighthouse Society
Variety
Video Business
Ward's Motor Vehicle Facts & Figures
Westminster Kennel Club
Wildseed Farms
World Association of Newspapers
World Bank
World Christian Database
World Cup Skateboarding
World Economic Forum
World Gold Council
World Health Organization
World Nuclear Association
World of Learning
World Tourism Organization

Picture Credits

[The publishers would like to thank the following sources for their kind permission to reproduce the photographs and illustrations in this book.

(Abbreviations key: t = top, b = bottom, r = right, l = left, c = centre)

Antonov ASTC: 199t.

Christie's Images Ltd: 102-103, 104, 105, 106.

Corbis: 14r Bettmann, 16-17t Rick Doyle, 17 Dean Conger, 18 Peter Guttman, 19t Pablo Corral V, 21t Warren Morgan, 21b Free Agents Limited, 25 Douglas Peebles, 28 Jim Zuckerman, 31 Bryn Colton/Assignments Photographers, 32-33 Bettmann, 33r Cath Mullen/Frank Lane Picture Agency, 35 Bob Gomel, 37 Pierre Holtz/Reuters, 38b, 39 Jeffrey L. Rotman, 40l Robert Dowling, 40r Lawrence Manning, 44l Darrell Gulin, 44r Frans Lanting, 45 Joe McDonald, 54t LWA-Dann Tardif, 57 Kevin Dodge, 61 Gianni Giansanti, 62 Tim Graham, 63l Patrick Ward, 63r Stephane Cardinale/People Avenue, 64t Richard Olivier, 67 Fat Chance Productions, 68 Hulton-Deutsch Collection, 69 t&b Bettmann, 70, 71t Hulton-Deutsch Collection, 71b, 72 Baldev, 78 Rafiqur Rahman/Reuters, 80l Abaed Omar Qusini/Reuters, 81r Saeed Ali Achakzai/Reuters, 82 David Zimmerman, 83t Tom Wagner/CORBIS SABA, 83b Bettmann, 86 Lake County Museum, NY, 87 Massimo Listri, 89 Jean-Philippe Arles/Reuters, 94b Chris Andrews Publications/CORBIS, 95 Alessia Pierdomenico/Reuters, 97t Helen King, 98l Ron Watts, 99 Steve Raymer, 100-101c Nik Wheeler, 103b Hulton-Deutsch Collection, 107 Reuters, 110t Seth Wenig/Reuters, 111 Bettmann, 112t Hans Klaus Techt/epa, 119 Michael Mulvey/Dallas Morning News, 120t Andrew Gombert/epa, 123r Elizabeth Kreutz/NewSport, 124 Bo Zaunders, 127 Micheline Pelletier/CORBIS SYGMA, 130 Bettmann, 131 Rupert Horrox, 136-137c Stewart Tilger, 139 Hamshere Keith/CORBIS SYGMA, 149b Warner Bros/ZUMA, 154 Christies Images Ltd, 155 Tobias Schwarz/Reuters, 157 Walt Disney Pictures/Pixar Animation/Bureau L.A.Collections, 158l G. Schuster/zefa, 158-159r Lester Lefkowitz, 163 Carlo Cortes IV/Reuters, 166 Lou Dematteis, 167 Jean-Pierre Amet/Bel Ombra, 169 Ming Ming/Reuters/, 175t Jose Fuste Raga, 176 Charles O'Rear, 179 Ed Kashi, 180-181 Skyscan, 188 Neil Rabinowitz, 190t Derek Trask, 195 Christian Charisius/Reuters, 196t Bettmann, 198b Bettmann, 199b Bettmann, 200 V.Velengurin/R.P.G./CORBIS SYGMA, 201 CORBIS SYGMA, 204l Bob Krist, 207 Reuters, 210l John Gress/Reuters, 211r John Kolesidis/Reuters, 212b Tobias Schwarz/Reuters, 213 Reuters, 216 Icon SMI, 218b Victor Fraile/Reuters, 222-223 Le Segretain Pascal/CORBIS SYGMA, 224 Reuters, 226t Michael Kim, 228t Michael Fiala/Reuters, 229 Marc Serota/Reuters, 230 Reuters, 234-235 Giampiero Sposito/Reuters, 236b Victor Fraile/Reuters, 238 Reuters, 240 Lucy Nicholson/Reuters, 241 Lucy Nicholson/Reuters, 242t Ina Fassbender/Reuters, 244b KCNA/epa.

Empics: 215 Steven Senne/AP, 237b Steve Etherington.

Frank Lane Picture Agency: 16 Norbert Wu/Minden Pictures.

Getty Images: 24 Jim Sugar, 58t Frans Lemmens, 73 AFP, 77 Robert Harding World Imagery, 114 Donald Kravitz, 117 Scott Gries, 186-187r, 187b, 190b, 192-193r AFP, 194 Yann Layma, 208 Menahem Kahana/AFP, 209 Javier Soriano/AFP, 231, 232 Joe Klamar/AFP, 243.

Ivan Hissey: 22–23, 28–29, 32–33b, 45b, 48, 86t, 88, 142, 178t, 178–179b, 206–207.

i-Stock: 19b, 22, 23t, 38t, 41, 42, 43, 48, 49, 50, 51, 52, 53l, 54, 55, 56, 58b, 59, 60, 61b, 64b, 66, 76, 79, 80-81, 84, 92, 93, 94t, 96, 97c, 98r, 100-101, 102l, 110b, 112-113, 116b, 118, 120b, 122, 125, 132t, 135b, 142, 146b, 147t, 148b, 149t, 150, 152, 156, 162, 164, 165, 166-167, 168, 170, 171, 172, 173, 174, 175, 177, 178, 182, 183, 186l, 191, 192l, 197, 198t, 204r, 210-211c, 212t, 214, 217, 218-219t, 219, 220, 221, 225, 226b, 227, 228b, 236t, 237t, 239, 242b, 244-245t, 245b.

Kobal Collection: 126 Miramax, 132b Columbia/Goldcrest, 133t Universal/Wing Nut Films, 135t Lucasfilm/20th Century Fox, 140 Dreamworks Pictures, 141 Nickelodeon Movies, 143 Warner Bros, 144 Columbia/Michaels, Darren, 145 Warner Bros, 146t 20th Century Fox/Dreamworks/ILM (Industrial Light & Magic), 147b 20th Century Fox/Appleby, David, 148t Miramax, 151 Lions gate/Sebastian, Lorey, 153 Warner Brothers.

NASA: 10t, 11t, 11ac, 11bc, 11b, 12c, 12r, 12l, 14l, 15, 189t, 189b.

NHPA: 36 Joe Blossom.

David Penrose: 23b.

Rex Features: 121 Richard Young.

Science Photo Library: 10b Mark Garlick, 53r Russell Kightley.

South African Astronomical Observatory: 13.

United International Pictures: 136b.

Publisher's Acknowledgments
Cover design: 'Ome Design

Packager's Acknowledgments
Palazzo Editions would like to thank Richard Constable and Robert Walster for their design contributions, and Ivan Hissey for the specially commissioned illustrations.